CINEMA AGAINST DOUBLETHINK

When is it OK to lie about the past? If history is a story, then everyone knows that the 'official story' is told by the winners. No matter what we may know about how the past really happened, history is as it is recorded: this is what George Orwell called doublethink. But what happens to all the lost, forgotten, censored, and disappeared pasts of world history? *Cinema Against Doublethink* uncovers how a world of cinemas acts as a giant archive of these lost pasts, a vast virtual store of the world's memories. The most enchanting and disturbing films of recent years – *Uncle Boonmee Who Can Recall His Past Lives, Nostalgia for the Light, The Act of Killing, Even the Rain, Carancho, Lady Vengeance* – create ethical encounters with these lost pasts, covering vast swathes of the planet and crossing huge eras of time. Analysed using the philosophies of Gilles Deleuze (the time-image) and Enrique Dussel (transmodern ethics), the multitudinous cinemas of the world are shown to speak out against doublethink, countering this biggest lie of all with their myriad 'false' versions of world history. Cinema, acting against doublethink, remains a powerful agent for reclaiming the truth of history for the 'post-truth' era.

David Martin-Jones is Professor of Film Studies, University of Glasgow, UK. His research uses philosophy to explore world cinemas. He is the author/editor of eight books, has published in numerous international journals (e.g. *Cinema Journal, Screen,* and *Third Text*), and edits the Bloomsbury series Thinking Cinema.

Remapping World Cinema: Regional Tensions and Global Transformations

Series Editors: Rob Stone, Paul Cooke, Stephanie Dennison and Alex Marlow-Mann

Remapping World Cinema: Regional Tensions and Global Transformations rewrites the territory of contemporary world cinema, revising outdated assumptions of national cinemas, challenging complacent views of hegemonic film cultures and questioning common ideas of production, distribution and reception. It will remap established territories such as American, European and Asian cinema and explore new territories that exist both within and beyond nation-states such as regional cinemas and online communities, while also demarcating important contexts for global cinema such as festival circuits and the discipline of film studies itself.

This book series is jointly coordinated by *B-Film: The Birmingham Centre for Film Studies* based at the University of Birmingham, the *Centre for World Cinemas and Digital Cultures* at the University of Leeds and the *Centre for Film and Media Research* at the University of Kent.

Advisory Board

Middlebrow Cinema
Edited by Sally Faulkner

The Routledge Companion to World Cinema
Edited by Rob Stone, Paul Cooke, Stephanie Dennison and Alex Marlow-Mann

Cinema Against Doublethink
Ethical Encounters with the Lost Pasts of World History
David Martin-Jones

For more information about this series, please visit: https://www.routledge.com/Remapping-World-Cinema/book-series/RWC

CINEMA AGAINST DOUBLETHINK

Ethical Encounters with the Lost Pasts of World History

David Martin-Jones

Routledge
Taylor & Francis Group

LONDON AND NEW YORK

First published 2019
by Routledge
2 Park Square, Milton Park, Abingdon, Oxon OX14 4RN

and by Routledge
711 Third Avenue, New York, NY 10017

Routledge is an imprint of the Taylor & Francis Group, an informa business

© 2019 David Martin-Jones

British Library Cataloguing-in-Publication Data
A catalogue record for this book is available from the British Library

Library of Congress Cataloging-in-Publication Data
Names: Martin-Jones, David, author.
Title: Cinema against doublethink: ethical encounters with the lost pasts of world history/David Martin-Jones.
Description: New York: Routledge, 2019. |
Series: Remapping world cinema; 3 | Includes bibliographical references and index.
Identifiers: LCCN 2018018292 | ISBN 9781138907942 (hardback: alk. paper) | ISBN 9781138907959 (pbk.: alk. paper) | ISBN 9781315694832 (ebook: alk. paper)
Subjects: LCSH: Motion pictures and history. | Motion pictures–Philosophy.
Classification: LCC PN1995.2 .M37 2019 | DDC 791.43/658–dc23
LC record available at https://lccn.loc.gov/2018018292

ISBN: 978-1-138-90794-2 (hbk)
ISBN: 978-1-138-90795-9 (pbk)
ISBN: 978-1-315-69483-2 (ebk)

Typeset in Bembo
by Deanta Global Publishing Services, Chennai, India

Printed and bound in Great Britain by
TJ International Ltd, Padstow, Cornwall

Para Elena

CONTENTS

FIGURES

ACKNOWLEDGEMENTS

Early research for this monograph was conducted when I was the Prowse Visiting Fellow at the Institute of Advanced Studies, Durham University, UK (October–December 2012). My thanks to everyone involved for their support and insightful input. This research was also supported by a grant from the Carnegie Trust for the Universities of Scotland, for a research trip to China (2012). I am grateful to former colleagues at the University of St Andrews and current colleagues at the University of Glasgow. I could not have wished for more supportive research milieus.

Thanks to Paul Laverty and Icíar Bollaín for generously speaking to me about *También la lluvia*. A huge thank you to David Deamer, Chelsea Birks, William Brown, Timothy Barker, Matthew Holtmeier, David Fleming, Robert Sinnerbrink, Dimitris Eleftheriotis, and David Archibald, and the combined efforts of the peer reviewers and series editors, for feedback on early drafts, as well as to Chelsea Birks (again!) for invaluable assistance in the book's final stages. Thanks to David Sorfa for a chance to present this as a keynote at *Film-Philosophy IV* (2011); to Robert Stam and Ella Shohat for their kind invitation to the *Transnational Cinema/Media Studies Conference* at NYU Abu Dhabi (2014); to Matilda Mroz for *Material Environments* at Greenwich (2015); and to Robert Sinnerbrink for the *Cinematic Ethics Symposium* at Macquarie (2016). In addition, for invitations to present at research seminars at UNSW, Manchester, Manchester Metropolitan, Lancaster, Liverpool, Belfast, Durham, Newcastle, and Edinburgh, thanks to Michelle Langford, Felicity Colman, Anna Powell, Helen Darby, Richard Rushton, Robert Porter, Andrea Noble, Kerstin Oloff, Ann Davies, Dan Yacavone, James Scorer, Tom Whittaker, and Jill Bennett.

I am indebted to several colleagues who generously spent time discussing ideas in development: Alia Al-Saji, Dudley Andrew, Davie Archibald, Guy Austin, Frederic Brayard, Bruce Bennett, John Berra, Jennifer Biddle, Chelsea

Birks, Lucy Bolton, Lorna Burns, Robert Burgoyne, Neil Campbell, Jenny Chamarette, Felicia Chan, Shohini Chaudhuri, Yun-hua Chen, Sinkwan Cheng, Felicity Colman, Paul Cooke, Amalia Cordova, Michael Crang, Sean Cubitt, Ann Davies, David Deamer, Rajinder Dudrah, Benoît Dillet, Dimitris Eleftheriotis, Stuart Elden, Thomas Elsaesser, Péter Érdi, Christine Evans, Peter Evans, Clifton Evers, David Fleming, Armida de la Garza, Elisabetta Girelli, Zoe Graham, Inderpal Grewal, Barbara Graziosi, Francisco-J. Hernández Adrián, Mette Hjort, Amy Holdsworth, Conn Holohan, Matthew Holtmeier, Heather Ingood, Dina Iordanova, Seung-hoon Jeong, Nike Jung, Tina Kendall, Anu Koivunen, Carl Lavery, Tarja Laine, Michelle Langford, Ji Young Lee, Tae Hun Lee, Robert Levine, Hsien-Hao Sebastian Liao, Laura McMahon, Patricia MacCormack, Gina Marchetti, Bill Marshall, Alex Marlow Mann, Matilda Mroz, Soledad Montañez, Jonathan Munby, Anna Munster, Andrea Noble, Kerstin Oloff, Darcy Paquet, Stefanie van de Peer, Yarí Pérez Marín, Adrián Pérez-Melgosa, Anat Pick, Patricia Pisters, Sandra Ponzanesi, Robert Porter, Ellen Rees, Tom Rice, Miriam Ross, Richard Rushton, Isabel Santaolalla, Kathleen Scott, Lisa Shaw, Ella Shohat, Robert Sinnerbrink, David Sorfa, Robert Stam, Veronica Strang, Rob Stone, Veronica Tello, Claire Thomson, Leshu Torchin, Maria Velez-Serna, Belén Vidal, João Luiz Vieira, Julian Ward, Chelsea Wessels, Catherine Wheatley, Udo Will, James Williams, Alison Wylie, Joshua Yumibe. Apologies, and thank you, to anyone I have missed.

Thanks most of all to my family, especially to Sol and Elena for putting up with so much absence.

Sections of the book develop upon, in significantly reworked form, the following previously published articles: 'Trolls, Tigers and Transmodern Ecological Encounters', *Film-Philosophy*, 20, 1 (2016): 63–103, published by Edinburgh University Press; 'The Cinematic Temporalities of Modernity,' *Insights*, 6, 1 (2013): 2–12; 'Personal Museums of Memory', *Latin American Perspectives* (Issue 188), 40, 1 (2013): 73–87 – thanks to María Soledad Montañez for allowing me to re-use part of work we developed together; 'Archival Landscapes and a Non-Anthropocentric "Universe Memory" in *Nostalgia de la luz/Nostalgia for the Light* (2010)', *Third Text*, 27, 6 (2013): 707–722 copyright © Third Text, reprinted by permission of Taylor & Francis Ltd, www.tandfonline.com on behalf of *Third Text*. I am grateful to the respective journals and publishers for allowing me to rework and reprint these works in developed forms herein. I can say with confidence that what is found in these pages is, ultimately, a very different idea indeed. The book was briefly 'trailed' in the companion which initiated the *Remapping World Cinema* series, Rob Stone, Paul Cooke, Stefanie Dennison and Alex Marlow Mann (eds.), *Routledge Companion to World Cinema* (London: Routledge, 2017).

PREFACE

What is this book about, in a nutshell? In science, many good ideas are transferred into popular consciousness through the use of a metaphor, or analogy, to enable greater access to complex knowledge for everyone. I will try to emulate this clarity as best I can, with an original short story about an installation artwork of my imagining, at the centre of which is a box which does and does not contain a cat, or cats. I make no claims to the genius of a Nietzschean aphorism, or to the succinctness of one of Slavoj Žižek's risqué jokes. Still, there is nothing like a ripping yarn, and stories and songs, after all, are how humans have always remembered histories. It should begin appropriately, then:

'Once upon a time …'

We enter a gallery space in a charming post-industrial conversion somewhere in a bustling metropolis, the capital of one of the world's former imperialist powers which remains embedded within the affluent Global North. We are told by a telescreen that world history is a lidded box. We can see the box on the floor, and notice that it is the size of a large shoebox. Inside, we are told, there is a pair of shoes. These shoes are an older version of the ones we are wearing now, which were worn by our forefathers. When our forefathers wore the shoes, we are told, they travelled great distances to build bridges and roads and cities and trains, all of which helped the world as we know it now to develop into the hi-tech state it is in. Our current shoes enable us to carry on in the footsteps of these forefathers. They are, effectively, an evolutionary update on the original pair, continuing in this developmental tradition: making us faster, enhancing our stamina and range, our resilience and our adaptability.

Many who visit the gallery believe this. Yet others think this may be a lie. Some because they have been told – elsewhere – that, in fact, their forefathers wore different shoes, or no shoes, or were killed by people in shoes that sound suspiciously like those in the box. Others because, no matter what they do, the shoes they wear no longer seem to give them an edge to enhance their lives, as they apparently did for their forefathers. Gloomy art critics are quick to point out the resonance between the very idea of such shoes being stored away and exhibited with such ancestor-worship-like veneration, and that of the bleak Orwellian image of the future – of a human face being trampled by a boot, in perpetuity. If the shoes are world history, they argue, then they encapsulate the violence of several centuries of what is, from the Renaissance onwards, a colonial (in many places, settler colonist) modern epoch.

Luckily, most people think these critics far too melodramatic, not to mention a little bit prone to showing off. In general people accept the story, or have a wee think about whether, or to what extent, they agree with it. Albeit, understandably some are too uninterested, busy, or tired, to really have the time to care. There are other things to think about, after all. So everyone just gets on with their day, making breakfast for the kids and so on.

In the usual run of things, such an artwork might expect to come and go within a few weeks or months. Except, on this occasion, something unusual happens. Something which, to this day, no one can definitively be sure was an intended aspect of the installation all along, or a genuine reaction to it. Whatever the case, suddenly, a dynamic guerrilla force called 'the filmmakers of a world of cinemas' (sadly, they decided their name by committee) break into the gallery one night. Following their radical new manifesto, they drill what appear to be ventilation holes in the box, and then place several small screens on its outside, showing moving images. These additions give the impression – to anyone who is curious enough to look at them, that is – that inside the box there seems to be a cat. It is only ever possible to catch a glimpse of the seeming cat as it moves about. Perhaps a piece of a paw pressing at the glass, or the swish of its furry tail, or occasionally a feline eye stares out of the box directly at the one looking inside. Then, it is gone. Moreover, whilst all the filmmakers seem to agree that it is a cat in the box, something about the cat seems a little different wherever in the world they are filming. And so the impression is of many different cats, all impossibly squeezed into the tiny box. Some visitors speculate that the cats might be, somehow, virtual cats.

The gallery decides to leave the artwork as it is. The guerrilla filmmakers have certainly captured the public imagination, and the artwork gets much more attention this way. So, the board concludes (the following quote is taken from the minutes), 'Well, you know, it's a win–win, isn't it?' They even extend its run, as its fame spreads, and it transpires that it has some longevity. As time passes, each screen goes blank, but in a few years there is another break-in, and another film about a cat reappears from somewhere else. It turns out each time that it is not exactly the same guerrillas. Sometimes it is a new generation who have been influenced by predecessors, but who are also bringing their own ideas, probably in a new manifesto. Others, however, strongly deny they have anything to do with such clandestine political agendas, and quite sensibly question why they have to break in every time they want to show one of their films. They argue instead that they are simply filming cats because it seems like the right thing to do, or, even, just a thing to do. Some filmmakers even joke that their interests are closer to those of gorillas than they are to guerrillas! Sometimes such protestations are disingenuous, but other times they are simply the truth. Although figuring out which can, at times, be confusing, mostly the filmmakers seem well intentioned. At any rate, at least in their earlier works.

The visitors to the gallery, for their part, wonder if it might be possible to get to know this cat, or rather these cats, in a more meaningful way. After all, they learn from interviews with the filmmakers, these films seem to have much more meaning in the contexts where they were made, where considering cats of the past seems an important way to think about the present, perhaps even the future. So, the visitors wonder, were they to open the box, might they encounter such a cat? And if so, might there be some value in so doing?

Sadly, were they to cross the line marked 'Do not touch the artwork' and lift the lid, they would not find a cat, or even cats, past or present, alive or dead. The situation, it transpires, is a little different from that of the famous thought experiment from the imagination of scientist Erwin Schrödinger. The cats on the screens were all lost long ago, and now only exist in such reinvented temporary glimpses. All the gallery patrons would find, were they to lift the lid on history, would be a rather unremarkable pair of leather shoes – rather different from the sweatshop-produced plastic footwear of many patrons – which look as if they have been cleaned long ago before being put away. There is no trace of dirt on the soles, and any suspicion that they may once have been marked by blood is not a supposition that could be proved after so long. Or rather, it probably could, due to the powers of science, but what could one do with this information (at best circumstantial evidence linked to a past which nobody is sure of anyway) in a situation where the descendants of the shoes' original wearers now own the gallery?

But, just thinking about how it is not shoes but a cat, or in fact so many cats, which may be in the box – alive, but dead to our ability to really know them – is enough to make the visitors *hesitate* with respect to everything they have ever been told about the shoes. Some even believe that elsewhere there might be ways to gain access to the cats. After all, the guerrilla filmmakers found out about them somehow. This hesitation is, one might say, a principle of uncertainty with regard to the veracity of the official story of history. And so minds begin to wonder about how the story of world history is variously told and undermined.

Some turn back to the gloomy art critics in the hope of insight, in spite of the rather intense philosophies they inevitably favour, and their accompaniment, as always, by overly long and mentally discombobulating sentences. Some such critics question whether the artwork exposes Orwellian doublethink and its strategic use of 'alternative facts' – in which the victors rewrite history into a one-sided 'official story'? Others, whether it is, perhaps more positively, an exposition of the Nietzschean/Deleuzian labyrinthine powers of the false – which recuperates the lost and forgotten histories submerged by such official history-making? Then again, yet more critics counter, isn't that how 'fake news' also operates, by inducing cognitive dissonance – such that it is difficult to tell truthful (history) from false – and making people understandably angry because no one knows what the hell to believe in anymore? So, as usual, such critics seem to be of limited practical use, meaning remains unresolved, and everyone goes back to making breakfast for the kids.

And all the while that this circuitous wondering goes on, the wind and rain picks up outside the gallery, making this a much more pressing issue today than perhaps it ever was before. Even so, sadly, the connection between the weather and the shoes just seems a little obscure to many people. Science may be in part to blame for this, but only in part.

The End.

Well, that was the story. Admittedly, it seems unlikely that what someone once dubbed 'Martin-Jones's-"prolier-than-thou"-art-gallery-installation-shoe-box-of-world-cinemas-thought-experiment' will catch on. It's hardly as neat as 'Schrödinger's cat' after all. But that's art for you, it's not science.

Still, the idea of this book is now hopefully clear: a world of cinemas asks us to rethink something we may believe we already know about history – or rather, Eurocentric world history. It asks us to 'unthink' doublethink. This is not necessarily because cinema is different in our post-truth era. Of course, the rewriting of history at odds with how so many have experienced it (doublethink), has been going on for centuries. Cinema, as a consequence, has been engaging with this topic for at least the last several decades of its short life. Indeed, whilst historical revisionism has been ongoing for more than centuries, it has a particular emphasis after 1492 that directly relates to the current state of the world, and it is this which a world of cinemas often resists. This effect, of a world of cinemas functioning against doublethink, is similar whether we encounter a film where it is made, or, like the visitors to this exhibition, many miles away. But, like an art exhibition, at once illuminating, it may also at times be frustrating in the way that its revelations tug tantalisingly at the very edge of our consciousness. It requires us to work at the creation of its meaning from only the glimpses of the fragments of the lost past that it can offer us. That is, ultimately, the point. On the upside, though, in this it is perhaps more useful than the mummifying of time which is found in a museum.

We embark, then, upon a quest to seek Macavity, knowing all along that the mystery cat will not be there. The value in so doing, nevertheless, is … the … hesitation … the search brings.

The Beginning.

[Or, perhaps, rather, as the phantom ladies said in that famous French film, a book like this should start thus:

'Twice upon a time …']

INTRODUCTION

One or many pasts?

A world of cinemas, incorporating films from all around the globe, is trying to tell us a story: several stories in fact. These stories belong to the world history which we all share. I refer to them here as transnational histories in that they are histories which pre-exist, or impact across, national borders, within this much larger, encompassing, world history.

What is remarkable is that these transnational histories are being examined by filmmakers from disparate locations worldwide in similar ways aesthetically. In Chapters 3–6, I outline how the stories of the following transnational histories are being told across a world of cinemas: the planetary history of the Earth (*Loong Boonmee raleuk chat/Uncle Boonmee Who Can Recall His Past Lives* (Thailand/UK/France/Germany/Spain/Netherlands, 2010) and *Nostalgia de la luz/Nostalgia for the Light* (Chile/Spain/France/Germany/USA, 2010)); the North Atlantic trade circuit (*Como Era Gostoso o Meu Francês/How Tasty Was My Little Frenchman* (Brazil, 1971), and *También la lluvia/Even the Rain* (Spain/Mexico/France, 2010)); the Cold War (*The Act of Killing* (Denmark/Norway/UK, 2012) and *Al pie del árbol blanco/At the Foot of the White Tree* (Uruguay, 2007)); and neoliberal globalisation (*Carancho/Vulture* (Argentina/Chile/France/South Korea, 2010) and *Chinjeolhan geumjassi/Lady Vengeance* (South Korea, 2005)). Before I turn to these examples, however, I will outline the book's argument in this Introduction, unpacking it in full in the chapters which follow.

Encountering lost pasts

Firstly, we need to consider how we watch. To illuminate this pattern, trend, or certain tendency towards the telling of the story of transnational histories across a world of cinemas, requires that we recalibrate how we group together films (how we categorise) when we analyse them. It necessitates a refocusing of our viewfinder away from individual nations, as is already the case with the transnational turn in Film Studies generally, but – as has *yet* to be the case – towards a broader conception of world history as the ground for such a hermeneutics. In this book, the worldview offered by influential Latin American philosopher Enrique Dussel (known for his work on ethics in relation to liberation philosophy; see Chapter 1), which draws upon world systems analysis, enables a greater understanding of how what is depicted on screen does not relate solely to a national-historical ground, but also to the transnational history (or histories), which traverse world history.

With focus thus newly racked we can also see how cinematic depictions of the past – specifically lost pasts (disappeared, censored, forgotten, eradicated) – are aesthetically structured like ethical encounters with others. A world of cinemas thus offers us *encounters* with lost pasts. In this way, what is revealed is not only that there are myriad other pasts submerged within world history (even if we may not feel they directly inform our present), but so too that the ethics required of us by recognition of these pasts is one which involves us all, as peoples of the world.

These encounters are most visible when staged between characters onscreen, as they are in many of the films discussed. But as importantly, they also offer an encounter to the viewer. This is not a cinematic encounter with an other necessarily (another human or even another species for example), as the status of self and other will depend on who is watching. Rather, it is an encounter which offers the realisation that such a person, or even species, *has* a history (in fact, a lost past) which belongs to the broader world history we all inhabit. What is important is that this realisation provides the viewer with the chance to hesitate, and potentially to recognise *the relative centrality of their own place in world history.*

For some, typically those closer to the location of filming, this may not be a world changing revelation. This, even if the process of considering the still-smouldering 'embers' of a lost past may be most crucial in such places (Sanjinés 2013). But for others, even if viewing from much further afield, this will create hesitation with respect to formerly held beliefs as to the place, perhaps even primacy, of the viewer (or their culture) within world history. In fact, this potential to hesitate with respect to what is believed to be normal regarding the past is open to all, and it is debateable whether it is felt more strongly by those nearer to, or further from, the film.

Acknowledging the existence of such lost pasts – histories now recalled only as memories, times, fabulous beings, songs, myths, fables – renders histories previously thought to inform the present, *universally*, now only one amongst many: whether human or nonhuman. For this reason, the transnational histories on film examined in this book are not understood to offer an ethical encounter with an other, but with another (lost) past. The reappearance on screen of these lost pasts challenges the hegemonic nature of Eurocentric views of history (whether this is a revelation to the viewer or not), and accordingly may make some feel uncomfortable in their own skin.

We may or may not be able to *know* these pasts. Indeed, for many viewers the experience may be, precisely, the realisation of an *inability* to know another, or another's past. Yet for others, such films offer a chance to hesitate with respect to what is known, via an encounter with a lost past.[1] A world of cinemas thus offers a hesitant ethics which seeks to address the historical foundations of global structural inequality – the perpetuation of capitalism via a deliberately unequal distribution of wealth, worldwide, which has persisted since at least 1492. Structural inequality is not solely the norm under neoliberal globalisation (today, even in the USA, the world's richest nation, there are 41 million people living in poverty, 9 million without cash income (Pilkington 2017)), but is inherent to a several hundred-year-old process which I discuss here, after Dussel and others, as colonial modernity (Coronil 2000, 369–370). As Chapters 3–6 illustrate via world cinemas, whilst, since the 1990s, the fall of the Soviet Union signalled freer trade across borders (and thus the period is pivotal in certain definitions of the emergence of globalisation), even so, the roots of the contemporary economic situation lie in the Cold War's 'Pax Americana' (a conflict which itself grew out of the last decades of the era of Western imperialism), a regress thereby taking this particular story of colonial inequality back at least as far as 1492 and the European discovery (for Dussel, 'invention' (1992b)) of the Americas. Thus, world history after this date, for Latin American philosophers like Dussel, is one of the intertwined nature of modernity with its propellant, coloniality – and this continues even today, under neoliberal globalisation. As a world of cinemas also indicates, the exploitation of the globe by the latter force, coloniality, is that from which the gains of modernity proceed, both historically and now.

For this reason, I claim that cinema is against doublethink. Doublethink is the Orwellian reduction of the myriad pasts of the world history to a singular narrative (such as that of the Hegelian view of history, discussed below) which retroactively bolsters the seeming legitimacy of the current world order, obscuring in the process the inequality via which it is fostered (the other lost pasts of world history).

The question is, why is this important?

The non-fascist life: Introduction to, or conclusion of?

George Orwell's *Nineteen Eighty-Four* (1949) famously imagines a bleak dystopian world in which the past is perpetually re-written in the present, so as to maintain authoritarian one-party rule at the expense of the lives and happiness of society's inhabitants. One of the most important literary works of the Twentieth Century, in the Twenty-first it has become an extremely pertinent text for Western society. Sales spikes occurred after the Edward Snowden leak of 2013 (revelations concerning the US National Security Agency's secretive monitoring of its own populace) and the 2016 US presidential election, specifically after the appearance of the term 'alternative facts' in the wake of the presidential inauguration (Stelter and Pallotta 2017).

In the conclusion of *Nineteen Eighty-Four*, Orwell outlines what doublethink means with respect to how the past is remembered, or, to how the story of history is told. As Winston Smith is tortured by party member O'Brien, he is confronted with a photograph which depicts an image from the past. The party now proclaims that the past never happened in the way the image evidently portrays. O'Brien incinerates the photograph and the following conversation ensues:

> 'Ashes,' he said. 'Not even identifiable ashes. Dust. It does not exist. It never existed.'
>
> 'But it did exist! It does exist! It exists in memory. I remember it. You remember it.'
>
> 'I do not remember it,' said O'Brien.
>
> Winston's heart sank. That was doublethink.
>
> *(Orwell 1949, 283)*

Doublethink, then, concerns the ability to convince ourselves that two contradictory statements are, simultaneously, true (40–41). It is how authoritarian regimes censor the past, leaving only one official story of history left, in spite of peoples' lived experiences to the contrary. The populace must adhere to the official story on pain of torture and death.

Examples of doublethink have been prevalent throughout recent colonial history. Remaining in a literary vein, Gabriel García Márquez's *One Hundred Years of Solitude* (1967) famously evokes the United Fruit Company's massacre of striking workers in Colombia in the 1920s (and its disappearance from history) as a stand in for a longer, often undocumented, history of such violence (298–319). The only surviving witness of the murders and the disappearance of all evidence of it is told: 'There haven't been any dead here [...] Since the time of your uncle, the colonel, nothing has happened in Macondo' (313–314). The soldiers wiping out all remaining trace of organised political opposition repeat the same doublethink mantra: 'Nothing has happened in Macondo, nothing has ever happened and nothing ever will happen. This is a happy town' (316).

In fact, doublethink has never been far away, and was especially apparent during the Cold War. It was a feature of Eastern European regimes, as per Orwell's fear for a future Britain in his novel, and spread throughout many parts of the so-called third world. Unsurprisingly, then, in the wake of the dictatorship in Argentina, for example, the film *La historia oficial/The Official Story* (1985) made precisely the point I am making here. Now, increasingly, doublethink is an everyday reality in Western liberal democracies. Whilst our eyes tell us that the US president's inauguration in 2017 was sparsely attended, the press and public are officially informed that it was the most well-attended inauguration ever. This is, precisely, the bracketing off of what we know to be true, in favour of an 'alternative fact' which we are told we must believe. This is what the term 'post-truth' often refers to, the prevalence of doublethink.

Framing this book is the spectre of this Orwellianism, which is explored via an analysis of how encounters with lost pasts create hesitation over the sense of our place within world history. This is because of a very specific cinematic feature of all of the films discussed, the similarities between the functioning of what Gilles Deleuze called the 'time-image' (1985) in what I am claiming is a hesitant cinematic ethics, and doublethink.

So, what is the time-image?

Deleuze's taxonomy of movement-images and time-images is now an integral part of the mainstream in Film Studies.[2] Deleuze's time-image categories (see Chapter 2) depict the temporal existence of the world directly (in the sense of, without subordination to movement through time, which produces a less direct, or spatialized form of time, or 'movement-image'). In Deleuze's time-image, especially in the concept of the crystal of time (in which we are able to glimpse the infinitely divisible nature of time, its perpetual splitting into a present that passes, and a past that is preserved), there is hesitation over the veracity of history. The crystal of time, *by definition*, contains the potential to offer an alternative view of the past, one which contrasts with that which we believe informs the present (see Chapter 2). I state 'by definition' because if time is forever splitting in this way, then what is stored in the (virtual) past is the infinite possibility of alternative histories to that of the one informing the (actual) present. Thus the crystal is a potentially destabilizing, deterritorializing, ungrounding force within history. Its purpose is to make us hesitate about the veracity of the present, by reminding us of alternative (or, lost) pasts.

Until recently this was thought to be a celebratory revelation, due to the challenge that the time-image poses to established histories. After all, the term 'alternative' has only very recently taken on the negative connotations it now has in the so-called 'post-truth' era. A brief example can show why the time-image's power to unground history was celebrated until now.

In Jacques Rivette's *Céline et Julie vont en bateau/Celine and Julie Go Boating* (France, 1974), history is revealed to be a patriarchal conspiracy that excludes women. This history is challenged by the two eponymous heroines, a magician, Céline (Juliet Berto) and a librarian, Julie (Dominique Labourier). They save a little girl from being murdered by returning to the past (see Figure 0.1). This past, dubbed the 'House of Fiction', is figured as both symbolic and societal, as well as informing of the personal histories of the heroines. It is, then, the virtual store of the past as totality, from which the official story of history emanates, but within which is also contained its alternatives – its other (lost) pasts – and, accordingly, its potential for change. Their travel to this past is undertaken via magic sweeties (candies) which enable an Alice in Wonderland style entrance into, or rather, passing through of, the crystal of time. The perpetually splitting nature of time is revealed to them in this way, such that they realise how the telling of this story of history can change: as they state succinctly, once upon a time can become 'twice upon a time'. To figure this out, however, is a work of historical detection on the part of the heroines, who must first of all hesitate

FIGURE 0.1   Saving the girl revives the lost past 'murdered' by patriarchy, in *Céline et Julie vont en bateau/Celine and Julie Go Boating* (Jacques Rivette, 1974).

with respect to the veracity of the truth of the story of history which they have known up to this point.

Ultimately, Céline and Julie are able to save the girl from a 'murder' symbolic of woman's entrapment in patriarchy from childhood. They thus enable the girl, and, by extension, themselves, to escape this fate and imagine a different future. Emerging during the second wave of feminism in the West, then, *Céline and Julie* explores the possibility that an alternative history can be offered to that of patriarchy. Hesitation, the time-image shows, is what happens in a moment where the veracity of history comes into question, allowing new futures to emerge.[3]

What is very apparent from this example, however, is that the operation involved, the positing of an alternative past which can inform the present, is not substantially different from that of doublethink. Albeit, we might argue that whilst doublethink attempts to obscure the reality of the past, the time-image actually attempts the opposite: the revelation of pasts that are obscured. Put another way, doublethink reduces history to one, the party line, whereas the time-image asks us to contemplate that history is multiple, labyrinthine, and potentially falsifying of the present (as opposed to fake). Even so, for those on opposing sides of this operation, there may well be an equal sense that what is being revealed or obscured (the effectively falsifying nature of the operation) is done with the best of intentions. Or at least, we can give actors at either end of the political spectrum the benefit of the doubt, for argument's sake. So, is the time-image any different, let alone any better, than doublethink?

Ultimately, the only difference between doublethink and the time-image is one of *political intent*. In an internet era which sees political discourse influenced by fake news in a deliberate attempt to create cognitive dissonance (Pynchon 2003, x) in the minds of voters (if we are unable to tell which of the 'alternative facts' presented is true, then how can we know who to vote for?), creating hesitation is now a political strategy used most effectively by the right to foster disengagement with the political process. Hence, it is now more important than ever to clarify how the time-image's political potential remains useful to our understanding of how the story of world history is told cinematically. To what extent can we still claim that the hesitation fostered by the time-image is ethical, in the face of doublethink, alternative facts, and fake news?

This discussion, of course, has some pedigree already (Corner 2017). Long before President Donald Trump's election led to claims that the right have stolen the crucial tools of philosophy in their surrounding of the truth with fake news (Williams 2017), in the wake of 9/11 and the resulting 'War on Terror', Bruno Latour had already noted the political right's capacity to hijack critical theory's tendency to debunk, deconstruct, unmask, and otherwise falsify accepted truths with alternative views of reality. Latour emphasised, especially, that purposefully maintaining a lack of scientific certainty (spreading doubt, effectively), in spite of the facts to the contrary, had already been established as a right wing tactic to deny climate change (Latour 2004, 226–227; Klein 2017, 67). Herein, then, lies the distinction between the importance of hesitation in the time-image, and in the cognitive dissonance fostered by fake news. For Latour, 'confidence in ideological arguments posturing as matters of fact—as we have learned to combat so efficiently in the past' (combatted, we can say, for example, via the time-image as challenge to patriarchal history in *Céline et Julie*) is now replaced by 'distrust of good matters of fact disguised as bad ideological biases' (as propagated by fake news denials of climate change) (227).

Yet, when Latour identifies the extinguishing of the lights of the Enlightenment, which had previously debunked so many older beliefs, by this 'same debunking impetus' (232) he is really, perhaps unwittingly, indicating the problem inherent to the news/fake news debate – namely, that the history of colonial modernity (which includes the typically lauded Enlightenment) builds its legitimacy upon doublethink.

So, what is colonial modernity?

Colonial modernity is a term used throughout this book to describe the history of global capital since the growth of Europe and the West (from the late Fifteenth Century onwards) to its present position of world dominance. It describes the emergence of modernity after 1492 on the back of colonial genocide, enslavement, torture, theft on an imperial scale, and the devastation caused by environmental exploitation for profit: all to provide the West with the wealth which accumulates from the managerial control of the resources and trade of the world system (Dussel 2003a, 62). As Walter Mignolo, indebted to Dussel, summarises, 'there is no modernity without coloniality' (2000, xii–xiii and 43), they being 'two sides of the same coin' (50).[4] The term 'coloniality', in fact, has a very specific meaning. It is drawn from Aníbal Quijano's argument that, distinct from colonialism as a historical category, the structure of domination which emerges with the rise to global dominance of Europe after the conquest of the Americas illuminates the 'coloniality of power' (2008, 101). 'Coloniality' includes colonialism's 'social classification of the world's population around the idea of race' within a global capitalist structure for controlling labour (Quijano 2008, 181), which remains ongoing under globalisation.[5]

It is for this reason that the eradicated histories which doublethink suppresses perpetually threaten to derail it, just as the ungrounding force of the time-image indicates the unstable nature of the Eurocentric view of world history – its instability being due to the subsisting histories which it has banished to the past. As García Márquez so succinctly notes, after all, empires have always hidden their crimes, justifying them in the name of the advances they supposedly bring.

For Western thought, it is the emergence of decolonial and postcolonial thinking, around the world, in particular after World War Two, which disturbs this orthodoxy.[6] Accordingly, the ungrounding of the history of colonial modernity via the time-image took place in the West at a moment when the left sought to uncover this great deception. It is no coincidence that May 1968, and second wave feminism, occurred as the global power of Europe's imperial nations waned, nor that Deleuze (perhaps erroneously), considers the time-image a postwar European invention in part for this reason. Yet, although the above subheading concerning a non-fascist life references Michel Foucault's preface to Deleuze and Guattari's *Anti-Oedipus* (1972), a book which Foucault believed provided an introduction to a life without fascism, looking back from the present under neoliberalism, this hope of a non-fascist life now seems, at best, optimistic.

Simultaneous to the intellectual development of the European left in the 1960s and 1970s, the CIA also realised the potential of French theory to boost the right's political project of deepening wealth inequality globally (Rockhill 2017). The attack on the young, which was a feature of the Cold War in many parts of the world, saw the right eradicating the potential for political opposition to capitalism across the third world, and preparing the ground for the global expansion of precarity which characterises neoliberal globalisation. With post-Cold War proclamations of a supposed 'End of History', there would no longer seem to be any alternative to neoliberalism, an economic model which – as was evident, for instance, in the 2016 US presidential election and the UK's referendum on its place in the European Union of the same year – fosters the conditions for a right wing populism verging on fascism. Noticeably, Orwell's doublethink, as Jonathan Beller observes, 'represented the collapse of any dialectical thought by the real, practical imposition of what he has already glimpsed as the end of history – the eternal domination of humanity by an immortal, relatively static, and ultimately unconceptualizeable totalitarian society' (2006, 288). So, under neoliberal globalisation, are we still able to realise a non-fascist life, and can a hesitant cinematic ethics help us to do so? Or has that potential been closed off by the right and the clock reset, perhaps forever, to a moment before the advances made by socialism and communism?

In this book I argue that all is far from lost. Neoliberalism suggests that if history cannot be known, all that remains is for people to adapt to the political status quo, accommodating themselves as best they can to a system which is the root cause of the quotidian exhaustion which distracts them from political engagement (Chandler and Reid 2016, 5). By contrast the time-image shows that people have the potential to react anew, to imagine a different future (different ways to inhabit society) by drawing on different ideas of history: hesitation, not to stultify, but to empower.[7]

This fine grain of difference is crucial to the political intent behind this use of hesitation. It is the same kind of understanding as that of the subtle differences between lying, sarcasm, irony, disingenuousness, etc, which we must learn to distinguish as children. This distinction is so difficult to explain to children because even though they are all the same operation – words spoken in a falsifying relationship with the truthfulness of their literal meaning (as any child will tell you, this is still basically lying) – they all have entirely different agendas with respect to the target recipient (deceit, hurtfulness, humour, gentleness, or as appropriate to context). As they all create cognitive dissonance, it is this *intention* which is the key to their difference. Whilst it might seem tempting to consider the playful tone of certain practices to work against their deceitful intent (i.e. to argue that only lying is really lying, and that the rest are all more innocent activities), in fact with all such practices there is the potential to wilfully deceive in line with a political agenda (e.g. irony can equally be a weapon of the right (Wilson 2017)). It is not tone that makes the difference, then, but the intent behind the use of what we might consider, after Mikhail Bakhtin, double voiced discourse (1981, 324–327).

The right may have co-opted thinking from the left to its own ends, but the idea that this nullifies the potential of the time-image to keep alive – and provide ethical encounters with – the lost pasts of world history should be treated with scepticism: it may well be right-wing spin. After all, the Eurocentric history of colonial modernity is, although the official story, also the ultimate in fake news. It is enunciated in the face of common sense and at the expense of the people it excludes – O'Brien requires Winston to believe that he is holding up five fingers even though Winston can clearly see four, or, the press are informed that the presidential inauguration was the most well attended ever, even though it very apparently was not. For contemporary thinkers like Naomi Klein, it may be possible to defeat such 'shock politics' (which seek to work via cognitive dissonance to open up a gap between 'events and our initial ability to explain them'), if we 'tell a different story from the one the shock doctors are peddling, a vision of the world compelling enough to compete head-to-head with theirs' (2017, 7–8). This includes, she notes, a vision of history which can expose the 'role played by the politics of division and separation' during the last five hundred years of colonial modernity (100). It is this process, of proposing a positive alternative (or alternatives), which a world of cinemas has been involved in for decades. Specifically, using time-images it seeks to create a hesitation with respect to the official story of Eurocentric world history: *cinema against doublethink*.

The time-image, that which Deleuze thought to express the potential for a new political cinema from the Global South (1985, 207–215), has the potential to speak for the underside of modernity (those excluded by colonial modernity). This is what the analyses of transnational histories in Chapters 3–6 variously illustrate. Rumours of the time-image's death, then, are greatly exaggerated.

To answer my earlier question: what is so important about cinema being against doublethink is that its opposition speaks with political intent to the heart of the struggle over global structural inequality. With this in mind, I now leave contemporary politics, and delve into cinema: to move from what is important about this, to how we can see it on screen.

For the remainder of this Introduction, I firstly detail this argument in more depth, signalling the theoretical areas which I will engage with in the two following chapters. I then provide one key example of what I am discussing, *El abrazo de la serpiente/Embrace of the Serpent* (Colombia/Venezuela/Argentina, 2016). This recent film clearly indicates what is at stake in the analysis found in Chapters 3–6, wherein are outlined different stories of transnational history being told across a world of cinemas.

Denying the denial of coevalness

What does it mean to encounter another past, even a lost past, on screen? This is not to say that we see someone else's past in its totality, and certainly not just by encountering a character with a potentially different background to that of the viewer. These are not pristine histories, if such a thing even exists. These are not 'prosthetic' memories, of pasts never experienced by the viewer but which can, once seen on screen, inform the viewer's present (Landsberg 2004; 2009). Nor are they quite the 'post memories' which we may try to invent to recuperate eradicated pasts, such as those of parents 'disappeared' by repressive political regimes (Hirsch 1997). Neither do they quite function as evocatively affective memory images of state terror, aesthetically rendered so as to resonate with similar memories, irrespective of the specificities of national experiences of torture and disappearance (Chaudhuri 2014, 84–114; see Chapter 2). Rather, in the films discussed herein, what is foregrounded is our *inability* to connect with someone else's history, or just, history, in a way that can inform the present (the inability of a lost past to function as prosthetic or post memory). What is glimpsed, instead, is something of the vastness of the world history in which we are immersed (hinted at by the fleeting encounter with the lost past), and therefore of the *relative* centrality of our own informing past within what we might consider a global, planetary, 'world memory' (Deleuze 1985, 95 and 113).

At best, encounters with other pasts are offered as fragments, stories, myths, hints or allusions, the sum of which are the leftover glimpses of a totality we will likely never recover: the virtual past, world memory. Even so, these encounters can be extremely powerful, and through them a world of cinemas is thus attempting to *deny* what Johannes Fabian terms 'the denial of coevalness' (1983). In this oft-quoted phrase, Fabian describes the refusal – attendant on colonial practices, but equally apparent in how the world is generally viewed from its privileged centres – to recognise that the histories of others are the same 'age' as those of the colonisers, ethnographers (and so on) who set out to conquer or observe otherness.

Fabian charts how a hegemonic conception of time – as progressive and linear – culminates in the naturalising of time by evolutionary thought with Charles Darwin (26). This creates a 'stream' of time, with some cultures 'upstream', some 'downstream' (17), effectively distancing the other from the (as it were, present point in) time of the observer (25). This view, of one time within which some cultures are more developed than others, has accompanied Western dominance of the world since '"universal Time" was [...] established concretely and politically in the Renaissance in response to both classical philosophy and to the cognitive challenges presented by the age of discoveries opening up in the wake of the earth's circumnavigation' (3).

Fabian's return to the Renaissance origins of colonial modernity, when Europe reoriented with respect to other cultures from a position relative in space to one relative in time (Mignolo 2003, xi) – is not coincidental. As Quijano notes of the way that Europeans categorised the indigenous Americans they encountered after 1492, banishing them to a primitive, under-developed past:

> Their new racial identity, colonial and negative, involved the plundering of their place in the history of the cultural production of humanity. From then on, there were inferior races, capable only of producing inferior cultures. The new identity also involved their relocation in the historical time constituted with America first and with Europe later; from then on they were the past [...] and because of that inferior, if not always primitive.
>
> *(2008, 200)*

The denial of coevalness, in the case of the Americas the expulsion of such sophisticated civilizations as that of the 'Aztecs, Mayas, Chimus, Aymaras, Incas, Chibchas' (Quijano 2000, 551) to the past, was the temporal dimension to the colonial exploitation which followed after 1492. As Michael Hardt and Antonio Negri argue, it was in the context of Renaissance humanism's confrontation with the discovery of the Americas that 'Eurocentrism was born as a reaction to the potentiality of a newfound human equality; it was the counterrevolution on a global scale' (2000, 77). Structural inequality, then, is at the dark heart of the last five centuries of the world history of colonial modernity, and it is justified by a view of time that banishes others to the past.

Now, however, due largely to decolonial and postcolonial thought, amidst a world of cinemas we are increasingly asked to decolonise such thinking by situating our own past in relation to the complexities of world history. We are challenged, five hundred years later, to refuse to see other pasts as backwards, primitive, or lost somewhere in the past: challenged to observe – as Mignolo has it – '*the denial of the denial of coevalness*' (2003, ix). Whilst decolonial and postcolonial thought brings this to the foreground, in addition the idea of the time-image (which Deleuze considers to emerge in post-war Europe) indicates that for many decades there has been a struggle over the eradication/remembrance of pasts across a world of cinemas. This is increasingly a 'trending' issue for scholars of a world of cinemas because of the importance of the Deleuzian idea of 'world memory' which underpins such scholarship (see Chapter 2). Even so, this is not universally acknowledged in the field. This is because, I believe, how we conceive of modernity directly influences how we understand cinema to negotiate the transnational histories stored away in world memory.

For example, consider Mary Ann Doane's rightly famous and illuminating exploration of how, under 'capitalist modernity' (2000, 4), film helped Western societies of the late Nineteenth and early Twentieth Century negotiate the contrary pulls between the rationalisation of time (the uniform standardisation of time by technological means in the realms of work, travel and communication) and temporal contingency (the heterogeneous nature of time which erupted in newly packed urban areas in chance or ephemeral encounters (10-11)). By contrast, we can equally understand these contrary pulls within cinematic time to negotiate the much larger concern of the perpetual disappearance of contingent histories from world memory, due to the rationalising forces of colonial modernity (the 'counterrevolution on a global scale'). As has already been explored with respect to specific postcolonial locations globally (e.g. Lim 2009), it is not the historically recent Western urbanisation of the Nineteenth Century, resulting from the industrial revolution, which created this struggle. Rather, it was the rise to global prominence of the West since the Fifteenth Century, via the eradication of the histories of all those from whom it took its wealth: colonial modernity. Thus the field of Film Studies may not universally recognise the wider issue, of the struggle over eradication/remembrance of world history, due to the worldview underpinning the analysis of some scholars.

The histories which are encountered in a world of cinemas are not necessarily those of others, then (as this depends on where you are looking from), but they do belong to the whole world, to world memory. They emerge in time-images which indicate the perpetual struggle that exists between the eradication of histories (forgetting), and the hesitancy with respect to what we believe to have been history under such circumstances (remembrance). This is the potential that the time-image has to keep alive the remembrance of lost pasts, with histories planetary, indigenous, political, and economic being illuminated (in Chapters 3–6) from across a world of cinemas. Together such different examples of pasts, 'bigger' than that of the nation, illustrate the international occurrence of current world cinematic engagements with transnational histories on film. But, as noted at the start of this Introduction, it depends on our worldview as to whether or not this is immediately apparent.

The closeness between these transnational histories and the planetary or world history which encompasses them is evident once considered in relation to colonial modernity. This is due to the convergence of ideas like that of the modern world system (from sociology) with those of the Columbian Exchange (environmental history), certain views on the Anthropocene (geology), the Capitalocene (ecology), all (like Latin American Philosophy) focusing around the pivotal date of 1492 (see Chapters 1–4). Even so, this is not to construct an, as it were, transnational universalism around colonial modernity.

Why not? How are we to be sure that this pitfall is avoided?

G. W. F. Hegel's Nineteenth Century notion of world history is now notorious. For Hegel, the 'development' of the consciousness of freedom, by the 'spirit', proceeds from supposedly primitive Asian origins to its apex in Western (surprise surprise, Hegel's own Northern, Protestant, Germanic) modernity's realisation of universal freedom in the nation-state (1837, 103). America, or European settler colonist America at least, is thus identified as the 'land of the future' (86). Hegel's denial of coevalness, intrinsic to his inability to appreciate the irony of a discussion of freedom in the context of massive global colonisation, is apparent in his negative estimation of the development of the indigenous peoples of the Americas. Noticeably, this argument emphasises military technology as measure: 'The weakness of the human physique of America has been aggravated by a deficiency in the mere tools and appliances of progress – the want of *horses* and *iron*, the chief instruments by which they were subdued' (82). Such a denial elides both the historical facts surrounding the advancement of African, Asian and American civilisations prior to the Fifteenth Century (for example, the indigenous peoples' of the Americas knowledge of zero long before it was known in Europe (Shohat and Stam 1994, 55–61; Mann 2005, 215–216)), and refuses to recognise, in the case of the Americas, the imported diseases (smallpox, malaria, yellow fever) which ravaged the indigenous populations.[8] Hegel, then, in line with Quijano's argument, banishes indigeneity to (Europe's) supposed past.

But of course, this is erroneous. As Dussel indicates, a non-Eurocentric world history focusing on migrationary patterns rather *literally* gives the lie to Hegel's worldview. Humanity moved Eastwards out of a centre in the Pacific (Neolithic people migrating from Asia to the Americas), long before the arrival of Europeans (1992b, 73–90; 1998b, 9–13; see also Mann 2005, 151–158). This before we begin to consider Hegel's denial of societal and cultural developments in the peoples that were eradicated by Europeans, conquerors so proud of the way their technology drove bloodthirsty coloniality. Yet Hegel's position remains informing of the normative story of world history – which runs through to late Twentieth Century thinkers of the supposed post-Cold War 'End of History', like Francis Fukuyama and Samuel Huntington (Stam and Shohat 2012, 62).

By contrast, exploring transnational histories on film is to follow Dipesh Chakrabarty in a search for 'a global approach to politics without the myth of a global identity' which can address the challenge of climate change to our grasp of history, but without, in contrast to a Hegelian universal, subsuming particularities (2009, 222). Chakrabarty asks:

> How do we relate to a universal history of life – to universal thought, that is – while retaining what is of obvious value in our postcolonial suspicion of the universal? The crisis of climate change calls for thinking simultaneously on both registers, to mix together the immiscible chronologies of capital and species history.
>
> *(2009, 219–220)*

As I demonstrate by introducing the viewfinder of a Dusselian ethics (see Chapter 1), a world of cinemas, in its examination of transnational histories, includes human histories within a broader, encompassing planetary history (see Chapter 3). It has become the archive of the world's memories, storing transnational histories in which the intertwined pasts of capital, humanity as a species, and the planet more broadly, are seen to be inextricably linked. This is the case whether these transnational histories predate the invention of the nation, with examples ranging from the several billion year planetary history of the Earth (in *Uncle Boonmee* and *Nostalgia for the Light* (Chapter 3)), to the several centuries' of the North Atlantic trade circuit as engine for Europe's rise to global centrality in the world system (Chapter 4, *How Tasty* and *Even the Rain*), or, because they involve various nations, as in the history of the Cold War (Chapter 5, *The Act of Killing* and *At the Foot*), or more recently of neoliberal globalisation (Chapter 6, *Carancho* and *Lady Vengeance*).

To glimpse the intertwined histories of capital and humanity within planetary history requires a recontextualisation of cinema's engagement with history, globally. An approach is needed which can grasp the local and global ramifications of transnational histories of exclusion – stepping beyond the 'limiting imagination of national cinema' (Higson, 2000) without creating an all-encompassing transnational universal. Taken together, these different transnational histories address what Chakrabarty indicates is the 'question of a human collectivity, an us, pointing to a figure of the universal that escapes our capacity to experience the world' (2009, 222). It is in this way, to answer my own question, that this potential pitfall can be avoided.

To ground this interpretation of transnational histories I turn to methods drawn from various disciplines, in particular, Latin American Philosophy. Dussel's work is not as well known in the UK as elsewhere, although his influence is evident in the works of much-discussed thinkers like Paul Gilroy, Charles W. Mills, and Mignolo. Naturally, this is far from the only possible way to proceed, but in Dussel we find an appropriate grounding for this hermeneutics due to the role of world systems analysis in his thinking. This is a paradigm, after all, which functions to 'reorient' us away from established Eurocentric conceptions of world history (Frank 1998). Dussel, by turns, is joined by a clamour of voices from elsewhere, including, in no particular order: Quijano, Mignolo, Chakrabarty, Gilroy, Mills, Hardt and Negri, Michel Serres, Carole Pateman, Rey Chow, Andre Gunder Frank, Arjun Appadurai, Heonik Kwon, Hannah Arendt, David Graeber, Giorgio Agamben, Maurizio Lazzarato, Étienne Balibar, Hayden White, Steven Shaviro, Alia Al-Saji, Eduardo Viveiros de Castro et al. Although the work of, to paraphrase Franco Moretti, 'distant viewing' (2001; 2013) undertaken herein (see Chapter 1), belongs to the heritage of Ella Shohat and Robert Stam's *Unthinking Eurocentrism* (1994) (this book can be similarly understood as involving us in the *unthinking* of *doublethink*), it is the specific combination of (a reconstructed) Deleuze with Dussel (and these various other voices) which reveals how a world of cinemas offers an ethics of hesitation with respect to normative assumptions about world history. As an introductory example of this, I now turn to *Embrace of the Serpent*.

Encountering other worlds

The Oscar-nominated *Embrace of the Serpent*, an internationally distributed art film with funding from the Hubert Bals Fund (the International Film Festival of Rotterdam) and Programa Ibermedia, is a movie some might consider 'familiar' to the festival circuit. It is a product of the complex geopolitics of the relationship between festivals and filmmaking in the Global South (Martin-Jones and Montañez 2013a). Whilst it might thus be tempting to dismiss such a movie, by emphasising the potentially self-serving loop involved in the film and resulting discussions of it (i.e. the view that the international festival circuit cynically fosters such 'views' of the world to 'develop' Western thinking at the expense of the others it continues to exploit for profit), I maintain nevertheless that there is much to be gained from a considered approach to this film.

Embrace of the Serpent is based on diaries of European colonisers encountering indigenous Americans (see Figure 0.2) (as is *How Tasty*, discussed in Chapter 4), and like all the films discussed herein it is a time-image. The action alternates

Give them a song.

FIGURE 0.2 Encountering a lost past creates hesitation over history, in *El abrazo de la serpiente/Embrace of the Serpent* (Ciro Guerra, 2016).

between two temporal planes (1909 and 1940), a story repeating itself of mankind's increasing inability to communicate with the natural world due to the exploitation of nature for material gain. This topic is a feature of the contemporary life of the viewing public, with ideas about ecology dating back to the 1960s (Sessions 1995, x) through a revival of interest in indigenous views of religion, society and place in the 1970s (Deloria 1972, 146), Gaia Theory (the 1980s) and the Natural Contract (the 1990s), to the now commonplace concern with environmental sustainability, or 'Green' politics (2000s onwards). *Embrace of the Serpent* links the colonial past to the globalised present with examples of armed conflict over the control of areas where rubber can be harvested, and the search for a plant (yakruna) which grows on the rubber (with properties exploitable for purposes medicinal or military). It thus evokes viewer awareness of the contemporary operations of multinational capitalism (so-called 'Big Pharma'), and the global reach of the military-industrial complex.

The viewer is aligned with the perspective of an indigenous protagonist,[9] the shaman, Karamakate (Nilbio Torres in his younger incarnation, Antonio Bolivar Salvador as an old man), who encounters two Westerners (one German, the other, Evan (Brionne Davis) from the USA), in the two historical periods. Karamakate initially believes that it is his destiny, as one of the last of the Cohiuano people, to continue their 'song'. At the close of the film, however, he passes it on as dream/ memory/knowledge to Evan, and also, directly to the viewer. As Karamakate hands Evan the yakruna potion he speaks his realisation, that his destiny was, in fact, to pass on knowledge of his people's 'song' to other people: 'I wasn't meant to teach my people. I was meant to teach you. Give them more than what they asked for. Give them a song. Tell them everything you see, everything you feel' (see Figure 0.2). As he prepares to blow the powder up Evan's nostrils, directly looking at the audience in close up, Karamakate states: 'You are Cohiuano'.

The cinematic vision which follows commences with a helicopter shot, moving rapidly over treetops, as though Evan were flying above the rainforest. The panorama slows, as we travel along the course of a mighty river, through a ravine, into vast canyons, and across mountaintops, all accompanied by chanting on the soundtrack. Finally we catch sight of the serpent which Karamakate told Evan he would meet – the winding river, seen from above. Suddenly the landscape is replaced by Karamakate as a young man, sitting crosslegged, against a luminescent light background. As he opens his eyes, and then his mouth, the light from behind him shines out through his face, obliterating his presence. The light is used to transport us, as via a match cut, to luminescent celestial starscapes, which morph by turns into brightly coloured renditions of shapes similar to those of rock paintings, and yet seemingly at one in terms of magnitude with the starscapes of the cosmos seen previously. The most striking of these is the final one, which positions a human stick figure amongst what appears to be an expanding cosmos.

This vision offers another way of remembering, from an oral tradition, which may better inform the present (exploitative) way of being in the world perpetuated by capitalism. This affective moment seemingly demonstrates how the history, or 'song' of Karamakate's people is at once of the Earth (the winding river), but also historically of the Universe (the patterns in the stars). Thus, we are shown, we can encounter the past, memory, history, myth, 'song' of another people (in this instance, of an indigenous tribe eradicated during armed conflict over the region's rubber), or more accurately, in such a cinematic glimpse we can encounter the knowledge that it once existed.

The highly mediated nature of the encounter with the past is significant regarding what we can and cannot know about the past from cinema. The scene is a mixture of the opening helicopter shots of forested landscapes of *Ten Canoes* (Australia, 2006) mingled with the psychedelia of *2001: A Space Odyssey* (UK/USA, 1968) and the cosmological emphasis of *Nostalgia for the Light* (see Chapter 3). The rather clichéd mashup of aesthetic elements from previous films serves to make of this history: a recognisably temporal otherness (as in the starchild sequence of *2001* evoked by the light emanating from the young Karamakate); an ethnic otherness situated in a specific place (as in the *Ten Canoes*-like helicopter shots); with a cosmological scale linking planet to universe (as in the celestial landscapes akin to those in *Nostalgia for the Light*). Indeed, the rather cinematic nature of this vision of another's past is emphasised by Evan's awaking the next morning in the rainforest, the sudden shift from night to day foreshadowing the emergence of the film's viewers into the light as they exit the auditorium. Thus we are clearly not supposed to understand this history, or Karamakate's worldview, in any detail. Only to realise its existence as different from our (or at any rate, Evan's) own.

Admittedly, when Karamakate says 'you are Cohiuano' it may well be intended as a suggestion of a prosthetic memory for those audience members able to connect with this cosmology. During the film Karamakate gives various indications as to his belief in what would seem to be a dynamic relationship which his people have with both the stars and the Earth. For instance, in an induced vision Karamakate sees a meteor, which he calls Watoíma, and afterwards relates that the Jaguar has told him that on hitting the earth it has been transformed into a boa. Both the Jaguar and the snake appear prominently in the film, in moments seemingly divorced from the human narrative – the point being, of course, that they are not disconnected from it at all even if there is no direct interaction with these species. For those who do understand these symbols, then, there may perhaps be the potential to take on Karamakate's peoples' memory as prosthesis – to become Cohiuano. Even so, it is not a given that such symbols will be understood, even in the region where the film was made, due to the effectiveness of several centuries of European colonial campaigns to burn all written sources of pre-Christian beliefs in the Americas (such as the Mayan sacred text, the *Popol Vuh*) and the reliance on oral history for the preservation of many such creation myths (Christenson 2003, 15–21). After all, one of the tactics used by the right in the USA, to create confusion surrounding climate change in the manner indicated by Latour, is to align with creationist beliefs that the Earth is only around 6000 years old. The very feasibility of such recourse to a Christian creation myth by a dominant settler colonist culture indicates the effectiveness of this systematic destruction of equivalent indigenous myths. In which case, what about those who do not have any way to connect to this history, wherever they may be? Those for whom it cannot act as a prosthesis?

It is possible to research the significance of what Karamakate says, of course. Answers might be found in ethnographic works of the period depicted, such as those of C. H. De Goeje (1943), which illuminates how, within a cosmology of eternal beings who are only encountered in dream (in which, say, the reality of a Jaguar which we may encounter in the forest is but an earthly manifestation of its associated eternal cosmic being (1-2)): Watoíma can be the name for both a meteor and a fire-spirit (47); the Jaguar may be a divine avenger possibly capable of devouring mankind at the destruction of the world (41); and the serpent might represent the mother goddess and founder of the universe, who can also be the essence of time (26). Yet few will undertake such research, or be privileged enough to be able to do so, and those who do are only able to imperfectly grasp the actual significance of the iconography.

Alternatively, curious viewers might turn to contemporary anthropological work to learn more about the Jaguar as *itseke* or 'dawn time being' in Amazonian cosmology, including its strong association with place (Heckenberger 2005, 79; 352 n13). Or, more likely than either of these approaches, of course, they might turn to emerging works exploring the film's attempt to reconsider how encounters with indigenous tribes in the Amazon are depicted cinematically (Berghahn 2018; Mutis 2018), or simply search the internet and uncover Peccadillo Pictures' accompanying press notes, where they might learn of the indigenous view of time (as 'a series of multiple universes happening simultaneously' (Anon. 2015, 5)) and an explanation for the final vision, as:

> A visual representation of the iconography of the Barasana tribe, the primitive drawings are representative of the childlike state and can only be accessed through the dreamworld therefore this scene invites the audience into a realm that merges past, present and future.
>
> (7)

But even here, the press pack's 'Amazonian Glossary' (10) does not provide a comprehensive answer to all these points surrounding animals and their possible cosmological or mythological significance. Rather, in line with the film's central premise, all that is garnered is a glimpse of a lost past – one which we cannot know through the film.

For perhaps the majority of viewers, then, this is not a transparent window into either Karamakate's culture or its past. What is very recognisable about the scene, rather, *is the very idea* that we are seeing a history being evoked cinematically. What is familiar is the cinematic *encoding* of such an encounter. There is a sense of enlightenment in the scene, as though a Road to Damascus conversion, of literally 'seeing of the light' for Evan. What he remembers is similarly coded as mythical: it takes place in a time before the present, as seen in the indicators of cosmology amidst recognisable cinematic markers of indigeneity. Thus Evan's revelation is not that of the *content* of another history, but *simply of its existence*. The revelation, recognisable to cinematic audiences worldwide, then, is that we are seeing the encoding of history as otherness.

The potentially varied viewing experience I am describing here is perhaps rather like that of encountering an Aboriginal map in an art gallery in, say, Australia. For those who can read it, it is a map. For others, it is possible to understand that it is a map, even if it is different from what one expects of a map (for some the painting on bark may resemble more an art work), and even if one is unable to read it or to understand the terrain it refers to. The fact that another visitor could easily read the map and envisage the contours of the land only emphasises the importance of the encounter with the *realisation of the existence* of a history which many do not (yet) know.

Indeed, what many may be confronted with, in both such a map and a film like *Embrace of the Serpent*, is an altogether different idea of what history is, than that of the linear, developmental model of colonial modernity. For many, the encounter, instead, is with a history invested in place, and a cyclical notion of time informing the present not uncommon to indigeneity in the Americas (Deloria 1972, 97–111). The reason we cannot know this history is because it is not a history to be understood after a Eurocentric fashion. Indeed it is not even necessarily clear whether Karamakate's people's song is a history per se, or whether it is actually more akin to a religious experience of a *place* in the cosmos, emanating as the vision does from a sacred site harbouring the last flower of the yakruna (280–282). In any case, it is a (lost) past, rather than a history: not only because colonial modernity denies equality to such pasts, and views of history, but also because it was never meant to be recorded in a linear, teleological fashion. What Evan and the viewer realise in this cinematic vision of the song of Karamakate's people, is another (spatial) relationship to history. So, whilst it is accurate to speak of transnational history (within the broader encompasser of world history), in a world of cinemas it is more accurate to speak of colonial modernity's lost pasts, than its lost histories.

For many, then, *Embrace of the Serpent* does not offer a prosthetic memory of the history of Karamakate's people. They have practically all been slaughtered anyway, and even Karamakate himself is concerned about how much he has forgotten of what he used to know. Rather, it is a glimpsed memory of another way of understanding humanity's place in the world, another view of history and of the interconnectedness of the universe. This realisation of difference is the recognition of coevalness, a chance to deny its denial.

What is made obvious is that, far from being a 'primitive' other to the modern European travellers, Karamakate possesses botanical wisdom beyond that developed by Western civilisation. This is precisely why he is sought out. The past of his people may not have 'developed' towards scientific discoveries (the gramophone player which features in the jungle is purposefully incongruous, indicating Hegel's mistaken insistence on the supposed superiority of Europe's technological development), but it did advance coeval with Western civilisation, as is evident in Karamakate's far superior knowledge of and engagement with the rainforest ecosystem. His Western visitors are, by contrast, ailing or incapable of completing their jobs there without him.

Thus the film seeks not to implant another memory, as prosthesis, but only to indicate the many (lost) memories which we may never know. This, so as to relativise the centrality of hegemonic Western understandings of history. As Karamakate tells Evan: 'I was not meant to teach my people, I was meant to teach you'. But what he is able to impart to his companion, and the viewer, is not an understanding of the culture and history of his people (their 'song'), but only the knowledge that it once existed, rendered as a cinematic 'revelation' of this fact.

What does this illuminate regarding a world of cinemas' opposition to doublethink? *Embrace of the Serpent* indicates the distinction between the argument I am making here and Rey Chow's analysis of what she calls 'liberal fascism', or 'the fascist longing in our midst' (1998, 15, 32), by which she describes an Orientalist binary evident in certain contemporary enunciations of multicultural difference. Like Chow, I also reconsider the history of theorising about fascism in light of the philosophical works of Deleuze and Guattari. With political events in 2017 increasingly suggesting that a non-fascist life may be more difficult to live in the near future, there is a distinct danger that the films discussed in this book might be understood to present unknowable pasts, because they bolster the mythical structure of unknowable otherness which Chow describes as emblematic of 'liberal fascism'. It is through this process, after all, that white consciousness constructs itself in relation to otherness by maintaining the belief that '*"we" are not "them", and that "white" is not "other"* […] which can be further encapsulated as *"we are not other"* […] fascism *par excellence*' (1998, 31).

Yet, rather than evidencing such a 'fascist longing in our midst', I argue that films like *Embrace of the Serpent* offer us a rather different revelation. Namely: '*other' pasts exist which are not ours, so our past cannot be the centre of world history.* This revelation, after all, leaves Western characters like Evan in *Embrace of the Serpent* shaken in their previous belief in themselves, and their exploitative relationship to the world: shaken in their adherence to colonial modernity as historical norm. This is not the same as the affirmation of the inviolable centrality of white supremacy via the encounter with an unknowable other. Whilst it would be idealistic (even in an age of increasingly universal precarity) to stretch this to the conclusion that, 'we are (also) other', nevertheless, there may even be, if only fleetingly, the revelation that '*we are coeval*.'[10]

Hence the argument I propose is not that we *cannot* know difference. Only, rather, that the first step to realising that difference is important *to the self*, is in acknowledging that the self exists in a relational position which challenges the contingent centrality of our own story of history. In short, these films ask us to 'get over ourselves' by realising our relative position in world history. As Paul

Gilroy argues, emphasising the importance of remembering the blood-soaked and ransacked colonial pasts in an era when such remembrance is discouraged unless as a form of 'whitewashed […] imperialist nostalgia' (2005, 3), it is no longer sufficient to look to gain self-knowledge through exposure to strangers. Instead:

> We might consider how to cultivate the capacity to act morally and justly not just in the face of otherness – imploring or hostile – but in response to the xenophobia and violence that threaten to engulf, purify or erase it. The opportunity for self-knowledge is certainly worthwhile, but, especially in turbulent political climates, it must take second place behind the principled and methodological cultivation of a degree of estrangement from one's own culture and history.
>
> *(2005, 67)*

It is precisely via a sense of estrangement from one's own centrality to the world, brought on by encounters with otherness in cinema, that the ethics required of the history of colonial modernity can be investigated. The remembrance of lost pasts, then, is not solely of importance for the cultures whose histories these pasts inform, but also for the re-appraisal of the 'centre', of that which is normative, by the making strange of the official story of world history.

This is not to say that a world of cinemas is oriented towards helping a white, male, Western viewer realise the normative nature of their assumed central place in world history. It is, rather, to argue that this can be the effect upon such a person (like Evan) of exposure to a world of cinemas. This, rather than any sense that they can appropriate memories of others as one can a prosthetic past – a position which, rather, might be open to just such a critique (that such films only exist to inform Western viewers of the pasts they have eradicated).

It is likely often the case that this provincialisation of the heritage through which coevalness is unthinkingly denied to others, is temporary. Like Evan in *Embrace of the Serpent*, ultimately we all awake and exit the auditorium. All we can expect to understand, realistically, these films illustrate, is that otherness – more specifically, other pasts – subsist along with us: that other histories (temporalities, cosmologies) exist parallel to our own. But this revelation is not provided so as to better separate viewers from such pasts, to consolidate an Orientalist self/otherness binary, as per Chow's observations of idealised visions of multiculturalism. Rather, together these films provide encounters with those excluded from colonial modernity, over its long and complex history, in order to foster remembrance of these lost pasts within our shared world memory.

After all, it is not necessarily the case that an indigenous audience will know the past hinted at in *Embrace of the Serpent*. Even in parts of Amazonia, with the ruins of pre-Columbian civilizations now lost to the jungle (Heckenberger 2005, 10), and, more generally in the Americas, so much indigenous heritage purposefully extinguished by colonisation (as noted above, through the burning of sacred texts like the *Popol Vuh*), the glimpse of a lost past may not serve so dissimilar a function as it does for a Western viewer. As also indicated above, the film seems to purposefully indicate this, by having Karamakate, the last of his nearly extinct tribe, observe that he has forgotten much of his own past. Indeed, indicating the complexities of how the lost pasts of the Americas can come to be 'remembered' via the Western invention of film (a film playing on an international film festival circuit whose biases are themselves geopolitically complex (Martin-Jones and Montañez 2013a, 29–30)), *Embrace of the Serpent* concludes with both a dedication to 'all the peoples whose song we will never know' and a simultaneous acknowledgement that the only record of many of these peoples may be the travel diaries of Western interlopers in the Americas (such as those which inspired the film).

The point for all viewers, then, is ultimately the same. *Embrace of the Serpent* indicates the former existence of the now lost past, so as to remind the viewer of the normative and naturalised (rather than normal and natural) nature of the history which they believe to be informing of their present. For those viewers willing and able to hesitate with respect to what such a revelation may mean for them, Eurocentric notions of history may become relativised, or 'unthought' (Shohat and Stam 1994).

Cinematic ethics, ecology, colonial modernity

The grouping of films explored here is reminiscent of the prevailing view of a world of cinemas, that it offers a 'cinema of resistance' to the consequences of economic liberalisation felt increasingly under globalisation. This is seen, for example, in post-Cold War festival films like *La promesse/The Promise* (Belgium/France/Luxembourg/Tunisia, 1996) and *Xiao Wu/The Pickpocket* (China/Hong Kong, 1997), through *Cidade de Deus/City of God* (Brazil/France, 2002) and *Tsotsi* (UK/South Africa, 2005), and on to the present with *I, Daniel Blake* (UK/Belgium/France, 2016). Such films belong to a heritage of political cinema which stretches back at least as far as the 1960s and 1970s, when third cinema (for Mike Wayne a 'cinema of liberation' (2016, 18)) emerged across the Global South, inspired by thinkers like Frantz Fanon (1961, 23), to resist inequalities in colonial, neocolonial and postcolonial contexts. My recourse to Dussel's philosophy of liberation (Chapter 1), suggests a direct link to this heritage, even if such struggles of the Cold War, and again today under globalisation, are understood (after Dussel and others), to be later phases in a five-hundred-year history of colonial modernity. Nevertheless, what this cinema of resistance might be resisting, I believe, is what is not so clear-cut nowadays. How we conceive of resistance affects our ability to grasp the transnational histories which a world of cinemas is engaging with, after Chakrabarty, at the intersection of the (ecological) histories of capital and humanity on Earth.

A direct address to the spectator by a face from within the film is a feature of nearly every film explored in the book. As *Embrace of the Serpent* emphasises when Karamakate breaks the fourth wall in the final scenes, the faces which stare out at the viewer in many of the films analysed are *evidently* those of the excluded, upon whose disenfranchisement (including genocide and enslavement) the West's global dominance was manufactured. Yet, across the films explored the list of such disappeared pasts is increasingly both *human and nonhuman*, and includes: animals, extinct species, spirits, mythological creatures, slaves, indigenous peoples, women, the disappeared and murdered, the poor, even the farmed landscapes and mined depths of the Earth itself. Thus, although films which use direct gazes to camera to reverse the imperial gaze have long been explored (Kaplan 1997, 154–194; Downing and Saxton 2010, 50–61),[11] current debates surrounding ecology give a different meaning to what is resisted in and by a cinema of resistance. Encountering such images is still to encounter global alterity (at least, for those viewers for whom the on-screen images depict otherness), but the underside of colonial modernity is far more inclusive of the histories of the Earth than definitions of political cinema as a cinema of resistance may typically acknowledge.

As the discussion of *Uncle Boonmee* in Chapter 3 illustrates, a character like the once-human but now monkey-spirit Boonsong (Geerasak Kulhong) indicates that the encounters on offer in a world of cinemas do not just include the face to face inter-human interactions discussed by Emmanuel Levinas, whose advocation of ethics as first philosophy has been so influential across disciplines in the early Twenty-First Century. Perhaps ironically, Levinas was inspired by his encounter with a dog, Bobby, whilst a prisoner of the Germans during World War Two (1967). Yet, in spite of the importance of another species in providing Levinas with his sense of humanity, the ethics which he ultimately formulated was not equally inclusive of all others (see Chapter 1). To grasp the extent to which Boonsong is representative of alterity, then, other philosophical voices are required. Dussel's ethics of liberation provides one way of realising Boonsong's otherness with respect to the correlation between colonial modernity and the Anthropocene (the relatively recent entwinement of human history with that of the planet; see Chapter 1), indicating that, because the denial of coevalness under colonial modernity extends beyond human others, so too must our understanding of the cinema of resistance.

This is to follow the emergence of a body of work on ecocinema since the 1990s, which asks us to view with, as it were, different eyes (for instance, those of another people, or even another species) what we think we already know about cinema (Pick and Narraway 2013, 8). It is to attempt to grapple with what Timothy Morton (2013) would consider the 'hyperobject' of, say, the Anthropocene, a history 'massively distributed in time and space relative to humans' (1) with a temporality so much larger than that of human history that we are only ever able to experience a (local) aspect of the much larger whole (1–4). A world of cinemas, then, is asking for an ethical engagement with the difficulties we face in the present moment of realising hyperobjects – like climate change, or the Anthropocene – as a product of colonial modernity (Chapters 1 and 3). It does so by demonstrating how various histories (which have all impacted transnationally across nations and national histories) are histories of unevenness, histories of the denial of coevalness upon which coloniality is established.

A world of cinemas and the Global South

The importance of the voice from the Global South offered by a world of cinemas, as García Márquez reminds us, lies in its potential to remember otherwise than the Eurocentrism of the official history of the world maintained by the West – that against which decolonial and postcolonial thought positions itself. The official story has a vested interest in forgetting this colonial legacy and its continuation in the contemporary world. Such forgetting creates the continued crises, economic and environmental, which threaten humanity's existence in order to generate immense wealth for a global minority. It is this which a world of cinemas increasingly attempts to challenge and resist. Enabling an unthinking of Eurocentrism, what Dussel dubs the 'superideology' of the modern world system after 1492 (1998b, 34; 2003a, 63), a view from the Global South needs to be understood as a geopolitical rather than a geographical categorisation. As noted above with respect to the degree of poverty in a wealthy nation like the USA, the fault line of inequality now runs directly through societies regardless of hemisphere, creating the ubiquitous cheek-by-jowl coexistence of Global North and South. The memory of the world's lost pasts is thus to be found in the cinemas of the Global South, wherever that may be.

I am not claiming that in staging the encounters with lost pasts these films are capable of liberating viewers, in the sense that liberation theology looks to liberate those excluded by modernity from conditions often equitable with misery (see Chapter 1). Before we celebrate the rejuvenative powers of world cinemas too unthinkingly, the distribution and consumption of films from around the world through portals like the international festival circuit has been critiqued, since the time of third cinema, for enabling a Western, or at least Globally Northern, consumption of misery – as though it were an option on the global cinematic menu, its realities all too soon forgotten after the credits roll (Rocha 1965). This geopolitics is not innocent, and accordingly I do not make claims for a cinema of liberation.

Rather, I argue that a world of cinemas upholds the 'liberation principle' by which ethical acts have the potential to transform the existing system (Dussel 1998b, 355–431; Mendieta 2003a, 13), by asking viewers to (re)consider their relationship with the excluded other of colonial modernity in a moment of hesitation. This is a pause in our lives during which past attitudes can be addressed, and the existing, normative view of history potentially relativised (see Chapter 2). By recognising the historical alterity (the lost pasts), of those excluded by modernity, a world of cinemas can thus assist in the denial of the denial of coevalness.

This realisation regarding a world of cinemas may offer something useful for our understanding of troubled times. Contemporary political events illustrate the continued relevance of liberation (in politics, ethics, theology, etc.), despite how dated the term may sound due to its association with postcolonial, Cold War, or third world origins. The political maelstrom in which parts of the West has become engulfed since the millennium is due to this longer world history which has its roots in the discovery of the Americas. In 2016 both the US presidential race and the UK's referendum on its place in the European Union indicated continued racial tensions, and a marked degree of imperialist nostalgia, in the discourses of the right. This outrage towards otherness on the part of white privilege (despite the global minority status of whites) throws into sharp relief the waning of its historical hegemony, in some part due, paradoxically, to the universal precarity encouraged by neoliberalism.

In addition, the almost quotidian regularity with which acts of terrorism are reported globally indicate the embeddedness of the Orwellian state of total war that has emerged since the USA's post-9/11 'war on terror' (Chomsky 2016, 239–258). Yet the correlation of many of these acts with colonial histories, and the continued resourcing of capitalism from 'peripheral' areas of the world (not least of which are oil-rich areas of Western Asia) is rarely acknowledged in the discourses through which such violent acts are explained in Western media outlets (Chomsky 2016, 256–257). This was very apparent in the indigenous American and climate change activist opposition to the Dakota Access Pipeline (which threatens sacred sites and the Sioux tribe's water supply) at Standing Rock in 2016. It took a Facebook 'check in' of over a million people in support of the protestors just to compel mainstream media outlets to cover in depth a story by then long circulating online (Torchin 2016). As the political manufacturing of consent turns to the manufacturing of confusion (deliberately fostered cognitive dissonance so as to leave many unsure how, or even whether, to vote), what is revealed is how post-imperialist white nationalism typically seeks to cleanse its chequered history via doublethink (Steele 2006, 107).

This context requires a more foregrounded appreciation of the world historical events which underpin contemporary conflict, and the inequalities which foster it. A world of cinemas, whilst it may not cause any revolutions (although it has taken part in a few), can readily contribute to changing perceptions. Amidst so much that is troubling, films offer a way to consider who 'we' are in relation to each other, and indicate the need to ensure inclusion and a more equally distributive flow to global wealth before the continued coloniality of neoliberalism (at home as much as abroad) ferments the widespread resurgence of fascism. But to grasp this begins with which films we watch, and how we regard them: the question of how we encounter other 'worlds' in a world of cinemas.

A meeting of worlds

In *Cinema Against Doublethink* the exploration of the *world* memory in which so many lost pasts are stored is joined by a grounding of interpretation in *world* history and *world* systems analysis, which by turns underpin a particular viewpoint on ethics taken from a *world* of philosophies (i.e. Dussel). Each of these worlds offers a dimension which seeks to enhance knowledge: by taking explorations of history in film beyond national to transnational history; film-philosophical work beyond European thinkers; and study of a world of cinemas beyond comparisons with world music and world literature (an approach roundly critiqued in the 2000s (Martin-Jones 2011, 4)), to world history and world systems. Thus, it challenges any too Eurocentric viewpoint on world history which does not account for the contrasting and competing experience of it, felt around the world (Kwon 2010, 7).

Discussing the world's memories is no longer the sole province of philosophy. For example, it is a topic emerging in history, surrounding questions over how we might consider a shared experience of 'remembering' world history as either 'global memory' or 'transnational memory' (Iriye 2013, 78–79), and again over the 'form in which we think of the past' as 'increasingly memory without borders rather than national history within borders' (Huyssen 2003, 4). A world of cinemas has a huge amount to offer such an interdisciplinary debate, as it can provide us with a shared experience of a history, or memory, which reaches beyond that of our collective national imaginings (Anderson 1983) towards those of our broader transnational mediascapes (Appadurai 1990).

Thus in the first two chapters I build the interdisciplinary methodology, whilst exploring the ramifications of the project's situatedness at the intersection of different areas of study. These include: in Chapter 1, the enhancement of the history on film debate with a world-historically grounded move from a national to a transnational emphasis, as well as the need to shift the focus in film-philosophy from Western to world philosophy; and in Chapter 2 the value of emphasising history in existing film theoretical debates surrounding time and ethics, along with the usefulness of the introduction of contract theory (from political philosophy) for the turn to transnational cinemas. We might say, a chapter of history and another of theory, albeit any such traditional distinction is now extremely blurry.

Together these opening two chapters demonstrate how the variously intertwined strands of the methodological approach coincide in the examination of the ethics involved in transnational histories on film, and how, thus entwined, they enable an intervention at the intersection of history and theory. These opening two chapters do not contain analysis of films – albeit some readers may be more pleased to hear that Chapters 3–6 are replete with detailed analysis. Rather, these chapters foreground the importance of situating this work at the intersection of the interdisciplinary concerns with which it engages, both historical and philosophical. Together they indicate that the historical and the ethical dimensions of analysis must both be attended to if we are to realise how transnational histories are staged as encounters with other pasts.

In Chapter 1, I argue that across a world of cinemas we find transnational histories (the engagement with histories deeper or broader than those of nations) emerging in similar forms aesthetically, despite differences in location, and that a worldview from the Global South (after Dussel) can illuminate how such histories are staged as encounters with the lost pasts of colonial modernity. In Chapter 2, a (reconstructed) Deleuzian understanding of time illustrates how a world of cinemas enables us to encounter world memory, asking us to hesitate and (re)consider our own past in relation to that of others. Finally, because grasping this multidimensional totality (ethics/colonial modernity, world memory/time, transnational history/liberation) means that we must taxonomise a world of cinemas in a new way, consideration is given to the idea of the contract from political philosophy. Contract theory looks to conceptualise how societies function, via contracts. Examining various social critiques within contract theory, which emphasise the underpinning (more accurately, undermining) exclusionary contracts which belie our everyday lives (natural, racial, social, individual, etc.) indicates how such a taxonomising can proceed, so as to unlock the encounters a world of cinemas offers with transnational histories.

Film analysis follows in Chapters 3–6, illustrating how transnational histories on film can be uncovered using this methodology. In each chapter, the use of the time-image is outlined first, to demonstrate how it constructs an, as it were, 'shorthand' version of history. The films are then discussed in terms of the ethical encounters they enable, not only with otherness, but also (due to the underpinning presence of the time-image) with another past, with a different conception of (world) history. In this way each of the chapters also illuminates one of the contracts (natural, racial, social, individual) operative in colonial modernity, fostering global structural inequality. Close analysis of two key examples from emerging trends then constitutes the bulk of each chapter.

Chapters 3 and 4 explore intertwined histories, of significant historical scope and scale. They indicate something of the depth of the *past* which is obscured by colonial modernity (to which past/present crystalline dyad, Chapters 5 and 6 add the *present* dimension).

Chapter 3 discusses *Uncle Boonmee* and *Nostalgia for the Light*. The encounters they offer are with the intertwined history of humanity and the Earth, or the Universe, respectively – histories billions of years in the making. Both use time-images to create affective spaces redolent with virtual powers and qualities ('*faceified*' landscapes which emerge from light or darkness in the films), through which we encounter the world's nonhuman memories – albeit enunciated by humans or former humans. In this way the viewer encounters the anthropomorphised face of the Earth as it asks us to consider its nonhuman history, requesting of us a natural contract (after Michel Serres (1992)) to mitigate the environmental cost of colonial modernity. This encounter with an occluded ecological past introduces what is at stake in the chapters which follow, namely, a cinematic ethics suitable for the Anthropocene (see Chapter 1), which emphasises the need to rescue all those excluded by colonial modernity since 1492, including that of the cosmological/planetary environment with which human history is complexly intertwined.

Chapter 4 analyses the Brazilian film *How Tasty* and the European coproduction, *Even the Rain*. These two films, made nearly forty years apart, take us back to the commencement of colonial modernity in 1492 so as to explore the transnational history of the North Atlantic trade circuit (which linked Europe with Africa and the Americas). Using the time-images of the opsign (*How Tasty*) and the crystal of time (*Even the Rain*), they explore the eradicated indigenous histories in the Americas after 1492, uncovering the intertwined (indigenous/ European) nature of the history of this region. This is a particular (transnational) perspective on the history of the engine which drove colonial modernity and took Europe to economic centre stage in the world, based on the exploitation of slave labour and raw materials from Africa and the Americas. Underpinning this world historical geopolitical formation, these films indicate, is the racial contract (after Charles W. Mills (1997)) which positions the indigenous of the Americas (amongst others) as the object of the white, European, male, coloniser's gaze. By bringing this transnational history of encounter and entanglement up to date (to the Cold War, in *How Tasty*, and neoliberal globalisation in *Even the Rain*), these films indicate the continuation in the present day of the structural inequality of the modern world system that began in 1492 (and the subsequent struggle for liberation of so much of the world's population).

These more recent historical moments bring us on to Chapters 5 and 6, which examine ongoing transnational histories from the latest of the overlapping phases (see Chapter 1) of colonial modernity. Their focus is on the continuing impact of colonial modernity on our present-day world (complementing the focus on the past aspect of the past/present crystalline dyad from Chapters 3 and 4).

Chapter 5 considers the *The Act of Killing* (made in Indonesia) against which is contrasted – as exemplar of a broader trend of documentaries about the erased histories of the still decomposing Cold War – the Uruguayan *At the Foot*. The two films explore the more than 70-year transnational history of this brutal phase of colonial modernity. The time-image evident in both films is the crystal of time, in *The Act of Killing* exposing the (perpetual) reterritorialising of the virtual as the actual, and in *At the Foot* illustrating the (perpetual) potential of the virtual to deterritorialise this actualising tendency of (linear) history. Thus, whilst Slavoj Žižek contends that *The Act of Killing* demonstrates how, under global capitalism, we inhabit a privatised form of public space, by contrast I argue that a film like *At the Foot* be considered the norm of the emerging trend in which time-images reinstall a public, collective sense of an occluded past, from a private memory or archive. This Uruguayan example, so different to the more notorious *The Act of Killing*, memorialises the collective nature of the public sphere by depicting the personal memories retained by individuals as though they were (once filmed) virtual museums of memory.

Both documentaries deal with the exclusion of a certain proportion of the population of a nation from the social contract (after Jean-Jacques Rousseau (1750)) under authoritarian rule – especially during the state of exception (after Giorgio Agamben (2003)). Thus in each, the historical analysis is of the 'failure' to render the social contract more equal, the 'failure' of communism to outlive the violence focused against it during the Cold War. Yet whilst they offer the viewer an encounter with the occluded political pasts of the Cold War, one tells the story of this transnational history from the perspective of the 'winners' (illuminating the obsessive need for the 'official story' of history to repeat in sameness), the other from the perspective of the 'losers' (wherein the eruption of difference in the retelling of history is a messy, unique, personally recorded/ salvaged, and against-the-odds singularity, or event).

Chapter 6 examines two contemporary thrillers from countries with recent histories of transferring from dictatorships to democracy (only to move swiftly to a disenfranchising of the populace under neoliberalism which many consider a continuation or worsening of the inequality fostered more brutally under military rule), the Argentine *Carancho* and the South Korean *Lady Vengeance*. Together they provide encounters with the transnational histories of the disenfranchised working- and middle-class bodies of neoliberalism (throughout its as-yet 45-year, and counting, transnational history) after the withdrawal of the state from guaranteeing even the already inequality-perpetuating social contract. The two films are exemplary of what Deleuze identified as the two poles of the time-image's cinema of the body: the everyday and the theatrical (*gest*). They reveal how the body exists in time, as a store of the past, and in the present constitutes a site of future potential.

Thus, although these are films set in institutions designed to enable or define a state-supported collective identity (the hospital in *Carancho*, the prison in *Lady Vengeance*), these spaces are refigured as crisscrossed by individuals, singularities whose futures rely on personal contracts (after Maurizio Lazzarato (2011; 2013)) negotiated through their very bodies in the present moment. For this reason, bodies beaten, broken, drugged, abandoned, kidnapped, incarcerated, tortured and abused in the present are the norm in these films, their futures entirely uncertain.

Across the four chapters of analysis, the intervention is, firstly, to see how a world of cinemas can be understood to illuminate not only national, but also transnational, histories from within a broader world history, and, secondly, to indicate how this is intrinsically related to ethics. Thus *Cinema Against Doublethink* uncovers how a world of cinemas can be read distantly (see Chapter 1) so as to expose the lost pasts of colonial modernity which remain submerged due to doublethink. Who we are in relation to others is something that can be informed by the hesitation over history informed by such encounters with other pasts. The four chapters of analysis, two focusing on the past (and the present), two on the present (and the past), thus formulate a crystalline approach to filmic analysis of the construction of crystalline (world) history, a topic which I now turn to explore in depth in Chapters 1 and 2.

Notes

1 This notion of ethical encounters with lost pasts which we cannot know, but which may unground our surety in established visions of world history, resonates with how a feminist epistemology might place non-being at the heart of being, as in Joan Copjec's Lacanian analysis of the ethics of the encounter in Hollywood melodrama *Stella Dallas* (2004, 6–7 and 130–131). I thank Christine Evans for this observation.

2 The web-resource deleuzecinema.com indicates the widespread global engagement with Deleuze's work on cinema, including over 30 books, and numerous other works on the topic.

3 Deleuze discusses Jacques Rivette's depiction of women as oscillating doubles, akin to the sun and the moon (1985, 11). This kind of oscillating, crystalline doubling remains evident in recent films which use this same idea – of two women who oscillate, like two crystalline facets – so as to recuperate the past for a more productive present. The two sisters in *Frozen* (USA, 2013) are a clear example. Anna's memories of the past have been altered, leaving her cut off from its virtual potential to inform the present differently. It is as though she is perpetually awakening in the very moment of the present that passes, to repeat (like a forgetful Sisyphus) her enthusiastic refrain: 'for the first time in forever'. Elsa, for her part, lives excluded from the passing present, concealed from the moment which Anna lives, trapped in the past that is preserved from which she desires release: 'The past is in the past [...]. Let it go'. Only when their crystalline facets are able to oscillate, is history repaired. I thank Soledad Montañez and Elena Martin-Jones for this realisation.

4 What I term colonial modernity is thus often referred to as 'coloniality/modernity' (Mignolo 2010a, 2010b; Escobar 2010).

5 This idea is redolent of Friedrich Nietzsche's assertion that the world is a 'will to power' (1891, 136), but perhaps recognises the historical reality of such a European idea of the 'will' as being but a one-dimensional view on the broader reality of coloniality. It also resonates with anthropologist Michael Heckenberger's consideration of the 'ecology of power' (2005) in his uncovering of pre-Columbian Amazonian history.

6 For a discussion of the distinction between decolonial and postcolonial thinking, and their respective (often complementary or related) emergence worldwide, see Walter Mignolo (2011, xxiii–xxxi). For the purposes of this work, I look to avoid conflating the two, considering the presence of decolonial thought (from the Caribbean/Latin America as far back as the Sixteenth Century at least (see Chapter 4)) and its historically Global South-North address, to be as important as that of postcolonial thought, and its, historically (Northern) East-West address. The difficulty of disentangling these trajectories is indicative of the need to consider the term 'post' in postcolonial with caution, and to appreciate the critique of the latent Eurocentrism in seminal works such as Edward Said's *Orientalism* (1978) found in Latin American philosophy.

7 If it seems whimsical to make such a claim in this internet era, then perhaps it is enough for now to remember just how many people around the world keep making such films to express this view (Brown 2018; Holtmeier 2018).

8 Not to mention the importance of various animals (not solely the military use of the horse) to the European invasion, as foodstuff and environment altering ally; the religious differences between European belief in a temporal, in contrast to the indigenous spatial understanding of history, and how this influences a people's relationship to land; nor the centuries of stout resistance to colonisation by indigenous and escaped slave communities (Deloria 1972, 61–111; Crosby 1972, 35–63; Crosby 1986, 172–194; Mann 2011, 99–151). Indeed, this bias continues even into the works of a thinker as opposed to the official history as Alfred W. Crosby (contemporaneous with Fabian), who considers the indigenous peoples which Europeans encountered after 1492 to belong to the 'Stone Age' (1972, 21; 1986, 21–22) using a scientific periodisation based on technological advancement which, like Hegel, denies the societal and cultural sophistication of indigenous populations. In fact, Europeans marvelled at indigenous technology, such as maize (a genetically engineered crop (Mann 2005, 191–203)), and also soon realised the initial relatively superior effectiveness of bows and arrows against guns (58). Inka metallurgy, weapons technology, transport and infrastructure, for example, was every bit as advanced as that of the West, only it was directed towards uses more suited to cultural and geological context. Hence its heritage, its development, its progress, was missed (perhaps wilfully) by European

observers (83–84). In their desire to identify a supposed prelapsarian primitiveness to the supposed 'state of nature' (see Chapters 2 and 5) of the Americas (noting their lack of animal husbandry for example), Europeans seemingly also failed to notice that the very ecosystems they encountered had been carefully shaped by the indigenous, in many cases using fire, so as to create a huge life-sustaining larder (Mann 2005, 148–252). It was not technological or military 'backwardness' which defeated the indigenous Americans, then, it was disease (87).

9 This distinguishes *Embrace of the Serpent* from its contemporary, *The Lost City of Z* (USA, 2016), a film which shares many similarities, but which explores this terrain from a perspective aligned with Western explorers.

10 This is again evident, both revelation and its fleeting nature, in the conclusion of *Even the Rain*, (see Chapter 4), another film to consider contemporary ecological concerns in light of the several centuries of history of colonial modernity.

11 I exclude from this tradition Tom Brown's *Breaking the Fourth Wall* (2012) which, perhaps sadly, replicates the pervasive invisibility of this decolonising heritage from the mainstream canon of Film Studies, as though it happened 'elsewhere' to a seemingly universalising tradition of Western films.

PART I

Decolonising entrances to the past

1

HISTORY/ETHICS

Interpreting stories from world history (Enrique Dussel)

This is the first of two chapters exploring how to ground a hermeneutics able to interpret transnational histories across a world of cinemas. The emphasis in this chapter is the history on film debate, to show how it can be broadened via more direct engagement with film-philosophy. The following chapter emphasises the ethical dimension of this intervention, more directly than the historical, but in both chapters the two dimensions – ethical and historical – are inextricably intertwined.

The Latin American philosophy of Enrique Dussel underpins the hermeneutics, due to both the importance of world systems analysis in Dussel's understanding of the history of colonial modernity, and to the ability Dussel provides for us to realise the correspondence between cinematic encounters with the past and their rendering on screen as ethical encounters. Simultaneously, the introduction of Dussel provides a new departure for film-philosophy, which typically engages with thinkers from the (Western) Analytical or Continental traditions. There is thus a (further) decolonisation of both the history on film debate, and the mainstream of film-philosophy with this interpretative work. It unlocks the inherent potential of both fields, due to the history on film debate having a similar (but rarely acknowledged) emphasis on liberation in its origins to that of a Dusselian film-philosophy.

History on film

There is a long tradition of scholarship exploring how films tell the story of history. This field is based on the premise that 'films can *do* history [...] can produce different but equivalent accounts of the past to those produced by historians' (Westwell 2007, 580). Typically this historiographical debate is understood to reach back many decades (for example, to include E. H. Carr's emphasis on interpretation in the writing of history (1961, 23)), with important interventions for the study of film in the 1970s (e.g. Marc Ferro's argument that cinematic constructions of history have the potential to challenge or oppose established or dominant understandings of the past (1977, 19–20)), and a gaining of momentum since the 1990s (Westwell 2007, 579–581; Treacey 2016, 2–3).

Hayden White remains an influential voice due to his observation regarding how history is constructed poetically, historians fashioning 'a "story" out of the "chronicle" of events contained in the historical record' (1973, 427). White foregrounded the constructed nature of both written and celluloid histories, arguing that: 'It is only the medium that differs, not the way in which messages are produced' (55). For White, history, whether in books or on screen, is a story (imperfectly) told, a point since developed by such pivotal figures as Robert Rosenstone, Marcia Landy and Robert Burgoyne.

Although recent texts on film and history illustrate the continued importance of the nation as the context which history films are commonly thought to negotiate (Carlsten and McGarry 2015, 10), the history on film debate has followed Film Studies' recent transnational turn by investigating histories beyond those of the nation.[1] For instance, in *Revisioning History* (1995a), Rosenstone argues that what he considers the 'New History Film', which is marked by a self-conscious complexity in its investigation of historiography, is a 'global phenomenon' emerging from 'postcolonial nations [...] societies where political systems are in upheaval [...] recovering from totalitarian regimes [...] [made by] ethnic, political, social or sexual minorities' (5–7). Other pertinent examples include Rosenstone's analysis of films from various parts of world which examine the Holocaust, deterritorialising his historical analysis from the national context (or at least, not engaging with them as works of national cinemas (134–153)), and Landy's examination of how popular genres construct counter-historical narratives using examples from various nations (2011; 2015). Albeit, importantly for this discussion, neither author attempts to ground such cross-border analysis within world history per se.

That said, what kind of history underpins the interpretative act is a question increasingly foregrounded by scholars addressing history on film. Rosenstone and Constantin Parvulescu's *Companion to the Historical Film* (2013) aims to give a 'worldwide perspective' (1), to relativise the importance of the nation with regard to the recognition of colonial legacies (transnational depictions of slavery, immigration, African histories, the European 'discovery' of the Americas). Yet precisely how, or rather, from where, such a 'worldwide perspective' is provided, is greatly influential with regard to the conclusions drawn.

An illuminating example of this problem is the difficulty with an argument made by White, shortly after the fall of the Berlin Wall. White's 'The Modernist Event' was published in Vivian Sobchack's *The Persistence of History* (1996). Sobchack's anthology is organised into three parts, the last of which is entitled 'the end(s) of history', evoking Francis Fukuyama's (1989) infamous pronouncement. As various critiques of Fukuyama, Samuel Huntington (1996), and others indicate, attempts to re-map the post-Cold War world as one in which the Hegelian future had arrived with US global supremacy (see the Introduction) served only to eradicate history from culture, and foster what Ali A. Mazrui terms '*global apartheid*' (1997, 29; see also Appadurai, in Elden 2009, 7–8). Yet the Eurocentric view of world history which enabled Fukuyama to draw such a conclusion regarding the end of history underpins White's argument and shapes his conclusions.

White argues that modernity has produced events in the Twentieth Century (the Holocaust enacted by National Socialist Germany, the nuclear bombings of Hiroshima and Nagasaki by the USA) that make it difficult for people to grasp, not the magnitude of history, so much as its meaning for the present. Whilst such events cannot be forgotten, nor can they be 'adequately remembered' such that their meaning for the present can be unambiguously assimilated by the collectives, communities, or societies affected. Due to the modern event, for White, films like Oliver Stone's *JFK* (France/USA, 1991) may provide uncertainty over what actually happened and the fictional recounting of it, offering the possibility that the two may become ontologically indistinguishable (1996, 19). For White, in such a situation the usefulness of examining the past to enable a better present (and by extension, future) is at risk: 'What is at issue here is not the facts of the matter regarding [historical] events but the different possible meanings that such facts can be construed as bearing' (21).

Yet, White's argument, that the 'holocaustal' events of the Twentieth Century 'could not possibly have occurred before', nor could any previous age have 'imagined' its 'nature, scope and implications' (1996, 20) displays a glaring absence in his understanding of world history concerning the centuries of genocide and enslavement enacted by European forces. As decolonial thinkers noted as early as the 1940s, the arrival of European technologies and diseases in the Americas provided just such a world-changing shift in people's lives (Ortiz 1940, 99). As Caribbean philosopher Charles W. Mills more recently observes, echoing predecessors like Aimé Césaire (1955, 36) and Paul Gilroy (1993, 213), the National Socialists' genocidal extermination of millions of Jews during the Second World War only brought home to Europe the same techniques for eradication of others which had been used globally against non-white populations since 1492. After all, Stam and Shohat note, the Twentieth Century's Holocaust was conceived of with previous European colonial atrocities in mind as concrete historical precedents (2012, 157–158). To demonstrate how un-unique the event was, Mills discusses 'the killing through mass murder and disease of nearly 95 percent of the indigenous population of the Americas [...] the single greatest act of genocide in human history' (1997, 98) alongside the 'slow-motion holocaust of African slavery' (99) and various other atrocities of colonial modernity (105). Thus, after Fernando Ortiz, Mills, and Dussel (who likewise describes the millions of dead indigenous Americans and enslaved Africans as the 'first holocaust of modernity' (2003, 177)), we can see the limitations of White's conception of what modernity is (his emphasis on technology indicating once again the

Hegelian view of history as 'development' and its attendant denial of coevalness (see the Introduction)), and how the resulting Eurocentrism of his 'worldwide perspective' limits the conclusions White draws from the films analysed.

In fact, what White's anxiety over the historical revisionism of films like *JFK* indicates is not the malaise of the supposed end of history, but the danger of the eradication of the past by a fake version of it: doublethink. The irony here, of course, is that this is precisely how Eurocentric visions of world history have eradicated genocidal colonial acts from the official record for centuries. Rather, then, understanding how transnational histories are created on film relates to various attempts which have been made to, historically, 'reorient' (Frank, 1998), 'provincialize' (Chakrabarty, 2000), 'recenter' (Iwabuchi, 2002), 'de-imperialize' (Chen, 2010), or 'decolonize' (Mignolo and Escobar, 2010) a globalised world.

Seen in this light, cinematic transnational histories offer ways to challenge, resist, and unthink the Eurocentrism of history. The supposed 'dead end' of history (Sobchack 1996, 11) only ever seemed as such from a Western perspective due to the prevailing Hegelian view of world history. What a world of cinemas offers, by contrast, is the opportunity to reclaim lost pasts from their eradication by doublethink. To better understand this, we need to grasp how what is depicted on screen can be understood to relate to a ground which is more world, than national, historical. And, indeed, how the worldview which offers this ground provides an alternative to Eurocentric conceptions of history. As one such way forward, I turn to world systems analysis.

World systems for a world of cinemas

A world of cinemas is often compared to other categorical constructions of 'worlds', such as world music or world literature, to illuminate the homogenising tendency of all such categorising of the West versus the exotic 'world' beyond it. By considering a world of cinemas with regard to world systems analysis, however, a more encompassing paradigm emerges within which to situate history on film. Yet why world systems, or rather (as this paradigm has already influenced engagements with a world of cinemas that draw upon Franco Moretti (2001; 2013) (e.g. Andrew 2006; 2010; Smith 2017; Caughie 2018) see further below)), why this model for transnational histories on film, from amongst the many possible ways there are to proceed?

Considering history in terms broader than the national is not new. Historians, for example, increasingly engage with the question of what it means to research history as a transnational or global phenomenon (Clavin 2005; Chakrabarty 2009; Sachsenmaier 2011; Iriye 2013; Frankopan 2015). Before this there have been countless examinations of history crossing borders, including, influentially, those focusing on trade in regions like the Mediterranean (Braudel 1949; 1998), the Atlantic (Glissant 1990; Gilroy 1993; Shannon 2004), or the Pacific (Jones, Frost and White 1993; Matsuda 2012; Armitage and Bashford 2014). What, then, is so special about world systems analysis?

Immanuel Wallerstein famously argues that a world system exists (a capitalist world-economy (2004, 17)) which is a product of Europe's expansion from the Fifteenth Century onwards (1974). This began, for Wallerstein, as a 'world' ('a spatial/temporal zone which cuts across many political and cultural units, one that represents an integrated zone of activity and institutions which obey certain systemic rules' (2004, 17)), but this 'world' ultimately expanded from its Atlantic roots to encompass the whole world (23). Crucial to the role that the development of this idea would play in the philosophy of Dussel (and other Latin American philosophers (see Mignolo 2011, xxv–xxvi)) was the role of the North Atlantic trade circuit in fuelling Europe's (and latterly the West's) transformation from global outlier to central world power block (Dussel 1998a, 9–13). This was the circuit via which ships left Europe bound for Africa, where their cargoes were unloaded and sold, and their holds filled with slaves. Once transported to the Americas the slaves were sold, and the ships' holds filled with the materials produced from the environment (land stolen from its former indigenous inhabitants) with the sweat of their labours (silver, cotton, tobacco, and so on).[2] These materials, once shipped back to Europe, were processed into goods to be sold at home and abroad. The North Atlantic trade circuit, then, was the murderous engine of colonial modernity, which shifted the global centre of economic power away from the Mediterranean (Dussel 1998a, 11) (see Chapter 4).

In the wake of Wallerstein's intervention, the ensuing debate illuminated the Eurocentrism to his findings. Was Europe at the heart of the first world system (world in the sense of an enclosed, border-crossing world), replacing an interstate system as Wallerstein argues? Alternative views suggest that the world system is closer to five thousand than five hundred years old (Frank and Gills 1993; Dussel 1998b) and that Europe's rise only transferred power from within the existing world system's centre in Asia, to the West (Abu-Lughod 1989; Chaudhuri 1990; Frank 1998).[3] Although such debates remain unresolved, the weight of evidence indicates the need to 'reorient', as Andre Gunder Frank (1998) puts it, our understanding of Europe's place in world history, and its reliance on centuries of exploitation (Galeano 1971). However the cloth is cut, Europe is a recently emergent superpower in a system (be it an enclosed entity or an interstate system) previously dominated by Asia – in particular the region now known as China which increasingly looks likely to re-emerge as the dominant global player.[4]

The most important points to take from Wallerstein, and the use of world systems analysis by Dussel, are: firstly, that modernity is not exclusively the domain of the Enlightenment, democracy, the Industrial Revolution, and so on, but commenced several centuries earlier in the Fifteenth Century; and secondly, that in the world system everything is related – centre and periphery develop together in a dynamic inter-related system, typically with centre growing at the expense of periphery. But to answer the question of what is so special about world systems analysis, it is less that this specific theory is so important, as it is that the engagement with it in Latin American philosophy (especially by Dussel, Aníbal Quijano and Walter Mignolo) developed it into the underpinning world history of a decolonising philosophy (Mignolo 2008). It is the role of world systems analysis in creating this particular 'worldwide perspective' that is key to its usefulness for interpreting a world of cinemas.

World systems analysis indicates that what is at stake in research into a world of cinemas (along with what is perhaps more obvious to Film Studies scholars, namely, of a more accurate understanding of the reality of film financing, production and distribution illuminated by the transnational turn) is the critique of what the nation means to the historical centrality of Europe in the world system. It is not solely the 'limiting imagination' of national cinema (Higson 2000) that is being rejected by the transnational turn, but also the imperialism of the nation as a historical construct. For Quijano, the origins of the modern nation-state lie in the emergence of 'small political nuclei that conquered their space of domination and imposed themselves over the diverse and heterogeneous peoples, identities and states that inhabited it', the first centralised states in Europe emerging 'simultaneously with the formation of the colonial empires' (2000, 558; 2008, 206). Similarly, Étienne Balibar observes of the notion of the border that, from the Seventeenth to the Twentieth Centuries onwards:

> Drawing 'political' borders in the European sphere, which considered itself and attempted to appoint itself the *center of the world*, was also originally and principally a way to *divide up the earth*; thus, it was a way to organise the world's exploitation and export the 'border form' to the periphery, in an attempt to transform the whole universe into an extension of Europe, later into 'another Europe', built on the same political model.
>
> *(2003, 7)*

Nationalism, the 'civic religion' (8), along with the European export of the notion of the border, thus leads to inequality in terms of who is included and excluded nationally, but also globally, during Europe's rise to global prominence (Dussel 2003a, 176). Balibar writes in the context of post-Cold War Europe, where, simultaneous with the redrawing of Europe's outer borders, immigration has moved the contact zone from the margins to the centre of the public sphere, creating an internal border between Global North and South which Balibar likens to apartheid (9). Thus, with the nation so integral to the Eurocentric control of the world system, departing from a focus on the nation is necessary to better understand how the stories of world history are told across borders, in a world of cinemas. Hence, what is special about world systems analysis is that, in underpinning Dussel's philosophy (providing the grounding for the 'worldwide perspective' which informs his ethics), it can also underpin the exploration of transnational histories across a world of cinemas.

Dussel's recourse to world systems analysis situates him between what might be considered the 'slow' and 'fast' models of transnational or world history. The former suggests that history be understood in broad historical sweeps. In spite of upheavals in social affairs, over the *longue durée* history appears to take place at 'a slower tempo, which sometimes almost borders on the motionless' (Braudel 1969, 33). Such a view is particularly attractive to the right of the political spectrum, as it suggests the impossibility of individual or collective action being able to change society. Thus it is evident in the thinking which underpins contemporary economic theories like neoliberalism (see Chapter 6) and its attendant denial of mankind's role in accelerating climate change (see Chapter 3). By contrast, the 'fast' view sees change, or its potential, as possible. Often deployed by those on the left, politically, it foregrounds the role which individuals and collectives can indeed play in changing history – for instance, Eric Hobsbawm's Marxist history of Europe, including *The Age of Revolution* (1962) which charts how the Industrial Revolution (originating in Britain) and the French Revolution together helped propel Northern Europe to a position of global economic centrality.

The complex coexistence of 'fast' and 'slow' is integral to historical works grappling with the Anthropocene (placing human history within a much larger nonhuman history of the Earth/Universe) (Christian 2004; Chakrabarty 2009) (see below and in Chapter 3), and is also a feature of Dussel's work. Whilst Dussel echoes Fernand Braudel's belief in the consistency of a longer term view of several centuries of mercantile capitalism (1969, 33) (after world systems analysis, which itself looks to the *longue durée* (Wallerstein 2004, 15–22)), Dussel also focuses on the role humans have played in shaping and changing this history. This is, in large part, what makes Dussel so useful for interpreting how the story of history is told across a world of cinemas. It is appropriate at this point, then, to introduce Dussel's work in depth, before returning to the history on film debate towards the close of the chapter.

Dussel, world systems, colonial modernity

Dussel is an Argentine philosopher who has been based in Mexico since his exile in 1975. Key texts from his immense oeuvre are increasingly being translated into English. For my argument here, impetus is drawn primarily from *Philosophy of Liberation* (1971), *The Invention of the Americas: Eclipse of the 'Other' and the Myth of Modernity* (1992), *The Underside of Modernity: Apel, Rorty, Taylor and the Philosophy of Liberation* (1996), *Beyond Philosophy: Ethics, History, Marxism, and Liberation Theology* (2003a), *Ethics of Liberation in the Age of Globalization and Exclusion* (1998b), the anthology *Coloniality at Large* (with M. Moraña, C. A. Jáuregui 2008), and selected relevant shorter works (2006; 2013). These particular works together illustrate what Dussel's philosophy brings to the study of a world of cinemas. This is because Dussel works at the nexus of a view of world history that develops upon world systems analysis, coupled with a post-Levinasian ethics of alterity which historicises otherness as a result of the global structural inequality fostered by colonial modernity. As such, it can expand our grasp of the hermeneutics involved in interpreting history on film, and in relation to film-philosophy can indicate the need to decolonise its current Western orientation.

Dussel is well known internationally for his work towards a philosophy of liberation, which is considered one of the driving forces behind the emergence of a distinct Latin American philosophy, one independent from the European canon (Martín Alcoff and Mendieta 2000, 19–21; Gandolfo 2013, 185–187; Márquez 2013, 301–307). This movement stems from the theology of liberation, outlined by Peruvian Gustavo Gutiérrez in 1971, which argues for the need for the liberation of the world's impoverished, within the context of a world economy which, by design, keeps the Global South indebted to the Global North (xxiv). Liberation theology remains a pertinent doctrine despite its denouncement by US President Ronald Reagan (Dussel 1996, xiii) and persecution of its adherents during the Cold War (such as the murder of Archbishop Óscar Romero, amongst others, in El Salvador in 1980), which exemplified the war waged against liberation theology under US foreign policy (Chomsky 2016, 11–13). For example, in May 2015, Pope Francis (whose own position during the Argentine military dictatorship remains unclear (Goni and Watts 2013)) invited Gutiérrez to speak in Rome.[5] Noticeably, liberation theology echoes the concerns of the earliest Christian decolonial critiques of colonial modernity, like that of Bartolomé de Las Casas (also an influence on Dussel's ethics) on his arrival in the 'New World' nearly five hundred years previously (1552, xxvii), not to mention indigenous critiques of colonial modernity and the role of Western philosophy in perpetuating it (e.g. Deloria 1972).

Dussel's philosophy of liberation follows a 'specific liberating rationality' which has developed over planetary history for many thousands of years (1998b, 3–9). Re-emerging from the Global South under colonial modernity, it offers hope for those at the periphery of the modern world system in its capacity for 'the *recovery* of a history that incorporates the counterdiscourse that is nonhegemonic and that has been dominated, silenced, forgotten, and virtually excluded – that which constitutes the alterity of modernity' (1998b, 46). For this reason it provides a suitable historical ground for the interpretation of how a world of cinemas offers viewers ethical encounters with different transnational histories – offers them the chance to recover the other face (or faces) of colonial modernity.

Dussel situates the commencement of modernity, and the origin of contemporary structural inequality, with the encounter with Europeans from 1492 onwards[6] (Dussel 1992, 9). Writing against the notion that Europe's rise to world prominence was due to its exceptionalism (creating a modernity which was then spread further afield), Dussel argues instead that modernity, whilst a European occurrence, 'originates in a dialectical relation with non-Europe. Modernity appears when Europe organises the initial world-system and places itself at the centre of world history over against a periphery equally constitutive of modernity' (9–10). Although Europe's expansion was based on a several centuries–long quest for access to the riches of Asian markets (Frank 1998), even so both modernity and capitalism are the result of Europe's discovery, and exploitation via the North Atlantic trade circuit, of the New World (1998b, 26).

Drawing on world systems analysis, Dussel notes the importance of recognising the first waves of European colonisation, involving the southern European nations of Spain and Portugal in propelling modernity. These tend to get written out of notions of modernity which emphasise the Industrial Revolution and the Northern European colonial powers which came later – Holland, Britain, and France (1992, 11; 2003a, 61), and then the USA (2003a, 61, 213). This longer time frame makes explicit the link between coloniality and modernity, as opposed to the more apparently 'detached' idea of modernity emerging from Northern Europe's rapid industrial, technological, and urban development in the West. For Dussel:

> Europe's centrality reflects no internal superiority accumulated in the Middle Ages, but it is the outcome of its discovery, conquest, colonization, and integration of Amerindia – all of which give it an advantage over the Arab world, India and China. Modernity is the result, not the cause, of this occurrence.
>
> *(2003a, 11)*

Understanding modernity as co-created via the interaction of the (initially European, latterly Eurocentric) centre – the 'West' – with its (colonised) peripheries, renders 'structural oppression', or 'structural servitude' (the structural inequality of capitalism) a direct product of the (co-)creation of modernity from coloniality (2003a, 223–224). Colonial modernity thus describes the manner in which the world system after 1492 is managed from a centre which exploits its peripheries – shifting recently with the growth of the Pacific Rim back towards East Asia (Frank 1998, 7; Mignolo 2010b, 14), notwithstanding the altogether harder to locate (geographically) model of multinational corporations able to exploit the Global South wherever it appears worldwide (Dussel 1971, 13; Wallerstein 1974, 99).

The world system helps us realise that colonial modernity relies upon an interconnection between Europe and its other. As Frantz Fanon succinctly summarises of the colonial plunder of Latin America, China and Africa: 'Europe is literally the creation of the Third World' (1961, 81). This is not to say that the idea of colonial modernity supersedes or is divorced from those of 'multiple modernities' or 'compressed modernity' which describe Asian experiences of, and engagements with, modernity – as its influence migrated from West to East (geopolitically speaking) (Chang 1999, 30; Lau 2003, 102). All such experiences of modernity are, in fact, connected world historically.[7] Nor am I arguing that a continuation of the then-existing world system, the Asian-centric hegemonic structure which had established itself prior to 1492, would necessarily have been better (or worse) than the modern world system. Rather, what is crucial about the interconnection between Europe and the rest of the world enabled by colonial modernity is that it indicates how the emergence of the world we now inhabit was a product of 1492. As the various contracts explored by the films analysed in the later chapters indicate, there is no escaping the fact that – for example, concerning the racial contract – the white supremacy which exemplifies Eurocentrism emerged as a global force with 1492 (see Chapter 4). If a world of cinemas is against doublethink, then, it is because it posits the historical reasons for colonial modernity's global dominance in the discovery of the Americas. Thus it is in Dussel's notion of transmodernity, which links directly to 1492, that we see how entwined his ethics is with this (world) historical viewpoint drawn from world systems analysis. This is not an ethics bidding for a nostalgic return to a perhaps imagined or utopian pre-Columbian state (regarding this kind of circuitous, potentially revolutionary logic, see further in Chapters 2 and 5 on the idea of the social contract), but one which considers, through the recognition of otherness (and in a world of cinemas, other pasts) how to imagine the future otherwise than doublethink.

Transmodern ethics

At times, misunderstanding may surround the term 'transmodernity'. Dussel's philosophy is familiar to many in the West because of his intervention into the postmodernity debate, including English translations of his works in several seminal anthologies (Beverley, Aronna and Oviedo 1995; Jameson and Miyoshi 1998; Dussel, Moraña and Jáuregui 2008). Yet, whilst Dussel does critique postmodernism for its Eurocentrism (1995, 75) he is more interested in moving beyond modernity (2002, 221), such that an alternative, inclusive, planetary vision can be offered instead. He states:

> The 'realization' of modernity no longer lies in the passage from its abstract potential to its 'real', European, embodiment. It lies today, rather, in a process that will transcend modernity as such, a trans-modernity, in which both modernity and its negated alterity (the victims) co-realize themselves in a process of mutual creative fertilization. Trans-modernity (as a project of political, economic, ecological, erotic, pedagogical and religious liberation) is the co-realization of that which it is impossible for modernity to accomplish by itself: that is, of an incorporative solidarity, which I have called analectic, between center/periphery, man/woman, different races, different ethnic groups, different classes, civilization/nature, Western culture/Third World cultures, et cetera, in the intertwined exploiter/ exploited aspects of Europe/Americas.
>
> *(1995, 76)*

Thus, Dussel considers his ethics to be 'transmodern' in that it seeks to encounter, engage, and liberate all those excluded from Eurocentric colonial modernity, globally. It is in this respect that Dussel's ethics is historicised rather differently to Levinas's. Dussel agrees with Levinas's emphasis on ethics as first philosophy, due to the Cartesian egocentrism of ontology – a 'philosophy of injustice' which reduces the other to the same (Levinas 1961, 43–46). Yet Dussel's philosophy does not offer the transcendental promise that Levinas holds to (the notion of an escape from the self in the encounter with the other), but rather of a transcendence of modernity (trans-modern) (Márquez 2013, 305). For Dussel, such an enterprise must 'always begin by presenting the historico-ideological genesis of what it attempts to think through, giving priority to its spatial, worldly setting' (1971, 1). Levinas's ethics sought transcendence in the encounter with the representative figures of alterity (often noted to be Biblical figures, although in fact they are historical as well[8]), of the stranger, widow and orphan (along with the poor) (Levinas 1961, 199–210). For his part, Dussel seeks a recognition not of a primordial otherness, but of colonial modernity in the encounter with modernity's 'colonised' or excluded other – understood historically and geopolitically (2003a, 26). Accordingly, Dussel's historicised other relates to the world system after 1492, encompassing: 'The poor, the dominated, the massacred Amerindian, the Black slave, the Asiatic of the opium wars, the Jew of the concentration camps, the woman as sexual object, the child under ideological manipulation' (1996, 80). Dussel's other, then, is a product of the world system which underpins colonial modernity, both historically and into the present. As Linda Martín Alcoff and Eduardo Mendieta observe: 'Dussel's argument is that the Other is concrete and historical, existing in time and space. In our time, the Other is the poor of the Third World, the populations that have been forcibly excluded from globalization and whose exclusion, through starvation or environmental genocide, is in fact necessary for the current form of globalization to be maintained' (2000, 10).

Globalization, on this view, is but the latest phase of colonial modernity (Dussel 2013, 5) (see Chapter 6). As Mignolo indicates, to arrive at globalisation, this five-hundred-year history has proceeded through various overlapping phases. From an initial Southern European Christian mission, to a Northern European civilising mission (mercantile, imperialist), then (in North America) to a belief in Manifest Destiny, before (post-World War Two) the emergence of (US-led) developmental and, finally, the market expansionary phase of transnational capital. Globalisation brings in a new phase of 'nonterritorial' or 'global coloniality', retaining the impetus and rationale behind the former phases (2000, 280–281). Under globalisation there remains a 'coexistence of successive global designs that are part of the imaginary of the modern/colonial world system' (Mignolo 2000, 280–281).[9] Dussel's historicised other, then, emerging from world systems analysis, along with his reconsideration of both Levinas and Marx is extremely pertinent for today's globalised world and its cinematic constructions of history.[10]

In colonial modernity we find the origins of the contested subjectivity and history which scholars note when contextualising the emergence of contemporary concerns with ethics: such as Rosi Braidotti regarding the importance of the women's movement for challenging the phallogocentric nature of subjectivity (1994, 125), and Thomas Elsaesser concerning precisely how universal such legacies of the Enlightenment and the French Revolution as human rights are, and over who in the postcolonial era has 'interpretative authority over, and thus the discursive ownership of the past' (2011, 2). Dussel's ethics is concerned precisely with the conjunction of these two points, at the origins of colonial modernity – the construction of the Eurocentric ego, after 1492, which, in its genocidal plunder of the Americas, banished the distinct histories of the indigenous peoples conquered to the 'primitive' past of Europe (as per the critiques of Johannes Fabian and Quijano explored in the Introduction). For Dussel, playing with the Spanish terms 'descubrir' (discover) and 'encubierto' (cover over or perhaps cover up), Europeans eradicated the difference (and different histories) of the indigenous people they encountered:

> By controlling, conquering, and violating the Other, Europe defined itself as discoverer, conquistador, and colonizer of an alterity likewise constitutive of modernity. Europe never discovered (*des-cubierto*) the Other as Other but covered over (*encubierto*) the Other as part of the Same: i.e., Europe.
>
> *(1992, 12)*

The Christian Europeans turned the other into the primitive version of the self-same (denying its coevalness by banishing it to Europe's past), obscuring its alterity, destining it for development or destruction (32). The genocide which followed was enacted against people considered not-as-yet fully human (35). In Levinasian terms, once deprived of its 'divine exteriority' (Dussel 2003a, 210), the other no longer enables the transcendence of the self, and the Christian prohibition against killing seemingly no longer applies. The other 'is reduced to the level of an idea. The meaning of the other is formulated in terms of the "I" who dreamed it into existence' (2003a, 30).

In his critique of Descartes, Dussel provides a specific origin to the Western emphasis on ontology as first philosophy observed by Levinas. The European arrival in the Americas originates the intertwined histories of the development of Eurocentric egocentrism (central to Western philosophy's emphasis on ontology) and the initial colonial interaction between Europeans and indigenous Americans. He states that: 'the use of the term "dis-cover" implies that the point of departure in this process is the European ego which is a constituent element of the historical event: "I discover", "I conquer", "I evangelise" (in the missionary sense) and "I think" (in the ontological sense)' (2003a, 221). Dussel's critique of the 'birth of modern subjectivity' (1992, 17) in the European invasion, sees the European ego surface 'in the person of Hernán Cortés'. In the conquest of Mexico, the conquistador's lust for gold reduces people to enslaved commodities to be traded for wealth in the mercantile capitalist economy (26 and 38). The Western ego's relationship with the world which it colonises, after all, stands in stark contrast to the pre-Columbian ethics of reciprocity between humanity and cosmos of indigenous cultures of the Americas, in which humans are understood to live in balance with the world (Maffie 2013, 11–21). In Cortés, and thereby from discovery via conquest and evangelical civilising, Western philosophy comes to privilege Descartes' solipsistic 'I think'.

> The colonizing ego, subjugating the Other, the woman and the conquered male, in an *alienating erotics* and in a mercantile *capitalist economics*, follows the route of the conquering ego toward the modern *ego cogito*. Modernization initiates an ambiguous course by touting a rationality opposed to *primitive*, mythic explanations, even as it concocts a myth to conceal its own sacrificial violence against the Other. This process culminates in Descartes's 1636 presentation of the *ego cogito* as the absolute origin of a solipsistic discourse.
>
> *(1992, 48)*

As a result, the Global South's role in the development of modernity was written out of its history by (Northern) European notions of exceptionalism during the Enlightenment. With a Hegelian narrative of Westward development over two centuries (from Italian Renaissance to Lutheran reform in Germany to scientific revolution to bourgeois political revolution in England, North America and France), the Global South became associated with Europe's 'past'. It was rendered seemingly unconnected from the apparently 'exceptional' thinking which leads to Descartes' solipsistic conclusions regarding thought and being (2006, 1–2).

By contrast, Dussel emphasises the vibrancy of the Sixteenth and early Seventeenth Century Atlantic crossings of philosophical thought between the newly colonised Americas and Spain and Portugal (2006, 13–14), focusing on the '*modern* Iberian-American philosophers before Descartes, who opened up the problematic of modern philosophy' (7). At the heart of the tradition which Descartes inherited were the Jesuits who, after arriving in the Americas in the mid Sixteenth Century 'drove the first steps of a modern philosophy in Europe' (13) in a context where the process of parsing humanity by race (Dussel notes Sixteenth Century debates in Spain regarding the ontological status of indigenous Americans) was being used to justify colonial violence (10–14), and, in part, from whose schooling in meditation arises Descartes' individualistic notion of being (5–7). Descartes' thought, and the Western emphasis on ontology over ethics, is thus the product of this longer history of colonial modernity. It emerges due to the influence of the first phase of modern philosophy, from the Transatlantic South, in Amsterdam, a city formerly a Spanish province, from a thinker schooled within a Spanish religious order (Dussel 2013, 10). Not as though seemingly out of a vacuum in a disconnected Northern Europe (Dussel 2006, 5).

Colonial modernity is thus Eurocentric both geopolitically (in terms of the world system) and philosophically (in terms of the privileging of ontology over ethics) (Dussel 1971, 34–35, 48). Moreover, with the birth to the modern world system in 1492, came the denial of 'ecological civilization, popular democracy, and economic justice' in the pursuit of the wealth which Europe would ultimately use to force its way into the centre of the world economy (116–117).

The concerns flagged by Braidotti and Elsaesser with regard to the reason for the contemporary emergence of a cross-disciplinary interest in ethics are thus both evident in what is excluded by Descartes – the otherness of the self, which can be discovered (after Levinas) in the encounter with alterity, and the otherness of history which can likewise be realised in the same encounter. That is, if the coevalness of the other is acknowledged it can be situated not as a primitive forerunner, but as the product of an altogether different history, inhabiting an altogether different, but copresent, 'time'. With such a viewpoint in mind, conjoining world history (from world systems analysis) with a historicised ethics of alterity which aims at the '*philosophical decolonization*' (2008b, 38) of the Western canon, I turn to what is at stake for the field (for Film Studies, and the interdisciplinary area of film-philosophy), in such a decolonising move.

A Dusselian ethics for film-philosophy

The ever-expanding engagement with ethics in film-philosophy has not produced entire agreement as to what a cinematic ethics entails. A broad working definition would be that it is less concerned with morality (a code defining right from wrong by which to live our lives) than it is with how an encounter with a film can change the way we consider our interaction with the world. In line with a long-standing argument that films can 'do' philosophy (Deleuze 1983 and 1985; Mulhall 2001; Wartenberg 2007), the ethical turn explores how films can prompt ethical change. For Jane Stadler, 'narrative film can be a source of ethical understanding [...] we reflect on, deliberate about, and discuss ethical situations rationally and lucidly by narrating and interpreting stories' (2008, 4). Cinema thus has 'the potential to bring about transformations in perspective, responsiveness and understanding' (6). Similar sentiments are echoed in subsequent works (Downing and Saxton 2010, 1; Choi and Frey 2014, 1; Sinnerbrink 2016, 3).

Levinas, an influential voice early on in this film-philosophy, remains prominent (Landsberg 2004, 151–152; 2009, 227; Cooper 2006; 2007; Downing and Saxton 2010; Girgus 2010; Hole 2016). Increasingly, however, a plurality of voices is in evidence, albeit as yet nearly all are drawn from the Western philosophical canon.[11] This proliferation is in itself encouraging, in the context of the worrying de-politicisation of theoretical work on film in recent decades – the privileging of approaches informed by analytical philosophy which 'attempt to redeem "theory" for film by placing it in the context of a philosophy of science' (Rodowick 2007, 98). Considering that Dussel is gradually being adopted in Film Studies (Bermúdez Barrios 2011, 1–2; Richards 2011, 201; Martin-Márquez 2011; Martin-Jones 2016; Brown 2016 and 2018), the role of a Dusselian ethics in enhancing this debate, providing a perspective from outside of the Eurocentric canon, is overdue.

The introduction of Dussel revivifies an until now submerged engagement with Latin American thought in Film Studies, stemming back to the third cinema manifestos (Rocha 1965; Solanas and Getino 1969; Julio García Espinosa

1969), through the use of the writings on cannibalism of Oswald de Andrade to analyse Brazilian films (Stam 1997, 70–78), to Dussel in the 2010s (Richards 2011; Martin-Márquez 2011). After all, the historical conditions which led to the third cinema debates remain as pertinent under neoliberal globalisation as they did during the Cold War. Whilst Dussel's category of 'the poor' ('poverty as the absolute limit of capital' (1998b, 40)) might seem sententious, the World Health Organization considers that around 1.2 billion of the world's seven and a half billion people live in extreme poverty (on less than one dollar a day),[12] with different estimates of global poverty ranging up to almost half of the world's population. Dussel's 'poor' summarises the historical fact of structural inequality as ongoing legacy of centuries of colonial modernity, his ethics thus resonating with previous writers on colonialism (e.g. Eric Williams, *Capitalism and Slavery* (1944)), as well as with many contemporary thinkers on globalisation (Guattari 1989; Hardt and Negri 2000 and 2005; Gilroy 2005, 9 (citing Dussel 1992); Appadurai 2006; Graeber 2011; Dabashi 2015).

Bringing Dussel to bear on this debate in film-philosophy, this book aligns itself with a broader consideration of what kinds of philosophy can best address the problems of globalisation. It moves beyond the dead end of attempting to engage the division in Western philosophy (between the so-called 'Analytical' and 'Continental' traditions) with the question of modernity (Pippin 1991; Glendinning 2006; Sinnerbrink 2008) towards a viewpoint that can encompass a plurality of approaches from a world of philosophies (Martin-Jones 2016). This is to address directly what Peter K. J. Park describes as the racism which shaped the formation of the Western philosophical canon (at the height of its imperial activities), such that, from 1780–1830 (from Kant to Hegel), Africa and Asia were written out of the history of the discipline (2013, 2).[13] The denial of coevalness, then, extended even to the world's philosophies, which were banished to the 'pre-history' of (European) thought (4–5).

Engaging with Dussel also aligns this film-focused project with existing decolonising critiques of Levinas, the problems in whose approach to otherness include: the normative position of patriarchy and the father-son relationship in his ethics (1961, 151–157 and 278–280); his difficulty acknowledging parity to all forms of global alterity (especially to Palestinians and to Africans) (Levinas 1989, 294; Bazzano 2016, 32); and, in spite of its usefulness for reconsidering subjects like ecology and postcolonialism (Sparrow 2013, 73–83; Drabinski 2011, xvii), the Eurocentrism of his worldview. As Dussel argues of Levinas's inability to see the Holocaust within a broader world history: 'Levinas remains inevitably Eurocentric, despite discovering the irrationality of the totalization of modern subjectivity, since he could not situate himself in the exteriority of metropolitan, imperial, and capitalist Europe' (2008b, 39). Dussel enables us to move past these issues with Levinas, who remains popular with film-philosophy scholars, when considering the ethics on offer across a world of cinemas.

Dussel also provides a perspective distinct from other post-Levinasian predecessors like Jacques Derrida (1967), Alain Badiou (1993), Sara Ahmed (2000),

Judith Butler (2004), or Slavoj Žižek (2006).[14] For example, Badiou critiques Levinas's 'pious discourse' on ethics, arguing that the absolute alterity of the other and the transcendence attained in the encounter with it is simply another way of considering the presence of God (1993, 22–23). Whilst Badiou might be right in arguing that alterity is simply '*what there is*' (25), such a conclusion, if viewed from the perspective of colonial modernity, must also include the similarly ubiquitous nature of inequality. Thus Badiou does not escape the Levinasian failure to recognise the geopolitics behind the structural unevenness which conditions global outlooks on alterity. Again, Žižek's conclusion, that 'others are primordially an (ethically) indifferent multitude' and that to rack focus on to the one, in the Levinasian encounter, is to deny justice to the 'faceless many left in shadow' (2006, 182) encounters the usual problems of Žižek's Hegelian dismissal of other world histories beyond that of Europe (136). Žižek's multitude remains, precisely, a primordial, and not a historically material one. Instead, Dussel can illuminate the very real transnational histories of colonial modernity, without retreating into an undifferentiated same (Badiou) or a blurry, abstract collective other (Žižek).[15]

Most importantly for this discussion, Dussel provides a way of understanding how a world of cinemas explores histories in a manner which requires ethical engagement. With a 'worldwide perspective' after Dussel, these two things – history and ethics – appear inter-related. Put simply, *to understand the importance of the lost pasts of colonial modernity is to realise that this requires the provincialisation of the centrality of our own history with regard to those marginalised by colonial modernity.*

Naturally, Dussel's ethics is not the answer to everything,[16] but it can at least unlock the relationship between Eurocentric views of world history and those evident in time-image films across a world of cinemas. Jennifer Lynde Barker argues, after Levinas, that films which provide us with encounters in which we are awakened to a responsibility for the other enable us to see the fascist in ourselves and resist it (2013, 85). But it is with Dussel that we can realise how this process is one in which the viewer can potentially resist, or at least reorient, a worldview historically. To summarise: if, in a Levinasian cinematic encounter we might realise the unknowability of the other (and be shaken from our complacency regarding the *centrality of our self to the world*), then the cinematic encounters explored in this book indicate the unknowability of lost pasts (after Dussel, shaking us out of any complacency regarding the *centrality of our past within world history*).

Distant viewing history on film with Dussel

With this introduction to Dussel in place, I return to the question of how to ground an interpretation of history on film in relation to colonial modernity across a world of cinemas. In the Introduction I briefly mentioned that this work would be an exercise in, after Franco Moretti, 'distant viewing'.

Famous literary theorist Moretti, influenced by world systems analysis, discusses the need to break away from close reading of texts within established canons. Instead, he argues for 'Distant reading: where distance [...] *is a condition of knowledge*: it allows you to focus on units which are much smaller or much larger than the text: devices, themes, tropes – or genres and systems' (2013, 48–49). To Moretti's list we can add histories or, more precisely, how time-images create transnational histories across a world of cinemas. In fact, Film Studies has been distant viewing across a world of cinemas for many decades, in various ways. Even amongst those scholars to recently undertake such a task, directly acknowledging the encouragement of Moretti's work, there are a mixture of approaches in evidence: some favour distance for the detachment from the text that it offers (Andrew 2006; Caughie 2018), some – like myself – prefer to retain a degree of close textual analysis even when distant viewing across a world of cinemas (Smith 2017). What is key for this study is not exactly how close or distant the position taken, however, but the worldview which influences the critical position adopted from distance.

Historically, scholarly attempts to draw connections between films across borders (with respect to themes, genres, and modes), often entailed the homogenising of a diverse range of auteur or art films from around the world: either through a focus on their aesthetic (Bordwell 1979) – which threatened to obscure the embeddedness of such aesthetic forms in national institutions, artistic heritage, and cultural discourse, all in spite of their international appeal (Neale 1981) – or through the positioning of, say, a Japanese director like Yasujirō Ozu as modernist, at least when considered in comparison to an assumed (seemingly globally) normative Hollywood aesthetic (Thompson and Bordwell, 1976). In fact, as more recent research reveals, Ozu's work engages with Japanese aesthetic tradition, translating this heritage into cinematic form (Geist 1994; Nagib 2006, 32). With such critiques now well known, this book emerges at a particular moment of historical development in the discipline, towards the increased observation across borders of 'the world's expanding storehouse of stories and storytelling styles' (e.g. Constanzo 2014, x), but with greater sensitivity to context (whether understood as national or transnational).

For instance, two influential predecessors for this book emerged in the early 2000s, examining (often disparate) diasporic histories. Laura U. Marks' *The Skin of the Film* (2000) posits that diasporic cinemas are becoming a transnational 'genre', with 'shared concerns about style and content' (2), and Hamid Naficy's *An Accented Cinema* (2001) likewise notes the shared features of films by exilic and diasporic filmmakers worldwide (their displaced situations creating the cinematic 'accent'), in spite of the very particular cross-border histories they navigate (3). In both instances the histories involved are, by definition, transnational, negotiating diasporic or exilic situations and memories of a now-distant homeland. This approach to uncovering transnational histories by focusing on diaspora is also discussed by Dina Iordanova as 'watching across borders', a process designed to free interpretative analysis from the limitations of situatedness in national contexts. The advantage of such an approach is that, for Iordanova, it can reveal 'the global processes that bring the whole phenomenon of migratory and diasporic creativity into existence' (2010, 61).

There are many reasons for this scholarly shift in perspective, causes geo-political and industrial in particular.[17] Yet this changing trajectory is also a reaction to a change in the manner of considering a world of cinemas which occurred in the wake of Ella Shohat and Robert Stam's *Unthinking Eurocentrism* (1994). This influential text indicated a way to explore films across borders whilst remaining sensitive to originary meanings, making connections across a 'history of multiply located oppressions' dating back to colonialist discourses commencing in 1492 (5). Shohat and Stam examine contemporary global inequality in relation to, amongst other global theories, world systems analy-sis (17). This text's influence is widespread, being evident in, for example: attempts to foreground the 'regional aesthetic styles' which national cinemas inflect (Chaudhuri 2005, 2); the development of 'positive', inclusive defini-tions of world cinemas without singular origin or centre (Nagib 2006, 34); the emergence of postcolonial cinema studies (Ponzanesi and Waller 2012); and re-mappings of a world of cinemas (along lines longitudinal and latitudinal) to negotiate 'how local tensions and worldwide transformations interact' (Stone, Cooke, Dennison, and Marlow-Mann 2018, 1).

What I am arguing for, after such predecessors, is that we maintain the rigour of historically embedded interpretation (understanding each film as, historically, the product of a national or transnational context, at least of production), but that we also feel encouraged to then lift films out of these contexts so as to examine their commonalities with movies from elsewhere. These new groupings, I would add, can be seen to explore transnational histories, themselves part of the much larger world history. Likewise, in Dudley Andrew's conceptualisation of (after Moretti) an 'atlas' of world cinema, he offers various ways of mapping the global terrain which complicate the fitting of cinemas within national borders. As he succinctly states: 'Displacement, not coverage, matters most; let us travel where we will, so long as every local cinema is examined with an eye to its complex ecology' (2006, 19). In this way, then, we can see how the study of a world of cinemas can be grounded world historically.[18]

History on film as liberation philosophy

The usefulness of a Dusselian 'worldwide perspective' for distant viewing world history in a world of cinemas returns us to the history on film debate. What I am arguing for here is a latent potential in this debate, even if it takes a reconsidera-tion of a world of cinemas, via Dussel, to reveal it. In spite of the Eurocentrism of White's perspective on world history outlined earlier, recent arguments for White as a historiographer of liberation align him with Dussel's philosophy of liberation, and indeed, the engagement with philosophy in the history on film debate in general. This is because, at its core, the history on film debate attempts the liberation of history from doublethink.

In *Metahistory* (1973), White considers history to be a form of writing which follows 'the path or paths of story-types endemic to the culture to which the discourse belongs' (xxvi–xxvii). Scholars construct histories stylistically via a *'combination* of modes of emplotment, argument and ideological implication' (28), such that different histories take generic forms (not unlike those of the romance, comedy, or tragedy). By turns, these forms are predicated upon ideas about what is real (different 'historical realisms' (39)), pre-existing in the understanding of the historians. History, as a story constructed poetically from the historical record, should be understood not with regard to its veracity in respect of the past, but for its moral and aesthetic values for the present (xxxii). It is, thus, with respect to the political intent behind our re-viewing of the past (in which respect White builds upon his previous discussion of the need for the historian to 'participate positively in the liberation of the present from *the burden of history*' (1966, 124)), that White's work indicates how cinema can work against doublethink.

In *Metahistory*, the reason for White's later conclusion in 'The Modernist Event' is evident with respect to the philosophy which inspires his thinking. White observes a critique, emerging in late Nineteenth Century Western thought from Friedrich Nietzsche onwards, of the prevalent historical consciousness. This critique solidifies following the mechanised slaughter of World War One, including in modernist art and literature. Hence, much later in White's career the same emphasis is placed on how 'holocaustal' events in the Twentieth Century require a modernist form of aesthetic treatment. The Eurocentrism of White's position aside, it is consistent in its search for a way of telling the story of history dynamically (considering the usefulness of the past for the present, for challenging accepted notions of historical reality), as opposed to reiterating historical facts to justify the present as *status quo* (1966, 133). White thus calls for 'liberation' from the past through a study of history which provides 'a specific temporal dimension to man's [sic] awareness of himself [...] less to remind men of their obligation to the past than to force upon them an awareness of how the past could be used to effect an ethically responsible transition from present to future' (132). Although I examine a world of cinemas in a different manner to that of White (the films herein are not the 'non-stories' he favours, but Deleuzian time-images), the emphasis on the temporal/historical and the ethical is precisely that of White, due to the emphasis on liberation which White shares with Dussel. As Herman Paul outlines, White produces in the 1960s and 1970s a 'liberation historiography':

> White envisioned a world in which historians would not do their work 'properly'[...] but would stop in order to reflect upon what is 'proper' in the face of social unrest and political injustice. In White's world, philosophers of history would [...] redefine the concept of history in such a way as to include those previously despised as 'people without history' [...]

> [T]he ideal that White defended in these years may be described as *liberation historiography.*
>
> *(2011, 55)*

White argues that choosing a history to inform the present is a moral and aesthetic choice. It has a political intent which, in line with Dussel's inclusive approach towards global alterity, indicates precisely the potential for cinema to oppose doublethink.[19]

The particular nexus being examined here, of liberation philosophy from the 1960s and 1970s, politics, history, and a world of cinemas, returns us to the question of this work's relationship to a cinema of resistance. The chosen films from a world of cinemas explored herein illuminate a critique that is not dissimilar to that of third cinema during the Cold War, in its engagement with the geopolitics of global structural inequality. As the subtitle of Teshome H. Gabriel's *Third Cinema in the Third World: The Aesthetics of Liberation* (1979) indicates, third cinema emerged in different parts of the third world as a form of resistance to global hegemony (whether to imperialism or neo-colonialism, or to the spread of neoliberalism after the early 1970s), seeking liberation for subjected peoples.[20] This similarity is in part due to scholarship on a world of cinemas building upon previous debates regarding third cinema. As Nagib indicates: 'the "national" project, in cinema, which was at the core of the Third Cinema movements of the 1960s as a reaction to and resistance to global capitalism [...] achieved their historical aims and needed to move forward towards closing ranks with movements of resistance across the world' (included in Fisher and Smith 2016). In this context, Nagib argues, a 'polycentric approach' can 'organise world cinema according to "creative peaks" and look at them through recurrent tropes [...]. Though strongly connected with a region, a nation and a culture, these films connect across borders' (included in Fisher and Smith 2016).

Scholarship on diasporas, third cinema, and Deleuze's concept of 'modern political' or 'minor cinema' (Sutton and Martin-Jones 2008, 51–64; Brown 2014; Holtmeier 2016) reveals the similarities of approach to globally shared concerns appearing in cinemas around the world. As Kathleen Newman summarises:

> What is now at stake in film studies is the question of how motion pictures register, at formal level of narrative, broad and long-term social transformations, that is, changes in the capitalist world-economy at the regional and global scales and over multiple decades.
>
> *(2010, 9)*

As this book exposes, a world of cinemas explores transnational histories which may account for several centuries of such transformations. To conclude this chapter, then, I consider how my approach to the story of history which emerges across a world of cinemas provides a slightly different kind of cinema of resistance to the 'capitalist world-economy' than such previous political conceptualisations of world cinemas (third cinema; minor cinema) have suggested. The distinction is that, when grounding such an interpretation in the 'worldwide perspective' provided by a Dusselian critique of colonial modernity, resistance becomes more broadly conceived as that which resists the global *capitalist world ecology*. To see why this is requires that the Cold War context in which such cinemas emerged be reconsidered as part of the longer history of both colonial modernity and the Anthropocene. This is the focus of this chapter's final section.

A cinematic ethics for the Anthropocene

The Road (USA, 2009), *Interstellar* (USA/UK, 2014), *Mad Max: Fury Road* (Australia/USA, 2015): science fiction films foretelling apocalyptic disaster for humanity are the kind typically used to illustrate discussions of the Anthropocene – the idea that we now live in an era defined by humanity's influence on the planet, evidenced by measurable geological traces of humanity's impact on the globe like radiation from nuclear detonations which can be found in rocks (Macfarlane 2016). This choice of films supports the type of narrative about the Anthropocene which emphasises the imminent collapse of contemporary society, what Christophe Bonneuil considers the 'eco-catastrophist' way of tell-ing the story of the Anthropocene (2015, 26–27). It also evidences a Hegelian pre-occupation with the link between technological development under moder-nity – in the West, a period still understood with respect to the imperialism and scientific discoveries since the Enlightenment, rather than the broader colonial modernity driven by Europe (and North America) since 1492. How scholars attempt to understand this ecological idea by selecting certain specific represent-ative films is very revealing of the structuring presence of Eurocentric views of world history within scientific thought, and the limiting grasp of what it means for a world of cinemas to resist global structural inequality. For example, Bruno Latour's (2015) choice of *Gravity* (UK/USA, 2013) to discuss the Anthropocene focuses us more on technology than ethics. Again, Selmin Kara (2016) coins the neologism 'Anthropocenema', to describe what she considers the 'becoming cinematic of the Anthropocene imaginary', analysing depictions of technological waste in the sci-fi films *Gravity* and *Snowpiercer* (South Korea/Czech Republic/ USA/France, 2013) (see also Kara 2014; Martin-Jones 2016).

As with scientific theories situating the commencement of the Anthropocene in the Industrial Revolution (Crutzen 2002) or the Nuclear Age (Carrington 2016), the focusing of our attention on technology in science fiction films both eradicates any sense that the Anthropocene is a condition inextricably linked to the uneven distribution of wealth (it keeps the focus instead on development), and perpetuates the questionable idea that newer forms of greener technology can stem the trajectory we are on towards environmental devastation (Hickel 2016) even in the midst of the acceleration of the world's sixth mass extinction event (Ceballos et al. 2015). If our long-held beliefs as to the potential of modernity to provide freedom from poverty are no longer self-evident (because the result of development would now seem to be environmental catastrophe), and the ones whose conditions are most likely to get worse initially are those excluded from modernity (Chakrabarty 2009, 208–216), then should the focus not instead be on liberation from the structural inequality of colonial modernity? It is here, in fact, that a Dusselian ethics chimes with recent attempts to date the Anthropocene to 1492, which, by turns, reveals something fresh regarding the cinema of resistance, and its accompanying cinematic ethics for the Anthropocene offered by a world of cinemas.

Simon L. Lewis and Mark A. Maslin (2015) suggest the possibility that the year 1610 might be considered for the commencement of the Anthropocene. This date refers back directly to 1492, linking such an idea not only with world systems analysis (which Lewis and Maslin mention in passing (175)), but also with the world historicised ethics of Dussel (who himself includes ecological concerns in his overview of colonial modernity (1998b 32; 2003a, 68) (see Chapter 2)). The argument put forward by Lewis and Maslin starts with the arrival of Europeans in the Americas in 1492 and the resulting reduction in the indigenous population by around fifty million people.[21] As a consequence of this staggering genocide, the same quantities of trees were no longer felled to create the space for farming or to provide fuel for cooking. The extensive regeneration of forest and grasslands that occurred over the following one hundred years thus resulted in a decline in atmospheric CO_2 levels between 1570 and 1620. This created the measurable impact of humanity on the environment – the so-called Little Ice Age – which is now recorded in Antarctic ice core records (175). This reforestation, along with the various other indicators of global change created by the meeting of the 'Old' and 'New' Worlds (misnomers illustrating once again the denial of coevalness), referred to as the Columbian Exchange (the globalisation of crops, animals, and diseases, as well as human travel, trade, and interaction (174)) lead Lewis and Maslin to conclude that: 'colonisation, global trade and coal brought about the Anthropocene' (177).

This correlation between the world system and the Anthropocene has a history, including in the emerging 'eco-Marxist' critique (Bonneuil 2015, 29). This direction finds its neatest academic expression in the concept of the 'Capitalocene' as capitalist world ecology (Moore 2003; 2015). Jason W. Moore draws on world systems analysis to describe an intertwined relationship between capitalism and nature which stems from the long Sixteenth Century (2003; 2015, 12). Capitalism, for Moore, is 'a way of organising nature' (2015, 2; 192). Nature is thus not something external to capital, which it controls or exploits exactly, but is the 'web of life' (3) within which capital operates: 'humans make environments and environments make humans' (3). Moore's conceptualisation of capitalism as 'world ecology' (3) provides a direct correlation with modernity, where the latter is understood very much as in Latin American philosophy: colonial modernity. The link between colonial modernity, the 1492 Anthropocene theory, and the need for an ethics which can engage with our intertwined historical relationship to others (whether people or species) is clear in Moore's observations regarding the coproduction of modernity by both humanity and nature (7): 'Modernity is a capitalist world ecology' (4). It is this, then, which a world of cinemas now resists.

To briefly give one example, illustrating how much more a world of cinemas can offer to the Anthropocene debate than just doom-laden science fiction films, *Embrace of the Serpent* (discussed in the Introduction) indicates that it is not 'greener' technology that we must turn to at a time of environmental devastation by capital, but to a different ethical relationship with otherness. This requires that we recognise the histories of those excluded by global structural inequality, which by turns requires a provincialising of the relative centrality of normative ideas of world history.[22]

What the depth of history to the eco-Marxist approach provides (correlating the 1492 Anthropocene theory with colonial modernity) is another way of thinking about the role of inequality, ethics and the denial of coevalness in the Anthropocene debate. Understanding 'modernity *as* environmental history', after Moore, reveals that it is not technology which is the problem (and so 'greener' technology is not the answer), but the coloniality of power upon which colonial modernity rests. Moore's discussion of the so-called 'Four Cheaps' – food, labour power, energy and raw materials (1008) – with which capitalism transforms nature, indicates how capitalism thrives by appropriating unpaid labour, including that of 'women or slaves' (in terms of humans – themselves, of course, a part of nature) or 'extra human natures, such as forests, soils, or rivers' (63). Moore's argument, then, effectively places Latin American philosophy's critique of global structural inequality within an ecological framework.

The contemporary focus of thinking on technology, in both scientific definitions of the Anthropocene and explanations of it which explore science fiction films, suggests that the threat we face is a recent one, relating to Western modernity's global expansion after the Industrial Revolution. This present-focused discussion obscures, for example, the massive global population growth (the horrendous death toll of the indigenous of the Americas and elsewhere notwithstanding) enabled by the spread of New World crops like maize, potatoes, sweet potatoes and beans in the centuries which followed 1492 (Crosby 1972, 165–207; Mann 2011, 210–303). The North Atlantic trade circuit, in effect, formed an 'ecological corridor' to enable the global spread and exchange of not only foodstuffs, but more generally of viruses, parasites, bacteria, crops, insects, and animals (Mann 2011, 43). The origins of colonial modernity, which gave Europe a comparative advantage over Asia as it rose to global prominence on the back of slave labour and indigenous genocide, was the millions of square kilometres of land they colonised in the Americas after 1492 (Dussel 1998b, 32). Yet now this 'civilizing process' is reaching its 'terminal crisis' in 'the ecological destruction of the planet and the extinguishing in misery and hunger of the great majority of humanity' (Dussel 2003a, 69). Thus, as Christophe Bonneuil and Jean-Baptiste Fressoz note, dating the origins of the Anthropocene/Capitalocene back to the Sixteenth Century enables us to grasp that it is the ecologically 'unequal' nature of the Columbian Exchange (2016, 225) which provides the origins of the technological leaps made during the Great Acceleration of the post-war period (leaps which, after all, increasingly exacerbate inequality due to the labour they render redundant). And it is here, then, that the Cold War origin of a global cinema of resistance is recast.

After World War Two, the natural resources of the third world were drained by the Western powers: 'the driving phenomenon of the Great Acceleration embarked on in 1945–73 was the tremendous ecological indebtedness of the Western industrial countries. These literally emptied the rest of the world of its materials and high-quality energy, a phenomenon that is key to the Cold War' (Bonneuil and Fressoz 2016, 250). *The emergence of a worldwide cinema of resistance during the Cold War, then, relates to the much longer history of colonial modernity, and its ethics, similarly, relates to the Anthropocene.* It is in ecological historical worldviews like those of Moore, and Bonneuil and Fressoz (themselves so close to Dussel's position), that we find the intersection of ethics with the importance of recognizing the impact of the denial of coevalness (that defining feature of colonial modernity) on our current state of global structural inequality. This is not often a feature of science fiction films, but it is of many others – like *Embrace of the Serpent* – across a world of cinemas, as Chapters 3 through 6 further illuminate.

The multitudinous plurivocality of global cinema considered *as a totality* offers a chance to shift our focus towards the recognition of coevalness, towards equality with others within the world we inhabit. This is not a case of art cinema vs Hollywood, or third cinemas vs first and second, but of understanding how transnational histories emerge across the cinemas of the world (in genre movies, art films, documentaries, and so on). To grasp this, we need to realise that the transnational histories being explored on film coincide with the ethics demanded by the denial of coevalness that is a feature of the ecological history of colonial modernity. Accordingly, in the next chapter I deepen the ethical dimension to this study by exploring the importance of hesitation in time-image cinemas.

Notes

1 The transnational turn in Film Studies has been ongoing since the late 1990s, Deborah Shaw outlining no fewer than fifteen different 'inter-connecting and overlapping categories' of the term transnational now in use (2013; Fisher and Smith 2016). A great diversity of views exist with respect to methodologies used, and as to which analytical dimensions meet in transnational studies of films (Fisher and Smith 2016). This may be because the transnational turn is the product of a much broader shift in the field towards the study of a world of cinemas. The earliest of the texts on transnational cinema, after all, explored Chinese cinemas (Lu 1997), Chinese and diasporic/postcolonial cinemas (involving France and the Maghreb) respectively (Higbee and Lim, 2010), and international coproductions involving a range of countries, including China/Hong Kong, France/Belgium/Tunisia, Denmark/Scotland (Hjort, 2010).

2 The silver which European powers mined from the New World using slaves (150,000 tonnes between the Sixteenth and Eighteenth Centuries, 80% of the world's output (Mann 2011, 189)), became Europe's chief export, enabling it to compete in the then Asia-dominated world market (Frank 1998, 5), and to pay off its structural balance of trade deficits (albeit the influx ultimately became inflationary and thus

increased inequality in Europe (74–75; 131–139; 277–283)). Specifically, Mexican and Peruvian silver funded the building of the Armada which gave the Spanish control over the Mediterranean from the 1570s (Dussel 1998a, 11; 1998b, 31; 2003a, 60).

3 Peter Frankopan's claims to an alternative view of history Eurocentrically overstates the originality of his intervention in light of this long-standing debate (2015, xix).

4 Chinese ships may have landed in the Americas earlier in the Fifteenth Century than Columbus, who may himself have been following a Chinese map (Menzies 2002).

5 The Pope's concern with inequality under capitalism's 'economy of exclusion' is evident in his Papal proclamations (Pope Francis 2013, 45; 2015, 1) (notwithstanding the irony of the Roman Catholic Church's wealth (Kirchgaessner and Watts 2015), nor its intertwinement with colonisation after the 1493 Papal Bulls of Pope Alexander VI seemingly gave permission for the enslavement of indigenous Americans (Minnich 2005, 281)).

6 Of course, Vikings had visited centuries previously, and likely the Chinese earlier in the Fifteenth Century (Menzies 2002). Other precursors include the possibility of ships from Japan, and long before them the Romans and Phoenicians (Deloria 1972, 110). Yet only the arrival of Europeans after 1492 would influence the world system so profoundly.

7 The idea of 'compressed modernity' usually refers to South Korea. The argument is that 'South Koreans have experienced Westerners' historical development of two or three centuries over merely three or four decades' (Chang 1999, 30). 'Multiple modernities', more broadly, explores how modernity has emerged differently in various East Asian contexts, 'Western modernity' having 'travelled to the East', before being 'transformed' due to the distinctive characteristics which have marked its emergence in different locales (Lau 2003, 102). Admittedly, Dussel's position, oppositional to European exceptionalism, could be said, paradoxically, to place too much emphasis on Europe. Challenging the view of Europe as an 'enlightened' beacon (shining the light of rational thought, scientific development, and democracy) risks only producing a dark mirror of this, of coloniality (Europe as engine of genocide and theft on a global scale) as sole world-changing agency. After all, world history since 1492 has seen many events which seem entirely unconnected to Europe's growth, and which many might consider just as problematic (e.g. the modernisation of Japan and the emergence of its empire in the Nineteenth and Twentieth Centuries, culminating in such horrors as the Nanking Massacre of 1937; or the growth of Communism in China, and the starvation of millions from 1959 to 1961 during the Great Leap Forward). In fact, the global perspective of colonial modernity can illustrate their connectedness. Behind the growth of the world system to encompass the globe lies the European desire for access to Asian markets. Herein lies the connection between the encounter with Spanish ships landing in the Americas in 1492; British ships in China in 1839 (the Opium Wars giving the British Empire its longed-for foothold into Chinese markets via the cession of Hong Kong, which in turn influences Chinese history dramatically – including the emergence of communism, and ultimately the millions of deaths during the Great Leap Forward); and with US ships in Japan in 1853 (opening up the closed kingdom to trade on terms determined by others, which influences Japanese history – including the emergence of the Japanese empire, and ultimately the war crimes committed at Nanking). Europe is not the sole causal agent of either of these Asian events. There is Asian agency as well. Yet in the world system, after 1492, even 'distant' events (distant from the newly emerging Atlantic centre) are all connected within it.

8 Dussel notes that Levinas' representative figures of alterity are from pre-Christian ethical systems in, for example, areas of the world like Western Asia (1998b, 8).

9 This history is part of a longer heritage of subduing nature and all other religious worldviews in Judeo-Christian culture, stretching back centuries prior to the modern world system (Deloria 1972, 107 and 183; Fabian 1983, 1–35; Serres 1992, 47–50). Yet, it is with 1492 that it influenced the entire world system.

10 Dussel offers an interpretation of Marx pertinent to 'a critique of globalized capitalism' (1988, xxxii), emphasising that in Marx's theories, surplus value under capitalism stems from the surplus labour of workers (the proportion of the labour they provide which is not valued by the wages they earn (xvii, xxvii, 3–8)). Living labour, then, is the exterior ground upon which capital rests: or put differently (colonial) modernity is fuelled by its excluded underside (18). For Iván Márquez, Dussel offers a 'new interpretation of Marx [...] not as a dialectician and heir of Hegel, but as an analectic thinker who tries to fight the totalising efforts of the most important totality of his time, i.e., capitalism' (2013, 304). Accordingly, whilst Dussel can be described as providing a 'Levinasian Marx' (Mendieta 2003a, 9), equally, he provides a 'non-Eurocentric' and 'proto-postcolonial' Marx (Martín Alcoff and Mendieta 2000, 22–23).

11 Downing and Saxton situate Levinas with Jacques Derrida, Michel Foucault, Alain Badiou, and Slavoj Žižek. In addition, see: Levinas and Deleuze (Girgus 2010; Grønstad 2016), Nussbaum (Stadler 2008), Kant (Wheatley 2009), Badiou and/or Rancière (Nagib 2011; Ling 2011; Elsaesser 2011), Deleuze and/or Cavell (Bogue 2010; Rodowick 2010; Boljkovac 2013; Chaudhuri 2014; King 2014; Sinnerbrink 2016), Aristotle (with Nussbaum) (Choi 2014), Foucault (Noortwijk 2014), Lacan (with Levinas and Badiou) (Piotrowska 2014), Nancy (with Levinas) (Scott 2014; Hole 2016).

12 http://www.who.int/hdp/poverty/en/

13 The Eighteenth Century view, that philosophy originated in 'the Orient' (Park 2013, 2) (typically focusing on its Indian and Egyptian roots (74)), was replaced, in an act of Eurocentric myth-making, with Greece, as the starting point of a timeline which was geographically focused on the European development of thought (as in G. W. F. Hegel's *Philosophy of History* (1837)) (Park 2013, 85; see also Quijano 2000, 552; 2008, 192, 200; Dussel 2000b, 465–466; 2013, 12).

14 Dussel's glaring absence from existing accounts of post-Levinasian critiques indicates the continued Eurocentrism of this field (Hand 2009, 109–121; Boothroyd 2013).

15 Both Dussel and Žižek, who share a disbelief in Levinasian transcendence and a grounding in Marx, explore the potential for a recuperation of Christianity to address global structural inequality. In both cases, critiques have revealed the homogenising nature of their respective understandings of precisely who those others are who are excluded by global structural inequality (an issue which is, by turns, the product of the flaws inherent to their respective philosophies). Žižek's idea of a Christian community, as it were, without faith, is of 'a fighting collective grounded in the reference to an unconditional universalism' (2003, 130). The historical precedent for this, evident in Žižek's reincarnation of St Paul as Lenin, is the Bolshevik Revolution (2003, 9). In this we see Žižek's continued emphasis on class as an undifferentiated mass (2000, 110–111; 2003, 48), indicating his failure of 'historical imagination' and how his 'Eurocentric perspective [...] blocks a materialist conceptualization of colonial history in relation to contemporary globalization' (Stam and Shohat 2012, 122 and 129). Although Dussel provides more nuance to his understanding of the region-specific nature of revolutionary movements like that of the Zapatistas (1998b, 385–388), even so, similar critiques are levelled at Dussel's postcolonial Christianity as they are at Žižek's pagan Christianity. Ofelia Schutte and Elina Vuola, for example, critique Dussel for the presumed lack of agency he gives to those in need of liberation, the possible return of God as philosopher in the one who thinks the underside of modernity seemingly from outwith the world system (and perhaps the one to whom the other presumably appeals), the difficulties Dussel has reconciling the liberation of alterity with a conservative and seemingly Catholic gender politics, and the authoritarianism of such an absolutist position on ethics, derived from religion (Schutte 1993, 175–190; Vuola 2000, 153–162).

16 Indeed, there is much more to the concrete *realisation* of Dussel's ethics than is necessary to outline for this discussion of cinema (Dussel 1996; 1998b; 2011).

17 Geopolitical: revolutionary movements of the Cold War enabling third cinema debates in Latin America; postcolonialism and third cinema debates in Africa; the end of the Cold War and the rise of neoliberal globalisation ensuring an increasing focus on diasporic, refugee, immigrant and other cross-border movements. Industrial: regional or global reach of industries like Hollywood or Bollywood; the increasing importance of multinational capital in globalising cinema; the increase in international coproductions and runaway productions globally; the growth and global reach of the film festival circuit as distribution platform and producer of 'world cinema' (Falicov 2007; Villazana 2008; Ross 2010, 2011; Martin-Jones and Montañez 2013a), the rise of online distribution, etc.

18 My approach is distinct from Franco Moretti's attempt to explore a world of cinemas in terms of a broader 'world system of culture' (2001, 101), which takes a rather one-dimensional economic approach. It is also different from Dudley Andrew's much more nuanced explorations of a world of cinemas via world systems analysis (which take Moretti as something of an inspirational jumping off point (2006; 2010)), due to the world historical/hermeneutical emphasis placed herein on the evocation of world systems analysis.

19 Several scholars working on history on film emphasise this film-philosophical heritage without acknowledging it as such. The legacy of Nietzsche's 'On the Uses and Disadvantages of History for Life' (1874) is apparent in the field, as is Michel Foucault's work on 'counter-memory' which he develops from Nietzsche. Counter-memory requires, for Foucault, an 'effective history' (affirming of 'knowledge as perspective') that is of use for the present, rather than affirming of first causes to history, which are often illusionary and retroactively posited (1977, 156–160). This legacy is evident in Deleuze's adoption of Nietzsche's text for his exploration of the historical film, White's emphasis on history's usefulness for 'life' in 'the present time' (which runs through the field generally) and attempts to read history on film as engaged in the construction of counter-histories. Deleuze, for his part, is utilised by several scholars (Landy 1996, 2001, 2015; Barta 1998, 9–10; Burgoyne 2008), his presence in the debate being acknowledged by the inclusion of the time-image in *The History on Film Reader* (Hughes-Warrington, 2011a).

20 Work on third cinema historically centred on Latin American and African cinemas (Gabriel 1979; Pines and Willemen 1989; Martin 1997; Wayne 2001; Guneratne and Dissanayake 2003), due to the emergence of three manifestos from Latin America in the 1960s advocating for various forms of resistance to the global hegemony of US and European cinemas (Rocha 1965; Solanas and Getino 1969; Julio García Espinosa 1969) and the importance of filmmakers like Senegal's Ousmane Sembene in the postcolonial growth of African cinema. There is much to challenge about this model, such as whether third cinema filmmakers see themselves in this way, whether works of second cinema may have as revolutionary an impact 'in spite' of their use of conventional forms, what role indigenous aesthetic traditions play (Ukadike 1994, 97–104), into which category to fit Bollywood (historically and now) and Nollywood, as well as indigenous filmmaking, so-called 'fourth cinema' (Barclay 2003), etc. Yet it remains an evocative way of using film-philosophy, often blending Marx and Fanon, to include within world cinemas 'a cinema of decolonization and for liberation' (Gabriel 1979, 1).

21 Some estimates suggest it may even have been double this amount, and if so, the toll may have accounted for the death – primarily by disease – of as much as 95% of the population of the Americas. This was perhaps around one fifth of the world's population at the time (Mann 2005, 93–94). Curiously, although the likelihood that much of the Americas was densely populated at the time of European arrival has been known to Western academia, and the general public, for some time (e.g. Heckenberger 2005; Mann 2005), even now reports of 'findings' to this effect, such as explorations of ruins in Guatemala and Mexico via Lidar scanning (aerially deployed laser technology), published in early 2018, are greeted in the West as breaking news (Davis 2018;

BBC 2018). This is a history, it seems, which we prefer to keep on losing, due no doubt to the inconvenience of this truth for a Western narrative of colonial intervention which prefers to emphasise a supposedly developmental (as opposed to, in reality, a murderous and exploitative profit-seeking) agenda. Or perhaps things are simpler even than this. Perhaps what is being celebrated, and what will be remembered here, is the achievement of Western technology in creating such laser technology, rather than the lost pasts – revealing, ironically, of the destructions wrought by Europeans in their supposed developmental quest to civilise the world – which it might uncover.

22 By contrast, it is rather ironic that the dystopian imagining of a settler colonial culture's future after a nuclear holocaust (a technologically produced disaster) in *Mad Max* movies effectively reduces the inhabitants of Australia to the same position which Europeans did to indigenous Americans after 1492. After all, European ideological displacement of the indigenous to the past, as noted in the Introduction after Quijano, mirrored the actual reduction of large and complex civilisations by disease, warfare and enslavement (in places such as the Amazon, now only recorded in archaeological traces) to what have become, by the Twenty-First Century, isolated, tribal, 'often fugitive [...] social groups' (Heckenberger 2005, xii), not dissimilar to those more fantastically imagined in *Mad Max* movies.

2

ETHICS/HISTORY

Hesitating in encountering lost pasts (Gilles Deleuze)

The previous chapter outlined how a certain historical worldview could provide the grounding for an interpretation of (world) history across a world of cinemas. The liberation philosophy of Enrique Dussel was introduced, beginning the process of integrating ethics into the discussion of history. This second chapter further develops this ethical dimension, to establish how, in the film analysis which follows in Chapters 3–6, cinematic engagements with transnational histories (staged as encounters with the lost pasts, the other stories of world history) create hesitation regarding accepted views of world history. Thus this chapter incorporates a temporal dimension, synchronising a reconstructed Gilles Deleuze (utilising his time-image categories but reconsidering his conceptualisation of history and manner of taxonomising) with Dussel (his post-Levinasian notion of the synchronic time of the encounter with the other) to explain the role of hesitation when encountering other pasts on film.

In addition, hesitation is understood to relate not only to the viewer's position in respect of world history, but also to their ability to realise the kinds of contracts which underpin global structural inequality. Such contracts – whether natural, racial, social, individual, et al. – focus the taxonomising process through which a world of cinemas' engagement with transnational histories on film is illuminated in Chapters 3–6. In both dimensions, the temporal and the contractual, transnational histories on film ask us to hesitate with regard to the recognition denied to those historically on the other, or under, side of the structuring contracts of (colonial) modernity.

The time-image and history I: The crystal history of world memory

Deleuze's time-image is integral to the depiction of transnational histories, due to its ability to create a shorthand view of (world) history. In spite of the

Eurocentrism of Deleuze's framing of his history of the emergence of the time-image in Western cinemas (Martin-Jones 2011), a 'reconstructed' Deleuze has emerged in recent scholarship engaging with a world of cinemas. This is due in particular to the usefulness of his conception of 'world memory'.[1] A brief introduction to the time-image, how it negotiates world memory (and contemporary uses of this idea to explore a world of cinemas) is thus necessary at this point.[2] This trajectory provides the first of several reconstructions of Deleuze which I undertake in this chapter, including of his cinematic ethics, and his cinematic taxonomising, respectively.

In the *Cinema* books, Deleuze built upon Henri Bergson's idea of time (1896; 1907) as a virtual whole, which is created by the perpetual splitting of time into a present that passes (actualised) and a past that is preserved (virtual). This relationship between the virtual and actual (the former subsisting and providing the latter with its potential for continual emergence and re-emergence in new forms) reflects the idea that time in its measured, quantifiable, actual form (space-time) is distinct from the constantly transforming or 'becoming' virtual whole of time (what Bergson dubs 'duration'). As a result, Deleuze states mid-way through *Cinema 2*, when discussing how the virtual whole of time is glimpsed in the films of directors like Orson Welles, Alain Resnais and Federico Fellini:

> Memory is not in us; it is we who move in a Being-memory, a world-memory. In short, the past appears as the most general form of the already-there, a pre-existence in general, which our recollections presuppose, even our first recollection if there is one, and which our perceptions, even the first, make use of. From this point of view the present itself exists only as an infinitely contracted past which is constituted at the extreme point of the already-there.
>
> *(1985, 95–96)*

Our lives are actualised manifestations of this virtual whole of time, of the past which subsists or insists along with them in virtual form, actualised as space-time. Thus we all exist in a giant world memory. Accordingly, rather than considering the representation of time on film, Deleuze effectively argues (like director Andrei Tarkovsky (1986)), that movement-images sculpt space-time, and time-images sculpt duration.

In *Cinema 1*, the movement-image's sculpting of space-time illustrates an anthropocentric focus when carving out of the world in actualised form. The trio of perception-image (what is seen), affection-image (what is felt), and action-image (what is done) are often used to create a sensory-motor continuity to the filmic world and human figures. Of these three, the affection-image exists in a particularly dynamic relationship with time, at the point between perception and action during which the virtual whole of time (duration) has the potential to intervene into, and potentially to break up, sensory-motor continuity (Martin-Jones 2011, 134–138). In the movement-image, for example, the close-up of the face magnifies the impact of sensations felt by a person, as though slowing time to consider the affective moment. In this instant we may reconsider the past, in order to alter how we behave in the present. This pause, or hesitation, may include a slip into the virtual past via a flashback, although in movement-image cinemas typically this potential is closed off in a seamless transition from perception to action, which retains the unitary, singular, and linear trajectory of time. In time-images, though, things are different.

In *Cinema 2*, Deleuze identifies several types of time-image which express our experience of existence in time, including 'pure optical and sound situations' or 'opsigns' and 'sonsigns' (moments in which we experience the passing of time in and for itself), 'crystal-images' (expressing the coexistence of virtual past and actual present, often at the moment of time's perpetual splitting (1985, 66–94)), layers or sheets of the past (e.g. when we travel through the layers of Bergson's cone of memory in flashbacks (95–121)), films about temporally labyrinthine multiple universes (122–150), etc. The time-image's various forms thus provide us with a glimpse of the movements of the virtual whole of time (Deleuze refers to this as the 'movement of world' (1985, 56)), which encapsulates humanity. Thus the previous anthropocentric emphasis on the progression from perception to action, of the movement-image, is gone. No longer the subordination of time to movement through space (movement-image), but the virtual movement of time itself (time-image). This is a relational difference, admittedly, from editing ordered around a continuous sensory-motor logic (movement-image), to discontinuous editing illustrating the shifts between different layers of time we experience when remembering (time-image). Hence the time-image types illustrate the various ways in which cinema's 'psychomechanics' can be said to 'think' about time (252). The glimpse of duration in the sensory-motor continuum of the movement-image, a moment of pause, or contemplation (such as a close-up leading to a flashback), in the time-image becomes the dominant logic of the montage. The viewer, accordingly, slips into the vastness of the virtual world memory, as though forever hesitating before the dynamic virtual movements of the past.

Deleuze's time-image, indeed the entire movement-/time-image taxonomy, thinks about time in a manner inextricably linked to how the story of history is told on screen. The movement-image and the time-image exist in a relationship of mutually exerting tension, in which contrary pulls seek to at once exert a reterritorialising pressure to create movement-images (straight lines through time), whilst, simultaneously, a deterritorialising disruptiveness seeks to diversify into time-images (to create a labyrinth of time). These contrary pulls correlate with the manner in which movement- and time-image films tell the story of history, with the movement-image particularly well suited to narratives of colonisation (the epitome of the action-image in the final chapters of *Cinema 1* is the US western) and the time-image to stories which throw into question existing beliefs regarding how the past informs our present (Deleuze focuses on postcolonial filmmakers in his discussion of the time-images of 'modern political cinema') (Martin-Jones 2006, 19–32).

Moreover, the virtual labyrinth of time contains within it the potential for the Nietzschean 'powers of the false' to falsify what we know of our current time, to propose an alternative past that might inform our present (Deleuze 1985, 122–150). Here we begin to realise its importance for the debate surrounding doublethink outlined in the Introduction. In the time-image, then, the potential to become lost in the virtual labyrinth of time does not only provide an opportunity to realise the forgotten pasts of world history, but also to reconsider the seemingly universal nature of the Hegelian *idea* of world history (the straight line of time, the movement-image) which is inhabited, by many, until the moment of encounter with the time-image. Hence, as we only ever perceive time in its actualised state, only ever live the present moment of the history which we do know, the time-image has the potential to indicate the very fact that there *is* such a virtual world memory subsisting along with the official story of history, thereby relativising its centrality to world history (offering the perpetual prospect of the powers of the false to unground our surety in the history that informs the present).

Engagement with Deleuze's time-image in scholarship on history on film (Landy 1996, 2001, 2015; Barta 1998, 9–10; Burgoyne 2008), as well as in the Deleuze and cinema community (Martin-Jones 2011, 69–131; Deamer 2009; 2012; 2014, 75–120), alongside the inclusion of a section of *Cinema 2* in *The History on Film Reader* (Hughes-Warrington 2011a) is thus apposite. The time-image is an aesthetic form which enables us to see as much the (temporal) aspect of world memory (that which Deleuze focused on) as it does the world history being negotiated onscreen. This is why it is so useful for exploring the kind of 'future historiography' which Hughes-Warrington postulates, at the intersection of cinematic constructions of time and history (2011b, 63). To fully grasp this, however, more detail is needed regarding the time-image category of the 'crystal of time' and its relationship to Deleuze's (and Deleuze and Guattari's) philosophy of history.

Deleuze and Guattari are known for critiquing, rather than celebrating, history. This is because of their negative view on history's role in the stratifying of (otherwise potentially smooth, or nomadic) space which accompanies the establishing of borders to a state (imperial, national, so on) (1980, 394). They prefer a 'geohistory' akin, they state, to that of Fernand Braudel (1991, 95), which can take account of geography and history. Indeed, the idea of a transnational history which I pursue herein, locating its grounding in world systems analysis (Wallerstein, after all, follows Braudel), can be understood very much in this way – as a spatially grounded idea of history. Nevertheless, in spite of their sometimes critical perspective, Deleuze's and Deleuze and Guattari's philosophy of history is now of increasing interest to scholars across disciplines, ensuring that its temporal dimension also becomes ever more apparent (De Landa 1997; Lampert 2006; Bell and Colebrook 2009; Lundy 2011). This dimension is of crucial import to any cinematic consideration of (transnational) history after Deleuze.

Eugene Holland describes Deleuze and Guattari's philosophy of history as a 'non-linear historical materialism' (2011, 17), which is predicated upon the Bergsonian notion of the past as a virtual whole 'omnipresent to itself' (22). Thus history for Deleuze and Guattari contains inter-related struggles, for the majoritarian actualisation of the virtual past (in the form of the official State narrative of history), and minoritarian becomings which reveal the potential of the virtual to destabilise or render discontinuous such a linear history: restoring 'its virtual potential to become otherwise' (Holland 2011, 26). History is thus made up of 'both a singular linear history and multiple non-linear becomings' (28).[3]

As Hanjo Berressem argues, the relationship between the actual and the virtual in Deleuze's philosophy can thus be equated with that between history (actual) and historiography (virtual), where 'actual history' is 'the history of pure change in and for itself [...] a chronic history of pure causes' and 'virtual history' 'consists of the temporal and spatial relations between singular events and their agglomerations' (2011, 207–208). Usefully for this discussion, Berressem has recourse to the time-image to explain what is at stake in Deleuze's philosophy of history:

> How to conceive of history when everything is adrift? If there are material contractions on the one side and immaterial contemplations on the other, and if these two series are to be kept radically separate, how can actual history and virtual history be brought to converge 'as much as possible?' [...] In terms of Deleuze's *Cinema 2: The Time-Image*: How to create a 'crystal history' in the sense that crystal-images are images that treat the 'smallest internal circuit' between the actual and the virtual: points of 'the indiscernibility of the actual and the virtual'; or, in historical terms, images of 'life as spectacle, and yet in its spontaneity'.
>
> *(211–212)*

At the smallest internal limit, where time is perpetually splitting into a present that passes (actual) and a past that is preserved (the virtual store of time, world memory), creating 'crystal history' is what the time-image *does* (see in particular Chapters 4 and 5). It offers the possibility of a new way of telling the story of history, the potential of historiography as described by Hayden White – to use the past to liberate the present (see Chapter 1). What this work on the temporal dimension of Deleuze and Guattari's philosophy of history indicates, then, is that the time-image is a potentially disruptive force, at once temporally and historically.

The world's time-images, then, provide entrances into world memory. Surveying a world of cinemas, the time-image emerges across borders to provide precisely this multi-dimensional (temporal, historical) critique of colonial modernity. Hence, worldwide, this aesthetic device is deployed to realise the 'crystal history' of a shared past which is far beyond that of individual nations.

With this idea of crystal history and its connection to world memory via time-images in mind, what is key, but also contentious, about Deleuze's taxonomy is the way in which he historicises it. Deleuze argues that the cinema of the time-image emerges after World War Two. It is expressive of a new way of understanding the temporal experience of late Twentieth Century life. Thus the time-image, for Deleuze, provides evidence of a post-war 'image of thought' (1968, 129–167), one more Bergsonian than Einsteinian (Durie 1999, v–xxi).

This is a transnational way of considering history, which includes many national histories within its sweep. Yet what is problematic about the way in which Deleuze frames his conclusion is, specifically, this Eurocentric focus on the Second World War as pivotal point of change. Regardless of how influential Deleuze's ideas, how evident his genius, how important his attempt to critique Eurocentric philosophical thinking, there is a Eurocentrism to the way he draws his conclusions in the *Cinema* books. This is due to the geographical range and type of films viewed, and Deleuze's perspective on 'whose' understanding of time changed in the Twentieth Century (a point made fairly regularly regarding Deleuzian interpretations of Asian cinemas (Berry 2009, 113; Martin-Jones 2011, 1–19 and 100–161; Martin-Jones and Brown 2012, 4–7; Deamer 2014, 16–20; Martin-Jones and Fleming 2014, 93–94)).

Deleuze's conclusions regarding his cinematic taxonomy thus require deterritorialising (to use a Deleuze and Guattarian term), such that the history which the time-image 'reflects' can be understood as more global than Eurocentric. This entails a shift from a time-image supposedly expressing a global change that stems from Western origins to a polycentric understanding of the world's time-images – each being viewed as equally expressive of a shock to thought which has emerged for different reasons in various locations. For example, in Hong Kong in the 1980s due to globalisation, but in South Korea and Argentina in the 1990s and 2000s due to the resurgence of filmmaking after the end of Cold War dictatorships and the need to re-examine the role of the national past under neoliberalism (Martin-Jones 2011, 69–161). A new way of understanding what connects so many expressions of the time-image across so many national cinemas is required, and contemporary scholarship indicates that the binding idea is world memory. Let us briefly consider how.

Patricia Pisters observes film's temporal archiving of 'history as collective memory, or "world memory"' (2012, 220), after Deleuze, the medium thereby offering the potential for future uses of the archive to reconsider the past. Similarly, Shohini Chaudhuri considers various works from a world of cinemas that focus on state terror, worldwide, arguing that:

> Film is not a repository of memory content, providing us with other people's memories; it constructs its own memory-world, which acts on and mediates our memories. Rather than a 'prosthetic memory', as Alison Landsberg has contended, film is a prosthesis *for* memory, capable of extending our sensory perceptions into our memories and shaping them in particular ways.
>
> *(2014, 87)*

For example, Chaudhuri argues of recent films to explore the disappearances during the Cold War military regimes of Chile and Argentina that, for those transnational viewers whose national pasts these are not, the films can nevertheless 'lure us onto sheets of the past', into 'memory-worlds, where memory becomes shared and multiple' (89).[4] Finally, Marcia Landy deploys Deleuze as methodological impetus (seeing counter history as the unthought which emerges in the time-image (2015, xv)) with a shift in focus from the national towards more transnational histories, albeit their connectedness as such is left mostly implicit. Landy thus explores how works of modern political cinema worldwide (following Deleuze, by definition, time-images) create minor histories which place the truth of history into crisis (123–184).

Importantly for this work, these predecessors indicate a broad shift in scholarly understanding of modernity, occurring due to this idea of world memory. As noted in the Introduction, this is evident in the difference between, on the one hand, Mary Ann Doane's exploration of how cinema negotiates the 'structuring of temporality in modernity' (2002, 11) through such devices as montage – in line with the emphasis on North America and Europe of the Benjaminian 'modernity thesis' (Gunning 1986, et al.) – and Bliss Cua Lim's (2006) Bergsonian/Deleuzian foregrounding of the role of various Asian genre films in manifesting the coexistence of multiple temporalities (often pre-modern in origin, postcolonial in expression), depicted in fantastic, supernatural, ghostly or monstrous forms. For Lim, who also draws on Dussel, these haunting temporalities coexist along with the homogeneous time of the 'world-historical project of modernity, which hinged on colonialism' (13)). From time in Western modernity as it is so often understood in its supposed isolation and exceptionalism (Doane), to the *times* denied by colonial modernity but stored in world memory (Lim). This shift of emphasis, also evident in works exploring time in national cinemas like those of China and India (Martin-Jones 2011, 201–233; 2014) stands in contrast to the separation of the West from the rest of the world via the denial of coevalness.

In world memory, for Deleuze, 'we plunge into a memory which overflows the conditions for psychology, memory for two, memory for several, memory-world, memory ages of the world' (1985, 115). What a reconstructed Deleuze shows, then, is that across a world of cinemas, world memory (which we enter via the time-image) focuses on keeping alive the lost pasts of colonial modernity. What is needed now is a deeper grasp of how the lost pasts are negotiated as transnational histories with the potential to create an ethically activating form of hesitation.

The time-image and history II: Hesitation

Like Film Studies, (Continental) Philosophy is also concerned with what a Bergsonian/Deleuzian understanding of world memory might mean for ethics. Accordingly, I take the idea of hesitation from Alia Al-Saji's philosophical examination, after Henri Bergson and Maurice Merleau-Ponty, of its potential to enable ethical transformations.[5] For Al-Saji, the interval created by the intervention of time into the sensory-motor continuum is hesitation, the opening up of time for thinking (2012, 351–358). Thus, Al-Saji constructs an argument for 'philosophy as prosthesis, as a means and a way of seeing differently [...] a transformative supplement, one that our bodily perception calls for and wherein that perception is recast. Rather than a fixed or assured view, this prosthesis holds open but does not fill the interval between affect and action, the interval in which thinking can take place' (352). This is, precisely as in Deleuze's *Cinema* books, the potential of the time-image to confront the viewer with the thought from outside. Indeed, Al-Saji considers the pause needed to reconsider the past which is opened up in the interval between perception and action much as Deleuze describes the powers of the false in *Cinema 2*. For Al-Saji:

> Though the past as a virtual whole pushes on each present, actualizing itself there, this past is dynamically reconfigured through the passage of events and through the creation of possibility that ripples back from these events (their virtualization). [...] Newness [...] arises not only from the openness to the future but from the way the past is remembered in the hesitation of philosophical vision.
>
> *(2012, 360)*

It follows from Al-Saji's Bergsonian position on hesitation (the pause which 'characterizes the work of philosophy as ontological organ or prosthesis' (358)), that it has the ability to enable a reconsideration of routine actions based on ingrained habits, including our reactions to others who are unlike ourselves.

Al-Saji elaborates elsewhere, drawing on Frantz Fanon and Aníbal Quijano, regarding the racialisation of time, and of being in time. The frames of reference of the racial imaginary used in the colonisation of the past 'differentially configure the kinds of past and fields of possibility available to subjects' (Al-Saji 2013, 4) such that coevalness is denied by the associating of colonised peoples with 'the stereotyped remnants, isolated fragments and colonized distortions extrapolated back from their oppressed and alienated state under colonialism' (6). These constructed images, 'the negative mirror of a white civilizational past' (9), replace the realities of precolonial pasts (6). For Al-Saji, the potential of hesitation is that it can provide the possibility of unlearning such habitually maintained prejudices, thereby enabling a recognition of coevalness. Hesitation's power is ethical and critical in relation to memory, as it enables the reconfiguration of

> memories of the past, my own past in its relations to the memories of others. [...] For affectivity to be opened up in the present, the past should also be worked through; memories of other pasts need to find voice, interrupting the ankylosed and dominant stories that are repeated there.
>
> *(2014, 148–149)*

For Al-Saji, then, hesitation can enable the realisation of our existence in a world memory, of 'a *shared* and *intersubjective* past' (2014, 161), and thereby reorient our relationship to a past which, historically, has been structured so as to keep us ignorant of this: doublethink.

As noted previously, the time-image, in its delaying and suspension of the sensory-motor continuum, offers an encounter with other histories, the shared and often intersubjective histories of the world. During this moment of hesitation, with the unthinking linearity of habit interrupted, the encounter with the virtual whole of time provides an opportunity for a reorientation of the past which can help us recognise (and unlearn) our historically conditioned responses to others.[6] This is not to say that every such encounter will transpire in this way, of course. As Sara Ahmed argues, the ways in which commodities (such as films) are consumed can often reterritorialise 'strangers' and 'strangeness' within established parameters that have been historically determined: 'the 'stranger as a commodity fetish through representation of difference' (2000, 116). As Al-Saji's work indicates, we are only discussing the *potential* of the time-image to create hesitation sufficient to reorient the past in ways that may counter those of the stereotypes and colonial distortions used to racialise the past.

Nevertheless, the hesitation offered by the time-image provides an opportunity to consider whether we should feel *uncomfortable* in our own skin. If necessary, to reconsider long-held beliefs, due to an encounter with the forgotten pasts of world memory. This is, Robert Sinnerbrink notes, echoing Paul Gilroy's observations regarding the need for cultural estrangement (see the Introduction), the potential of a cinematic ethics to create 'emotional *estrangement* through which conflicting, clashing, or incompatible ideas, commitments, or beliefs can be revealed' (2016, 8). Thus, what a Dusselian approach to the kind of hesitation which Al-Saji outlines provides is not an indication that every viewer needs to unlearn racism (as every individual encounter with world memory will be different), nor that every film will actively work to open the viewer to world memory without some form of qualification along the lines noted by Ahmed. Rather, it provides only the possibility that through hesitation the multiplicity of experiences of world history which co-exist can be understood to be coeval. It is this possibility, this gap in history which indicates the illusory nature of the very idea that there is one single history (like that of colonial modernity), which the time-image keeps open.

With the role of hesitation in the construction of crystal history in mind, it is now possible to consider how Deleuze and Dussel mesh in respect to time and the other. For Dussel, in the encounter with the other there is a synchronic temporal relationship which refuses the denial of coevalness, in spite of the historical reality of the colonisation of time by this very denial.

> Economic, technological, semiotic history is diachronic. Times passes while one waits for future proximity, inspired by the remembrance of past proximity. But in the immediacy of proximity itself, time becomes synchronic: my time is your time, our time; our time is your time, the time of fellowship in justice and festival. The synchrony of those who live proximity becomes timeless. In the instant of proximity, distinct and separate times converge and dissolve in the joy of being together. The timelessness

of the instant of proximity is, nevertheless, the point of reference for history; it is where ages and epochs begin and end.

(1971, 19)

Dussel's notion of time is developed in distinction from Levinas's. For Levinas, who wishes to counter the idea of sequential past, present and future, time is realised in the encounter with the other, because the time of the other disrupts the time of the self. In *Time and the Other,* Levinas states, 'the "movement" of time understood as transcendence towards the Infinity of the "wholly other" [*tout Autre*] does not temporalize in a linear way' (1947, 33). Rather, alterity 'opens time' (36), time being 'the very relationship of the subject with the Other' (39). In the encounter there is a realisation of temporal noncoincidence (the subject's time is not that of the other). Yet in the encounter, both subject and other are contained within the '*always* of the *relationship*', its brush with the infinite (Levinas 1947, 32). Thus, for Levinas, whilst the chronological time of the subject is synchronous, the time of the transcendent encounter is diachronic. It is here that the distinction being drawn by Dussel is clear. The diachronic axis of time, for Dussel, is that of history, whereas the encounter with the other is one in which – in a conclusion directly opposite to that of Levinas – the time of the subject and the other are synchronous. Rather than together in infinity (Levinas), the encounter brings people together in the moment (Dussel). In Dussel the synchronic moment thus contains the possibility of the denial of the denial of coevalness. It is the moment of hesitation, prompted by the encounter, in which history can be reconsidered.

The time-image and history III: Deleuze's ethics

This reconstructed Deleuze outlined so far – after Al-Saji, and aligned with Dussel – is preferred to Deleuze's own cinematic ethics, which considers the crisis of the action-image and the emergence of the time-image to indicate a broader shift in thinking with respect to humanity's ability to act meaningfully upon the world (Bogue 2010; Rodowick 2010; Bernstein 2012; Boljkovac 2013; King 2014; Sinnerbrink 2016). Deleuze's position, of the need to encourage engagement with the world, is one held against nihilism (as Sinnerbrink notes, 'evoking a Nietzschean affirmation of art in response to pervasive forms of historico-cultural nihilism' (2016, 55)), and as such it is very much involved in the European tradition which it reconsiders. At the heart of this transformation is the role of World War Two in apparently disconnecting us from the world.

> The modern fact is that we no longer believe in this world. We do not even believe in the events which happen to us, love, death, as if they only half concerned us. It is not we who make cinema; it is the world which looks to us like a bad film. [...] The link between man and the world is broken. Henceforth this link must become an object of belief: it is the impossible

which can only be restored within a faith. [...] Only belief in the world can reconnect man to what he sees and hears. The cinema must film, not the world, but belief in this world, our only link. [...] Restoring our belief in the world – that is the power of modern cinema (when it stops being bad).

(Deleuze 1985, 166)

For Deleuze, the cinema of the time-image can restore faith in our ability to reconnect to the world. It presents us with limit situations to which we cannot react ('to make us grasp something intolerable and unbearable [...] something too powerful, or too unjust, but sometimes also too beautiful, and which henceforth outstrips our sensory-motor capabilities' (17)), asks us to choose to react, to choose to choose as a 'mode of existence' (171). D. N. Rodowick clarifies that, due to Deleuze's adherence to the Spinozist idea of the univocity of Being, Deleuze's cinematic ethics advocates 'the choice to believe in *this* world, the world in which we exist now, alive and changing, and not some transcendent or ideal world' (2010, 100). In this respect, Deleuze's ethics is quite different from that of Levinas's recuperation of the transcendent in the encounter with the other. As Dave Boothroyd argues: 'For Deleuze, ethics *is* ontology, moreover political ontology, whereas Levinas locates ethics 'beyond Being' and therefore, the scope of any ontology' (2013, 34). Thus the time-image offers reconnection to the world, typically for Deleuze, through the access that montage offers to the virtual whole of time. Through its relinking of images in new ways, the time-image enables the thought from the outside to intercede into the interstices between them.

When Deleuze seeks out exemplars of this ethical demand of the time-image, he considers directors often explored in discussions of third cinema (Glauber Rocha, Ousmane Sembene, Yilmaz Güney, Haile Gerima, Youssef Chahine (1985, 207–215)) to describe what he terms modern political cinema (also known as minor cinema (Sutton and Martin-Jones 2008; Brown 2014; Holtmeier 2016)). What the crisis of the action-image shows, then, is the faltering of the belief in action so important to imperialism (in its US incarnation, from the myth of Manifest Destiny onwards (Martin-Jones 2006, 67–73)). For such cinemas, Deleuze's argument makes complete sense. From Italian neorealism, through the various European new waves, to US independent filmmakers like John Cassavettes, Martin Scorsese and Robert Altman in the 1970s, there is an evident attempt to connect differently with reality, due to the circumstances of global conflict during the Cold War (which ultimately caused the faltering of the American Dream: Vietnam, the Watergate scandal and so on (Martin-Jones 2011, 71)). Yet the revolutionary and oppositional cinemas of the post- or neocolonial contexts which Deleuze cites were not reconnecting with the world due to some sense of a *recently* lost capacity. World War Two is not the cause of their disconnection. They are engaging in a recurring attempt to overcome the situation of subjugation, to reconnect with the world they were deprived of for several centuries by colonial modernity.

Accordingly, one might consider whether *disbelief* in the world does not seem a rather privileged Western position. Nietzsche's concern with nihilism emerges due to the Western philosophical tradition's realisation of the death of transcendence, perhaps not coincidentally, at the height of Northern Europe's global colonisation. Yet, and thus, for filmmakers of third cinema, the realisation that one's actions might not meaningfully affect your world was, surely, long ingrained before World War Two, due to histories of colonialism. If there was a motivating factor for the attempt to consider how to reconnect (how to create what Deleuze calls of modern political cinemas a people yet to come (1985, 207-215)), then for pioneers of third cinema it was, presumably, inequality, or simply hunger (as per the title of Glauber Rocha's famous manifesto (1965)), rather than the kind of middle-class ennui evident in the films of François Truffaut or Michelangelo Antonioni (in which 'we' do not believe in love anymore). Deleuze's recourse to World War Two in determining the emergence of the time-image indicates that his thinking follows that of, amongst others, Hayden White's Eurocentric worldview (see Chapter 1). Western cinema's evidencing of a lack of belief in the world in the post-war era is simply its realisation of its relative centrality to global power, in an era of growing postcoloniality. This (Eurocentric) shift in thinking about humanity's relationship with the world being due to the shocks of the Holocaust and Hiroshima (Alain Resnais' *Hiroshima mon amour* (France/Japan, 1959) features in Deleuze's discussion of Hiroshima and Auschwitz (1985, 200–201) and subsequent works on Deleuze and ethics (Bernstein 2012; Boljkovac 2013)), and intellectual attempts to grapple with their ramifications for long-held beliefs in what Europe stands for (the Enlightenment, the supposedly progressive nature of modernity, etc.) does not hold up to scrutiny considering the atrocities of the centuries-long history of colonial modernity. As noted in Chapter 1, the Holocaust is not an inexplicable modern event, but the latest of many after 1492. Only this time, it took place in Europe (Césaire 1955; Gilroy 1993; Mills 1997). Like White, Deleuze demonstrates a Eurocentric pre-occupation with the supposedly suddenly overpowering capacity of technology to determine our lives. But the nuclear era is not itself the reason for a need to reconnect with the world. It is just another phase of colonial modernity.

So, if the time-image enables a reconnection to the world and this is not due to World War Two, then why is it? *It is because of its re-activation of world memory.* For this reason we find time-images emerging all around the world at different moments, as various locations reconsider their place within not only national, but also world, histories which have excluded (parts of) their populations. The notion of modern political (or minor) cinema being able to develop a 'people yet to come' is, precisely, one which relates to those excluded by colonial modernity. The time-image emerges in post-war European cinema simply because it was then that the Western middle classes began to find themselves included in this exclusion (the Holocaust already being indicative of this for many), as their capacity to influence the world began to diminish along with their imperial wealth. Just as Levinas' affirming of ethics in the wake of the Holocaust showed

Europe's reaction to the returning to its origins of the same genocidal practices it had developed elsewhere since the encounter with indigenous Americans, so too does Deleuze's understanding of cinema's ability to reconnect 'us' with the world reflect European philosophy's relatively recent dissatisfaction with the failings of modernity. For many around the world, these failings have been a lived reality for centuries.

Yet amidst this critique of Deleuze's cinematic ethics there is something to be recuperated. What attracts many to Deleuze's position is that a person might be changed by their encounter with film, and with Deleuze we can understand this as a temporally informed transformation which functions in relation to world memory. Rodowick notes: 'films or other forms of art express for us or return us to our past, current and future states' (2010, 99). As films are able to change how we consider our own pasts to inform our present, Deleuze's cinematic ethics is unlike Levinas's. The encounter enabled by the time-image is not one which provides transcendence (due to its emphasis, instead, on connecting with this world), but it is one which is compatible with a Dusselian ethics (which also eschews transcendence in the encounter for a historicised understanding of the occluded other of colonial modernity). The time-image, after all, occasions the re-alignment of the temporally divided I (the I forever splitting into a virtual past and actual present which emerges when we hesitate) with an awareness of the world history of inequality upon which colonial modernity rests.

Thus a reconstructed Deleuze – as noted, after Al-Saji and in line with Dussel – reveals that the time-image, rather than offering an opening onto infinity (after Levinas), or a chance to reaffirm faith in *this* world per se (after a strict reading of Deleuze), instead asks us to hesitate in relation to the manner in which our past has been oriented by colonial modernity. It encourages us to consider whether we should reorient the informing pathway through the world's memories which shapes our present-day actions and interactions, to question whether we should affirm, or in fact critically reconsider, our faith in our relationship not with *this world*, but with *this world's history*. The reason why the time-image is crucial to realising the existence of transnational histories on film, then, is not because it indicates a shift in thinking about, or the experiencing of, time after World War Two. Rather, it is because it keeps open the possibility of encountering the multiple coeval histories of world memory. This renders my use of hesitation to describe cinematic ethics rather unique amongst related ideas.

For example, the hesitant ethics of a world of cinemas is distinct from the temporal hesitation in our being in time described by Boris Groys (2009). Groys discusses hesitation in terms of indecision and postponement in a present divorced from its history, due to a disbelief in the supposed progressive linearity of modernity (the argument regarding so-called postmodernity) – as Groys states, after Deleuze's *Difference and Repetition* (1968), the creation of 'a non-historical excess of time through art' (Groys 2009). Rather, what I argue for here is a hesitation which (whilst understood in terms of temporality after a reconstructed view on Deleuze's *Cinema* books) concerns the understanding of a position with regard to world history. A hesitation born not of the supposed end of history (as noted in Chapter 1, Dussel critiques the postmodernity discourse for its Eurocentric focus on a linearly progressing modernity that supposedly enters a 'post' phase (1995, 75)), but of the realisation of the present moment's relationship with a much longer, global, colonial modernity.[7]

This particular Deleuzian/Dusselian assemblage also provides a different perspective to, for example, Kristin Lené Hole's analysis of the films of Claire Denis (after Levinas and Nancy) as illustrating an 'ethics of interruption' (2016, 11–17). Interruption, like hesitation, also enables a physical 'unlearning' of 'expectations' and 'received knowledge about the world' (3). Yet, rather than the Nancian sense that interruption interrupts the totalising narrative of myth to prevent 'meaning from being fixed' (Hole 2016, 12), instead, I argue that temporal hesitation enables a reconnection with world history as world memory, encouraging us to reconsider ingrained habits which would typically have us deny the coevalness of the time of the other.

This is also what distinguishes my conclusions from those of a Levinasian approach to cinematic ethics. For Sam B. Girgus, a film like Frank Capra's *Mr. Smith Goes to Washington* (1939) evidences Deleuzian time-images which illustrate how (due to Levinas's assimilation of a Bergsonian model of time with his ethics, with duration providing access to infinity): 'Time in the form of Levinasian diachronicity and transcendence persists as a crucial part of the film's significance in conjunction with the predominance of montage and the movement-image' (2010, 57). But, after Dussel and Al-Saji, it is not infinity which is found in the experiencing of duration, but the world history in which the relationship to the other is defined via a racialising of the past. In the moment of hesitation, to return to Dussel's notion of synchronicity, the encounter with the other enables a realignment of the past in the crystal of time – a crystal history taking place in a very real historical moment but able to deracialise time. Indeed, whilst neither Levinas nor Dussel maps entirely onto the Bergsonian/Deleuzian model of time with *absolute* cohesion, Levinas's past 'immemorial', which is in actual fact the 'history of humanity, in the past of others, who "regard me"' (1947, 112), is too anthropocentric to enable a full exploration of the encounters with alterity (including with other species, and the very history of the Earth or the universe) available in the world memory archived by a world of cinemas. This last point brings us, then, to taxonomy.

The time-image and history IV: Taxonomies

The preceding critique of Deleuze indicates, finally, that the manner of choosing the films analysed from the myriad examples available across a world of cinemas greatly influences the conclusions drawn. The final step in reconstructing Deleuze for the exploration of transnational histories, then, is a reconsideration of the process of taxonomising. For instance, when discussing the potential of hesitancy for cinematic ethics, it would seem self-evident that the films explored may well encourage hesitation precisely by being 'slow' – as per Manohla Dargis and A. O. Scott's 'defence' of slow cinema for the chance it gives for contemplation (2011), apparently denied by 'faster' commercial cinema, and the emerging discussion of 'slow cinema' in general (Shaviro 2010; Jaffe 2014; de Luca and Barradas Jorge 2016; Kendall 2016). As Asbjørn Grønstad notes, duration in cinema offers 'a condition of possibility for intrinsically ethical acts, such as recognition, reflection, imagination and empathy' (2016a, 274). Indeed, some of the films explored in the pages which follow might be considered works of slow cinema. Yet here is where more nuance is needed. To term the diversity of films which follows 'slow' would artificially homogenise a range of films which include fiction and documentaries (not forgetting that in some countries where a film industry has historically been absent, documentaries can be considered the national cinema, and hence the mainstream in that location), and – whilst there are art films (e.g. *Loong Boonmee raleuk chat/Uncle Boonee Who Can Recall His Past Lives* (Thailand/UK/France/Germany/Spain/Netherlands, 2010)) – there are also more traditional popular genre movies (e.g. the thriller *Carancho/Vulture* (Argentina/Chile/France/South Korea, 2010)), not to mention (as is more the norm nowadays, making the prolonging of art/popular distinctions rather obsolete) several films which are not so easy to categorise (e.g. *Como Era Gostoso o Meu Francês/How Tasty Was My Little Frenchman* (Brazil, 1971), *Chinjeolhan geumjassi/Lady Vengeance* (South Korea, 2005), and *También la lluvia/Even the Rain* (Spain/Mexico/France, 2010).

The diversity of films demonstrates something of the multiple ways in which the Global South (I reiterate, a geopolitical rather than a geographical category) tells the story of colonial modernity. Whilst it is no coincidence that the character types which often recur in festival films (as Thomas Elsaesser notes, 'ordinary folk, children, orphans, peasants, and suppressed women' (2005, 509)) are remarkably close to Dussel's excluded of colonial modernity, to focus too much on the global art film alone would be to obscure the much larger picture which this book attempts to bring into focus. Instead, when viewed together these various films illustrate the transnational nature of the histories explored. Whilst what unites these films is their creation of time-images that encourage hesitation, they have myriad 'faster' and 'slower' manifestations. After all, even in Deleuze's own formulation of the crystal of time in *Cinema 2* there is discussion of such fast-paced comedies as Jean Renoir's *La règle du jeu/The Rules of the Game* (France, 1939) (which also appears in his discussion of the pre-war movement-image in France in *Cinema 1* (1983)) and Federico Fellini's *Amarcord* (Italy/France, 1973) (1985, 80–94).

What is more important than the notion of slowness, then, is how the time-image enables hesitation to work on memory and, thereby, to reconstruct history. Amongst the various emerging works on slow cinema, Rob Stone and Paul Cooke (focusing on slowness in the heritage film genre), engage specifically with Deleuze's crystal of time and its role in the construction of history. They argue that 'slowness in heritage cinema can make a crystal-image visible' (2016, 318), thereby foregrounding the process of historical re-alignment in which time-images are involved. Echoing Berresem's idea of a crystal history, Stone and Cooke discuss how a traumatic scene in *12 Years a Slave* (USA/UK, 2013) – in which the protagonist Solomon Northup (Chiwetel Ejiofor) is depicted hanging from a tree, his life likewise hanging by a thread – enable audiences to reterritorialise 'one's awareness and its remapping in relation to the immediate and wider context of a film's viewing', to collaborate in the 'complex, evolving meanings occurring between the virtual and the actual' (318). Through such moments of slowness, then, the past is addressed in relation to the present in a historiographical manner. This is a process in which, I would argue, the hesitation involved also enables the viewer to reorient their position in relation to the intertwined coeval histories which construct world memory.

In which case, how to sort the most relevant films for analysis from amidst the magnitude of a world of cinemas? If Deleuze's taxonomy proceeds from a Eurocentric view of world history, then what type of taxonomising can illuminate the engagement of a world of cinemas with transnational histories? Regardless of how suspect the very idea of taxonomising may seem (due to its colonial heritage, its place in the capitalist reorganisation of nature, etc.), it nevertheless plays a crucial role in how we understand such phenomena as time, history and ethics to be negotiated in cinema.[8] The answer to the above questions, in fact, is given in the notion of the encounter itself: a taxonomy of transnational histories emerges from a world of cinemas once we attend to how colonial modernity operates in a manner which can be explained using an idea that emerges with the encounter: the contract. As I will demonstrate in detail in Chapters 3–6, transnational histories on film, creating encounters with lost pasts, typically also evidence a focus on a related, if not defining, contract for that particular history.

Contract theory can be traced back to differing origins, including Ancient Greek thought and Medieval European Christianity (Lessnoff 1990, 1–26; Boucher and Kelly 1994, 1–34), through Enlightenment European scholars (Thomas Hobbes, John Locke, David Hume, Immanuel Kant and Jean-Jacques Rousseau), to thinkers like John Rawls in the late Twentieth Century.[9] This area of political philosophy does not discuss actual contracts, of course. Rather, it considers the idea of the contract as a way of conceptualising how governance is established in society – who consents to participate, and who is excluded 'contractually'. Even so, this is not so much metaphorical as it is a way of describing a system which – whilst it may not be formally ratified – nevertheless evidences its structuring logic, and its operation, ubiquitously (much as it is possible to critique the, as it were, invisible presence of patriarchy – not least through its very concrete effects on people's lives – without considering it a metaphor).

What unites contract theorists from the Enlightenment to the present is exploration of how a supposed state of nature transforms into a society of people abiding by agreed rules, seemingly without coercion by force (Boucher and Kelly 1994, 13) (see Chapter 5 in particular). Yet, from the 1980s onwards there have emerged critiques of the exclusive nature of the social contract (exclusions, including coercion by force, that are inherent to societal governance), most notably in perspectives offered by feminist, ecocritical, decolonial and political thought (Pateman 1988; Serres 1992; Mills 1997; Pateman and Mills 2007; Lazzarato 2011; 2013). Together these critiques provide the taxonomising emphasis of this book's exploration of transnational histories on film.

We can begin with the social contract. In *A Discourse on Inequality* (1755) Rousseau reveals that the social contract is a naturalised (as it were, invisible but widely upheld) idea of who precisely should constitute society. It functions as though a contract has been drawn up (and imposed upon what he considers humanity's natural freedom in the so-called state of nature), designed to keep the elite rich and the poor excluded from wealth. Then, recent critiques of the social contract illuminate the many varied exclusions enacted by it: against women (Carole Pateman), nature (Michel Serres), race (Charles W. Mills), and ultimately even individuals (Maurizio Lazzarato). Together, these critiques of how such tacit but everywhere naturalised contracts perpetuate inequality reveal broader transnational histories of exclusion (closely corresponding with the exclusions of colonial modernity) fostered by the emergence and dominance of the nation-state on the world stage with the rise of Europe. This is because, during the Seventeenth Century (with the Peace of Westphalia in 1648 especially):

> The state became the principal moral entity through which the interests of individuals are expressed in the international society of states. The primary obligation of the citizen *de facto* belongs to the state, and that of the state to its citizens, and only to humanity as a whole as a secondary consideration.
>
> *(Boucher and Kelly 1994, 14)*

The underside of colonial modernity is thus constituted of all those excluded due to the contracts it (as it were, invisibly) imposes upon others (those sexual, racial, and natural, in particular). Dussel's critique of colonial modernity indicates as much:

> What presuppose the liberation of diverse types of oppressed and/or excluded populations are the over-coming of *cynical management reason* (planetary administrative), of capitalism (as economic system), of liberalism (as political system), of Eurocentrism (as ideology), of machismo (in erotics), of the reign of the white race (in racism), of the destruction of nature (in ecology), and so on. It is in this sense that the ethics of liberation defines itself as trans-Modern (since the postmoderns are still Eurocentric). The end of the present stage of civilization shows itself some limits of the 'system of 500 years' – as Noam Chomsky calls it.
>
> *(2003a, 68)*[10]

The social contract, noted by Rousseau to deliberately exclude the poor, is a product of liberalism 'as political system', whilst the underpinning (more accurately, under*mining*) contracts which variously give the lie to the seemingly benevolent and protective veneer of the social contract are equally present in Dussel's description: contracts sexual ('machismo') as outlined by Carole Pateman in terms of its exclusion of women; racial ('the reign of the white race') as defined by Charles W. Mills with regard to the exclusion of people of skin colour deemed non-white; natural ('the destruction of nature') by Michel Serres concerning the exclusion of nature; individual (at the intersection of the economics of capital and the politics of liberalism), by Maurizio Lazzarato. Under neoliberalism, the dominant contract is that between individuals, as the nation–state withdraws its responsibility for the welfare of its population under the pressure of rootless capital.

It becomes clear in the process of analysing films across a world of cinemas that a focus on any one of these contracts ultimately leads to exploration of its intertwined existence with several of the others. This is due, precisely, to the exclusionary nature of the history of colonial modernity. The 'destruction of nature (in ecology)' is not a separate issue from 'capitalism (as economic system)' or 'liberalism (as political system)'. In fact, such contracts are by nature overlapping, as Pateman and Mills (2007) observe by bringing together the racial and sexual contracts for a multi-dimensional exploration of their interaction (3). For this reason, examining any one such 'way in' to how films enable us to encounter the other of colonial modernity is to bump up against more than one such contract: tracing any one transnational history confronts us with colonial modernity's deliberate disenfranchisement of so many, via these various contracts. Thus the idea of the contract as a means of understanding the structures which foster inequality, globally, provides a way of taxonomising which can reconcile the intertwining of the seemingly nonhuman nature of planetary history and the multitudinous transnational histories which emerge in colonial modernity (to return to Chakrabarty, as noted in the Introduction, the 'question of a human collectivity, an us, pointing to a figure of the universal that escapes our capacity to experience the world' (2009, 222)). The four chosen contracts explored in Chapters 3-6, then, ground the taxonomising which I undertake because together they illustrate a hesitant cinematic ethics, found in the transnational histories being constructed amidst a world of cinemas.[11]

The correspondence of transnational histories, and such tacit but informing contracts, throws into stark relief the naturalised, and often unacknowledged, structuring presence of a different contract which informs several existing works on ethics and politics in film-philosophy: the settler contract. The settler contract relates to the colonial appropriation of lands considered *terra nullius* (e.g. Australia and North America, amongst others) a term taken loosely to mean (depending on the context), nobody's, empty, virgin, uninhabited, uncultivated, or waste, land. This, even if it is already inhabited by somebody, just not in the way that European setters recognise.[12] The settler contract is perhaps the most literal actualisation of the ideal of the social contract, which considers society to have developed upon a previous state of nature (Pateman and Mills 2007, 36):

> The settler contract is a specific form of expropriation contract and refers to the dispossession of, and rule over, Native inhabitants by British settlers in the two New Worlds. [...] When colonists are planted in a terra nullius, an empty state of nature, the aim is not merely to dominate, govern, and use but to create a civil society. Therefore the settlers have to make an original – settler – contract. [...] The state of nature disappears as soon as the contract is concluded and is replaced by civil society.
>
> *(38–39)*

For this reason, Pateman argues after Hannah Arendt, there is an obsession in settler colonial cultures with the reiteration of rituals surrounding the foundation of the nation, and the acts of its founding fathers, so as to obscure the lack of legitimacy of this moment, historically (54–55). The invisible structuring presence of the settler contract creates an ignorance of the excluded other who loses their homeland in the one-sided establishing of the contract. The influence of this tradition is apparent in certain works of film-philosophy, a fact which provides impetus for the – different – taxonomising by contract undertaken herein. Two recent works can stand as representative examples of this tendency. In both, the absence of discussion of the original inhabitants of the *terra nullius* creates a defining (haunting, challenging) absence from a scholarly engagement focused entirely on and within the settler colonist culture.

Firstly, Sam B. Girgus' *Levinas and the Cinema of Redemption* (2010) includes analysis of John Ford's *The Searchers* (1956), a film oft-discussed for its exploration of the taboo of miscegenation underlying the triumphalism of the USA's founding rape–revenge narrative (Martin-Jones 2006, 121–124). Girgus's project is the identification of a Levinasian multinational cinema of redemption which 'enacts the struggle to achieve ethical transcendence by subordinating the self to the greater responsibility for the other' (4), and which operates through 'the ethical engagement with the other, rather than the triumph of the self' (7). Yet, curiously, he argues that the Levinasian encounter in *The Searchers* is that between the settler colonists and Ethan Edwards (John Wayne), the initially mysterious rider who approaches the homestead from the 'wilderness' in the film's opening (10–11). As has been extensively discussed of this scene, classical Hollywood westerns use formal properties like editing and cinematography to hold in opposition binaries like civilisation and wilderness. They thereby maintain a unity of ideological identity to the (supposedly) self-same settler colonist nation (Eleftheriotis 2001, 109–115). It is obviously the case, then, that the most challenging ethical encounter in this supposed *terra nullius* of the US Western frontier was that between settler colonists and the indigenous population they massacred. So it is surprising that the encounter which the film offers with the indigenous Americans, such as Chief Cicatriz (or 'Scar' as the settler colonists call him (Henry Brandon)), culminating in his death at the climax of the film, is not mentioned (or critiqued) by Girgus. Instead, Girgus makes the ethics of redemption an issue for the settler colonists. Girgus's analysis, although extremely sophisticated, and laudably aiming to recuperate the positive potential of Levinas in spite of his sexism (17–20), demonstrates how pervasive a blind spot exists – with regard to colonial modernity – in the philosophical discussion of ethics.

Secondly, Richard Rushton's *The Politics of Hollywood Cinema* (2013) discusses how Hollywood films explore politics. Yet the idea of 'politics' which structures the approach is only that of how democracy functions in the West and cinema's role in exploring this (2013, 2). The several centuries of exclusion from political representation of so many people under colonial modernity (including under democracy, until suffrage was won through hard and bloody struggle, and still not everywhere) is rarely if ever mentioned. Instead, there is a recurring Eurocentric celebration of the French and American revolutions, the latter of which famously declared all men (but not women) equal at a time of enslavement and racially motivated genocidal wars which rendered millions captive or dead.[13] Seeking to celebrate the birth of the 'subject as citizen' (Rushton 2013, 176) then breaking their bonds of servitude to monarchy, Rushton retains the silence of the global *terra nullius* across which Europeans supposedly benevolently spread democracy. This approach directly influences the results of the film analysis, in which the denial of inequality which is a feature of the history of colonial modernity is not recognised, due to the limiting nature of the chosen taxonomical focus.

Rushton's analysis of *Mr. Smith Goes to Washington* (1939), for instance, considers Jefferson Smith's (James Stewart) opposition to the proposed building of a dam – with a filibuster including a reading of the Declaration of Independence and the United States Constitution – because it will flood land on which he wishes to situate a National Boy's Camp, noting that: 'democracy is precisely about never taking things for granted and never accepting "how things are", that the basic virtue of democracy is its instability and uncontrollability, that "how things are" is never fixed but always open to change and transformation' (151). As might be expected of a 1930s Hollywood movie, the film displays a studied ignorance of the history of the land and the eradication of its former inhabitants (referenced only through clichéd 'Red Indian' music used to poke fun at Smith for the parochial ridiculousness of his bushcraft skills), whilst the racial contract is evident in the African-American actors relegated to the roles of station porters and waiters. By focusing only on the settler colonist's perspective on how democracy should function, Rushton neglects to consider the historical underpinning of the politics, celebrated in the diegesis, of the inequality-fostering settler contract. As a result, Rushton's exploration of the kinds of political thinking which Hollywood films may express or inspire ignores how such films deny agency to indigenous peoples (in a similar manner to Girgus's analysis) and thus obscures the reality that for many centuries after 1492 white settlers in the Americas were in the minority compared to indigenous Americans and African slaves (Mann 2011, 424). Aside from the exclusionary politics of the film, any number of politically oriented cinemas worldwide – whether genre or art films – could have acted as comparative examples to Rushton's focus, providing a more nuanced case for understanding classical Hollywood's position (with respect to inspiring political thinking), globally (see Holtmeier 2016; 2017). Instead, tacitly expressing the prominence of the view of history established by the settler colonist contract, Rushton seeks to pursue a positive view of democracy in films which operate on a historically unequal playing field.[14]

Film-philosophy is far from alone in this. For example, a similar historical blinkeredness enables Steven Pinker to cheerlead for modernity, without recognising its cost to those in the underside of (colonial) modernity.[15] In a similar vein, the works of Girgus and Rushton together demonstrate a tendency within film-philosophy to problematically universalise topics such as ethics and politics through the choice of films used to explore them. The field, then, requires a decolonisation of a mindset that remains beholden to Eurocentrism as 'superideology' (Dussel 1998b, 34; 2003a, 63). It is the settler colonial heritage, historically, which has led to the neocolonial global wealth divisions of neoliberalism, which echoes so closely that of the enslavement and exploitation upon which colonial modernity is established (Klein 2017, 184). The settler colonist contract, after all, provides the ultimate in doublethink. Although the evidence is clear before the settler colonist's eyes that there is another history enmeshed in the land, they are able to simply pretend it does not exist, state the validity of their own as providing sole claim on this otherwise history-less territory, and make it theirs.

To explore new pathways away from the settler contract, in this book four very different contracts are chosen to structure the taxonomy of transnational histories analysed. They are, in decreasing longevity towards the present, from Chapters 3–6: humanity's exploitation of the Earth (the natural contract); the North Atlantic trade circuit (racial contract); the Cold War (social contract); and neoliberal globalisation (individual contracts).

This approach to taxonomising transnational histories, via contracts, reveals how a world of cinemas is developing a hesitant cinematic ethics for the Anthropocene through its engagement with the lost pasts of those excluded from colonial modernity. The contracts, after all, are clearest in the encounters they indicate: planetary encounters (with locations – and the species which inhabit them – that are repositories of the Earth's or Universe's memories), colonial encounters (Europeans face to face with indigenous Americans and the history of their attempted eradication), political encounters (rediscovering forcibly disappeared pasts in which other possible political futures were still possible), physical encounters (with human bodies as physical stores of the past in a seemingly disconnected, but actually historically informed, present). Together, the films exploring these contracts expose us to the awareness of pasts lost to colonial modernity: of exterminated species, the history of slavery and genocides enacted against indigenous peoples, the disappeared of Cold War dictatorships, and those marginalised under neoliberalism to the point where their bodies have become reduced to the status of meat. These transnational groupings of film, by contract, provide a (partial, at least) picture of the world's memories, the recognition of which can potentially challenge viewers over their certainty with respect to the version of world history they inhabit.

Whilst staggering in terms of the depths of history they explore, these transnational histories are also closely related to how the last seventy years inform the present. This is the recent history of colonial modernity's development from empires (under imperialism) to what Hardt and Negri term 'Empire' (2000) (under globalisation). In this latest phase of colonial modernity's five-hundred-year global 'civilizing design' (Mignolo 2000, 279), we find the emergence of environmentalism since the 1960s and with particular emphasis since the 1990s (Chapter 3), of postcolonial histories from the 1960s to the 1980s revisited due to events like the 'Water War' in Cochabamba, Bolivia, in 1999–2000 (Chapter 4), the 'decomposing' (Kwon 2010) Cold War as it precariously persists today in some parts of the world (Chapter 5), and the legacy of the emergence of neoliberalism since the 1970s and 1980s in others (Chapter 6).

The emphases of the four chapters, in addition, together create a crystal of time through which to explore (crystal) history. Chapters 3 and 4 explore the past that is preserved, and are indicative of a world of cinemas' attempts to recuperate two of the key lost pasts of colonial modernity (as an archive of world memory involved in the preservation of the past which occurs in the splitting of time in the crystal). Chapters 5 and 6 for their part are concerned more with the subtle nuances of preserving the present that passes, in the moment of time's splitting. Hence, the four transnational histories together reflect how the emergence of colonial modernity as capitalist world ecology, and its latest phases (Cold War/neoliberalism), are equally involved in the eradication of other pasts: whether, on the one hand, that of the Earth which is denied a natural contract, or of the peoples denied coevalness by the racial contract (past that is/is not preserved – Chapters 3 and 4), or, on the other hand, the disappeared political opponents and economic victims of more recent decades who are denied the possibility of even an unequal social contract in favour of individual contracts (present that passes – Chapters 5 and 6). In all such cases, what we see is a world of cinemas attempting to archive within world memory the pasts eradicated by colonial modernity, as it understands this process in the present, looking backwards into history.

In this way, a world of cinemas illuminates what Michael Hardt and Antonio Negri consider a five-hundred-year-old process in which a global potential for revolution is repressed, yet its memory somehow never fully extinguished:

> The development of Renaissance thought coincided both with the European discovery of the Americas and with the beginnings of European dominance over the rest of the world. Europe had discovered its outside. [...] On the one hand, Renaissance humanism initiated a revolutionary notion of human equality, of singularity and community, cooperation and

multitude. [...] On the other [...] the same counter revolutionary power that sought to control the constituent and subversive forces within Europe also began to realise the possibility and necessity of subordinating other populations to European domination. Eurocentrism was born as a reaction to the potentiality of a newfound human equality; it was the counterrevolution on a global scale. [...] European modernity is from its beginnings a war on two fronts. European mastery is always in crisis – and this is the very same crisis that defines European modernity.

(2000, 76–77)

Hence, in Chapters 5 and 6, the often murderous global eradication of the left as a political force during the Cold War, which results in the writing of this absent past on the exhausted bodies in the neoliberal present, crystalizes, in Chapters 3 and 4, with the genocide, slavery and exploitation of nature which enabled the colonising of the Americas. Across the four chapters together, then, the world history of colonial modernity emerges as a crystalline history.

What we find by thus distant viewing a world of cinemas is not only how different cinemas explore shared issues that cross borders (e.g. environmental change), but also similar reactions to shared histories, or rather, to histories which cross borders (transnational histories from within world history). This is the case whether the 'local' situations involved are even aware that there are other locations where similar things are occurring, or not. The four examples of transnational history thus provide a planetary perspective on the several centuries of world history of colonial modernity, a critique capable of informing a cinematic ethics for the Anthropocene.

Notes

1 This 'reconstruction' of Deleuze in film-philosophy is also apparent more broadly with respect to his philosophy. Deleuze and Félix Guattari are known for an infamous declaration with respect to the inability of cultures beyond the West to produce what they define as philosophy (1991, 93). Unsurprisingly, perhaps, Gayatri Chakravorty Spivak's 'Can the Subaltern Speak?' (1988) famously critiques Deleuze and Deleuze and Guattari. However, in the 2010s several scholars have indicated how successful Deleuze (and Deleuze and Guattari) were in creating intellectual lines of flight 'away' from the Western philosophical tradition precisely because of their engagement with non-Western thought. This includes the ideas and beliefs of indigenous peoples of the Americas and Africa, Ancient Chinese thought, and in general what might be considered the 'outside' of the Eurocentric canon (Deleuze and Guattari, after all, situate their own thinking amongst the canon's most 'marginal' thinkers) (Viveiros de Castro 2010, 219; Robinson and Tormey 2010, 32–35).

2 Greater depth can be found in various existing works, such as: Rodowick 1997; Bogue 2003; Sutton and Martin-Jones 2008; Colman 2011; Deamer 2016; or the myriad works catalogued at deleuzecinema.com.

3 In *Deleuze, Cinema and National Identity* (2006), I mapped this struggle onto cinematic narratives which employ time-images to de- and reterritorialise narratives of national identity (see above regarding the relationship between the reterritorialising line and the deterritorialising labyrinth). Historical time is that of Chronos, and is actualised

in the movement-image, whilst the time of the event is Aion, glimpsed in the time-image (Patton 2009, 37; Deamer 2009, 170).

4 I reach the opposite view to Chaudhuri, considering how a world of cinemas' encounters with 'other' or 'lost' pasts impact upon the viewer. Whilst we both agree that these are not prosthetic memories, as Landsberg argues, where Chaudhuri sees encounters with onscreen pasts as evoking similarities, or at least resonances with the pasts the viewers know, I see them as indicating a need to consider the difference of other pasts, to meditate upon the coevalness which they have otherwise been denied. For instance, for Chaudhuri, many films about disappearances under Cold War military regimes 'impress upon us multiresonant images that can summon memories of similar patterns of disappearance across national borders, or trouble memories of complicit societies' (2014, 91). The act of triggering or disturbing a viewer's recollection of the past, then, relies upon some degree of similarity with another past which is evoked (113). For my part, I consider such films to evoke difference rather than similarity, encounters with the lost pasts of those excluded by colonial modernity indicating the relative centrality of established memory within a much broader understanding of world history.

5 To date in Film Studies, Al-Saji's work has been used by Kathleen Scott to consider how the affective nature of certain types of extreme cinemas ('cinemas of exposure' which purposefully confront us with images of women suffering) has a critical-ethical function, due to its 'potential to alter modes of spectatorial perception by revealing gendered blind spots and bio-political prejudices structuring and limiting vision' (2014, 33). Here, however, I shift focus from the phenomenological dimension of Al-Saji's work to its engagement with Bergson and memory, which provides the necessary link to the Deleuzian model of time.

6 The hesitation described here is distinct from that which Tzvetan Todorov considers emblematic, generically, of the fantastic. For Todorov, the fantastic requires the reader to hesitate over what they understand to be the real and imaginary (1970, 31–33), before this dilemma is resolved, one way or the other, by the text (157). The time-image, as Deleuze argues, retains the confusion between the two 'not because they are confused, but because we do not have to know and there is no longer even a place from which to ask. It is as if the real and the imaginary were running after each other, as if each was being reflected in the other, around a point of indiscernibility' (1985, 7).

7 This is also what distinguishes the hesitation I outline from that discussed by László Strausz with respect to national history in Romanian cinema (a book published when this manuscript was practically complete). For Strausz, hesitation is encouraged in the viewer as an interpretative strategy, before images foregrounding the complexity of history. For example, with respect to the rapidly repeated rewriting of history during the Cold War, under Nicolae Ceauşescu (doublethink, effectively), hesitation emerges in film as 'a reaction to the official production of culture and history' (2017, 2–3). Hesitation foregrounds the complexity of history, then, in contrast to proposed uniform certainties with respect to the past (11). Whilst the role of cinema to counter doublethink is a shared aspect of our respective analyses, this work seeks to understand how transnational histories are evoked on screen in ways which reorient viewers towards their own position in relation to world history. Not the rendering visible of the complexities of national history in the making, then, but of the (disappeared, forgotten, erased) virtual labyrinth of other times which belie the official Eurocentric story of world history.

8 Floyd Merrell goes so far as to question whether thought is even possible without taxonomising, the process providing the framework and parameters for investigation of a defined field (quoted in Deamer 2014, 273–274).

9 Amongst these various thinkers there are different approaches, whether the focus is on a contract between ruler and people or one which unites the people (Lessnoff 1990, 5–15) (Rousseau provides a key example of the latter approach), or whether the

contract is understood to be moral, civil, or constitutional (Boucher and Kelly 1994, 1–34), amongst other differences.

10 The reference to 'erotics' in Dussel's work refers to his discussion of how face to face encounters come to be gendered, and the relationship of this practice to coloniality (specifically in the perpetuation of the man as subject and the woman as object under patriarchy) (1974, 55–59).

11 I do not focus on the sexual contract in a standalone chapter in part because of this intertwining, but also because of the wealth of material which already exists engaging with a world of women's cinema (initially using Deleuze), which illustrates its engagement with the transnational history of women's lives under patriarchy (Butler 2002; White 2015). Recent work in this area has already considered the 'interruptive' nature of a feminist cinematic ethics of encounter, via Levinas and Nancy (Hole 2016, 12). Instead, this existing body of work on women's cinema as world cinema, and its ethics, provides inspiration for the work undertaken here on the much less discussed contracts in Film Studies: social, natural, racial, individual.

12 Patemen differentiates the settler contract, historically, from the assumed right of conquest (the Spanish conquistadores) and right of husbandry (the seizure of indigenous lands across various continents by the Dutch and British empires).

13 Rushton enthusiastically contextualises Kant's writings in relation to the emergence of democracy (2013, 176), failing to recognise the contradictory coincidence of the French Revolution and the Declaration of the Rights of Man and the Citizen in 1789 with the application of the racist *Code Noir* as governing law in the French colonies (Dussel 2013, 8), nor the link between democracy and the colonial development of the nation-state in the USA (Quijano 2000, 560–561), the struggles for liberty of 'maroon' communities (often constituted of indigenous peoples and escaped African slaves) in the Americas, long before white settler colonists conceived of the Declaration of Independence (Mann 2011, 466), or the racism inherent to Kant's works in the context of the brutal colonial projects then ongoing worldwide (Park 2013).

14 More curiously, for Rushton, whilst it is all right for settler colonists to stand up for their equal rights (as per Mr Smith in the movie), pointing out that such films are themselves denying the voices of others in a way which reinforces an imperialistic worldview is frowned upon. This is due to Rushton's questionable view that discovering inequality only ever exacerbates inequality (196–197). Rushton thus seeks what Dussel terms a '*univocal universality*', in place of the reality of the 'pluriverse' (Dussel 2013, 18). The pluralistic model of world cinemas now in play in the field (after Lúcia Nagib and others; see Chapter 1) renders Rushton's anxiety over the other ways in which cinema can function politically – as though the politics of a world of cinemas can only be seen in relation to a Hollywood bogeyman – rather nostalgic for the time when this was the case in scholarship (the high point of the third cinema debate, several decades past, for example).

15 Steven Pinker argues that the global rate of (human-on-human) violence is declining as a feature of the historical progression of humanity, basing his argument in large part on statistical evidence, for example those measuring homicides and wars. Pinker's argument, however, is framed in terms of its benefit for our capacity to make sense of modernity (2012, xix) and champions Enlightenment humanism and the role of the state in controlling violence (after contract theorist Thomas Hobbes), with no regard for their connection to coloniality (155–227). Pinker simply believes modernity to transcend the previous (more violent) state of nature which humanity left by forming societies (xxii–xxiii). Pinker's position, then, is blinkered by his equation of modernity with the Enlightenment, and the advancement of the West, without realising the deeper connection with 1492 and the world system (see Chapter 1). Aside from the rather obvious denial of coevalness in Pinker's too-literal portrayal of the pre-modern state of nature as anarchical, three points of critique indicate the flaws in his reasoning. Firstly, Pinker is unable to realise the founding violence of colonial modernity, the genocide of the indigenous and the enslavement of Africans

in propelling the growth of Europe within the world system, as being integral to the history of violence he surveys. That modernity relies upon the violence of global structural inequality passes Pinker by, his bias being most apparent in such conclusions as this: 'A world in which war continues in some of the poorer countries is still better than a world in which it takes place in both the rich *and* the poor countries, especially considering the incalculably greater damage that rich, powerful countries can wreak' (2011, 304). The people living in the 'poor' countries, of course, may well disagree, especially those during the Cold War in which the purposeful containment, if not active pursuit, of violence was perpetuated by the 'rich' countries draining resources back to the Global North. Secondly, then, and related to this, Pinker fails to realise the violence of the border, whether between nations or the Global North and South, nowadays maintaining a wealth division akin to global apartheid, as critiqued by, amongst others, Étienne Balibar (2003, 7). In this second respect, a thinker like Slavoj Žižek (2008) provides a more nuanced appreciation of the ubiquity of violence in the perpetuation of the capitalist world system, as was borne out by events like the police violence against civilians during the illegal referendum in Catalonia (evocative of the functioning of an Agambenian state of exception (see Chapter 6)) in 2017. Thirdly, the clearest flaw in Pinker's thinking is that the evidence of 'a species retreat in violence' (2011, xxii) which he foregrounds in terms of declining rates of human-on-human violence, pales in comparison to the Sixth Mass Species Extinction event in which we are living – the culmination, and continuation, of centuries of violence by humanity against other species. The whole point of the focus on ecology within the posthuman turn is thus ignored by Pinker. The culmination of considering these three major flaws in Pinker's thinking is the reminder that violence is inherent to the exclusionary nature of colonial modernity: as Hardt and Negri summarise, it is 'the counter-revolution on a global scale' (2000, 77) (see the Introduction, and further, below).

PART II

Encounters with the past that is/is not preserved

3

4.54 (TO 13.7) BILLION YEARS

Planetary history, the natural contract, encountering earthly pasts

This is the first of four chapters of film analysis which constitute the remainder of the book. It proceeds by: outlining the type of time-image evident in the films analysed (the chosen two being key examples from a broader trend); considering the type of transnational history which they together illuminate if read distantly; and drawing out the type of contract that is evident in the encounter with the past on offer. Then, the films in question are analysed to illustrate the argument textually. This same structure remains across Chapters 3–6.

In this instance, the two films indicative of a broader transnational trend are *Loong Boonmee raleuk chat/Uncle Boonmee Who Can Recall His Past Lives* (Thailand/ UK/France/Germany/Spain/Netherlands, 2010) and *Nostalgia de la luz/Nostalgia for the Light* (Chile/Spain/France/Germany/USA, 2010). Both films are marked by the time-image which Deleuze describes as the any-space-whatever. They indicate the qualities and powers of expression of the landscape as though it were communicating on behalf of the Earth – enunciating the memory of the Universe, stored by the Earth – rather like a human face might when speaking of its recollections. These temporal landscapes provide entrances into the Earth's 4.54-billion-year (*Uncle Boonmee*) and Universe's 13.7-billion-year (*Nostalgia for the Light*) histories. In doing so they address how this nonhuman history is intertwined with that of human history. These any-space-whatevers illuminate planetary history, then, but emphasise in so doing the intertwined human/non-human nature of this past in the Anthropocene. Thus this transnational history emerges from humans or former humans who are depicted as integral to their environment. Situated within the landscape, they temporarily become the mouthpiece for the Earth (or Universe) as gigantic archive of matter in which is stored away nature's memories. The films thus provide the viewer with encounters with the intertwined past of the Earth (in the Universe) and humanity, otherwise obscured by colonial modernity's exploitation of nature. They offer a chance to consider the need for (after Michel Serres) a natural contract.

In *Uncle Boonmee*, which I interpret as an ecocritical story, it is through darkness that we are invited to understand this archival property of the Earth and the intertwining nonhuman and human memories it stores away. In *Nostalgia for the Light*, conversely, it is through light. In both, any-space-whatevers construct '*faceified*' (*visagéifiée*) (Deleuze 1983, 90) landscapes – dark and light respectively – which provide ecological encounters with the intertwined nature of human and nonhuman history. In these films, then, the memory of the Earth greets us from the landscape. We do not learn about the Earth's or the Universe's history per se (see the Introduction), but rather, we encounter the awareness that colonial modernity denies coevalness to all nonhuman pasts, creating a one-sided history of the Anthropocene. This is a hesitation-inducing revelation with regard to what we may otherwise think we know of our own place in world history.

Time-images: Planetary pasts

There is a global trend for films which explore the intertwined human and nonhuman pasts of planetary history via affective landscapes. This includes the Norwegian monster movie *Trolljegeren/Troll Hunter* (Norway, 2010), the Australian thriller *The Hunter* (Australia, 2011), the independent US film *Beasts of the Southern Wild* (USA, 2012), the Chilean postcolonial shamanistic slasher movie *Gritos del Bosque/Whispers of the Forest* (USA/Chile, 2014), amongst others (Martin-Jones 2016). In each case, landscapes address the viewer, often via the temporary mouthpiece of an endangered or extinct species, a shaman, mythological creature, spirit, ghost, or other being – whether human, part human, nonhuman, or former humans. Such landscapes function as, following Deleuze's taxonomy, any-space-whatevers, affective spaces which provide entrances to time. The characteristic time-image, then, is the affection-image as any-space-whatever.

Affection-images function slightly differently in movement- and time-images. As noted in Chapter 1, in *Cinema 1* (1983), Deleuze outlines the sensory-motor logic of the movement-image, charting the progression from perception-image (what is perceived), to affection-image (how what is perceived produces affects) and action-image (the consequences of these affects). Affection-images express powers or qualities. They express feelings in their as-yet non-actualised form, prior to the moment when 'power becomes action or passion, affect becomes sensation, sentiment, emotion or even impulse. [...] These are qualities or powers considered for themselves, without reference to anything else, independently of any question of their actualization' (1983, 100). The affection-image is thus an image which illustrates possibility, the potential of the virtual (whether of the unthought, the unfelt, the untimely), 'potentiality considered for itself as expressed' (101). Affection-images inhabit the pause between perception and action within which hesitation can occur.

The affection-image, epitomised by the close-up of the face (see Chapter 4), also includes images which are *faceified*. *Faceification* occurs when objects or places take on the quality (a reflective surface with the ability to marshal several features to express a single affect) or power (the micro-movements of different features that shift expression from one quality to another) of the face. A *faceified* image, including any-space-whatevers, can be defined as such when 'it looks at us [...] even if it does not resemble a face' (Deleuze 1983, 90). A landscape, then, can be *faceified*.

In the movement-image, the any-space-whatever grants limited access to the virtual realm of duration which subsists with the actual world we perceive (after Henri Bergson, see Chapter 2). The close-up of the face, for example, may reveal a subjective flashback, or 'recollection-image'. However, this conventional device is clearly signalled, and does not break the movement-image's linear sensory-motor continuum. Instead, it only looks to posit a causal explanation for the present from the past by actualising a linear pathway through time, one that clearly connects past (cause) to present (effect) (1985, 46). It is when affection-images become abstracted or deconnected from spatial-temporal coordinates – as they do in the time-image – that they become entities in their own right (Deleuze 1983, 98). It is now that spaces can become any-space-whatever, with the (virtual) potential for conjunction with any other space (Deleuze 1983, 106).

When Deleuze discusses his categories of time-images, the any-space-whatever re-emerges as an idea identifying emptied spaces, no longer connecting up what came before and after (as per a sensory-motor logic or a linear sense of temporality as in the movement-image), but as 'an amorphous set which has eliminated that which happened and acted in it. It is an extinction or a disappearing. [...] It no longer has co-ordinates, it is a pure potential, it shows only pure Powers and Qualities, independently of the states of things of milieu which actualise them (have actualised them or will actualise them, or neither the one nor the other – it hardly matters)' (Deleuze 1983, 123). In the time-image, the 'virtual conjunction' between any-space-whatevers enables the viewer to 'enter a "system of emotions" which is much more subtle and differentiated, less easy to identify, capable of inducing non-human affects' (113).

Prior to the *Cinema* books, Deleuze and Guattari discuss 'faciality', in a manner which helps unlock Deleuze's discussion of *faceified* landscapes in film. They argue that the face in human beings is the 'inhuman', and as such human beings must look to 'escape the face, to dismantle the face and facializations, to become imperceptible [...] by quite spiritual and special becoming-animals, by strange becomings that [...] make *faciality traits* themselves finally elude the organization of the face' (1980, 171). Deleuze and Guattari argue for such a decomposition of the face, due to its association with the iconic figure of Christ in the development of the category of 'the White Man' (182), a representative of what we might consider (bearing in mind the influence of Christianity on colonial modernity) the coloniality of power[1] (see further in the Conclusion).

The *faceified* any-space-whatever of the time-image, then, would imply that the viewer is encountering an other in this affection-image (consistent with the idea of the face, in close-up, as paradigmatic of the affection-image), or rather, they are engaging in a mutually imbricating deterritorialisation/reterritorialisation with the image (1980, 174). Indeed, existing critiques indicate how, via any-space-whatevers, time-image films offer an encounter with a becoming-animal, or becoming-imperceptible, a chance to deterritorialise away from the face (e.g. Jeong 2013, 144–183; see further below). Yet, what we find in the two films analysed is not quite this. The material conditions explored in these landscapes, especially the intertwined human and nonhuman histories which are archived in them, render such an idea of becoming-imperceptible more akin to a forcibly violent disappearance. After all, in both films the recent histories of place include those of the Cold War, whose disappeared victims haunt the landscapes we encounter. This virtual presence is, by turns, equated with the extinction of various species (including, ultimately, humanity) attendant on the Anthropocene since 1492.

Instead, then, a temporary (anthropomorphising) reterritorialisation of the landscape into a face is undertaken by the films, to stave off any sense that becoming-imperceptible may mean an eradication of endangered histories (this is the opposite of the merging with otherness of Deleuze/Deleuze and Guattari's position). What is identified in these time-images, rather, is another form of *faceified* landscape altogether. It cannot be adequately explained by a Levinasian approach (it is not a face opening onto infinity), nor a Deleuzian/Guattarian one (it is not a face on a line of flight towards a becoming-imperceptible), but it can by a Dusselian one (it is the face of the Earth, retelling the memories of those excluded by colonial modernity during its many phases – as is emphasised by the equation of Cold War political disappearances with species extinctions due to the Anthropocene).

I thus consider the films in question – as I have argued elsewhere of other contemporary time-image films (Martin-Jones 2006; 2011) – to capture the moment in which the virtual is becoming-actual. I analyse how their *faceified* landscapes briefly reterritorialize into a humanoid face, to provide a mouthpiece through which the Earth can speak of the need for a natural contract which can regulate (the historical condition of) human/nonhuman interaction in the Anthropocene. In contrast to Deleuze and Deleuze and Guattari's desire to avoid anthropocentrism, I will draw on Steven Shaviro's work to argue that these films deliberately anthropomorphise nature to this effect.

With this anthropomorphising in mind, what the viewer encounters in a *faceified* any-space-whatever landscape is an expression of the pure powers and qualities of world memory. These any-space-whatevers are shown to populate the surface of the planet, and through them we can encounter the archived memories of the history of the planet. The reterritorialised faces, then, are nonhuman centres of indetermination (as a Bergsonian/Deleuzian understanding of time suggests humans are, cutting out their experience of the world as images, making linear sense of the passing of time through perception, affection, and action-images), but adrift in the virtual whole of time which forever threatens to disrupt this actualised progression via the opening offered by the affection-image. The Earth, then, becomes the contingent centre of nonhuman indetermination which, momentarily, has the potential to speak to us: it temporarily becomes-actual to give voice to the 4.54-billion-year planetary history of the Earth (and indeed, its place within the 13.7-billion-year-old Universe (Marshak 2015, 12–35)), in relation to the human/nonhuman intertwining of history in the Anthropocene.[2]

Transnational history: Planetary – intertwined human/nonhuman

The Anthropocene debate offers various possible ways of identifying the origin of this epoch in geological records (see Chapter 1). It is concerned, then, with how the Earth, as material archive, provides evidence of the planet's nonhuman/human past. This is perhaps unsurprising. Jussi Parikka, drawing on John Durham Peters' work, notes how in the Nineteenth Century scientific advances in astronomy, geology and evolutionary theory led to the Earth being considered 'a sort of a recording device', in which the planet's history within the Universe was stored (2014, 2). As Durham Peters has it, in terms which evoke Deleuze's description of the any-space-whatever as 'an extinction' or 'disappearing' devoid of the co-ordinates of linear history: 'For Darwin and Lyell, the Earth is a recording medium – a profoundly fallible one. At best it inscribes ruins, enigmas, and hieroglyphics; at worst, blank sketches of oblivion' (2003, 402). Such a view can inform analysis of filmic depictions of the Earth as storage device, in their engagement with the planet's (by definition) transnational history.

This engagement takes place, in the films analysed, via the landscape. As noted in the Introduction, my approach to a world of cinemas shares much common ground with that of Lúcia Nagib. However, there are also differences, and they illuminate how I uncover this particular transnational (planetary) history on film via any-space-whatever landscapes. Nagib draws on Alain Badiou to provide a unique take on ethical filmmaking, studying 'filmmakers who use the film medium [...] to produce as well as reproduce reality' (2011, 8). Following Badiou's inclination towards fidelity or faithfulness to the event, Nagib seeks to explain how certain films are able, due to the filmmakers remaining faithful to 'the truth of the profilmic event' (12), to, literally, make 'history' in the production of an 'ethical reality' (15). Discussing what she calls the 'end of the other' in cinema (19–73), Nagib identifies certain shared characteristics in films from different contexts, in particular exploring how casts and crews 'drive to merge with the phenomenological real' (10). Here, Nagib argues that lengthy scenes of running – in *Les quatre cents coups/The 400 Blows* (France, 1959), *Deus e o Diabo na Terra do Sol/God and the Devil in the Land of the Sun* (Brazil, 1964), *Yaaba* (Burkina Faso/Switzerland/France, 1989), and *Atanarjuat: The Fast Runner* (Canada, 2001) – are 'related to recognizing, experiencing, demarcating and taking possession of a territory, and, in so doing, defining a people and its culture' (19). A commitment to realism when filming the physically demanding event places 'a people and its culture' at the centre of the film and its story and thus refuses the position of 'otherness' for cultures often marginalised cinematically. For Nagib, what is at stake in the foregrounding of the 'actor's bodily existence as it slowly migrates from fact to fiction' (29) is the placing of bodies at the centre of the event being filmed. This is important in films from postcolonial or neocolonial contexts, where the refusal by filmmakers to see the self as an exotic object is a politically charged geopolitical issue (32). There is a strong sense in Nagib's argument, then, of a (re)connection of people with their histories, which have been recorded in the landscape.

Yet, if we shift the focus from the running figure in the landscape to the very landscape against which their journey is figured, then suddenly things seem different. The way in which these landscapes function as repositories of human memories becomes the subject of an ethical encounter, this time one on the part of the viewer. As a result, a different grouping of films also suggests itself from amidst a world of cinemas. We might consider *Huang tu di/Yellow Earth* (China, 1985), *Yeelen/Brightness* (Mali/Burkina Faso/France/West Germany/ Japan, 1987), *Seopyeonje/Sopyonje* (South Korea, 1993), *Ten Canoes* (Australia, 2006), *Seachd: The Innaccessible Pinnacle* (UK, 2007), *La teta asustada/The Milk of Sorrow* (Spain/Peru, 2009), amongst others. In this grouping, the running figure is not always present, but we always find the landscape alive with the memories that it stores. For example, in *Yellow Earth*, a Chinese soldier is sent to a remote rural area in Shaanxi province, to collect folk songs, for repackaging as communist rallying anthems. As he surveys the landscape he hears singing, but there is no discernible human source for the sound. It is, literally, as though the landscape were singing.

Again, the opening of *Ten Canoes* depicts the Australian outback from an aerial perspective whilst the voiceover explains that: 'I am going to tell you a story. It's not your story, it's my story' Thus, before the story descends to the level of humans walking the land, the opening suggests that the tale is told by the very landscape itself. The opening of this film, especially, is less about what happened when (at least in any linear sense of history), than what happened where. The union between a story (or song) and the landscape, emphasising its role in materialising memory, is a feature of oral culture in which – as in *Ten Canoes* – stories store knowledge of how landscape can maintain life (for instance, by recording the places where the best hunting or fishing can be found during different seasons). This suggests the spatial, rather than temporal, understanding of history of some indigenous cultures, providing a view of humanity amidst nature (Deloria 1972, 81–89). Various African films, including Cissé's *Brightness* have also been considered in relation to oral storytelling traditions (Ukadike 1994, 254–262; Nagib 2011, 53–54).

Approached from a Dusselian perspective, this engagement with the storing of the past in place, akin to that of oral cultures, indicates that place, understood as a temporal memory bank, retains the occluded histories of colonial modernity. Distinct from Nagib's view that these are films in which a people 'are sovereign over their land before time' (42), this analysis suggests instead that the interaction between humans and land is determined by an ethics of reciprocity that inter-twines humans and cosmos (as in indigenous cultures in the Americas prior to the arrival of Europeans (Maffie 2013, 11; see the Introduction)), if not that the very land may be sovereign over the people whose pasts it stores.

Ultimately the films explored in this chapter go further, offering an encounter with the memory of the Earth, or Universe, as archive or recording device. Here, landscape is not, or not solely, the repository of orally recorded pre-modern pasts. Rather, it is the archive of nonhuman history, which landscapes give voice to directly, using humans or former humans (in the broader trend we also find animals, spirits, shaman, or mythological creatures) as its mouthpiece. Thus the transnational history evident here is that of the intertwining of humanity and nature, as has become more apparent in consideration of the impact of the Anthropocene (however we determine its origin) on the planet.

Encountering the Earth: The natural contract

This encounter with the Earth brings us to the first of the four contracts dis-cussed in the remaining chapters: the natural contract. Serres argues that human-ity is at war with nature. 'We so-called developed nations are no longer fighting among ourselves; together we are all turning against the world' (1992, 32). In contrast to the idea of the social contract through which we can understand how humans organise society, humanity can similarly be understood to lack, or deny, a natural contract with the Earth. Indeed, Serres notes that the origins of humanity's conflict with nature lie in the same Cartesian rationale critiqued by Dussel for propelling several centuries of colonial modernity (32). In such a state of affairs, Serres argues, a natural contract between humanity as a species (rather than a collection of nations) and the Earth, is of the same necessity as a social contract (1992, 15; 2008, 83).

> To be sure we don't know the world's language, or rather we know only the various animistic, religious, or mathematical versions of it. When phys-ics was invented, philosophers went around saying that nature was hidden under the code of algebra's numbers and letters: that word *code* came from law. In fact, the Earth speaks to us in terms of forces, bonds, and interac-tions, and that's enough to make a contract.
>
> *(1992, 39)*

Although there is much that is debateable in Serres' argument, not least whether humanity attacks nature or rearranges it for profit (as Jason W. Moore argues, see Chapter 1),[3] in the films discussed in this chapter an ethical encounter is pro-vided with the Earth, illustrative of the link between human and ecological his-tories now found in works addressing planetary history (e.g. Dipesh Chakrabarty (2009), see the Introduction). The encounter provided is suggestive of the need to acknowledge the tacit, structuring nature of an absent natural contract, allowing the devastation humanity wreaks on the planet. For this reason, in standout moments, the world memory archived in the landscape is temporarily given a face and voice in the any-space-whatever, as, for Serres, 'the Earth speaks to us' (1992, 39).

Amongst the rapidly growing field of ecocinema criticism, although there have been very few attempts to engage with Serres' ideas (Barker 2012), nevertheless much analysis already considers how humanity is integrally connected to nature, or able to communicate with nature. My work aligns with these predecessors. For example, Sean Cubitt analyses the complex imaginings of ecological themes and environmental politics in film and television, placing such issues in relation to the human (economic, industrial, technological) aspects of the earth as ecological system. Exploring the mediation between humanity and nature, our biopolitical existence within the world's eco-system, Cubitt states:

> Nature communicates with us as surely as we do with it, but to do so it must mediate. Nature cannot tell us the idea behind a volcano in any way other than through a volcano. In this case it is not so much nature, nor even the volcano that speaks, but the same physical processes that work in the human body and its sensorium.
>
> *(2005, 134)*

It is this message, as much as this process, which the films in question visualise – that nature requires a conduit through which to mediate its history, its memories, its request for a contract.

With regard to how such encounters might be offered by films, most useful is the position of Anat Pick and Guinevere Narraway, who argue that 'film screens nonhuman nature as both revelation and concealment' (2013, 2). Thus,

> reading films with an ecological eye partly means learning to see beyond the confines of narrative and story, whose natural tendency, as it were, is to suppress the nonhuman elements by relegating them to the role of setting, background or prop. At the same time, it means no longer viewing landscape – itself already a laden human construction – as passive or mute.
>
> *(8)*

In determining our ability to view films with an 'ecological eye', ecocinema criticism is engaged with the same questions which concern recent developments in philosophy, such as speculative realism and object oriented ontology. These new trends attempt to understand how humanity might conceive of the world without adhering to the so-called 'correlationism' of Western philosophy since Descartes (and most especially since Kant), which posits that the only way humanity can know the world is imperfectly, through its human experience of it (the correlation between thinking and being (Meillassoux 2006, 5)). A speculative approach is attempted instead, to understand what the outside world might be thinking or feeling, independent of a human filter.[4] Ecocinema criticism and speculative realism, then, indicate the rejuvenation of ways of understanding the existence of 'mind in matter' (Skrbina 2007, 2) found in the Western philosophical tradition of panpsychism, or the animist traditions from which panpsychism attempts to distance itself (19). All such thinking serves to focus our attention on the existence of 'mind in nature' (223) which is deliberately anthropomorphised in the films under discussion.

Hence, I am not claiming that the Earth actually attempts to communicate with humanity. This would seem unlikely. Even if it did, how could we possibly understand what was being said? As Tom Sparrow (2013) observes of the idea that Levinas's concept of visage might be applied to 'the face of nature', whilst the otherness or the infinity of the face in Levinas's visage may evoke the similarly unknowable character of nature, nevertheless amidst the interconnectedness of everything which ecological thought emphasises 'there is no adequate perspective on the environment that would enable us to look it in the face. The environment faces us from every angle; it is everywhere we look, and everywhere we don't' (Sparrow 2013, 81). There can be no doubting, then, that when *faceified* landscapes appear in films, there is a filter mediating between humans and nature: namely, humans have made these films, have anthropomorphised nature.

Indeed, anthropomorphism can be a useful feature for decentring too humanist a worldview. As Steven Shaviro notes, a 'certain cautious anthropomorphism is necessary in order to avoid anthropocentrism. I attribute feelings to stones in order to get away from the pernicious dualism that would insist that human beings alone (or at most, human beings together with some animals), have feelings, whilst everything else does not' (2014, 61). He continues: 'the accusation of anthropomorphism rests on the prior assumption that thought, value and experience are essentially, or exclusively, human to begin with' (90).[5] John Mullarkey even argues that an 'absolute anthropomorphism' might enable humans to realise their parity with animals, and vice versa (2013, 24).[6] The anthropomorphism of the films discussed here, then, considers a message sent to the species that is destroying the environment (a call to remember the intertwining of nature and humanity in the Anthropocene, a call for a natural contract), or rather, it is as some filmmakers imagine the Earth might look were it to try to send such a message to humanity.

The transnational history of human and nonhuman entanglement in planetary history (in particular during the Anthropocene), and the encounter with nature depicted as though it were looking for a natural contract, is clearly by human design. Filmmakers have anthropomorphised the Earth, attributing communicative powers or qualities to its nonhuman representatives via *faceified* landscapes. Yet, this does not detract from the importance of these films asking humanity to understand the Earth's ability to record the past, to consider the need for a natural contract. In a situation where human and nonhuman histories intertwine, these films suggest that it is possible to deny the denial of coevalness by relativising the centrality of human history amidst planetary (or Universe) history.

If this sounds fanciful, then consider again Timothy Morton on 'hyperobjects', phenomena like global warming which require of us 'thinking on a planetary scale' (2013, 119) (see the Introduction). As Morton observes: 'The reality is that hyperobjects were already here, and slowly but surely we understood what they were already saying. They contacted us' (201). This is the reason for the anthropomorphisation we see on screen, the attempt to visualise what it means, for humanity, to have such a revelation with respect to its own contemporary existence within the Anthropocene.

The encounters staged in these films, then, are not best understood as a speculation on what the world is like beyond or outside humanity, as this is (precisely as is the case with other histories, or 'lost pasts' more generally) something we can never attain. Rather, they offer a critique of humanity's ignorance of its own place in the world by providing a glimpse of nature's precarious relationship to an exclusive colonial modernity. For Shaviro, after Thomas Nagel, 'Likeness-in-human terms, if it is projected imaginatively enough, may work to dislocate us from the correlationist position of understanding [...] other entities only in terms of their resemblance, and relationship, to ourselves. But it can never actually attain the inner being of these other entities' (2014, 91). Thus the films meditate on how, as Serres observes, humanity might learn 'the world's language', and resituate itself as one animal amongst many (one history amongst many) in the context of the Anthropocene (Serres 1992, 39).

In the analysis which follows, then, I consider how any-space-whatevers speak to us of the world's memories, of transnational history (a planetary past reaching back long before nations and, indeed, humans) which has relatively recently entwined with humanity. The Earth is depicted asking for a natural contract (via temporary apertures which it opens in the landscape through which to speak of its memories via human/former human mouthpieces), to save it from the ravages of colonial modernity. The encounters the any-space-whatevers offer with world memory, then, necessitate the reconsideration of the centrality of our own (understanding of) history and, indeed, of the exclusionary relationship between colonial modernity and nature.

Uncle Boonmee Who Can Recall His Past Lives

Uncle Boonmee begins with one of the most captivating images in cinema history. The initial scene follows a water buffalo escaping from its human owners, being recaptured, and led out of shot. The camera lingers on the seemingly empty jungle at dusk. A cut then reveals, framed in the trees, a humanoid silhouette: dark black against the foliage, with two burning red eyes.

Or, is this what the viewer sees initially? Having seen the entire film, the viewer knows in retrospect that this is a (once human) monkey-spirit. Yet it is hard to recapture the moment of surprise and cognition during which the image was first processed. Perhaps one does immediately see a humanoid shape. Or perhaps one sees a patch of shadow in the trees, with eyes, which is then reconstituted as a humanoid shape. Or, just maybe the viewer's first expression may be of a pair of eyes looking out at them from the jungle itself. *Uncle Boonmee*, then, confronts us with a landscape that produces nonhuman creatures who will speak to us of the entwinement of humanity within the Earth's longer nonhuman history, providing a glimpse of the Earth as virtual centre of indetermination amongst loosely connected images (see Figure 3.1).

Uncle Boonmee has an episodic narrative, many of the scenes being interspersed with, or internally fragmented by, a prolonged shot of the countryside. The film begins with a slow-paced introduction to the life of Uncle Boonmee (Thanapat Saisaymar). He is suffering from kidney disease and receives medical attention from a Laotian immigrant in his employ, Jaai (Samud Kugasang). Boonmee is visited by Auntie Jen (Jenjira Pongpas) and Tong (Sakda Kaewbuadee) from Bangkok. That night, at dinner, the ghost of Boonmee's wife, Huay (Natthakarn Aphaiwonk) (also Jen's older sister), materialises slowly before them. They are then joined by monkey-spirit Boonsong (Geerasak Kulhong), the human son of Boonmee and Huay, who disappeared years previously. Boonsong describes his discovery of monkey-spirits living in the jungle through the lens of a camera, his decision to join them, and his transformation after mating with one of them.

The episodes that follow include: a scene at Boonmee's tamarind farm during which he wonders whether his health is suffering due to karma brought on by killing too many communists during the war and too many bugs on his farm; a scene set in an unspecified moment in the past concerning a lonely princess (Wallapa Mongkolprasert) who mates with a talking catfish (again, entwining humanity with another species); Boonmee in the present, being nursed by the ghost of Huay; a womb-like cave where Boonmee unexpectedly encounters Boonsong and other monkey-spirits (Boonmee states that he was born in that cave in a previous life

FIGURE 3.1   Encountering earthly pasts, in *Loong Boonmee raleuk chat/Uncle Boonmee Who Can Recall His Past Lives* (Apichatpong Weerasethakul, 2010).

he does not recall, but is not aware whether it was as a 'human or an animal, a woman, or a man'); a photo montage accompanying Boonmee's recounting of a recent dream of a 'future city' where 'past people', if caught, are made to disappear through the shining of a light on them until their past lives have been played out on a screen behind them (as though the eradication of their histories erases their existence as other, in a scene conflating both those who disappeared into the forest to avoid state violence during the Cold War[7] with all the species other than humanity who are now disappearing in the forest – the captive is a man in a gorilla suit, evocative of monkey-spirit Boonsong – due to the cultivation of the land by Uncle Boonmee and others); Boonmee's Buddhist funeral, after which Jen, Tong and Roong (Kanokporn Tongaram) meet in a hotel room where, as they prepare to go out for food, they leave behind alternate (seemingly temporally virtual) versions of themselves, sitting watching television.

Weerasethakul has variously discussed the importance of the village of Nabua to the film's evocation of memories of the Cold War stored in place (Weerasethakul 2009; J. H. Kim 2011). Indeed, in existing works on this much-analysed film, various scholars have explored this link: by considering the film to meditate on the history of the region (including its staging of the repression of communism from the 1960s to the 1980s) via 'dream, time travel, reincarnation and transformation' (Chung 2012, 217–218); as ingeniously melding 'a slice of Thai history with that of the fictive life of Uncle Boonmee', in which the animals and spirits dwelling in the forest are seen as obliquely referencing the victims of the region's troubled history during the Cold War (Suter 2013, 51); and as depicting the jungle as a haunted space which 'during the Cold War [...] became a space of flight, danger and the habitation of spirits [...] insofar as its density and depth could conceal communists, insurgents and others fleeing the security apparatus' (Ingawanij 2013, 96), as well as part of a broader argument about 'presentations of animism's historicity' in Weerasethakul's films (91).

However, other scholarly views reach beyond the national: situating *Uncle Boonmee* amongst Weerasethakul's transnational, hybrid cinema which 'seeks to reconstitute itself in the shadow of modernity by excavating an alternative vision of "Thainess" not only in local folklore and popular culture, but also in new and contemporized conceptions of the sacred' (O'Hara 2012, 188); as illustrative of a queer sensibility (producing a 'queer disturbance of meaning', a 'refusal to make sense') which exists across many national cinemas within contemporary global art cinema (Galt 2013, 65–66); and as a meditation on memory and time (Lovatt 2013, 61; Deamer 2016, 317–319). This is before we consider the various pieces about the *Primitive* project art installation, out of which *Uncle Boonmee* grew, and, indeed, the many pieces on his other movies.[8] Thus there would seem to be a productive tension in the film between its situatedness in a specific place where history is very much alive, and the broader, global processes with which this local/national history converges.

It is a little surprising, then, that amongst such varied writings on *Uncle Boonmee*, one interpretation is absent: an ecocritical one focusing on two of the influences which Weerasethakul identifies for the film (one literary, one cinematic). Whilst many scholars mention that the film was influenced (in part) by Buddhist monk Phra Sripariyattiweti's book *A Man Who Can Recall His Past Lives* (1983) (and whilst this seems to fit *Uncle Boonmee* neatly alongside the engagement with Buddhist thought in Weerasethakul's previous films (Quandt 2009, 25–26)), nevertheless, another book also influenced the film's conception, Terry Glavin's *Waiting for the Macaws* (2006) (Weerasethakul 2009, 192). Again, whilst the range of modernist and avant-garde influences on Weerasethakul's cinema are often discussed (e.g. Chris Marker's *La Jetée* (France, 1961)), the inspiration he took from the Amazonian adventure, John Boorman's *The Emerald Forest* (UK, 1985), like Glavin's book, is rarely if ever mentioned. Both of these influences on the film's development, however, would indicate the importance of ecological concerns in the film.

In *Waiting for the Macaws*, which discusses how the earth archives 'stories' (14) (and contains a chapter entitled 'The Ghost in the Woods' about humanity's ability to drive species to extinction throughout history), Glavin explores the rapidity of species extinction in the modern world (around one species being lost every ten minutes (3)), and, simultaneously, humanity's attempts to preserve, catalogue and archive rapidly disappearing pasts in zoos and botanical gardens (40–41).[9] For its part, *The Emerald Forest* provides a loose template which *Uncle Boonmee* reprises: both films are about fathers reunited with sons long lost to the forest (living with an Amazon tribe in Boorman's film, a monkey-spirit tribe in Weerasethakul's), from whom they learn that the profit they make from exploiting nature, whether as a US engineer building a dam in Boorman's film,[10] or a Thai farmer expanding his land in Weerasethakul's, also effects those who live in the forest. Both films foreground a choice between a capitalist view of the natural world (as suitable for (re)organisation for productivity, as per Jason W. Moore) or an alternative possibility involving reciprocal living arrangements with those in the forest, for a more sustainable future.

Accordingly, an interpretation focusing on the film's engagement with the ecological exclusion of the Earth by colonial modernity seems extremely pertinent. *Uncle Boonmee*, like the other films in the transnational trend outlined at the start of the chapter, considers how humanity, through the engine of colonial modernity, pushes animals and spirits to the edges of the Earth, forcing many to extinction. The Chris Marker–style photo montage of the future, a clear homage to the post-apocalyptic *La Jetée*, is a prime indicator of this. Thus an interpretation with an 'ecological eye', as Pick and Narraway advocate, does not reside apart from those listed above, but rather includes the excluded other of nature (its endangered species) amidst the many ghosts in the woods (including the mysterious and legendary beings of pre-modern myth), subsisting in the shadows along with colonial modernity's more political outcasts (the lost imperial subjects, the disappeared of the Cold War).

Such an approach also illuminates how *Uncle Boonmee* establishes an ethical encounter with the Earth as it calls for a natural contract, especially in the instances where the monkey-spirit Boonsong appears. In these moments, any-space-whatevers provide glimpses into the Earth's planetary past, and reveal that *this* is the virtual centre of indetermination which belies the loosely connected episodes which constitute the narrative. As in the opening scene, these are encounters, ultimately, with blackness, from which a humanoid shape emerges to indicate the relatively recent importance of humanity to planetary history, and the need for it to re-engage with nature as contractual partner.

The landscape, as archive, thus provides the coherence to the episodic narrative. Before we see any images, the opening epigraph to *Uncle Boonmee* reads: 'Facing the jungle, the hills and vales, my past lives as an animal and other beings rise up before me.' Thus this film about memory, oral history, and reincarnation, which unsettles the boundaries between humans and animals (and indeed, Cartesian selves and themselves), is inextricably linked to the landscape as repository of nonhuman history. The various episodes, often seemingly disconnected, rely upon the notion that within the surrounding landscapes there are nonhuman memories which can be encountered by humans.

Firstly there is the ghostly Huay and the arrival of Boonsong from the jungle (analysed further below). The latter informs Boonmee that 'There are many beings outside right now [...] spirits and hungry animals.' Then there is the scene of inter-species copulation between the princess and the catfish, which begins with an establishing shot of the countryside. For its part, the death of Boonmee occurs in a cave which he travels to through the jungle, as though returning to the depths of the Earth to become a part of its memories (there he encounters ancient cave art, fish evocative of the talking catfish, and the monkey-spirits). Boonmee's confessions with regard to the communists he killed during the war relates to the ghost- and spirit-inhabited environment on which his tamarind farm now sits, but seems to be mentioned only to pointedly interweave this level of human history amidst the many other nonhuman histories with which it overlaps in the forest. It is precisely as Boonsong says: 'There are many beings outside right now' – many past histories of exclusion which become resurgent when 'facing the jungle'. Thus the centre of indetermination which holds the episodic string of stories together – themselves evocative in their varied styles of a cinematic archive, from a tribute to the Thai 'Royal Costume Drama' genre (the tale of the princess and the catfish), to the evocation of other cinematic jungles shot in day for night (like Boorman's), to the Chris Marker–influenced ending (J. H. Kim 2011, 52) – is the virtual archive of the Earth's entwined human and nonhuman histories, stored in the landscape.

Darkness: Seeking a (nonhuman) natural contract

Two standout instances directly equate Boonsong and his fellow monkey-spirits with dark holes in the landscape, suggesting they are temporary mouthpieces through which the forest speaks. These affection-images consist of a dark shadowy space, the reflective *quality* of the Earth's face. The darkness emphasises the

Earth's ability to absorb light, to store matter as world memory. The red eyes that appear from the darkness, staring out, are the Earth's affective *power*, its ability to desire an encounter with humanity, its hope in seeking out a natural contract.

Firstly, when Boonsong appears at the dinner, his arrival in the house is preceded by two shots of the surrounding landscape. A prolonged long shot of an image of a nearby hillside is first, a shot akin to those which often precede shifts in physical and temporal location throughout the film. Then, a medium shot follows, of the jungle immediately outside the house. It is an image of, quite literally, darkness. Just an opening in the trees from which we cannot detect light: we see only shadow, with the faintest of movements in the leaves which frame the gap. In this image of darkness, the any-space-whatever expresses the Earth's virtual potential to archive the nonhuman past, enabling its return at a later date in the form of nonhuman history. This potential to record world memory is what the any-space-whatever enunciates. This is its affective quality. The mouthpiece it uses to enunciate its affective powers is Boonsong, who emerges as though from the darkness of the jungle to tell us how he transformed from human to monkey-spirit, thereby indicating the intertwining of human and nonhuman history. Notably, as he enters the house he is again depicted as eyes emerging from darkness.

Boonsong tells of how his first glimpse of his (now) fellow monkey-spirits was in a photograph he took, the leaping form he magnifies being barely distinguishable from the leaves of the trees they inhabit. His attempts to create a photographic record of the monkey-spirits led him to become a part of the natural archive himself, by mating with one of their number. When Boonmee brings out his photo albums at this precise moment, to show his acquisition of land for his bee farm, there is a stark contrast created between the natural archive of the Earth and its threatened nonhuman inhabitants (Boonsong himself) and the scientifically produced photographic record of human expansion into nature (Boonmee's photo album). The affective power of the Earth, its desire for a natural contract is missed by Boonmee, who stays focused on human history and the colonising of the land. But the film is clear about the intersection of these histories.

The Earth's affective quality, its potential to archive, is emphasised even more clearly in the scene in which Boonmee dies in the cave. Amidst the ancient cave paintings and the tiny fish in their rock pool (suggestive of the stories stored in the landscape which we have been watching until now), a completely dark cavity within the cave is punctuated by the appearance of Boonsong's red eyes, moving across the darkness. They evoke at once the shimmering points of luminescence, so evocative of far-off stars, previously encountered as the humans make their way through the cave, and the image of the moon seen through the opening in the roof of the cave: they are, again, points of light which give expression to a reflective surface of the Earth's face, eyes providing the micro-movements across the *faceified* image, a demonstration of its affective power as it seeks out humanity to establish a natural contract. Once again, then, in the cave scene the Earth is rendered as an any-space-whatever with the potential to record the nonhuman in its depths. As the eyes appear, Boonmee is comparing the cave to a womb, a place from which the lives he remembers (and does not) are born, whether as human or as animal. Then, as he recounts his dream, the monkey spirit appears again in the Marker-esque photo montage. The future sees the death of the last of its species, after it is captured by soldiers and its image retold using a cinema-like projection machine.

As we return to Boonmee lying dying in the cave, we are shown the landscape outside, standing vigil, as though regarding him or bearing witness to his death. Slowly, five sets of red eyes appear in the darkness, the black bodies of the monkey-spirits blending in with the darkness such that the image appears to be simply a landscape full of eyes. In this way, the Earth appears to speak, through the darkness, of its ability to store the stories of human and nonhuman lives alike. It asks for humanity to recognise this quality.

A similar conclusion to this is reached by Seung-hoon Jeong, with regard to Weerasethakul's previous films. However, the difference between our final viewpoints is telling. As part of a sophisticated intervention into the debate surrounding 'suture' (a several-decades-long discussion about the extent to which viewers can be said to be 'stitched' into narrative film via its aesthetic techniques), Jeong explores how certain of Weerasethakul's films provide us with glimpses of the 'unsutured unconscious of the world itself' (2013, 108). *Sang sattawat/Syndromes and a Century* (2006), for instance, is viewed as a 'civilizational suture of the impersonal desire and relationship between any disparate types of being', which enables us to 'sense inhuman eyes viewing all human desires from an ontological ground' (108). Again, in *Sud pralad/Tropical Malady* (2004), a film that features an ambiguous relationship between humans and animals manifest in the shamanistic transformation of man into tiger, 'the tiger […] seems to remember even thousands of years' impersonal desires shared by former lives' (108). Of the film's close-ups on the tiger's face in the Thai jungle at night, Jeong writes: 'while the steady panoramic camera unfolds ecological space, a crucial shift often occurs through cut-in or zoom-in that guides the viewer unaware to the face of a nonhuman gaze' (120).

Yet, crucial to Jeong's exploration of suture are what he terms 'quasi-interfaces' which, Jeong argues, 'evoke but do not represent the medium interfaces of camera, filmstrip and screen' (14). These 'quasi-interfaces' include a range of objects on screen, such as a solar eclipse for a (quasi-)camera, a strip of windows for a (quasi-) filmstrip, and the sky as a (quasi-)screen. The last of these in particular, which we might consider in terms of landscape, is pertinent for this discussion.

For Jeong, the sky enables the viewer to encounter the plane of immanence created of 'the open whole of all screened images in ceaseless change. […] Pure memory is that of this immanence in multi-layered temporality, and it appears as already actualised and always present in the case of the sky positioned behind molecularly moving images; it is the case of pure matter' (112). This very specific sense of the plane of immanence (outlined in *Cinema 1* as 'the infinite set of all images [...] the Universe as cinema' (Deleuze 1985, 61)), appears onscreen, for Jeong, through the 'quasi-interface' of the sky as screen, rendering the ecological environment analogous to cinema. Through such quasi-interfaces 'the actual state of the world is desutured into its virtual verso' (Jeong 2013, 110). However, whilst brilliant intercessors in terms of what they offer Jeong's argument regarding what cinematic suture may mean in the Twenty-First Century, Jeong himself acknowledges that these analogies may not be 'intended' or 'clearly convincing' (111). As it is debateable whether they are intended to function as such, or whether all viewers will be convinced that they do, an alternative conclusion is worth considering.

The darkness of the black holes in the jungle in *Uncle Boonmee* do not evoke a camera, filmstrip, or screen, or any such 'quasi-interface'. Rather, they indicate something of the Earth's ability to archive nonhuman history, a function which contrasts with humanity's attempts to record the history of its own expansion and the everyday extinction of nonhuman species that trails in its wake. Here Weerasethakul's debt to Glavin's *Waiting for the Macaws* is most evident, as he grapples with how cinema can engage with the recording of the rapid disappearance of nature due to colonial modernity. This is perhaps not yet a million miles away from Jeong's conclusion. However, let us think on further. It is noticeable that *Uncle Boonmee* contains a foregrounded emphasis on ecological concerns which is absent from *Tropical Malady*. If we were to explore the any-space-whatevers of *Uncle Boonmee* using Jeong's ideas, this would be to catch a glimpse of a human or animal centre of indetermination (de)suturing back into the plane of immanence, via the any-space-whatever: a face 'decomposing' as it were, becoming-virtual. As Jeong puts it with regard to the becoming-animal of the man confronting the tiger's face in *Tropical Malady*:

> he enters the uncanny plane of infinite, immanent connectedness to the animal, the ghost, namely all virtual life, while becoming naked, imperceptible, and clandestine. Cinema then stops facializing the landscape. We see not a film but rather a cinematic interface that amalgamates the ontological others, staring blankly into the disappearing traces of faces.
>
> *(Jeong 2013, 183)*

Jeong thus follows Deleuze and Guattari's view of the need to escape the organisation of the (inhuman) face, which, as noted previously, I depart from in my analysis of anthropomorphised faces becoming-actual (organising into *faceified* landscapes) on screen. My own position finds similarly in aesthetic terms to Jeong, then, but with regard to the broader picture I look to bring into focus (concerning the transnational histories emerging across a world of cinemas, and the negotiation of different contracts via which they become visible), my interpretation is, literally, the opposite of this. The encounter is not with a decomposing but a *composing* 'face of nature'. One which, after Sparrow, we can understand to be effectively impossible (due to the environment's ability to regard us from every angle), unless anthropomorphised. Whilst Jeong is careful to avoid anthropomorphising cinema in his emphasis on becoming-virtual, by contract, to realise *Uncle Boonmee*'s engagement with humanity's place in planetary history it is necessary to depart from a strict Deleuzian or Deleuze and Guattarian theoretical position, so as to accurately describe what is happening on screen. Rather than a human or animal centre of indetermination decentring back into the plane of immanence (becoming-virtual), in *Uncle Boonmee* we see instead the Earth as centre of indetermination (becoming-actual, making a face), to request a natural contract.

For the Earth to address us in the anthropomorphising cinematic form (that which gives the illusion of agency to the Earth), it must take a form which we can recognise. Thus the any-space-whatever composes a *faceified* landscape, central to which is a becoming-actual humanoid form that acts as its mouthpiece. As Jeong's reading of Weerasethakul's earlier films is so compelling, the importance of this distinction is not immediately apparent. Yet when we remove *Uncle Boonmee* from Weerasethakul's oeuvre, to view its similarities with other of the cross-border examples from the transnational trend, it becomes apparent that Weerasethakul's approach is different in this later film than it was in *Tropical Malady*. The choice of former human Boonsong as aperture through which the Earth can speak provides an agency and purpose to the Earth in its attempt to make contact with humanity.[11] Boonsong, after all, appears in order to tell his father of his life since he disappeared into the forest and to try to gain recognition for the history of the rapidly disappearing spirit-monkeys which has been obscured by human development of their land. Through Boonsong we do not learn much, if anything, about the history of the monkey-spirits as a species. Rather, the point is to provide an encounter with a lost past (in this case, of another species) which prompts either the realisation, for some viewers, or remembrance, for others, that there is such a history intertwined with others: a transnational planetary history of entwined human and nonhuman pasts.

Due to the presence of this anthropomorphising focus, the Earth is not so much caught in the act of becoming virtual, desuturing into its cinematic verso, as Jeong argues. Rather, it is caught in the act of becoming-actual. Not the disappearing traces of faces in the landscape, but precisely the opposite, their temporary appearance – from the virtual world into the actual – seeking an encounter. Like the man-becoming-tiger in *Tropical Malady*, Boonsong is also becoming-animal. Yet, whereas in the former film the encounter we are offered is with the fully transformed tiger (the complete dissolving of the human into becoming-animal, as Jeong observes), Boonsong pauses in, or temporarily retreats from, his trajectory towards the monkey, to communicate with humans. He briefly reterritorialises again, to return as a humanoid form able to explain his history. In a context where, to reiterate Serres, 'we don't know the world's language, or rather we know only the various animistic, religious, or mathematical versions of it' (1992, 39), *Uncle Boonmee* uses Boonsong as an anthropomorphised aperture through which to request a natural contract.

Jeong's interpretation could be said to illustrate how Weerasethakul's earlier films indicate, as Bruno Latour famously has it, that we have never been modern (in that they disrupt the idea of the separation of human and nature upon which colonial modernity rests). But, in *Uncle Boonmee*, a more direct address appears to the viewer who is, in many cases, likely to believe that they are in fact separate from nature, and thus that for modernity there is no contract with nature. The latter film, then, is perhaps more evocative of Vilém Flusser (2014, 98–104) in its attempt to clearly differentiate between, but also show the importance of realising the coexistence of, on the one hand, those planting the land (Uncle Boonmee's tamarind farm) as a way for humanity to control history, and, on the other hand, those living in relationship with nature (Boonsong and the monkey spirits) as a means for understanding the world ecologically. To provide nature with a voice, it is rendered familiar. The interface provided (to use Jeong's term a little against the grain) is not cinematic (or an inhuman eye in the sense that, say, the black hole of an air vent is (Jeong 2012, 211)), but rather, is that of a becoming-actual, becoming-human form that emerges out of the darkness to (impossibly) constitute the 'face of nature'. In summary, instead of seeing humans deterritorialising away from the face, towards a becoming-animal or becoming-imperceptible (as Jeong illuminates of *Tropical Malady*), in *Uncle Boonmee*, animals momentarily reterritorialise as humans so as to relay the Earth's message that human and nonhuman histories are interlinked in world memory.[12]

In *Uncle Boonmee*, the encounter offered is with the occluded ecological past, suggesting the need for a natural contract to rescue nature from colonial modernity. The becoming-animal of the one confronting the face, the 'dissolve' of the human into nature which Jeong observes in *Tropical Malady*, can now be reassessed as the relativising that such an encounter enables of any too central a sense of *human history* informing their being. The reason to consider what is on screen to be such a *faceified* landscape is the Dusselian ethical position from which this reading stems (see Chapter 1), that which places nature amidst all those in the excluded underside of colonial modernity. From such a position, why would we not think it capable of asking for its past to be recognised along with ours, for a natural contract that would deny the denial of coevalness? Or, more accurately, why would we not think filmmakers capable of depicting it as such?

Nostalgia for the Light

The documentary *Nostalgia for the Light*, whilst very different to *Uncle Boonmee*, also explores the connection between human and nonhuman history, putting human history in perspective by encapsulating it with the billions of years of existence of the matter of the Universe (see Figure 3.2). The film positions the Earth in a dynamic encounter with the Universe, recasting the concern with the natural contract evident in *Uncle Boonmee* (of the Earth addressing humans through Boonsong) into the broader arena of Universe memory (of the Universe speaking through humans). Once again the any-space-whatever provides the

FIGURE 3.2 Enunciating disappeared pasts, both recent and long ago, in *Nostalgia de la luz / Nostalgia for the Light* (Patricio Guzmán 2010).

entrance to this nonhuman archive of memory in matter, exploring the virtual temporal connections between the Earth (humanity being but a part of the matter it archives as world memory) and the Universe. This time, however, the ethical encounter offered is not with the Earth per se, but with the matter of the Universe of which the nonhuman histories of the Earth, and humanity, are intertwined aspects.

In *Nostalgia for the Light* the any-space-whatevers also express the Earth's ability to record, store or archive memories as an affective quality. This time, however, rather than darkness, this is evidenced through light. Indeed, rather than their affective powers expressing a desire for interaction with humanity, instead their wish is to reveal what has been recorded to the Universe as a whole. This includes, most recently, the intertwined human and nonhuman histories of the planet. As opposed to the darkness of the recording surface and the micro-movements of red eyes across them of *Uncle Boonmee,* in *Nostalgia for the Light* the red desert earth becomes the plate, which offers up world memory into the light of Universe memory. Thus a film ostensibly about history conceived of as national (recent Chilean history, including in particular the recent Pinochet dictatorship) and regional (Latin America's history of colonial extermination of indigenous peoples and diasporic settlement) ultimately opens up onto the Universe in its exploration of how the intertwined human and nonhuman history of the world (conceived of as a heritage of universal matter that stretches back beyond human origins) encounters its other in the Universe.

Unlike the national focus of many of Guzmán's previous documentaries, *Nostalgia For the Light* (the first part of his third trilogy) quickly establishes that it will meditate on how the personal (Guzmán's memories of childhood) connects not only to the history of the nation (or not *solely* of the nation), but also the history of the Universe. The opening segues from an old German telescope, which Guzmán's voiceover credits for his personal interest in astronomy, to a domestic setting evocative of his childhood. The montage moves us, via a graphic match, from the cratered surface of the moon to the play of light and shadow caused by the movement of the leaves of a tree. The tree is situated outside the window of a house with sufficient period detail to remind Guzmán (the voiceover indicates) of his youth (White 2012). Guzmán describes this period of his life in a way that seems idyllic, before, during the Cold War, a *'coup d'état* swept away democracy, dreams and science'. As Guzmán's voiceover relates this personal story, the house evocative of his childhood is gradually obscured by dust, blowing across the screen, reflecting light back at the camera in twinkling patterns against a black backdrop. It is described as 'star dust' by Guzmán.

This non-anthropocentric force, that of the matter which constructs the Universe, reappears at several points during the film to illustrate the all-consuming nature of Universe memory – the stuff of which humanity is created and to which they return in death. We are pointedly informed by scientist George Preston that the calcium in our bones 'was made shortly after the big bang' and that accordingly: 'We live among the trees but we also live among the stars. We live among the galaxies. We are part of the Universe. The calcium in my bones was there from the beginning.' The matter in the landscape, then, from meteorites to the bones of the dead, is part of a giant archive which at its broadest limit encompasses the Universe. The memory, of which Chile's past is a part, is thus considered to be a much larger phenomenon. This, not only due to the film's introduction of the transnational movements of diaporas and exiles in the present, through to the nomadic, pre-national movements of prehistoric man, but back even further, to the origins of all life in the big bang. The personal extends into a universal (in the literal sense) concern with a nonhuman view of history and humanity's place within it.

As with *Uncle Boonmee*, *Nostalgia for the Light* is a film which has captured the imagination of many scholars: Patrick Blaine explores the film as the latest entry in Guzmán's oeuvre's political analysis of events in Chile, including a foregrounded examination of the complexities surrounding time, memory and absence in national history (2013); Shohini Chaudhuri, as part of an examination of how films about state terror worldwide 'foster audience identification with memories they have never had', examines the film's ability to 'summon us to remember and make connections between different violent histories' (2014, 20 and 104); Selmin Kara, similarly departing from the national context, places *Nostalgia for the Light* amidst a cross-border (on the American continent at least) grouping of films evocative of a 'speculative realist aesthetic', mixing human and nonhuman temporalities (Kara 2014); and Asbjørn Grønstad, drawing on the first iteration of the following analysis (Martin-Jones 2013b), argues that *Nostalgia for the Light* promulgates 'a planetary ethics' which is 'mostly materialist, as evidenced in the film's suggestion that memory resides in matter', and as such indicates the potential for a cinematic 'ethics of the Anthropocene'

(Grønstad 2016b, 224 and 13).[13] As with *Uncle Boonmee*, the position I take on *Nostalgia for the Light* makes common cause with aspects of these predecessors, but does so in order to emphasise its place in the broader transnational trend of films exploring the intertwining of human and planetary history via an encounter with the Earth's past.

Nostalgia for the Light is set in the Atacama Desert in Chile, and interweaves two narratives. One details the activities of astronomers watching the heavens from the desert's arid landscape. The other explores the desert landscape for the traces of its lost history, both as part of a nation called Chile and for thousands of years beforehand. The desert is first introduced as a landscape as alien as that of the planet Mars, before the documentary focuses on the history contained within its barren expanse. In both aspects – looking up to the sky and down into the ground – the documentary meditates on what it means to research the past.

On the one hand, astronomer Gaspar Galaz, who features as a talking head throughout, explains his view that to scan the Universe through a telescope is to explore the past, because it is to examine light which takes a long time to reach the Earth. He compares astronomers to archaeologists, historians, and geologists. Galaz extrapolates, further, that due to the time it takes for light to reach us, even from objects very near to us, we all exist in the past.

On the other hand, at ground level, the various people whose lives cross the Atacama Desert are shown to belong to the past. This ranges from the artefacts and physical remains of people who inhabited the region 10,000 years ago, to former political prisoners of the Pinochet regime who were held captive in the desert, to the elderly women (the Women of Calama) who routinely search the desert for fragments of the remains of the disappeared (the political victims of the Pinochet dictatorship from the 1970s and 1980s, executed and buried in the desert).

Due to this weave, in the film's final moments a crystal of time is constructed to encapsulate much of the film's play with memory, landscapes, and the past seen in light. Guzmán's voiceover states:

> I am convinced that memory has a gravitational force. It is constantly attracting us. Those who have a memory are able to live in the fragile present moment. Those who have none don't live anywhere. Each night, slowly, impassively, the centre of the galaxy passes over Santiago.

The words are spoken over a panoramic image of the city of Santiago de Chile as a nightscape of shimmering neon lights against a black backdrop. It is as through the city were reflecting back to the Universe its own glittering firmament, as seen in so many impressive shots of the Universe scattered throughout the film. The city becomes a star-scape, crystallizing with the Universe. In such a crystal-line structure, the virtual and the actual facets of the crystal are Universe and Earth (or, if you prefer, Earth and Universe). The indiscernibility of these two sides, as they reflect each other, makes sense of the two related narratives of the film. They are crystalline facets of the same story. One is a search into the past through astronomy, looking up into the sky through telescopes (the Universe as 'mobile archive', as John Durham Peters would have it (2003, 404)), the other a search into the past through archaeology (looking into the ground for buried histories) (for Peters, the Earth as 'recording medium' (402)). In both instances, the landscape – whether the Universe or the Earth – is the virtual past as archive through which we search. The Earth archives world memory, within a much broader archival process of Universe memory.

Thus *Nostalgia for the Light* notes the need to focus as much on the history of the planet as we do on that of the stars above, so as to realise that the past below our feet, whose 'voice' also comes to us from afar, is also that of the Universe more broadly. In this respect the film's treatment of the landscape is key, because, as in *Uncle Boonmee*, it is from the landscape that the call comes to recognise the Earth's archival qualities, its need for a natural contract and the recognition of humanity's place amongst the other histories occluded by colonial modernity. In the opening, the landscape's position as an enunciator of the Earth's archiving qualities emerges when, over a montage of striking images from the desert, Guzmán states:

> I imagine that man will soon walk on Mars. This ground beneath my feet bears the strongest resemblance to that faraway world. There is nothing. No insects, no animals, no birds. And yet it is full of history. For 10,000 years this region has been a transit route. Rivers of stone provide natural paths. The caravans of llamas and men came and went between the high plains and the sea. It is a condemned land, permeated with salt, where human remains are mummified and objects frozen in time. The air, transparent, thin, allows us to read this vast open book of memory, page after page.

Here there is a literal evocation of landscape as archive ('page after page') which is explored in more detail thereafter. We are told that there are meteorites below the surface. We see the remnants of petrified fish and molluscs amidst the dunes, which are depicted in close succession with the ruins of an indigenous American fortress. We are introduced to rock carvings by archaeologist Lautaro Núñez, significantly of faces, from 'pre-Columbian shepherds' who used the desert as a transit route over 1,000 years ago. Núñez notes the layered nature of this landscape by observing how the modern road they drive down is laid directly atop a prehistoric one. The desert also contains a Nineteenth Century graveyard of dead miners, a former mining complex later used as a prison during the Pinochet era, and perched atop these layers of history are the astronomers, in the latest high-tech observatories, searching the sky for the Universe's past. The desert landscape, then, is introduced as a giant archive constituted of the same matter as the entire Universe – as Guzmán argues, 'our roots' are 'up above, beyond the light' – within which the human and nonhuman coexist.

Like *Uncle Boonmee, Nostalgia for the Light* permits access to the material archive of the desert through a recurring *faceified* any-space-whatever. The film cues us towards such a reading through the various images of faces in the landscape: from the ancient rock carvings to the pictures of the disappeared laid upon the desert floor, to Guzmán's use of cinematography to conflate planetary landscapes with a human skull. However, the standout moments are those in which one of the women searching the desert for the remains of a loved one, Violeta Berríos, is depicted against the desert landscape, speaking of her quest for the bones of Mario. It is here that, via a human mouthpiece, the intertwined human and non-human histories of the planet are most clearly evident.

Light: Revealing the archived world memory to the Universe

Several times during the film, Berríos is framed against a distinctive backdrop of desert rock (see Figure 3.2). She speaks with great emotional sincerity about her quest for Mario's remains. This can be a very difficult moment to watch, and I do not wish to detract from its importance in terms of national history or, indeed, gender politics. There is clearly a level of interpretation of this scene in which Berríos's testimony is integral to that of the survivors of the Cold War military regime and those they lost. After all, at several points, Guzmán depicts the people he interviews in tableau, as though bearing witness to their struggles with the past.[14] However, as noted previously, this is a film which does not look to reterritorialise its story in the nation, but in the Universe. It is immediately noticeable, for example, how different *Nostalgia for the Light* is from Guzmán's previous trilogies, which very directly explore Chile's recently traumatic national history (Martin-Jones 2013b, 708). *Nostalgia for the Light*, for its part, commences with the auteur's memories of childhood and broadens out into a meditation on the nation of Chile's place within the history of the Universe. In this process, national history and politics remain integral, but are seen from a perspective which relativises the centrality of humanity to the nonhuman history of the Universe. It is with this in mind that the following interpretation is offered, with an 'ecological eye'.

Through choice of location and framing, Berríos' form blends with the landscape to suggest that her human story also belongs to the desert, and also speaks from the nonhuman landscape's historical archive. Berríos is filmed in medium shot, seated cross-legged on the ground. She is interviewed about her continual search for Mario. Behind her the uneven desert landscape closely frames her body, such that no horizon is visible above her head. The pink hue of the rock blends with Berríos's tanned face and her pink shirt, as a result of which she seems to blend in with the colour palette of the shot. The landscape which frames her is a striated section, in which layers of the past are visible. The effect of this closely framing background, which places Berríos literally within the ground, suggests on one level that her human life has become one with her search for graves. However, her place within the red earth equally emphasises her role as a voice that speaks from and for the nonhuman desert. Barríos's seventy-year-old face is extremely animated at points as she expresses the anguish she feels at never having recovered Mario's body. The darker sunken cavities of her face (eye sockets, nostrils) and those created by the folds of skin on her neck, echo the pitted and pockmarked cavities in the rock wall behind her. There is a clear sense here that the landscape speaks through Berríos, whose emotional strength is apparent, the affective landscape thus appearing as a face talking of the occluded past whose secret it keeps.

The choice of Berríos as the human voice piece for the Earth is similar to the way in which *Uncle Boonmee* uses Boonsong to draw equivalence between the recently disappeared of the Cold War, and the broader species extinction of life in a jungle which is being increasingly colonised as farmland. Berríos, as someone who seeks recognition for the disappeared histories of the Cold War (the bones of Mario in this case), is similarly of those *recently* excluded by colonial modernity, and so her plight aligns with that of transnational history (of colonial modernity's much longer exclusion of the Earth from a natural contract), which the Earth enunciates with and through her. She is thus the most appropriate voice piece through which the Earth can tell of its disappeared pasts. Her personal past opens up to a Cold War history, which is but a recent phase of the broader history of colonial modernity, and so we track back through time to the former mine workers, to the indigenous history of the landscape, and then further still, until we reach the limit of history in the origins of the Universe itself. This is, after all, precisely the same journey on which Guzmán takes us at the start of the film – from personal history, to Cold War, to Universe.

With this in mind, it is clear how the film's depiction of the desert landscape expresses its capacity, as an any-space-whatever, to archive Universe memory. In the early montage sequences, the Atacama Desert is introduced in all its weird and wonderful rock, sand and salt formations: from its isolated rocks to its mountain ranges, its hard-packed dry and flat-ridged surfaces to its wind-blown dunes, its ruined fortresses (whether evidence of the indigenous human past, precisely, or whether of the colonial destruction of the coevalness of other pasts) and its 1,000-year-old carvings to its high-tech observatories. In these sequences the desert is rendered precisely as any-space-whatever, 'a perfectly singular space, which has merely lost its homogeneity, that is, the principle of its metric relations or the connections of its own parts, so that the linkages can be made in an infinite number of ways. It is a space of virtual conjunction, grasped as pure locus of the possible' (Deleuze 1983, 113). Hence, Berríos's testimony, as one whose own past has been denied coevalness by colonial modernity, gives voice to the Earth as centre of indetermination via a *faceified* landscape. Thus the any-space-whatever of the desert attests to the virtual layers of archived matter that exist in time and to the potential for virtual conjunction in new formations throughout the ages past and to come.

Yet this is not to say that Berríos's moving speech, nor her terrible grief, should be considered somehow absent from the *faceified* landscape. This is where viewing with an 'ecological eye' needs to be considered with care. Guzmán does not, to be clear, attempt to obscure or subsume Berríos's personal history, or the political history of the disappeared, within the history of the Universe. Rather, these scenes indicate precisely the intertwining of human and nonhuman histories since 1492. There is no attempt to render human histories – such as those of the disappeared of the Cold War – somehow less important or relevant by aligning Berríos's voice with that of the Earth. I do not think Guzmán is trying to say that once we all return to dust, we will be forgotten (albeit the film does indicate that this is part and parcel of the recording of life's passing in the desert). Rather, in this instance, 'an ecological eye' leads to the realisation that human and nonhuman histories are entwined in planetary, and Universe, history.

This does not necessarily entail the annihilation of humanity. Instead, the choice of Berríos has the opposite effect. Berríos, a woman whose (human) life has seemingly been irrevocably damaged by a recent phase of colonial modernity (the Cold War), is aligned with, gives voice to, the same denial of acknowledgement that the Earth has suffered during the Anthropocene. It is precisely because of her personal trauma and grief that Berríos can represent the Earth's request for a natural contract, via a human form. In Berríos, human history is shown to be closely intertwined with the nonhuman history of the Earth, indeed, with the Universe.

It is not only the composition of the shot that creates this effect. Berríos's story appears as though spoken by the landscape precisely because Berríos has physically become a part of it through her repetitive actions. Of her perpetual searching she says:

> I no longer count the times Vicky [Saavedra] and I have gone into the desert. We set out full of hope and return with our heads hanging. But we always pick ourselves up, give ourselves a shake and set off again the next day even more hopeful and more impatient to find them.

Berríos is shown to be a physical repository of the past, of memories of searching the desert which have been stored up through repetition.[15] Berríos exists in a habitual relationship with the landscape, as though her identity were becoming-nonhuman, through repetition, to the point where she merges with the desert. Her personal testimony demonstrates how entry into the archive of the Universe's memory is offered by human bodies, which are physical repositories of memory, just as the landscape is. Contrary to the subtitled translation ('heads hanging'), here Berríos uses an expression usually meant to describe an avoidance of the truth, 'con la cabeza metida en la tierra' ('with my head in the ground'). This phrase indicates an ostrich-like retreat from reality, as Mario's remains will likely never be found. Yet it also illuminates that she is searching so hard that she has become subsumed within the ground. Her head has effectively been forcibly pushed into the ground by the unremitting search for Mario (his remains have likely been removed from the dessert by the military, to unknown whereabouts). Berríos, again, is at one with the landscape: human and nonhuman history intertwined.

Through Berríos, then, the landscape speaks its oral testimony, of its secrets and lacunas (e.g. where is Mario?), but also of its desire to archive, to record history (Berríos cries in her most emotional moment: 'Some people must wonder why we want bones. I want them. I want them.'). Here, in addition to her moving personal need to have the forgotten history of Mario recognised, Berríos also gives a voice to the landscape, which equally seeks recognition for its own archival qualities: a natural contract to preserve its planetary past as part of the Universe. The choice of Berríos to speak both for herself (and those traumatised by the Cold War) and also for the Earth, in the any-space-whatever, thus ties the desert's wish for bones back to the documentary's construction of a Universe memory which archives matter: the calcium in Berríos's bones, and those of her lost Mario, are the same as that which was formed shortly after the big bang. This Universe memory reaches out, then, through a human mouthpiece, to indicate humanity's implication in this broader nonhuman archiving of history during the Anthropocene.

To conclude this chapter: a landscape of red eyes addressing us from the darkness, telling of the immanent eradication of the histories of endangered species with which humanity is intertwined. A voice emerging from within the landscape, enunciating the lost pasts of those excluded by colonial modernity which are archived underground – from the disappeared, back in time to the miners, then back again to the indigenous, and even to the very minerals of the Earth itself. This chapter has explored these cinematic encounters with the transnational history of humanity's entanglement with the planet: a history now of great import due to the Anthropocene debate, but one which only further foregrounds the history of ecological exclusion that is colonial modernity (from 1492 to the Cold War and beyond). These are key examples from a category of films about the natural contract. In the next chapter I focus on the transnational history of the world since 1492, on colonial modernity's origins, and their imbrication with the racial contract.

Notes

1 It may be that Deleuze intended *visagéification* (1983, 90) to evoke Emmanuel Levinas's *visage* (discussed in Chapter 2), or indeed, considering Deleuze and Guattari's equation of the face with Christ, as a critique of it. I thank Bill Marshall for pointing this out.

2 This idea, that films provide an encounter with a nonhuman landscape, has featured in previous Deleuzian analyses, albeit my argument is distinct from these predecessors (Beugnet 2007, 137–139; Pandian 2011, 53; Deamer 2014, 38–44; Jeong 2013, 104–110; McMahon 2014, 2–6).

3 As outlined in Chapter 1, Jason W. Moore's conceptualisation of modernity as 'capitalist world ecology' (2015, 4), like Serres' position, proceeds from a critique of Descartes's creation of an artificial separation of humanity from nature. Yet Moore positions his idea of intertwined humanity and nature (capitalism being a way of organising nature (2)) in contrast to ideas surrounding 'capitalism's war on the earth' (Foster, Clark and York 2010), which is also Serres' position. Moore indicates how the emergence of differentiations such as modern class, gender, and racial relationships are all forged in the intertwining of capitalism in the 'web of life', as 'bundles of human and extra-human natures, interweaving biophysical and symbolic natures at every scale' (9). What links Serres and Moore are their respective critiques

of humanity's banishment of nature to the past (whether understood as a war or a re-organisation), denying it coevalness. This is typified by contract theory's recourse to a long-departed state of nature out of which the social contract supposedly emerges (Lessnoff 1990, 7).

4 There have been speculative realism-inflected considerations of how contemporary films speculate as to what a nonhuman world or Universe might look like (Kara 2014), but they have not managed to provide a comprehensive argument with respect to the ethical consideration of humanity's engagement with nature found across a world of cinemas (Martin-Jones 2016).

5 It is not unusual for scholars to discuss films with respect to their anthropomorphisation of landscapes (Prager 2010, 97).

6 See also the contributions to Lorraine Daston and Gregg Mitman's *Thinking with Animals* (2006).

7 The sequence is set in Nabua, situated in the region where state security and communist forces first fought in the 1960s (Weerasethakul 2009, 196–197; Ingawanij 2013, 106–107).

8 *Uncle Boonmee* relates to the installation film *A Letter to Uncle Boonmee* (2009) (Kim 2010). Writings on Weerasethakul's other films, which explore the reception of his films in Thailand (Anderson 2009), emphasise his work's position within a 'contact zone' between Asia and the West (Ingawanij and MacDonald 2006), its Buddhist view of human reintegration with nature (Ferrari 2012, 173–174), its status as an 'itinerant cinema' of the 'nation's under-represented others' (Teh 2011, 609), and the role still images and stillness play in the aesthetic in the context of the slow cinema debate (Davis 2016).

9 The archiving of species undertaken by London's Kew Gardens (one of Glavin's examples of an 'ark' for botanical preservation (2006, 207)) is not an altogether altruistic enterprise. For example, in Kew Gardens, British imperialists looked to cultivate rubber seeds stolen from the Americas, which would then provide them with a secure supply of the plant with which to produce rubber in their Asian colonies (Mann 2011, 335–341).

10 Part of Brazil's economic expansion, including the construction of the Trans-Amazon Highway (Franco 1993, 82–83).

11 This is not unlike the agency which Jonathan Burt considers film able to give to animals, in relation to humans, due in particular to the capacity for the encounter with the animal's gaze to position the viewer within nature – as opposed to outside, looking in (2002, 15 and 47). This specific point emerges within Burt's broader argument regarding the potentially 'transformative aspect' of cinematic depictions of animals (15).

12 This technique is again evident in Weerasethakul's later film, *Rak Ti Khon Kaen/Cemetery of Splendour* (Thailand/UK/Germany/France/Malaysia/South Korea/Mexico/USA/Norway, 2015). To emphasise the coexistence of the present along with the spirits of those who lived before and the virtual layers of the past they inhabit (from ancient warrior kings, back as far as the dinosaurs), the film multiplies its use of humanoid mouthpieces: sleeping soldiers, a psychic medium, the spirits of dead princesses, etc.

13 For further background on the development of the scholarly idea of a cinematic ethics for the Anthropocene, prior to this book, see also an article I published in the same year (Martin-Jones 2016).

14 In other works, I interpret several Latin American films which consider recent history in terms of their memorialisation of this traumatic past (Martin-Jones 2011, 69–99; 2013b).

15 This is as Bergson described in *Matter and Memory*, of the storing up of pasts through repeated habitual actions (1896, 77–131).

4

500 YEARS

The North Atlantic trade circuit, the racial contract, encountering others' pasts

This, the second of four chapters of film analysis, explores two films about intercultural encounters across the Atlantic which meditate on colonial modernity's origins and contemporary form: *Como Era Gostoso o Meu Francês/How Tasty Was My Little Frenchman* (Brazil, 1971), and *También la lluvia/Even the Rain* (Spain/Bolivia/Mexico/France, 2010). The films cover early Sixteenth Century colonial interactions between Europeans and indigenous Americans, with implicit resonances for the then Cold War present (*How Tasty*), and the neo-colonialism of contemporary globalisation (*Even the Rain*). These films are characterised by the time-images of the opsign and the crystal of time, respectively. They both conclude with an affection-image in which a direct address to the viewer breaches the fourth wall. The five-hundred-year transnational history on display in these time-images is that of the North Atlantic trade circuit. The films together explore how the entangled histories of white Europeans and indigenous cultures from 1492 onwards – histories integrally linked to the exploitation of the environments and natural resources they traverse (specifically brazil wood (*How Tasty*) and water (*Even the Rain*)) – have been rendered 'lost pasts'.

The encounter with these lost pasts enables viewer hesitation with regard to what Charles W. Mills calls the racial contract, the role of which in determining this period of world history continues into the present. In *How Tasty*, the encounter with an eradicated indigenous past momentarily turns the racial contract on its head, as those typically excluded by it usurp the place occupied by the coloniser. The viewer is thus, perhaps unsettlingly for many, aligned with the position of the colonised. *Even the Rain*, similarly, emphasises the difficulty Europeans have engaging with the other (during the history of colonial modernity, as today), whilst foregrounding the crystal histories though which access can be granted to the lost pasts of world memory. In neither film do we learn about the history of the North Atlantic trade circuit per se. Rather, we encounter the awareness that it has denied coevalness to the people upon whose exploitation the global centrality of Europe was built after 1492.

Time-images: Others' pasts

In *How Tasty*, the encounter between a would-be European coloniser in the early Sixteenth Century and an indigenous tribe of Tupi Indians in what is now Brazil occurs in a pure optical situation (or opsign). Opsigns are discussed by Deleuze amongst his time-image categories, to describe situations in which characters are unable to act so as to influence their destiny. Opsigns are actual images, but in them we see the passing of time for itself because they do not function within a sensory-motor oriented progression of images. In opsigns we encounter situations in which the continuity from perception to action has been suspended. Thus the inhabitant of the interval between the two becomes a (hesitant) seer, unable to act decisively upon what is perceived (as might a doer in the movement-image (1985, 1–2)). Tellingly, this suspended temporal moment, in which the European discoverer of the New World finds himself without the capacity to construct history, is positioned at the origins of colonial modernity.

In *Even the Rain*, the defining time-image is the crystal of time, which encapsulates the coexistence of an actual present that passes and a virtual past that is preserved (1985, 66–94). A film-within-a-film conceit is used to indicate how present-day events under globalisation mirror those of the initial colonial encounter between Europeans and the New World. Whilst corporations have replaced conquistadores, the struggles over ownership of natural resources (gold in the Sixteenth Century, water in the Twenty-First), and the resistance of the indigenous population against exploitation, are indiscernible.

Both of the time-images introduce an uncertainty to history – European colonisation inverted, with a Frenchman enslaved and eaten by indigenous Americans (*How Tasty*); globalisation's exploitation of the Global South as a resistance struggle which (albeit temporarily) includes Europeans (*Even the Rain*). The hesitation which this viewing experience creates culminates each time in an affection-image in which the persistence of the possibility of another's past is emphasised. However, there is a marked difference in the type of affection-image, and the way it functions, to that of the any-space-whatever explored in the previous chapter. Here, an affection-image directly confronts the viewer with the gaze of an indigenous American, representative of all those from the underside of colonial modernity. The affection-image confronts us with the knowledge that another past exists (more concretely, that other pasts exist) subsumed within colonial modernity. In this case, a past in which European and indigenous cultures were – and are – intertwined.

As noted in Chapter 3, the close-up of the face typically belongs to the anthropocentric sensory-motor regime of *Cinema 1*. In the movement-image, the most rudimentary of cinematic journeys into the past, the flashback (conventionally commencing with a facial close-up) affirms a linear timeline. This is a temporal regime distinct from the more associative, non-linear slippages between the virtual sheets of the past of the time-image. Yet, what these close-ups do in the films analysed here, appearing at the close of stories in which Europeans encounter indigenous Americans, is to confront viewers with the moment of the (re)emergence of a lost past, its virtual, latent possibility, before it is reterritorialised into any one (or anyone else's) history, as it would be in the movement-image.

As Amy Herzog clarifies with regard to the temporal uncertainty in the affection-image, it 'exists as a kind of tableau vivant, vibrating immobility, in a perpetual state of inbetween-ness. [...] The face as affection-image marks a threshold between worlds, a moment of forking time where various potential paths, actions and lines of flight intersect' (2008, 68–69). Hence, what looks out at us from the screen in *How Tasty* and *Even the Rain* is a temporal hesitation, a possibility of another history which by definition cannot actualise. This is because, by definition, affect is something forming, but not formed. As Gregory Flaxman and Elena Oxman indicate: 'in cinema [...] the face can become a hesitation, an affective intensity that prolongs itself in an expression in relation to something "as yet" to be seen' (2008, 46). Yet, more specifically, these affection-images cannot actualise by definition, both because the faces emerge at the end of the films (leaving no narrative time left for actualising the potential of the pasts), but – more crucially – because of the exclusion of the people whose faces we see from Eurocentric history. Hence, in these films the faces of indigenous Americans provide an encounter with the possibility of the myriad human pasts of world history which belie the recent destructive past of colonial modernity.

From these faces we do not learn much, if anything, of the excluded histories they represent: only that such (lost) pasts exist. The faces staring back at us from colonial history, then, deny the denial of coevalness by indicating the possible, virtual histories which subsist along with the accepted history of colonial modernity. Hence these two time-image films provide different examples of a similar process of historical reconsideration, undertaken from different geographical and geopolitical perspectives, on the history of the North Atlantic trade circuit.

Transnational history: The North Atlantic trade circuit

From the Fifteenth Century onwards, the North Atlantic trade circuit altered the world system in favour of European dominance (Dussel 1992, 11, 88; 1998a, 5).[1] The circuit was a triangular route. Ships leaving Europe would find port on the coast of Africa, take on board slaves, and sail on the trade winds to the Americas. Their cargoes were sold and the holds filled with the mineral wealth mined from the ground, along with the tobacco, sugar, cotton and other such fruits of slave labour. Westerly winds and the current of the Gulf Stream propelled their return to Europe. The raw materials of the Americas were manufactured into goods (textiles, rum, etc.) destined for the next fleets leaving for Africa. This triangular route was the engine which moved the world system, facilitated the Columbian Exchange, and commenced the Anthropocene (see Introduction).

The study of Atlantic history is widespread (Shannon 2004; Egerton et al. 2007; Canny and Morgan 2011, et al.), propelled by post-war work on colonial history and the African diaspora in particular (Egerton et al. 2007, 3). One of the most famous texts remains Paul Gilroy's *The Black Atlantic* (1993), in which he explores this 'intercultural and transnational formation' to reveal the complexities of how the slave plantations of the Americas (as such 'inside modernity') remained connected to premodern histories (e.g. via oral histories of African ancestry) 'outside' modernity. Accordingly, the Black Atlantic is, for Gilroy, at once inside and outside of modernity (57–58). Thus Robert Stam and Ella Shohat explore the term 'Atlantic Enlightenment' (2012, xiii) to indicate how post-World War Two 'culture wars' across the postcolonial Atlantic can be understood as part of a struggle over colonisation/decolonisation of the region, which stretches back to 1492 (1). Not only the Black, but also the White and Red Atlantics, respectively, all indicate a history of being influenced by, and influencing, colonial modernity: transnational histories intertwining Europe, Africa, and the Americas in the North Atlantic trade circuit. In this chapter, the focus remains primarily on (how the films explore) the White Atlantic.

Aníbal Quijano argues that the discovery of America brought new 'intersubjectivities' (2000, 547), new relationships between European, American and other peoples. European wealth based on the exploitation of labour and resources from Africa and the Americas ensured that new, intertwined identities emerged between 'modern' Europeans and 'primitive' non-Europeans. As noted in the Introduction, the claims to legitimacy of the former position relied entirely on the maintenance of the supposed veracity of the 'primitivism' of the latter, a view built upon hierarchical racial cartographies which emerged after 1492. Hence, for Quijano, the Americas and Europe have a shared history of development as modern geocultural entities, Europe's emergence as a new global centre being intertwined with the encounter between Europeans and others in the exploited global periphery. '[S]tarting with America, a new space/time was constituted materially and subjectively; this is what the concept of modernity names' (2000, 547; 2008, 195).

It is this intertwined Atlantic history which is negotiated in the two films under discussion. Thus, whilst they can be grouped with period films about Atlantic discovery or encounter – *Aguirre, der Zorn Gottes/Aguirre, Wrath of God* (West Germany, 1972), *The Mission* (UKI/France, 1986), *Black Robe* (Canada/Australia/USA, 1991), *1492: Conquest of Paradise* (France/Spain, 1992), *Sankofa* (USA/UK/Ghana/Burkina Faso/Germany, 1993), *Brava gente brasileira/Brave New Land* (Brazil/Portugal, 2000), *The New World* (USA/UK, 2005), *Embrace of the Serpent* (Colombia/Venezuela/Argentina, 2016), *The Lost City of Z* (USA, 2016) – the two under discussion, which focus on the intertwining of European and indigenous histories (the White – experience of the – Atlantic), actually belong with a different trend that considers intertwined subjectivities under colonial modernity much more broadly (see further below). In a context wherein the intertwining of cultures from centre and peripheries which characterises the history of the Atlantic is now played out globally, this trend focuses on the intertwining of histories, as much as people, all over the world (Global North and South now co-existing, globally). It does not solely concern the historical nature of the North Atlantic trade circuit, then, even if the two chosen films here do, but the racial contract which underpins the history of colonial modernity more broadly (encompassing the Atlantic initially, but then spreading globally as per the world system). The two films explored herein are just the most explicit in connecting globalisation's rendering precarious of Eurocentrism (and its attendant white supremacy) to the origins of the rise of Europe via the North Atlantic trade circuit.

Encountering the other: The racial contract

This particular transnational history is marked by what Caribbean philosopher Charles W. Mills considers the (unacknowledged) racial contract which underpins (or more accurately, undermines) the social contract. Mills, like Dussel, opposes the developmental narrative which sees the West's centrality to the globalised present as the result of European exceptionalism. After all, the Enlightenment, the industrial revolution, the emergence of democracy with the French Revolution and the American Wars of Independence (as well as the idea that the social contract elevates humanity out of a supposed state of nature and the introduction of 'race' as a category (the idea of modernity)), all coexist with the chequered history of European colonialism (1997, 62–64). Instead, then, Mills details how the racial contract privileges white people over all others (7). It effectively uses the idea of a preceding state of nature to delineate between those humans who are deemed to have left it, and those (more akin to animals) who still dwell within it. For Mills, the racial contract is thus 'the truth' of the social contract (64).

Like Dussel, Quijano and others, Mills considers the racial contract to be 'clearly historically locatable in the [...] events marking the creation of the modern world by European colonialism and the voyages of "discovery" now [...] more appropriately called expeditions of conquest' (1997, 20). It is the underside of modernity, precisely, which is subjugated by the Christian, supposedly civilising mission emanating from Europe after 1492 (22).

> [W]e live in a world which has been *foundationally shaped for the past five hundred years by the realities of European domination and the gradual consolidation of global white supremacy.* Thus not only is the racial contract 'real', but – whereas the social contract is characteristically taken to be establishing the legitimacy of the nation-state, and codifying morality and law within its boundaries – the racial contract is *global*, involving a tectonic shift of the ethicojuridicial basis of the planet as a whole, the division of the world, as Jean-Paul Sartre put it [...] between 'men' and 'natives'.
>
> *(20)*

In 1492, just as Spain was expanding Westwards though colonialism, it was equally securing the borders of Christian Europe with the *Reconquista*, a military campaign imbricated as it was in 'Judeophobia and Islamophobia' (Shohat 2013, 51). For Ella Shohat, the way of considering otherness in the behaviour of the conquistadores towards the indigenous peoples of the Americas was not very different from that shown towards those 'from' areas to the East of Europe (50–55). For this reason, as Mills notes, the racial contract should be understood as global, and as spreading historically with the growth of the Eurocentric world system.

The racial contract enables a more distinct interpretation than is typical when films about encounters with the New World are explored – even when diverse examples are considered from a world of cinemas with a view to engagement with pasts silenced from official historical accounts.[2] Usually, the emphasis remains on how American history was impacted upon by the intertwining of cultures brought about by European colonisation (e.g. McAuley 2013, 515). Even when the Columbian Exchange is visualised in a film like *The New World*, scholarly engagement typically explores its re-imagining of not the transnational history of the phenomenon, but of American history (e.g. Burgoyne 2010, 120–142). By contrast, the chosen films are analysed with respect to a proliferation of contemporary movies about encounters between different cultures under globalisation (far too numerous to enumerate in full) as diverse as *Calendar* (Armenia/Canada/Germany, 1993) and *La Promesse/The Promise* (Belgium/France/Luxembourg/Tunisia, 1996) in the 1990s, through to *Un cuento chino/Chinese Take Away* (Argentina/Spain, 2011) and *Le Havre* (Finland/France/Germany, 2011) in the early 2010s. Such films illuminate the intertwined nature of human histories (from colonial pasts to neoliberal presents), in our contemporary, global border-crossing world. Hence, in the two examples focusing on Atlantic history, we see the historical depth which belies this feature of globalisation, in the normative construction of Eurocentric/other (world) histories characterising colonial modernity.

How Tasty Was My Little Frenchman

How Tasty is set in 1557, in what is now the State of Rio de Janeiro. The protagonist, if he can be called that, is Jean (Arduíno Colassanti), a French sailor. On his arrival in the New World without a wife, Jean attempts to become friendly with the indigenous Americans. For this impropriety he is accused of mutiny by his puritanical brethren and dumped into the sea in chains. Miraculously, he re-emerges onto dry land (see Figure 4.1) and is captured by Tupiniquim Indians, allies of the Portugese. Forced to fight alongside them due to his expertise with cannon, he is recaptured by rival Tupinambá Indians (allies of the French), who believe him to be Portugese. The Tupinambá decide to keep Jean alive for eight months before sacrificing and eating him. During this time, he is the lover of Sebiopepe (Ana Maria Magalhães) whose husband has been killed in battle. Jean integrates into the tribe, using his skill with cannon to fight alongside

FIGURE 4.1   History hesitates, before it is washed away as by the tides of time, in *Como Era Gostoso o Meu Francês/How Tasty Was My Little Frenchman* (Nelson Pereira dos Santos, 1971).

the Tupinambá against the Portugese, but he is unable to escape. Amusingly, his attempts to hijack Tupinambá myths of ancestral origin to establish himself as a god-like figure (emulating the mythical ancestor Mair, who taught the use of fire, food and weapons (Peña 1995, 197; Sadlier 2003, 66)) are spurned by the tribe. Similarly when Jean murders a French trader in a squabble over a stash of gold and jewellery taken from the grave of another murdered trader, his attempts to escape with it are foiled by Sebiopepe, who shoots him in the leg with an arrow.

The final scenes see Jean sacrificed in a ritual for which he is prepared by Sebiopepe. Yet, with his last words Jean refuses to play his allotted role as sacrifice, and instead foretells the coming eradication of his Tupi hosts at the hands of the Europeans. The final credits are preceded by intertitles in blood-red lettering, containing a letter from the Governor General of Brazil, Mem de Sá, proudly detailing the (historical fact of the) extermination in battle of the Tupiniquim. Between Jean's death and the intertitles, however, is one of the most distinctive endings in the history of cinema. Sebiopepe, gnawing with relish on Jean's barbequed neck, breaks the fourth wall and stares directly at camera (see Figure 4.2). Her dark eyes fill the screen in close-up, framed by colourful ceremonial face paint. Then, the camera lingers over a tableau of the Tupinambá, paying homage to their existence – and genocide – in this historical moment. Finally, there is a shot of an empty beach. This location is integral to the film because it provides the pure optical and sound situation which Jean encounters at the start of the film and reappears here to bear testimony to the passing of the Tupi. In the letter that follows in the closing

FIGURE 4.2 Having an old friend for dinner, in *Como Era Gostoso o Meu Francês/How Tasty Was My Little Frenchman* (Nelson Pereira dos Santos, 1971).

intertitles, just such a shoreline is described by the Governor General as littered with the dead Tupiniquim he has vanquished.

Nelson Pereira dos Santos is one of Brazil's most influential directors. He spent an influential two months in Paris in 1949, where he saw several neorealist films (Traverso 2007, 173). In the 1950s he made socially committed films like *Rio, 40 graus/Rio, 40 degrees* (Brazil, 1955) and became one of the key members of Cinema Novo movement with *Vidas sêcas/Barren Lives* (Brazil, 1963). But *How Tasty* stands out from these earlier films, both for its dark humour and its direct engagement with colonial history. There are various ways in which *How Tasty,* which appeared in the same year as the Uruguayan Eduardo Galeano's *Open Veins of South America* (1971) and the Cuban Roberto Fernández Retamar's *Caliban* (1971) (both reconsidering Latin America's history and its relationship to Europe), can be explored in relation to history. In this, the film's original literary source is important to consider.

How Tasty is based on the diary of a German, Hans Staden, who claimed that he lived for a while as a captive of indigenous Americans, in 1556, awaiting his fate in the same manner as Jean. Unlike the protagonist of Dos Santos's film, Staden, if his story has credibility, escaped to tell the tale. He frames his account, in fact, as one in which his Christian God intervenes to save him, describing the sickness which carries off many indigenous people as an act of God working towards his (Staden's) salvation (tacitly indicating precisely how the horror of colonisation comes to be re-written as a supposedly civilising mission (1557, 69)).

Existing scholarship typically notes that *How Tasty* changes Staden's identity from German to French to recognise that the French colonised the areas seen in the film (Stam 1997, 248–249) and to reflect the role of French culture in Brazil since the early Nineteenth Century, in spite of the initial, predominantly Portugese, colonisation (Sadlier 2003, 63). We can add that the Portugese and the French were fighting in this part of the world over trade in brazil wood (Staden 1557, ix). Thus, Frenchman Jean is pushed off the map in the first place due to his desire to profit by transforming nature (see Jason W. Moore, in Chapter 1). This historical reimagining relates directly to the moment of the film's making. The film conflates the discovery of the Americas with the shifting political moment of the Cold War, and in particular the economic expansion favouring the global marketplace at the expense of national assets like the Amazon and its indigenous cultures (in the devastation wrought in the building of the Trans-Amazonian Highway (Sadlier 2003, 70–71)), in which Brazil under military rule was embroiled. As was the case with colonialism, it was evident that such Cold War developments were intended to enrich the few at the expense of the many. This understanding of the film is evident in the extensive existing literature, from which two indicative arguments can be highlighted (Xavier 1993; Peña 1995; Stam 1997; Young 2001; Sadlier 2003; Nagib 2007; Gordon 2009; Pérez de Miles 2013).

Firstly, *How Tasty* is indebted to *Tropicalismo*, which impacts on its depiction of Brazilian history. The Tropicalist Movement of late 1960s Brazil reacted against the military government (1964 onwards), resurrecting aspects of the Cannibalist Movement of the 1920s, as typified by Oswald de Andrade's 'Manifesto Antropofago/Cannibalist Manifesto' (1928). Andrade advocated cultural cannibalism, in which Brazilian identity is constructed through the consumption (cannibalist consumption, that is) of cultural aspects from inside and outside the nation. These aspects are then incorporated into the autonomous national culture. In *How Tasty*, cannibalism is used as a metaphor that turns on its head the previous labelling of native Brazilians as primitive and therefore justifiably exterminated by European colonisers. Indeed, Staden's book was first published in Brazil in 1900, and was an influence on de Andrade, so it is not surprising that – coming later on in this legacy of rethinking the past – the film actively debunks the notion that Staden might have escaped due to his Tarzan-like ability to transcend the indigenous culture with the help of his Christian God (Staden 1557, x–xvi). Instead, as per the notion of cultural cannibalism, in *How Tasty,* Brazilian cannibals enslave and then eat the European, their bodies becoming intertwined just as their identities were in the founding of Brazil. This is one apparent meaning of the film's final images, of Sebiopepe staring out at us as she eats Jean's neck, inviting audiences in Brazil to consider their identity as Brazilians in the eating of 'my' (or 'our') little Frenchman. *How Tasty*, then, aims to engage the audience in its construction of a people, just as the Tropicalist Movement did (Peña 1995, 194; Stam 1997, 250; Nagib 2007, 68–69).

Secondly, *How Tasty* is typically interpreted at the convergence of broader Latin American reconsiderations of the continent's history and the experience of Brazilians under the military regime. It critiques the recurrence of the same uneven power structures of colonisation under the Brazilian economic policy and military crackdown enacted by the US-backed dictatorship. Here, the film's opening scene is much discussed for its deconstruction of colonial history formations, the myth-making they involve, and the casual loss of life on which they are built. This it does by juxtaposing ironically conflicting image and voiceover accounts of the arrival of Europeans under Nicolas Durand de Villegagnon, the leader of the French Protestant settlers of Guanabara Bay. The voiceover history we hear is at odds with the images we see – the film contrasting two different accounts of historical events (Sadlier 2003, 61), to humorously undercut the veracity of the historical record, both with regard to colonisation and the contemporary treatment of political opponents of the military regime (Stam 1997, 250; Sadlier 2003, 70–71; Nagib 2007, 71). Looking back from an era of fake news, what we recognise here is a playful engagement with cognitive dissonance in the enunciation of official history.

What can be added to this existing body of work on the film's playful questioning of the veracity of history, then, is the role of the time-image in situating such a narrative within Atlantic history, itself part of a world cinematic history of intercultural encounters during colonial modernity which continues under globalisation.

Opsign, off the colonial map

The time-image appears early on in the film, and is used to express the moment of European encounter with the New World. The film's ill-fated French protagonist, Jean, emerges from his attempted execution at the hands of his European comrades and wanders along the shore, accompanied by the sounds of native flutes, his movements impeded by the ball and chain attached to his ankle. In this moment, after being pushed off the colonial map, he meanders along alone in a pure optical and sound situation (opsign). After his effective banishment from the settler community, Jean encounters a situation to which he is unable to adequately react, and becomes instead a seer. Jean has lost his ability to perpetuate a linear historical narrative, lost the mastery of the world which accompanies Eurocentrism. Indeed, his banishment from the temporality of the European settlers is a punishment for fraternizing with the indigenous in the first place, for abhorring his place within the colonial order by attempting to enter into a more intertwined relationship with the naked native women. It is not a coincidence that, at this point, Jean is captured by the indigenous Americans.

In *How Tasty*, then, it is very explicitly the discovery of America – as a moment out of history – which is expressed through the use of a time-image. This also indicates, by turns, how European identity is grounded on the establishing of one dominant view of time at the expense of myriad others. In *How Tasty*, Jean's life becomes intertwined with that of the Tupinambá in a manner that expresses Quijano's view of modern intersubjectivities, albeit in an inverted parody as Jean is the Tupinambá's slave. In this time-image, Jean, the seer, is a witness whose sensory-motor interruption illustrates precisely the intertwined (albeit, unbalanced) mutuality of the experience of colonial modernity. However, Jean, wandering along the beach on his arrival, explores the same space which we know, from history, will soon be littered with dead Tupi. Thus this opsign encapsulates the existence of other times to that of European modernity, but simultaneously recognises the reality of the death of the other (and other times) that this encounter brings.

For Deleuze, the time-image has the ability to demonstrate the temporal division of the self, the realisation that time is a labyrinth in which 'I is another' replaces 'Ego = Ego' (Deleuze 1985, 129). *How Tasty*, by focusing on the time-image of the empty beach at the beginning and end, asserts the temporal division of the self-same that occurs in the intercultural colonial encounter so as to undermine the Cartesian certainty upheld by Eurocentric versions of history. The resurgence of the opsign of the deserted beach shows how only the eradication of the other (the dead, absent now, but historically littering the beach) can create the illusion of a singular self and a singular linear history. Prior to this, however, history hesitated. It was initially suspended in the opsign, when other possibilities still existed (Jean's stay of execution, his life with the Tupi). In *How Tasty* the encounter between Jean and Sebiopepe demonstrates how the Eurocentric myth of the unassailable ego, based on the relegation of all others and their times to the primitive past (with the discovery of the Americas) is at odds with the reality of the intertwined histories of the Atlantic and the world system more broadly. It demonstrates the unstable, illusory position of the Western ego by juxtaposing the myth of its historical construction (in the initial colonial encounter) with the reality of its intertwined history of development along with the Americas.

Face to face with Sebiopepe

This time-image narrative, providing a shorthand way of thinking about five hundred years of colonial modernity, sets up the closing affection-image in which the ethical encounter with a lost past is offered. In the film's most iconic moment, Sebiopepe eats Jean's neck, the most sought-after part of the human by the Tupi. As she chews hungrily, her gaze directly to the camera challenges viewers to consider their relationship to this history and their role in the process by which the other becomes consumable material. At the time of the film's release this image was primarily intended to address Brazilian spectators, engaging directly with the cannibalism of the Tropicalismo movement. It questions Brazilian identity in relation to the indigenous American, as opposed to the European coloniser. As Stam notes, *How Tasty* asks the viewer to consider whether the cannibalism of the Tupinambá is anything like as devastating as the economic 'cannnibalism' of colonisation (1997, 251). Yet, as the focus of recent scholarship on this scene with respect to the film's portrayal of women indicates (Gordon 2009; Pérez de Miles 2013), this image of Sebiopepe also offers an unusual viewing experience in contrast with the usual Eurocentrism, or rather, globalcentrism, of metropolitan audiences. Sebiopepe's gaze suggests that the viewer takes the position of the powerless European, Jean, unable to assert a meaningful identity in the time-image. Instead they are confronted with alteriority: pre-modern, indigenous, woman, cannibal. All that Tarzan should be able to command is eating Tarzan, and with relish. The historical construction of the looking/looked-at relationship of Europe and the Americas over several centuries of Western art (of the clothed European man imposing his history upon the unclothed body of the indigenous American woman (Beardsell 2000, 14)) is not only inverted, but openly ridiculed. The import of this realisation is given an even stronger temporal dimension in the images that follow.

After Sebiopepe's confronting gaze, the film offers a stylised moment of contemplation, a striking tableau in which the Tupi tribe stand still in ranks, and the camera pans across them, whilst loud chanting is heard on the soundtrack. This image is immediately followed by the end titles, which describe De Sá's massacre of the Tupi: 'I fought on the sea, so that no Tupiniquim remained alive. Laid along the shore the dead covered almost a league.' This ending provides an encounter with an indigenous American history which was first relegated to the past, then all but extinguished through massacre (in this specific instance by the Portugese), in order that the European ego could become the dominant form. What the viewer encounters, then, is not solely another identity, but – as per the potential of the time-image to enable a becoming-other via the connection to another (lost) past – an occluded history. This image provides a chance to encounter this lost past, intertwined as it is in Atlantic history.

The temporal dimension of this ethical encounter ties together the Deleuzian time-image with a Dusselian ethics, to illustrate how the construction of the self-same European ego is founded upon the denial of the intertwined histories of the world system. The affection-image here includes, literally, the 'tableau vivant' which Herzog discusses as indicative of its potential as 'a threshold between worlds, a moment of forking time where various potential paths, actions and lines of flight intersect' (2008, 68–69). It is so effective because it arrives at the culmination of a film in which the expected conventions of the encounter movie (in which a Tarzan-like coloniser subdues primitive natives) are inverted (Peña 1995, 193; Stam 1997, 249). Jean's captivity does not provide the space for a masterful anthropological observation of the other, but rather situates him at a distance from his usual place within a narrative of teleological progress. As Nagib indicates, this is apparent in the way that the film is edited, so as to avoid privileging any one unified point of view throughout (2007, 71–72). For instance, early on Jean is observed from the perspective of a Tupi crouching in the jungle, making him the object of the gaze which controls that territory. This is precisely because, when falling off the colonial map, he encounters an opsign and lives his remaining months as a seer in a situation which he is not able to act to change. Instead, he can only witness the possibility of another history, which relativises the supposed centrality of his own.

Thus the affection-images, of Sebiopepe devouring Jean, and the tableau of the now exterminated tribe who held him captive, offer a glimpse of the other pathways through history denied coevalness by colonial modernity. Of course, Jean's final prophecy at the moment of his execution does come true ('my friends will come, to revenge me. No one of yours will remain upon this land'), as we are shown in the opsign of the now deserted beach which was, soon after Jean's death, laid end-to-end with dead Tupi. Colonial action, decidedly, replaced the uncertainty of the seer, as the opsign was conquered by a narrative of progress offered by the Europeans' civilising mission. Nevertheless, the reason for Jean's arrival, as a sailor involved in the international wood trade, emphasises the coincidence of colonial modernity with the Anthropocene, and the correlation between European denials of coevalness (the destroying of other possible pathways through history) and the attendant practices of colonial enslavement and extermination in the North Atlantic trade circuit.

How Tasty, as well as negotiating what was a shifting economic and ecological historical moment, adds the ethical shift, which was occurring simultaneously. The affection-image that concludes the film asks us to consider, how were societies organised along lines of mutual endebtedness, prior to the racial contract? As David Graeber argues of the rise of capitalism in the Fifteenth Century (which he effectively aligns with the growth of the world system), along with Europe's exploitation of Peruvian and Mexican precious metals, the conquistadores like Hernán Cortés were often deeply in debt and sought New World plunder as a result (2011, 307–325). Both the human toll of the murderous intent of colonial modernity and the ecological damage caused by extracting profit from nature are therefore inextricably intertwined in the origins of the Anthropocene. The arrival of Europeans in the Americas destroyed or irrevocably transformed societies in which people were connected in networks of mutual indebtedness, through the imposition of impersonal relationships of credit and interest, including those extended to would-be adventurers on foreign soil (332). This was, for Graeber, the result of capitalism's rise along with colonisation (with colonial modernity, in fact), which rendered people strangers to one another (slaves, for example, become objects once removed from their embeddedness in societies of networked obligations (347)), and through the establishing of relations of credit/interest which encouraged slavery, genocide and ecological devastation in the service of transforming nature into profit (307–360). The North Atlantic trade circuit, after Graeber, can be understood as a 'giant chain of debt obligations' (347).

Jean's time with the tribe, and his execution, indicate the very different sense of contractual reciprocity (including a mutuality to being in balance with the world) upon which pre-Columbian indigenous American societies were often ethically aligned (Graeber 2011, 136; Maffie 2013). For Eduardo Viveiros de Castro, a voice surprisingly unreferenced in existing discussions of the film, the cannibalism of the Tupinambá society is not to be understood as simply a vengeful measure providing a restorative function to society (i.e. one warrior is sacrificed to replace another). This is too simplistic. Rather, the physical incorporation of Jean in the ritual cannibalistic act can be understood, after Viveiros de Castro, as part of a wider social relationship of reciprocity amongst the Tupi – who were intertwined through their mutually defining relationship to war and the consumption of the flesh of their enemies (1986, 273–306).

Cannibalism for the Tupi had a creative function. It was only possible to reach the status of an adult man able to procreate by killing another in battle (279). Thus society could only reproduce because of the reciprocity, amongst tribes, of death – death of others, and at the hands of others (283). For this reason, being killed and eaten in such a ritual was not considered as unpleasant a form of death as was, for example, passing away peacefully at home (288–289). This was because, through warfare and cannibalism, 'individual death' served as 'the fuel for social life' (290). In a situation where 'one is always and before all else the enemy of someone, and this is what defines the self' (284), what is eaten in the ritual in which Jean is consumed (albeit, tellingly, he refuses to play the allotted role in it, foreshadowing the destruction that Europeans would bring to such reciprocally intertwined cultural norms) is the very position of being an enemy: of enmity (286). The role which the sacrificial victim should have played, and in which Jean was instructed (Sebiopepe taught him to say, at the point of death, 'when I die my friends will come to revenge me'), suggests precisely the ongoing nature of this reciprocal intertwining. The victim is almost reassuring his captors that the vengeance which will follow (although it may mean the death of his captors) will nevertheless ensure the continuation of the Tupi.

Tellingly, this role is refused by Jean in favour of a different idea of revenge, one which validates instead the dominance of the European ego over the indigenous. His 'friends', as he predicts, in a proclamation in French which his captors cannot possibly understand, do indeed return to avenge him and, as Jean prophesises, to the point where no Tupi are left alive. Thus in the extermination of the Tupi, whose fate has disappeared from the empty beaches of the closing opsign, the Europeans establish the inequality of worth (one European life can be avenged by millions of indigenous lives) that is the racial contract, founding it directly upon the very eradication of this former, more reciprocal, ethics of cannibalist consumption.

What the racial contract also excludes from history, then, as *How Tasty* illustrates by situating its story in an opsign, is the possibility that society might be organised differently, ethically. This, whether in the specific manner of the Tupinambá which Viveiros de Castro outlines, or more broadly, as it was when, as Graeber argues, endebtedness was a way of organising mutually reinforcing community relationships, rather than of accruing personal wealth (2011, 207–208).[3] Noticeably, due to this very different functioning of the society which Jean encounters in the opsign, in which a contrasting idea of contractual obligations exists to that of the racial contract (one in which Jean can live with the dead man's wife as if she were his own), he is unable to know how to act so as to change his situation.

Finally, who does this affection-image address nowadays? At the time of the film's production, the title of the film indicates with its emphasis on 'my' little Frenchman, the intended target of this gaze was Brazilians. The film attempts to make Brazilian audiences complicit in the consumption of an alternative origin that might inform national history, an intertwining of cultures, rather than a colonial imposition.[4] Yet, even at the time of its release in Brazil, the film, which was subtitled because the dialogue is either in Tupi-Guarani (the country's dominant language prior to the arrival of Europeans) or French, would have seemed to represent the old adage that the past is a 'foreign country', even to Brazilian audiences (Stam 1997, 250; Nagib 2007, 69). Nowadays, as we can no longer be so sure of the film's contemporary audience, as it circulates globally on DVD and online, the viewer who is stared at, as they look in on the past, has been pushed off the colonial map. Like Jean, they must wander in the opsign, there to encounter a forgotten history of the Atlantic. They can but recognise, in Jean's failed attempts to impose himself upon the tribe as their coloniser, the historically constructed nature of the normative position of the European ego which forms after 1492. Sebiopepe's gaze, in fact, returns us to the origins of the Anthropocene, in the story of a European caught up in a historical moment in which the escalating tensions between indigenous tribes caused by the arrivals of the Europeans (and the competition to source brazil wood) led to the destruction of another society, another ethics.

Jean's murder of a fellow Frenchman who makes his living by trading with the Tupinambá, over a small quantity of jewels and gold, suggests something of the greed for mineral wealth of the conquistadores. Yet this is to obscure the greater worth of the natural world being stolen by the Europeans. If we view *How Tasty* with an 'ecological eye' (see Chapter 3), for much of the film we are watching events set in a natural world, where trees are omnipresent, and a human environment constructed entirely from wood. Brazil wood, then, is the resource for which the Europeans will commit genocide. With the inter-tribal warfare that accompanied the European demand for brazil wood, the desire for gunpowder would grow amongst the Tupi tribes

> into a sort of dependence as tensions between the indigenous American tribes – in this case the Tupiniquim and the Tupinambá – were exacerbated by the Europeans. This creation of a dependence economy, based upon the technological superiority of the Europeans, gave them the upper hand in commercial dealings with the tribespeople.
>
> *(Peña 1995, 195)*

Thus it is in Jean's mastery of cannon (which saves his life for a time, rather than Staden's Christian God) that the equation between colonial modernity and the Anthropocene is most evident. Via the trading of gunpowder for brazil wood, *How Tasty* alludes to the reorganising of nature via what Moore calls the 'Four Cheaps' of the capitalist world ecology emerging after 1492 (see Chapter 1).

Sebiopepe stares at us from out of the past, then, to request a remembrance of this lost past, a reminder of indigenous genocide, of ecological imperialism, but also of another possible (lost) past and its equally lost ethics.

Even the Rain

The second film provides a European perspective on the transnational history of the North Atlantic trade circuit. The encounter it offers is also with the inglorious European past of colonisation and (indigenous) American resistance to it, but with a focus on how this past is reflected in present-day struggles and how this can be *realised* from a European perspective (see Figure 4.3). *Even the Rain* (written and directed by Paul Laverty, from Scotland, and Icíar Bollaín, from Spain)[5] is set during the water war which erupted due to the privatisation of water in Bolivia. It takes place during the riots in Cochabamba, in April 2000, between protestors (the Coalition in Defence of Water and Life) and the police and army (Laverty 2011, 7–8). The film is structured in *mise-en-abyme*. A Spanish film crew arrives in Bolivia to shoot a historical drama about the discovery of the Americas by Columbus in 1492, and gets caught up in the demonstrations and violence against the people. The crew learns first-hand about the events they become embroiled in, a process which also provides the viewer with access to knowledge about the actual historical events of the water war.

Once again, this story of colonial modernity, exploring the transnational history of the Atlantic, has a strong ecological dimension. *Even the Rain* examines how the latest phase in colonial modernity (that marked by neoliberal economic doctrine, during which multinational corporations exclude local populations from their own natural resources with the complicity of an elite political class) is intricately linked to the global environmental changes of the Anthropocene which commenced with Spanish desire for gold in 1492. In Bolivia, in line with the US-backed exposure of Latin American economies to global market forces during the latter stages of the Cold War, the New Economic Policy established

FIGURE 4.3   Colonial modernity – then as now, in *También la lluvia/Even the Rain* (Icíar Bollaín, 2010).

in 1985 opened the door to the privatisation of state industries and natural resources, with the approval of the IMF and World Bank. Water war activist Oscar Olivera, a spokesman for the Coalition in Defence of Water and Life, argues that such neoliberal activities cost the Bolivian people more in terms of debt accrued than any of the previous dictatorships (2004, 12–15). The title of the film, then, alludes to the capping of private wells and banning of the use of water tanks to collect rain water, under laws passed by the government in support of the purchase of the nation's water by a multinational consortium (Aguas del Tunari – renamed Aguas de Bolivia in the film – which included the US corporation Bechtel) (Olivera 2004, 58–60). Ordinary Bolivians found themselves facing exorbitant prices for water (even rainwater was not theirs by right) and took to the streets in protest. Ultimately the water war ended with the deal with Bechtel cancelled, a rare but now touchstone success in the resistance of organised people, united against neoliberalism and multinational corporations controlling their natural resources.

Whilst turn of the Twenty-First Century Bolivia is not a part of the North Atlantic trade circuit as it would be understood historically – albeit there was plenty of trade from the West coast of South America during the same period – even so the point the film makes, by having the filmmakers choose to set their recreation of the discovery in Bolivia due to the reduced costs it offers, is that the same exploitation occurs under globalisation as it did during former phases of colonial modernity. All that has changed is that arrival is by aeroplanes not caravels, the exploitation by multinationals not colonial states. The effect, however, remains the same: the struggle against inequality (increasingly, for survival, as the Earth's natural resources grow scarcer), which defines existence for those excluded from colonial modernity, means that the attempted eradication (or reassertion in the present) of indigenous history is a battle that recurs down the centuries.

Even the Rain has already received considered critical attention, typically as a Spanish film, due to Bollaín's role as director. Its foregrounded reconsideration of colonial history leads many scholars to focus on transatlantic history, the potential transformation of Eurocentric viewpoints through encounters with different cultures under globalisation, ethics (as a result of the former), human rights, and ecology (Santaolalla 2012; Cilento 2012; Hageman 2013; Wheeler 2013; Hulme-Lippert 2015; Weiser 2014). Whilst conclusions drawn with respect to the film's appeal to Spanish audiences are useful (e.g. Duncan Wheeler argues that 'Bollaín is trying to make Spanish audiences more aware of their trespasses in the past and present in order to inculcate an ethics of humility' (2013, 251–252)), of particular relevance are two pieces which consider the film's transnational appeal in ways which approach my own conclusions.

Firstly, Santaolalla, noting the film's place amidst a longer heritage of Spanish films to consider Spain's relationship with the Americas and its place in Bollaín's career trajectory (which sees similar concerns with intercultural exchanges under globalisation in films like *Flores de otro mundo/Flowers from Another World*

(Spain, 1999)), discusses *Even the Rain*'s self-consciousness with respect of its 'transatlantic imperialism', and how it questions the 'assumptions and positions of dominance' of Costa and its other European protagonists (Santaolalla 2012, 211–212). Santaolalla argues that 'with the fusion of Daniel and Costa, of white European and Latin American Indian perspectives, the film tries to appeal to transatlantic as well as to peninsular audiences. Very importantly, *También la lluvia* is not just neutrally transnational. Its transnationalism is inspired by its concerns with socially conscious, postcolonial sensibilities, and variations on perspective' (219). Secondly, Andrew Hageman analyses the film alongside others that depict the water war, considering it a work of 'ideological ecocriticism' that offers 'a glimpse of capital in desperation' (2013, 75). The failure of events in the neo-colonial present to entirely match with those in the colonial past (the multinationals fail where the Conquistadores previously succeeded in their exploitative projects) indicates for Hageman something of the breaking point of global capitalism due to 'catastrophic unemployment and ecological devastation' (75).

Whilst sharing common ground with these predecessors, my interpretation is a little different. Although the film's headline star is arguably Mexican Gael García Bernal, playing director Sebastián, *Even the Rain* primarily focuses on the reconstruction of the film's Spanish producer, Costa (Luis Tosar). He learns that the colonial history they are recreating for the film is one he himself is involved in perpetuating in the present. The film-within-a-film is intended to redress Eurocentric visions of world history. The film's depiction of Columbus as a gold-obsessed, insatiably cruel soldier reconsiders a long history of cinematic depictions of this legendary European explorer.[6] Moreover, the film crew is repeatedly shown recreating the exploitative power dynamics of colonialism and historical revisionism: for instance, by brushing over the casting of Quechua-speaking Andean Indians as Taíno Indians (from the Caribbean), which language to use, how much the language will have changed in the interim, and so on. In this way, the mise-en-abyme structure meditates openly upon the difficulty of depicting the initial moment of colonial contact as a historical drama (Laverty 2012). But it also enables the narrative arc of Costa's reconstruction, key moments of which take place in time-images in which the film formally contrasts past and present in a crystalline manner.

Costa is initially depicted as the most cynical of all the film crew, happy to exploit the local populace in order to produce his film cheaply. He describes Bolivia as 'full of starving Indians', who are 'all the same'. Ultimately, however, Costa decides to help the Bolivians in their struggle for the right to their own water, including Daniel (Juan Carlos Aduviri), an Andean indigenous American, and his family. Daniel is a leader of his people in the water war and is also chosen by the filmmakers to play Hatuey, a Taíno Indian leader in the film-within-a-film (historically, Hatuey led a rebellion against the Spanish and was burnt at the stake for it in 1512). As rioting erupts and the film crew flee for their safety, Costa returns to Cochabamba to use his privileged position as a Westerner to bring Belén (Milena Soliz), Daniel's daughter (who has been badly injured during the protests), through the roadblocks to medical assistance. As Isabel Santaolalla notes, in spite of the Judeo-Christian imagery and references interwoven throughout the film, Costa actually plays 'a secular redemptive role' (2012, 212–213). His reconstruction, then, speaks to ideas of liberation as a historical, rather than spiritual or transcendent, condition by its framing within the history of colonial modernity. In part for this reason, the film deliberately indicates that the reconstruction of Costa is likely a temporary one, as he returns to Spain at the film's conclusion and indicates an unwillingness to return. Like so many films set in the Americas, a Western perspective is thus offered as an entrance point to the film for viewers from beyond the region where the film is set. Yet for Costa, like Frenchman Jean before him, what promises to be a potentially Tarzan-like entry point ultimately becomes that of one whose control over the land he encounters falters, in his realisation of the intertwined nature of his history with its. In this way, the assumed centrality of Eurocentric world history to his personal worldview is challenged.

The difference between this reading and the existing field can now be seen. Firstly, it places as much emphasis on Laverty's influence as scriptwriter as it does on Bollaín as director, because of the resonances between Laverty's influences and this book's Dusselian-inspired interpretation of a world of cinemas. Secondly, whilst – like Hageman – my cross-border analysis creates a distant view, unlike his broader rationale for grouping films around a contemporary event like the water war and a concern with ecology, here the taxonomising is propelled by the uncovering of how different films depict transnational history. This is also what distinguishes my focus on transatlantic history from Santaolalla's perspective on the film within Spanish or Hispanic traditions. Indeed, whilst I also examine the film in terms of an ethics, I do not consider this to necessarily be a matter solely for Spanish audiences, as in Hageman's position. More important than any of these differences, and where I commence my argument, is that this analysis focuses on the film's deployment of a time-image in the construction of transnational history on film.

Crystal, Sixteenth Century colonial/Twenty-First Century neoliberal

The time-image that characterises *Even the Rain* is that of the crystal of time in which is glimpsed the coexistence of past and present. The film uses its crystalline structure to repeatedly draw parallels between the events in the historical past and those in the present. The virtual image of the history of the European conquest of the Americas and the resistance of the indigenous Americans (the film-within-the-film) comes to oscillate with the actual present-day protests of the water war so as to demonstrate their indiscernibility (Deleuze 1985, 66–121). Then, as now, this equation indicates, it was a struggle for wealth derived from the natural resources of the Americas in which different cultures, histories, and times become intertwined.

There are many examples of this in the film. Columbus's meeting with Hatuey and other indigenous Americans (in which he announces the levying of a tax in gold on every indigenous 'Indian' over fourteen) is reflected in confrontations between Daniel's community and corporation workers sent to cap their well. Similarly, the recreation of the Dominican Friar Antonio de Montesinos's famous sermon of 1511 – in which he denounced the Spanish for their mistreatment of indigenous Americans and questioned, rhetorically, 'Are these not men? Do they not have rational souls?' (Pagden 1992, xxi) – is immediately mirrored in the present by Daniel's speeches during the water war in which he stirs up his countrymen, saying, 'What are they going to steal next? The vapour from our breath? The sweat from our brows? All they'll get from me is piss!' Again, the depiction of the Spanish conquistadores' use of attack dogs to hunt down and kill the indigenous Americans in the Sixteenth Century finds its present-day mirror in the presence of dogs accompanying the Bolivian police and military as they run through the tear gas clouded streets to engage the water war protestors.

Of all such instances, the pivotal scene (its most direct image of time), occurs when shooting is disrupted by the arrival of the police in the present, to arrest Daniel on the set (see Figure 4.3). Here, the previous technique of cross-cutting between past and present events gives way to a more general confusion between virtual and actual layers of time, such that they become indiscernible. In the film-within-a-film, Daniel is playing Hatuey, the indigenous American who led a rebellion against the Spanish colonisers, and the scene in question is his public execution by immolation, along with twelve of his co-conspirators. His verbal defiance of the Spanish engenders solidarity and resistance amongst the assembled indigenous Americans, who chant his name as he dies. Then, as the shoot wraps, the Bolivian police arrive to arrest Daniel, who is still dressed as Hatuey. Their modern-day police van seems incongruous against the lush green setting (filmed in the Chapare jungle (Santaolalla 2012, 201)), in which signs of contemporary civilisation are absent from the film crew's viewfinders.

Continuing this surreal effect, as Daniel/Hatuey is bundled into the back of the police van, the rest of the cast, also dressed as Sixteenth Century indigenous Americans, come to his rescue, tipping over the van so that he is released. As Costa and Sebastían intervene to stop the scared police from shooting anyone, Daniel/Hatuey is aided in his escape by his friends. In this scene, more than any other, the conflation between events in past and present foregrounds how the 'policing' of the indigenous Americans by the Spanish conquistadores in the past is recreated by the actions of the anonymous police serving the elite (who profit from collaboration with the multinationals, in the present). The rebellion by the indigenous Americans is likewise literally repeated in the present, as the extras aid Daniel/Hatuey in his escape. In a nutshell, the crystal shows, the struggles of the Bolivians to retain access to their water is the same as that of the indigenous Americans to retain control of their land and natural resources over five hundred years ago.

Sebastían and Costa are complicit in Daniel's near-arrest, as it is they who convinced the Bolivian police to release him temporarily, to enable them to shoot the final scenes of their movie. This implication of the film crew in the exploitation of the indigenous Americans is crucial for the film's conclusion, in which Costa finally develops empathy for the struggle of Daniel and his family. The crew's realisation of their own actions as, effectively, slave traders in the Americas, is integral to the film's contention that the history we glimpse in the present is the same global struggle which followed the discovery of the Americas: that between the multitude and the 'counterrevolution on a global scale' (Hardt and Negri 2000, 77) (see Introduction and Chapter 2).

It is not coincidental that a key figure in the execution scene in question is Bartolomé de Las Casas. Las Casas was a Dominican Friar who arrived in the Americas in 1503, was ordained a priest in 1510, but was initially involved in obtaining wealth from colonial oppression. He later went against the Catholic Church and began to argue against the devastation that the colonial project caused to the indigenous American tribes (Pagden 1992, xviii–xxii). Accordingly, he remains a historical precursor to contemporary liberation theology and philosophy (Dussel 1996, xviii–xxii). The film references events described in Las Casas's *Short Account of the Destruction of the Indies* (1542), which details his experiences during the initial colonial encounters. This work provides a stark account of the genocide (the slaughter, torture, slavery and disease) wrought on the indigenous Americans by the Spanish. The film dramatises and condenses certain of the events detailed in Las Casas's account, including the dramatic scene of the thirteen sacrificial pyres to represent Jesus and his twelve apostles (which precedes the bungled arrest of Daniel/Hatuey), Hatuey's last words (that he would prefer to go to hell than reside in heaven with the Christians) and the use of attack dogs to kill indigenous Americans (Las Casas 1552, 15–17, 28). Indeed, in the film-within-a-film, the character Las Casas (Carlos Santos) appears prominently at the execution of Hatuey, in the film's pivotal time-image.

The appearance of Las Casas in the film can be traced to various origins: he features in the first chapter of Howard Zinn's *A People's History of the United States* (1980), the original inspiration for the film, and Laverty's personal background included formative years spent in Latin America during the 1980s, during which he encountered trades unionists and human rights activists influenced by the theology of liberation (whose courage to act on their conscience he found in the outspoken critics of colonialism amongst the Dominican priests, like Las Casas (Laverty 2012)). Key to understanding the ethics of the concluding affection-image, however, is that the decolonial critique of Las Casas was influential in the formulation of both Gustavo Gutiérrez's theology of liberation in the late Twentieth Century, and, as a result, Dussel's development of his philosophy of liberation. For Dussel, the '*first head-on critic of modernity*' (2006, 16) Las Casas refused to deny the indigenous Americans their status as equals, refused to deny their coevalness (1992, 69–72). As a figure to appear in the film, then, Las Casas is indicative of the centuries of intertwined histories (domination/revolution) of colonial modernity, which are caught up in the crystal of time in *Even the Rain*.

Face to face with an anonymous taxi driver

The encounter with the past offered in the final stages of *Even the Rain* is more indirectly rendered than in *How Tasty*. The finale of *Even the Rain* takes place in a taxi, and shows two gazes that do not meet. Moreover, the gaze which breaks the fourth wall is, very deliberately, heavily mediated. As a result it confronts the spectator rather obliquely. By rendering the frontal gaze in this way, *Even the Rain* dramatises the unequal nature of the conflict, domination/revolution, the intertwining of peoples it entails, the global inequality it fosters, and – most especially – the lack of recognition it provides for the many histories which it excludes from the official record. Unlike the confrontational optimism of *How Tasty*, confident in its assertion that there is another history, another way into the labyrinth of time which can be signalled by the presence of a direct gaze to camera in the affection-image, in this case the access to this past is given as, literally, a glimpse. Just a glance, in fact, which the European, Costa, misses in his preoccupation with his own reconstruction. Thus *Even the Rain* is scrupulously honest in its depiction of this particular perspective on the legacy of the North Atlantic trade circuit. It illuminates that there is a forgotten history to be uncovered, but emphasises that it is one which speaks to the unthinking of Eurocentrism precisely for Eurocentrics. Some more detail is needed at this point.

The final scene in the taxi directly follows a scene in a warehouse, in which one of the film's many crystals of time is repeated so as to demonstrate the completed reconstruction of Costa and his previously Eurocentric understanding of history. The first such scene takes place around thirty minutes into the film, when Costa speaks to Daniel in the warehouse. There, the filmmakers have constructed a replica of an early Sixteenth Century Spanish caravel, of the type Columbus sailed in. The framing of Costa in dialogue with Daniel conflates his initial attitude with that of the Eurocentric legacy of colonisation. Costa is trying to persuade Daniel to withdraw from his role as a leader of protestors in the water war until the film is over. He is interrupted by a phone call from one of the film's backers. The camera tracks Daniel moving through the props, which include the guns, knives and cannons of the colonisation, as Costa, speaking in English (which he assumes that Daniel cannot understand), boasts about how cheaply he can make his film in Bolivia. 'It's fucking great [...] two fucking dollars a day, they feel like kings. You can throw in some water pumps, some old trucks when you're done and hey presto, two hundred fucking extras!' Daniel understands English, having spent time working in the US, and angrily confronts Costa. As he leaves with Belén, Costa, crestfallen at being caught out, is framed from Belén's point of view, with the caravel and a large crucifix behind him. As he then turns to leave, the film cuts twice in quick succession, firstly to a shot of the entire warehouse of props, the caravel taking up the middle ground, and then again to the recreated scenes of the indigenous Americans panning for gold – precisely the two hundred extras of which Costa boasted. In this way, through the use of cinematography, *mise-en-scène* and editing, Costa's exploitative position on the Bolivian workers, and indeed the reality of cross-border labour in the present day, is positioned as part of a five-hundred-year-old legacy. Costa in the present is effectively equated with the conquistadores in the past.

This scene is then replayed just before the film's final moments, set in the taxi. Costa and Daniel repeat their face to face encounter in the same warehouse, which is now abandoned except for the remains of the model Spanish caravel (see Figure 4.4). In this instance, Costa and Daniel share genuine emotion and friendship, and Costa's conversion from his previous Eurocentric position, due to his interaction with Daniel and his family, seems complete. They exchange parting gifts: Costa a print-out of a headline from the Spanish newspaper *El Correo*, which includes a photo of Daniel, declaring the victory of the Bolivian people in the water war, and Daniel, a small wooden box. As they do so, Costa is framed with the caravel behind him, once again conflating him with the history of colonisation and modernity, but this time in tatters.

When Costa first spoke to Daniel in this scene, he was surrounded by the armaments of colonisation, which Daniel fingered gingerly, and flanked by the imposing Spanish caravel. The second time, however, this informing milieu is in ruin. As a time-image it precisely illustrates that Costa's informing virtual history of colonial triumph (which the film earlier equated with Costa's mistreatment of the Bolivian actors in the film) has been 'ruined' by his acknowledgement of his connection to Daniel, his family, and his rights. Costa now has to rebuild his informing history (that which had previously framed his arrogance towards Daniel, as seen in the image of Costa framed by caravel and crucifix), due to the loss of his Cartesian self-same self. This loss, noticeably, he has experienced through his Dusselian ethical encounter with the intertwined histories of European self and indigenous American other. Put simply, Costa can no longer act in a manner as though he is informed by an unproblematic acceptance of his colonial past. Having entered into an ethical relationship with Daniel, that particular labyrinthine pathway through time, alone, cannot inform his actions.

FIGURE 4.4 The ruins of Costa's (unthinking) Eurocentrism, in *También la lluvia/Even the Rain* (Icíar Bollaín, 2010).

The *mise-en-scène* shows that his previously informing past is now in tatters, due to the present-day realisation of the ongoing historical reality of European entanglement with indigeneity.

Daniel, for his part, has been provided with a positive, fictional, virtual past by the arrival of the film crew (his is also a labyrinthine powers of the false), when his Hatuey side escaped from the Bolivian authorities in the present and replayed the past differently. After all, this is just as the Bolivians did when they won the water war, defeating the multinationals being a standout success in the centuries of colonial modernity. Daniel's words to Costa evoke the history of the colonial struggle of modernity as one of constant battle. He states that it: 'Always costs us dear, every time. It's never easy. I wish there was another way.' When Costa then asks him what he will do next, Daniel responds: 'Survive, like always. What we do best.'

Yet the seeming stoicism of these words does not do justice to how the film portrays the refusal on the part of the Bolivians to accept the role or history of a colonised, subjected people. The sentiment, visually, seems more akin to Dussel's point, that the indigenous of the Americas were never conquered, and revolt against colonial modernity (Hardt and Negri's perpetual revolution/counterrevolution) is ongoing precisely due to the structural inequality inbuilt into the system (2003a, 225). After all, in both film-within-a-film (where the extras refuse to recreate actual moments from their history of colonisation, and where Daniel escapes from the authorities in a refusal of the fate of Hatuey who died at the stake) and the film itself, a postcolonial powers of the false is activated in the present so as to rewrite a Eurocentric history of domination as, instead, one of perpetual struggle and intertwining of cultures. Thus, from the time-image, another history is seen to emanate, one in which Daniel/Hatuey survives the past in order to lead his people to victory in the water war. This newly emerging other history impacts directly upon Costa's liberation. When Belén is injured during the protests, her mother, Teresa's (Leónidas Chiri) actions in seeking out Costa's assistance provide the present-day counterpart to the refusal on the part of the Indians acting in the film to repeat past events (such as sacrificing their infants by drowning). Costa, then, becomes an integral part of this new history of liberation, in which the colonial forces of neoliberal multinationals are overthrown by protest movements which have been described, again echoing Hardt and Negri, as a 'flexible organizational network' able to mobilise the various people who constitute 'multitude', in opposition to neoliberalism (Linera 2004, 74).

This brings us back to the scene in the taxi, following immediately after the touching scene in the now deserted warehouse. As Costa leaves for the airport in the taxi, he opens the gift given to him by Daniel. Inside the box is a small vial of water. Significantly it is about the same size as the containers which the conquistadores (in the film-within-a-film) force the indigenous Americans to fill with a quota of gold on pain of dismemberment. Previously, during their several interactions, Costa has only ever discussed money with Daniel. Daniel's gift is chosen to teach Costa that the war for water is the same war that has been waged since

1492, only with gold replaced by an arguably more significant natural resource. When Costa sees the vial of water, he speaks a Quechua word for the first time: 'yaku' (water). This is significant because, previously, whilst certain members of the crew were keen to learn Quechua, Costa held himself back from engagement with the indigenous culture he was exploiting.

Along with the perhaps more trite interpretation that offers itself (that Costa has learned that some things are more valuable than money), Daniel's gift indicates the significance of water for Bolivians, which is held to be a sacred right, rather than a commodity, in a tradition related to community preservation that stretches back to the Incas (Laverty 2011, 10–11 (see Figure 4.5)). Here, the evocation of the former levy of gold imposed by the conquistadores, in an equation with the small vial of water, illustrates the greater spiritual dimension of colonisation and the devaluing of indigenous American culture and tradition by Western thinking. As Costa speaks the film's final word in Quechua, the anonymous taxi driver looks into his mirror, and we see his eyes in close-up as he reacts to Costa's use of Quechua (see Figure 4.6). In this moment Costa, by speaking

FIGURE 4.5   Fleetingly realising that another('s) history exists, in *También la lluvia/Even the Rain* (Icíar Bollaín, 2010).

FIGURE 4.6   Ephemeral ethical encounter, in *También la lluvia/Even the Rain* (Icíar Bollaín, 2010).

a Quechua word which has a meaning that he has come to understand to mean life (Daniel's gift is to thank Costa for saving Belén), has an opportunity to enter into an ethical relationship with the other. However, Costa does not spot this opportunity. He is thinking about what has happened to him and looks out of the window as the taxi drives through the streets of Cochabamba. This returns Costa to his initial position, at the very start of the film, of newly arrived (colonial) observer of Bolivian life through an automobile window, the imperialist tourist-like gaze, isolated from those upon which it lands. The potential of this affection-image to offer an entrance to another understanding of the past, one of interaction between cultures, is thus lost.

Noticeably, the gaze that regards Costa, and briefly also the viewer, is mediated through a mirror, playfully foregrounding once again the virtual/actual temporal relationship with which the film has been toying in its exploration of colonial modernity. The look of the taxi driver comes from the virtual history of the colonial encounter. Costa, however, fails to notice or return the gaze. Ultimately, then, *Even the Rain*'s European perspective on this transnational history is – as stated above – an honest one. Despite focusing on Costa's reconstruction, the film foregrounds the limitations of European involvement in Bolivia, noting that only because of Costa's privileged position can he assist Daniel's family. After all, he does not play any active role in the Bolivians' struggle during the water war, and departs soon afterwards. Although Costa, perhaps like the European film viewer, can temporarily inhabit the crystal of time, his actions ultimately maintain the difference between European and Bolivian worlds. As Olivera notes, the water war was won, but this was only one small step in an ongoing struggle against neoliberalism in Bolivia. A giant victory against the odds, it is true, but all that was won was the maintenance of a basic natural resource (2004, 46). Costa's departure shows, ultimately, that whilst there may have been some unthinking Eurocentrism, some reconsideration of the national, colonial past, for many Europeans this is a past conceived of as having taken place hundreds of years ago. The actions of the multinationals, now, can therefore appear rather disconnected from any sense of ongoing responsibility. Costa does learn that it is wrong to oppress others (as it was in colonial history, so too is it now under globalisation) or turn his face away when others need help – hence his return during the rioting. Even so, the film emphasises, his ethical encounter is limited to a (temporary) unthinking of his own Eurocentrism.

In *Even the Rain* as in *How Tasty*, an attempt is made to indicate how the entangled histories of white (European) and indigenous cultures from 1492 onwards illustrate a lost past, so often forgotten by Eurocentric history. It is for Europeans, and their diaspora, that these films provide an encounter with the lost past which was, and is, intertwined with theirs in colonial modernity. The history of the exploitation of the Global South, which necessitates such entwining, and upon which the exploitation of which the Global North depends, is 'unseen' by the Global North due to its Eurocentric view of history.

Yet finally, as was the case with *How Tasty*, although *Even the Rain* was intended to speak to specific audiences (in this case intended primarily for Western viewers, as the film's distribution illustrates) it also has resonances for many others. Two years after its release, Laverty notes that in conversation with Olivera he learned of the film's afterlife. In pirated form it was being screened across the Andes, to factory workers for instance, with a following debate and discussion (Laverty 2012). This would seem to bear out something of Santaolalla's contention that *Even the Rain* may be a potential prototype for a future Hispanic cinema, able to speak to audiences in both Spain and Latin America (2012, 220). This extra-life of the film, its passing on by hand in the manner evoked by Laura U. Marks as illustrative of the 'skin of the film' that unites communities (2000, 20–21) – in its political connotations akin to that of *La battaglia di Algeri/Battle of Algiers* (1966) (which famously served as a visual aid to recruitment and training for guerrilla-style resistance movements worldwide (Pisters 2012, 230)) – cannot be explained in terms of reconsiderations of Eurocentrism. Aside from the fact that the film depicts the water war as one that was won by the protestors, and there are not a myriad of such examples to choose from for people looking to organise resistance (in spite of the existence of a very similar Bolivian film about a European film crew making a film about the colonisation, *Para recibir el canto de los pájaros/To Hear the Birds Singing* (1995) (Wheeler 2013, 248)), presumably Latin American audiences are responding to other aspects of the film than European viewers. Alongside the likely appeal of certain well-known Loachian/Lavertian aspects (e.g. depictions of democratic decision-making amongst diverse communities with common aims, and the focus on the potential for success of collective action), *Even the Rain* also appeals in the different perspective on modern colonial history which it offers in the time-image – and indeed the observation it makes with regard to the inability of Europeans to engage in the ethical encounter with Bolivians. Thus, whilst the film could be considered to offer a Spanish or more broadly European audience what Wheeler describes as an 'ethics of humility', it may also offer Bolivians a chance to consider the likelihood (or *lack* of it) that Europe will ever pursue an ethical position on the liberation of the Americas that is of practical assistance in everyday struggles under globalisation.[7]

In the pivotal time-image scene in which Hatuey is executed, but Daniel escapes, the Spanish soldiers force a local crowd to gather to watch the agonising execution of the indigenous who have resisted their brutal rule. As the thirteen condemned men shout their defiance of the Christians, and in return the crowd chants Hatuey's name, the dialogue at this most affective of moments is in Quechua. For viewers who do not speak the language, there are no subtitles to assist (in either the original Spanish version, or the English subtitle track) until it has been translated into Spanish by an indigenous American working for the Spanish. This will place many viewers in something of an alignment, albeit perhaps an uncomfortable one, with the soldiers, who grow visibly worried as the crowd grows restless. For viewers unable to understand what is being said by

Hatuey and the crowd of indigenous Americans who have gathered to witness his execution, there is only the initial facial anxiety of Las Casas, and then of the soldiers, through which to register the affective nature of the event. That is, until Las Casas shouts, interpreting, for the soldiers (and many viewers), what the assembled crowd of indigenous are chanting: 'His name! Thanks to you, it will never be forgotten!' Yet, this same scene, for speakers of Quechua, will inevitably provide a very different alignment, and affective tension, with the imperilled resistance fighters. This, perhaps, explains something of the afterlife of the film in the Andes.

This final example, which links the origins of colonial modernity with our present era under globalisation, begins the transition towards Part III, and Chapters 5 and 6. But first, a brief recap of this chapter. An indigenous woman in the early Sixteenth Century stares directly at us as she devours a would-be French colonist, addressing us from a past now eradicated by genocide. A film crew shooting the execution of a Sixteenth Century indigenous freedom fighter by Spanish colonists is interrupted by state police seeking to arrest a Bolivian water war activist resisting a multinational corporation – the past and present coalesce to the point of becoming indiscernible. This chapter has explored these cinematic encounters with the transnational history of the North Atlantic trade circuit. Specifically, the entanglement of European and indigenous histories which occurred as the world system propelled Europe to global dominance, and their continued entwinement today under globalisation. These are key examples from a category of films about the racial contract, which focus on this transnational history using the White Atlantic as entry point, as subject to deconstruct.

In the next two chapters, the chosen cinematic explorations emphasise less the environmental changes brought by the Anthropocene, as I explore with more focus how the legacy of the systematic destruction of political opposition to colonial modernity during the Cold War (Chapter 5) is felt today under neoliberalism in and on the bodies of those who have experienced it (Chapter 6). These are films exploring transnational histories which ensured firstly the policing of the social contract (eradicating the possibility of communism for many in the so-called third world during the Cold War) and, as a result, the dominance of the individual contract under neoliberal globalisation. Let us, then, look further into the most recent transnational histories that are not supposed to be remembered, those within living (world) memory.

Notes

1 Commencing with increased trade between Europe and the West Coast of Africa, the colonisation of islands off the coast of Africa (Crosby 1986, 70–103) and then the discovery of the Americas in 1492 (Egerton et al. 2007, 2).

2 Dan Flory's reading of a 'noir Atlantic', bringing together films from the USA, UK, Brazil and South Africa (2008, 303) has some similarities with the approach taken here, illustrating the 'global connectedness of various oppressions, as well as an awareness of shared values, ideals and possible solutions that might remedy the social

problems posed by such oppressions' (303). However, engaging with the time-image herein indicates a different historical dimension, that the encounters which illuminate the reality of the racial contract's underpinning/undermining presence in colonial modernity are not solely between different peoples, but between intertwined pasts.

3 Pre-Columbian societies typically did not emphasise private property as the newly arriving Europeans did (Zinn 1980, 16–22).

4 The film's perhaps rather prudish rejection by the Cannes International Film Festival may have also initially limited its circulation beyond the nation (Stam 1997, 250).

5 Laverty spent ten years working on the story, which was set to run as an HBO series based on Howard Zinn's *A People's History of the United States* (1980), and later as a feature film directed by Alejandro González Iñárritu. The three majority funders were Morena Films (Spain) and Mandarin (France), followed by Alebrije (Mexico) (Wheeler 2013, 245), along with support from Ibermedia, TVE and Canal Plus. When shooting in Bolivia, the production engaged in mutually agreeable payment arrangements, in direct contrast to the mercenary arrangements pursued by the film-makers in the diegesis. The extras received a negotiated rate of US$20 a day, and, as with Laverty's experiences in Nicaragua on *Carla's Song* (UK/Spain/Germany, 1996), other forms of payment were provided to the local communities (e.g. support for a local film school, bricks for a local school, library computers and €40,000 towards a water truck (Santaolalla 2012, 18; Laverty 2011, 18)). The film was fairly successful for what can loosely be considered a European art film (an early scene of a huge crucifix being helicoptered into the jungle provides a direct nod to the helicoptered Christ of Federico Fellini's iconic *La dolce vita* (Italy/France, 1960)) with a budget of US$6.8m (around €5m), premiering on the festival circuit, garnering three Goyas (Spanish Oscars) and a theatrical run in the USA. Howard Zinn's *A People's History of the United States*, the inspiration for the film, has repeatedly been the subject of attempted bans from the school curriculum in the USA (Khan 2017).

6 Previous films focus on his supposedly 'enlightened' attributes: his connection to Christian beliefs, science, and modernity – even, anachronistically, portraying him as a democrat (Shohat and Stam 1994, 62–63).

7 It was not until March 2012 that the World Council of Churches repudiated the centuries-old Doctrine of Discovery which legitimised the destruction of non-European peoples.

PART III

Encounters with the present that passes

5

70 YEARS

The Cold War, the social contract, encountering political pasts

This and the following chapter of film analysis bring the exploration of how cinema depicts the transnational histories of colonial modernity up to date, to the late Twentieth and early Twenty-First Centuries. This chapter examines two contrasting documentaries, *The Act of Killing* (Denmark/Norway/UK, 2012) and *Al pie del árbol blanco/At the Foot of the White Tree* (Uruguay, 2007). The dominant time-image in each case is the crystal of time, which encapsulates the perpetual splitting of time into (virtual, preserved) past and (actual, passing) present. This recurring image re-imagines, or re-aestheticises, the lost pasts of the Cold War, a seventy-year period of world history (sometimes referred to as a Pax Americana), which impacted transnationally. Ostensibly a standoff between superpowers, the Cold War covered a geopolitical terrain which crossed national borders. It also included, however, myriad wars fought in the 'margins' between the Soviets and the US (and their respective allies), as ideological battles traversed borders within the so-called 'third world'. In this historical period, the line which had previously demarcated colonial modernity's beneficiaries from its underside during its colonial phases, a 'colour' line indicative of the racial contract (see Chapter 4), shifted to an ideological one. Thus the Cold War is understood to be a global civil war, which some consider to be ongoing or only now decomposing (hence this is a seventy-year history, bleeding into globalisation today, this latter being the subject of Chapter 6).

Like many recent documentaries from around the world, the two chosen films explore what can be known of the history of brutal eradication of political opposition by authoritarian rule. The time-images show that there was another facet or virtual pathway to the past – since forgotten, obliterated, murdered, censored, disappeared. They respectively indicate either the supposed legitimacy of its eradication with repetitious certainty (*The Act of Killing*) or its virtual potential to re-inform a different understanding of the present (*At the Foot*). This is the chapter, then, in which the notion of a crystal history is clearest.

Both films provide encounters with political pasts, requiring viewers to hesitate with respect to their knowledge of how contemporary world history was formed during the Cold War: of how complete it can be (how much of the past has been lost?), and how aware we are of the alternative histories which might have occurred instead. It is the role of the social contract suspended during a state of exception which is at stake in each case. The existing social contract, designed under colonial modernity to perpetuate inequality, was threatened during the Cold War by the rise of communism. *The Act of Killing* celebrates the eradication of another possible past (communism) at that time. For its part, *At the Foot* offers a glimpse of an otherwise lost alternative past (of resistance to military rule, which included communism) of this period.

In *The Act of Killing*, the time-image's potential to explore the indiscernibility between past and present is evident in carnivalesque recreations of the past (recreated through the filter of Hollywood genres), which demonstrate how state-employed killers remember their own murderous past: the virtual past of their memories literally blurs with the virtual cinematic past of the movies they enjoyed during their time as killers. In *At the Foot*, time-images are constructed from old photographs of the period (some of the only remaining traces of this alternative past, belonging to a communist newspaper) in order to restore an absent layer of history able to inform the present. This kind of patchy archival retrieval, and recreation in locations resonant with past political actions, is a recurring strategy in many such documentaries. In both instances, it is not that we learn about the history of the Cold War per se, but that we encounter the awareness that it denied coevalness to those who might have politically opposed the continuation of colonial modernity – at least in its capitalist guise – during this moment in its history.

Hence, *The Act of Killing* is analysed differently than it typically is, not as exemplary, but as the exception to a broader trend. *At the Foot*, rather, is exemplary of the broader re-aestheticisation of lost or disappeared pasts of the Cold War in contemporary documentary. Contrary to Slavoj Žižek's position on *The Act of Killing* (that it depicts how public space has been privatised under globalisation), I argue that in both films what is considered through the time-image is the role of private pasts in informing memory in the public sphere, the importance of individual recollections in informing world memory when state violence eradicates oppositional political histories. Both films, in fact, despite their huge differences in emphasis, are involved in remediating traumatic pasts, as virtual museums of memory.

Time-images: Political pasts

Many documentaries produced in the 2000s use time-images to rediscover, reimagine, or recreate lost Cold War pasts, including: *Los rubios/The Blonds* (Argentina/USA, 2003), *Al pie del árbol blanco/At the Foot of the White Tree* (Uruguay, 2007), *Wo sui siqu/Though I Am Gone* (People's Republic of China,

2006), *The Act of Killing* (Denmark/Norway/UK, 2012), *S-21, la machine de mort Khmère rouge/S21: The Khmer Rouge Death Machine* (Cambodia/France, 2003) and *L'image manquante/The Missing Picture* (Cambodia/France, 2013). This is per- haps unsurprising. During the Cold War, documentaries offered ways of rais- ing political consciousness in politically contested moments, significantly in the Latin American films *La hora de los hornos/The Hour of the Furnaces* (Argentina, 1968) and *La Batalla de Chile/Battle of Chile* (Venezuela/France/Cube, 1975). Documentaries continue to offer an affordable mode of production, including in contexts where national industries may not have developed or where state con- trol may render uncensored cinematic exploration of the past challenging. The crystal image appears in such films due to its capacity to hold open, even if only momentarily, the possibility of the coexistence of an alternative political past which might inform the present differently.

As noted in Chapters 3 and 4, in the crystal we see the splitting of time at the heart of duration, with virtual past and actual present appearing as though two facets of a crystal. The crystal is 'a bit of time in the pure state' (Deleuze 1985, 79). As David Deamer clarifies, the crystal image 'must necessarily link the actual image to a virtual correlate' (2016, 149). Thus the crystal image cre- ates the links needed between disconnected actual images (e.g. an opsign) and virtual correlates (e.g. a sheet of the past which corresponds to the present), so as to ensure that there is still a form of narration possible in the time-image: 'crystalline narration' (Deleuze 1985, 124).

There is thus a story of history being told in crystal images: a crystal history (see Chapter 2). Crystal images show how actual history is always mirrored by a virtual past which offers the potential for a re-engagement (of this alternative labyrinthine pathway through history) in the present, via a new re-aestheticisa- tion of the past in the time-image. In these documentaries the past is, precisely, re-aestheticised in the crystal of time. Either the past which is preserved is maintained as singularly linear – in an Orwellian manner – once again reac- tualised in the same form so as to re-affirm the unquestionable veracity of the actual present that passes (*The Act of Killing*), or it is recreated as the glimpse of a virtual alternative that can potentially newly inform the actual present that passes (by falsifying the existing view of history which exists in the absence of any evidence to the contrary (*At the Foot*)). Both instances provide an oppor- tunity for hesitation with respect to the centrality of the actual history which we know, by indicating the virtual remnant of the (in this case, political) past which was eradicated in the establishing of what is known as history. Both cases? Yes. Even when watching the fictional, and fantastical, recreation of the supposedly one 'true' past in *The Act of Killing*, the haunting possibility of the virtual labyrinth of possible pasts which could have existed threaten the (in this case, gangster) storytellers of history.[1] The crystal thus shows the contingency of history which comes to the fore during armed struggles in which one side of history is forcibly eradicated. The right to tell the story of history in another way is here denied, ideally (ideally as understood by those creating the state of exception (see further below)) by silencing – whether through imprisonment, exile, torture or murder – all those whose existence might demonstrate the existence of an alternative history to that of the status quo: doublethink. What these documentaries show, then, is not solely the eradication of alternative pasts during the Cold War, but also (in the crystal, by keeping alive an alternative past, in its scattered fragments) the impossibility that the so-called 'end of history' followed in the wake of the Cold War: an alternative to capitalism does still exist, these films show, or rather it virtually subsists as alternative (lost) past in (and to) the present.

Transnational history: The Cold War

The Cold War is typically understood as a stalemate over nuclear superiority between the USA and the USSR. John Lewis Gaddis (1992) famously called it a 'Long Peace' between the two empires. It is typical for Film Studies to mirror this historical consensus. In *Cinematic Cold War* (2010), Tony Shaw and Denise J. Youngblood examine, as their book's subtitle states, 'the American and Soviet struggle for hearts and minds' in an 'intensive, multidimensional battle of images between the Soviet and American film industries that lasted well into the 1980s' (4). Here the usual historical and geopolitical structuring focus is evident in the two chosen film industries, albeit Shaw and Youngblood do acknowledge the broader geopolitics of the global conflict fought in the margins between these two superpowers. Even so, a book about that 'other' Cold War (which would have to include a great many more cinemas of the world) would look remarkably different in terms of the aesthetics explored. How, then, can the impact of the Cold War's struggle for the supremacy of (ultimately) the global free market, a transnational history still ongoing in many places which emerges as a later phase in colonial modernity, be understood differently?

Anthropologist Heonik Kwon (2010) outlines an alternative view of the conflict, arguing that the Cold War did not end for all the nations of the world with an outright 'victory' for capitalism over communism. Contrary to the 'end of history' thesis which followed the fall of the Berlin Wall in 1989, Kwon racks focus from the broader geopolitical standoff to a question of social order, and explores nations at the 'periphery' of the conflict between the superpowers, such as Korea, Vietnam, and Indonesia.[2] Kwon sees the Cold War as still in a state of 'decomposition' (8) taking place at different rates in different places.

Kwon reconsiders the Cold War as a conflict illustrative of the 'hierarchical dimension of the global bipolar order' (4), that is, effectively, colonial modernity:

> The 'contest-of-power' dimension of the cold war has been an explicit and central element in cold war historiography; in contrast the 'relation-of-domination' aspect has been a relatively marginal, implicit element. [...] [T]he history of the cold war is increasingly about a particular power structure of domination, invented and realised along the bipolarization

of modernity, rather than singularly about the contest of power waged
between opposing versions and visions of modernity.

(2–4)

Considering the Cold War as a history of domination focuses us on the 'decomposing' histories illustrative of Dussel's underside of modernity and affirms Dussel's
view that the Cold War was a conflict for the 'leadership of capitalism', which
began in earnest around a decade after World War Two, and saw the end of state
capitalism and the rise of multinational corporate capitalism (2003a, 137). During
the Cold War, the demarcation of societies via the racial contract – which accompanied the imperialism of European nations after 1492 (see Chapter 4) – gave way
to a new division along ideological lines: capitalism/communism.[3]

Crucial to this discussion is Kwon's exploration of the state of exception, and
how it relates to the social contract. Kwon effectively argues that there was not
one Cold War, but many, as different societies experienced political bifurcation
differently (2010, 7):

> [F]or many new postcolonial nations [...] the onset of the cold war meant
> entering an epoch of 'unbridled reality' characterized by vicious civil wars
> and other exceptional forms of political violence. [...] [T]he cold war [...]
> engendered a perpetual condition akin to what Giorgio Agamben calls
> 'the state of exception' – the suspension of the rule of law as a rule of the
> political order. In certain parts of the world, the beginning of the cold war
> coincided with the end of imperial and colonial rule, whereas in other
> parts these two epochal political forms were disturbingly entangled and
> became practically inseparable.

(6)

In addition to the millions who died in the preceding centuries due to colonisation and imperialism, the much briefer Cold War produces another 'forty
million human casualties of war' (8) (the vast majority of them in the Southern
Hemisphere (McMahon 2013, 7)), giving the lie to the notion of this era as one
of a long peace. It was, rather, one of 'total war' which drew into the underside
of colonial modernity those now ideologically excluded from history (Kwon
2010, 8). In this new order of empire, the racial inequality of what W. E. B.
Du Bois calls 'the colour line' becomes entangled with ideological conflict: the
colour line of the Cold War was 'Red'/'Not Red' (Kwon 2010, 38). Although
in some cases 'state violence against individuals who were believed to harbour
subversive political ideas took on and was justified by the idioms of biological
or racial difference' (39), in others the new colour line encompassed societies
previously on different sides of the older colonial line (42). This is no longer
a transnational history marked by the racial contract, then, but by the (suspension of the) social contract in a state of exception designed to counter the
spread of communism.

With this in mind, let us return to the question of how to consider the cinematic Cold War differently. In line with scholarship which addresses the documentary's transnational potential to enable the democratic ideal of 'intervention in public debate' (Chanan 2007, 16), this chapter finds that documentaries from these zones of perpetual war use time-images to deal with the 'mass destruction of human lives and political displacement of the victims' memories of this destruction' (Kwon 2010, 11) in similar ways aesthetically – using crystal images to create virtual museums of memory. This is the case in spite of their unique cultural and social backdrops. Thus these time-image documentaries demonstrate the complexity of each national experience of the Cold War's decomposition, as part of a still emerging transnational history.

Encountering the (eradicated) political past: The (suspended) social contract

What is encountered in the crystal of time is the moment in which the social contract is suspended, or in many cases eradicated, in the state of exception. The idea of the social contract in political philosophy is traced back to different historical starting points, its current manifestation emerging in Enlightenment Europe in the works of John Locke, Thomas Hobbes, Immanuel Kant and Jean-Jacques Rousseau. Of these thinkers, it is with Rousseau that the idea of popular sovereignty emerges (Boucher and Kelly 1994, 16). In *The Social Contract* (1750), Rousseau attempts to explain why individuals enter into a social contract, giving up 'natural freedom' (60) in exchange for the 'social freedom' offered by the collective, the state (61).

Rousseau critically uncovered the (as it were, invisible) contract through which society is structured via economic inequality. His *A Discourse on Inequality* (1755), indicating the correlation between private property and inequality, is exemplary in this respect (Mills 1997, 5). Here Rousseau outlines how the social contract is designed to maintain the elevated status of the rich over the poor, noting 'the equality which nature established amongst men and the inequality which they have instituted amongst themselves' (1755, 57). During the Cold War (when the theology and philosophy of liberation as we know them today were forming), the spread of communism across the third world threatened the inequality fostered by the social contract under capitalism. In many places, the resulting 'state of siege' which suspended the social contract, excused as a bulwark against the spread of communism, ensured that large sections of the population – typically left wing citizens – could be eliminated, along with their potential to alter the inequality built into the system.

This is perhaps unsurprising. *The Social Contract*, a text most famous for the observation, 'Man was born free, and he is everywhere in chains' (49), has also been blamed for inspiring a manifestation of popular sovereignty which led to the worst excesses of France's revolutionary Reign of Terror: 'Robespierre was Rousseau in action' (Jennings 1994, 121). This is because, towards its conclusion,

Rousseau draws on examples from antiquity to indicate that under certain circumstances the social contract may be suspended, and either an extension of the power of law or a dictatorship ('with the power to silence all the laws' (Rousseau 1750, 171)), imposed. Rousseau qualifies that this measure should be undertaken 'only in the greatest emergency', 'when the safety of the fatherland is at stake' (171), and limited to one term in duration (173). Even so, this clause is indicative of the difficulty inherent to the social contract that is based upon the need for a certain section of the population to decide against the possibility of change offered by another. What is evident in Rousseau's caveat is that the legitimacy of the social contract is only ever based upon its relationship to another state – a seemingly less desirable alternative, or a (mythical) origin from which the social contract departs – a 'state of nature' (Cranston 1984, 42; Lessnoff 1990, 7).

In fact, the state of exception only really makes extremely clear that the social contract excludes by definition: it is structured by, and fosters, inequality. To suspend the existing social contract via the imposition of a state of exception is, as Giorgio Agamben argues, effectively to return to the supposed state of nature which pre-exists the social contract ('the state of nature is in truth a state of exception' (1995, 109)) and establish a new exclusive contract by eradicating its potential opposition. As Hannah Arendt explains, this juxtaposition of a supposed state of nature, which is *followed* by a social contract, is not a literal 'historical fact' (1963, 9–10). Rather, the notion of a state of nature indicates the need for an idea that society *has* a starting point. This imaginary of a former state of nature thus gives impetus, Arendt argues, to the notion that a revolution can return a society to this 'year zero' and rebuild it.[4] The social contract, understood in this manner, rests on the need to perpetually repeat its normativity in order to suture over the lack at its heart, to thus obscure that its beginning is as arbitrary as its inequalities. There is always the possibility of its repetition in difference, always the possibility that another social contract could be written should enough people wish to, as Arendt has it, turn the clock back to 'year zero'. Understanding this is crucial to the analysis of the films which follows, because what is true for the social contract is also true for the way the story of history is told, and it is this which the crystal of time illuminates.

This potential of ungrounding, or rather the *condition* of ungrounding, which lies at the heart of the social contract, is the subject of Agamben's *State of Exception* (2003), on which Kwon draws. Agamben theorises the state of exception as existing in a grey area between law and politics, noting its close relationship with 'civil war, insurrection and resistance' (2). He discusses how the state of exception can be considered a 'legal civil war' in which the state controls the majority of the resources necessary to eradicate its political opposition, and any sectors of the population which it cannot integrate into its political system (2). The state of exception (or 'state of siege' or 'martial law') is the moment of the suspension of the rule of law, and thereby the 'threshold' or 'limit concept' of the law (4).[5]

Although most of Agamben's examples of the state of exception are drawn from Twentieth Century European history, his intention is to indicate the emergence of a state of exception in US policies drawn up after the 9/11 attacks, such as The Patriot Act (2003, 3–7). Yet his early references to Arendt's *On Revolution* indicate that Agamben considers the state of exception to be the feature of an ongoing 'global civil war' (2003, 3), progressing since World War One, which has now reached its 'maximum worldwide deployment' (86–87). There is, however, a Eurocentric myopia in Agamben's thinking with respect to modernity's place in world history. In *Homo Sacer* (1995), he posits the origins of the extending of the state of exception to all of society in the European colonial powers' concentration camps of the late Nineteenth and early Twentieth Century (166). Although Agamben does not align with the European tradition critiqued in Chapter 1, of considering the Twentieth Century Holocaust to be an exceptional event, nevertheless, his argument that Nazi concentration camps exemplify 'the hidden paradigm of the political space of modernity' (123) is not entirely accurate.

What Agamben is observing is but a recent manifestation symptomatic of coloniality's perpetual marking out of the boundaries which police its exclusion of modernity's underside. The origins of the Twentieth Century's Holocaust do lie in colonial aggression, it is true, but, as Charles W. Mills indicates (in uncovering the racial contract which emerges after 1492 (see Chapter 4)), the apartheid which first exemplifies the subsistence of coloniality along with modernity (modernity's real 'hidden paradigm') was the genocide of fifty million indigenous Americans, and the enslavement of millions more Africans. If the 'truth' of the supposedly egalitarian social contract is the inequality fostered by the racial contract (ongoing since 1492), then – as Kwon indicates – all that changes with the Cold War is that the line of demarcation shifts from solely racial to (primarily) ideological distinctions. It is less that the Twentieth Century's concentration camps in Europe exemplify the pervasive and seeming without-origin violence of contemporary life, as Agamben argues, than that the violent exclusion of some from the benefits of colonial modernity (over the last five hundred years) found its Twentieth Century European expression in the camp (see Chapter 1).

The above notwithstanding, what Kwon's recuperation of Agamben indicates is the incisiveness of the idea of the state of exception (as suspension of the social contract) for the current critique of Cold War histories on screen. This is because the state of exception, functioning as though the return to a (mythical) state of nature, is in fact 'continually operative in the civil state in the form of the sovereign decision' (Agamben 1998, 109). This explains the seeming paradox in Rousseau's formulation of the social contract, namely that it may, at times, need to be suspended and replaced by dictatorship, in order to survive. Agamben discusses the state of exception as a 'non-place' (2003, 51) or 'zone of anomie'[6] in which the usual ethical standards of society are suspended, stating:

> The state of exception is not a dictatorship (whether constitutional or unconstitutional, commissarial or sovereign) but a space devoid of law, a

zone of anomie in which all legal determinations – and above all the very distinction between public and private – are deactivated.

(2003, 51)

The 'non-place' of the state of exception is a 'fictitious lacuna', one which ultimately upholds the norm which is claimed to be at threat. For Agamben, this suspension of the law does not make for unlawful acts (as they 'escape all legal definition' (51)), but only for acts necessary to maintain the law, and the norm which it legislates, against the potential threat of revolution. Thus the state of exception 'traces a threshold' which creates the 'complex topological relations' that inside and outside enter into, when sovereignty suspends the rights of some in order to ensure its continuation against the threat that they pose (1998, 19). In a zone of anomie it is the collective identity of political opposition that is under attack, a collective perceived to be a danger to the law (a revolutionary collective, or the possibility that a collective may become revolutionary) and – the key point for the documentaries under discussion – *it is their ability to remember themselves as such that must be eradicated.*

The two chosen documentaries thus return to events at the height of the Cold War (in the wake of the Cuban Revolution, coinciding with the US war in Vietnam), when it most infused third world struggles (Parker 2013, 132). *The Act of Killing* focuses on the infamous violence of 1965–1966 in Indonesia, in which hundreds of thousands were massacred, particularly communists and their families, along with other organised political opposition groups (Oppenheimer and Uwemedimo 2012, 287). *At the Foot* attempts to resurrect footage of events from the period leading up to the Uruguayan coup d'état in 1973, the culmination of political disturbances going back a decade, in particular involving the Marxist guerrilla force, The Tupamaros. From a time when the collective was deligitimised, criminalised, and often 'disappeared' by means of violent repression, these documentaries attempt to recreate this virtual layer of the public past, whether to fantastically re-assert the veracity of the official history in a carnivalesque celebration of the origin of contemporary history (*The Act of Killing*), or by drawing on what, by definition, can only be left behind after the eradication of opposition (the scraps of evidence which relate to the personal, and its interaction with the public), to provide a glimpse of the lost alternative political past (*At the Foot*).

The Act of Killing

Joshua Oppenheimer, Christine Cynn and the director known as Anonymous's *The Act of Killing* focuses on the murderous history upon which General Suharto's (President from 1967–1998) Indonesia was founded. It targets Anwar Congo, a former gangster turned death squad member from Medan (North Sumatra), current associates, and some friends with whom he committed multiple murders during the infamous political crisis of 1965–1966. These gangsters are now

Peace! Happiness! Smile!

FIGURE 5.1 The carnivalesque past gets the Hollywood treatment, in *The Act of Killing* (Joshua Oppenheimer, Christine Cynn, Anonymous, 2012).

celebrities – at least they are hailed as heroes by the Pemuda Pancasila paramilitary organisation and its three million members, and welcomed by the governor of North Sumatra.

Congo and his former comrades re-enact events of the time, including massacres and executions, in the style of their favourite genre movies (see Figure 5.1). The visual strategy is to reflect the psychology, or mental state (whether imagined, remembered, or 'real') of the killers (Oppenheimer refers to it as a 'documentary of the imagination'). They describe committing murders, routinely, after watching Hollywood movies at a nearby cinema. They were 'killing happily', Congo remembers, whilst still in the mood created by, say, the latest Elvis musical. At points, the ageing gangsters debate, sometimes somewhat nervously, the veracity of the version of history which sees them as saviours of the nation. Nevertheless, they want their version of this story of history to be told.

The film ends with a contentious scene in which Congo, revisiting a location where he committed many executions, begins to retch uncontrollably. The camera films his physical difficulties in long take. It is unclear whether Congo's physical tribulations occurred towards the close of the film's shooting. The scene's placement at the film's end creates the suggestion of a narrative arc in which Congo, after working through his past, feels empathy for his victims (or at least feels guilt), and demonstrates contrition physically. It is impossible to tell, though, whether this is just another act, 'an act of contrition' (Hoskins and Lasmana 2015, 263). After all, we also see movie-lover Congo dancing in the same space, hence undercutting the implication that such a redemptive conversion took place.[7]

The historical events recreated in *The Act of Killing*, whilst undeniably traumatic for the people of Indonesia, indicate the transnational nature of the Cold

War history negotiated on screen. This tumultuous year, during which Suharto gradually seized power from Sukarno in 'a creeping coup d'état [...] disguised as an effort to prevent a coup' (Roosa 2006, 4), saw the elimination of what was then 'the largest nonbloc Communist Party' in the world, the Partai Komunis Indonesia/Indonesian Communist Party (PKI), who were erroneously blamed for an aborted coup (Simpson 2014, 53). As Bradley R. Simpson notes, since 1964 the PKI had been 'tilting openly towards China' (53) and intensifying rural class struggle. This was partly due to, Chen Jian also reminds us, the influence of Chinese foreign policy, emphasising revolution in the world's rural areas as a prelude to revolution in the cities (Simpson 2014, 57; Chen 2014, 91–92). In a climate of economic decline and inflation (Booth 1999, 110), with the PKI at three million members and perhaps a further eighteen million followers taking part in mass organisations (Anderson 2012, 271), an anti-Communist military terror campaign was conducted in 1965–1966 (predominantly October 1965 until April 1966), with the covert support of Britain and the USA (Simpson 2014, 52; Westad 2007, 186). It claimed the lives of an estimated half-million to million alleged communists or sympathisers at the hands of the military, anti-Communist militia and civilians incited to violence by Special Forces against a demonized PKI (Kwon 2010, 39–40; Roosa 2006, 26–29). Many disappeared, their bodies still to be exhumed from mass graves, whilst others were imprisoned without charge or trial.[8] As a result, Indonesia under Suharto's dictatorship was a country in a 'constant state of emergency' (Roosa 2006, 13), ever alert to the threat of communism.

The Act of Killing, then, is a film which explicitly deals with the manner in which this period of Cold War history is remembered from the perspective of the side which 'won' after perpetrating wide-scale disappearances and clandestine massacres 'meant to be forgotten' (Roosa 2006, 30). Indeed, *The Act of Killing* is one of several recent documentaries to investigate this troubled period in Indonesian history, a few of which have received international attention, including the more conventional *40 Years of Silence* (USA, 2009) and Oppenheimer's sequel (actually shot prior to the release of *The Act of Killing*), *The Look of Silence* (2014). Such works offer an alternative to *Pengkhianatan 30 September PKI/The Treachery of the September 30th Movement of the Indonesian Communist Party* (1984), a widely viewed four-hour state propaganda film of the Suharto years, mandatory viewing for school children, which was for decades the only visual representation (the official history) of the murderous social turmoil.

Yet, of all these, *The Act of Killing*'s provision of a platform upon which the murderers can tell their story of history is exceptional. Indeed, it stands out both within this recent documentary reconsideration of the period in Indonesia, and in the broader trend outlined above of documentaries exploring Cold War pasts. Even so, there is really nothing exceptional about its view of history. Although the viewing experience may be challenging, there is little that is shocking about the revelation that this murderous history underpins the present-day state. *The Act of Killing* only addresses head-on the way in which the contemporary world is the product of the global ravages of colonial modernity, and how the world history that many hold to be true is based on just such ruthless endeavours. After all, as Mills observes with respect of science fiction stories and novels based on the premise that Germany and her allies won the Second World War, the many acts of genocide upon which colonial modernity established the global centrality of Europe mean that 'we live in an actual, nonalternative world where the victors of racial killing really *did* win and have reconstructed and falsified the record accordingly' (1997, 104–105).

Tellingly, when questioned about the morality of their actions, the gangsters answer by querying with, amongst other examples, the fact that the genocide of indigenous Americans was something that no one has ever answered for. In so doing, they identify a period in history in which European state powers which identified as Christian were prepared to suspend their religious beliefs to murder and enslave during what was the defining state of exception of colonial modernity. There is little difference, the gangsters are indirectly indicating, between the way they prefer to remember their story of history, and how a US western inverts history to portray colonists as embattled heroes saving the nation from supposed indigenous savagery (Shohat and Stam 1994, 114–121). This equation goes to the very heart of the killers' recreation of their murders as though in the style of Hollywood films. Why would they not think it legitimising, after all, to tell their story of national history exactly as the most powerful nation on the planet does its own, through genre movies?

Due to its complex engagement with history and ethics, the scholarly interest in *The Act of Killing* has been widespread, including special issues of *Film Quarterly* and *Critical Asian Studies* (Anderson 2012; Chaudhuri 2014; Sinnerbrink 2016; Nagib 2016a).[9] Most famous of these reactions is undoubtedly Slavoj Žižek's (2013) argument that the film illuminates how, under contemporary capitalism, we inhabit a privatised form of public space. This conclusion is in large part determined by the role that the movies played in the killings during the 1960s, and again during their enactment in Oppenheimer's documentary. As well as 'killing happily' in the style of the movies they watched, the gangsters also incorporated ways of killing taken from movies. Thus Žižek notes: 'The protective screen that prevented a deeper moral crisis was the cinematic screen: as in their real killings and torture, the men experienced their role play as a re-enactment of cinematic models: they experienced reality itself as a fiction' (2013). Accordingly, Žižek concludes that the actions of the killers are a result of 'the dislocating effects of capitalist globalisation which, by undermining the "symbolic efficacy" of traditional ethical structures, creates such a moral vacuum' (2013).

Drawing on a dizzying variety of examples from across history and geography,[10] Žižek concludes that the actions of Congo and his friends are illustrative of the behaviour encouraged by the privatisation of public space under market capitalism:

> The animality with which we are dealing here – the ruthless egotism of each of the individuals pursuing his or her private interest – is the

paradoxical result of the most complex network of social relations (market exchange, social mediation of production). That individuals are blinded to this network points towards its ideal ('spiritual') character: in the civil society structured by market [sic], abstraction rules more than ever. [...] It is often said that today, with our exposure to the media, culture of public confessions and instruments of digital control, private space is disappearing. One should counter this: it is the public space proper that is disappearing. The person who displays on the web his or her naked images or intimate data is not an exhibitionist: exhibitionists intrude into the public space, while those who post their naked images on the web remain in their private space and are just expanding it to include others. The same goes for Anwar and his colleagues in *The Act of Killing*: they are privatising the public space in a sense that is far more threatening than economic privatisation.

(2013)[11]

For Žižek, the implication is that the Cold War killings which Congo and his friends re-enact were responsible for constructing the contemporary society in which their invasion of the public space continues to this day in their celebrity. Indeed, once Suharto had consolidated power, the New Order did turn to neoliberal policies (following advice from several US-educated economists (Booth 1999, 111; Klein 2007, 68–69)), which increased foreign investment, export sales of natural resources, and increased manufacturing for export to Western markets (Elson 2008, 271–273; Roosa 2006, 197). This was a dramatic about-face for a country which had been experiencing workers' seizures of US-owned plantations and oil wells and which seemed to be moving towards increased nationalisation (Roosa 2006, 13–14, 194). The killings eradicated opposition to the free entrance of global capital, the ideological motivation provided by Hollywood gangster films being, presumably, the aspirational fantasy of wealth accumulation that includes even the commodification of public space. Žižek's conclusion suggests that Arendt's prophesy of a 'century of revolutions', won by those 'who understand revolution' (1963, 8), has been borne out by the victory of the global counter-revolution – that same force which (as noted in Chapter 2) Hardt and Negri identified as emerging with the discovery of the Americas.

Yet a very different conclusion can be drawn with respect to *The Act of Killing*, and indeed, the global cycle of films under discussion. If we follow Kwon, it is too simple to conclude that market capitalism 'won' the Cold War. This, in spite of the effectiveness of the suppression of communist opposition during this time, which provided the springboard for the global spread of neoliberalism. All the films in question, even *The Act of Killing*, actually demonstrate that the Cold War is only decomposing, its battles still being fought in the vestiges of their contested remembrance.

To begin with, it is worth stating an obvious, but rarely mentioned point. What the killers express in their recreations of the year of 'killing happily' is a degree of nostalgia for an exciting time in their lives. It is worth remembering, after all, that even from the opposite end of the political spectrum such times are very often enjoyable for some. The Chinese Cultural Revolution is a case in point. During such times of murderous turmoil, for some there emerges a chance at advancement which did not exist otherwise (White 1991, 94–96). This would seem true regardless of the ideology propelling the state of exception. This excitement would go some way towards explaining the incredibly surreal feel to the film, as the gangsters recreate their murders as though enjoyably recounting a wild party, one which continued for many years and culminated in hero status for the executioners. Their recreation, then, is of the state of exception as carnival.

In formulating the concept of the state of exception, Agamben draws on Karl Meuli's description of the charivari or the carnival of the medieval and modern world. These periodic festivals invert the normal social order for a limited period of time, fools becoming kings and vice versa. The carnival, seen as an accepted transgression by commentators like Mikhail Bakhtin (ultimately functioning to shore up the established order in the longer term (1965, 1–58)), when understood after Agamben's evocation of Meuli on the carnival or charivari, does not provide as positive or optimistic a formulation as Bakhtin's (1965, 18–24). Rather, after Meuli, Agamben draws a parallel between the supposedly temporary situations designed to uphold the norm (carnival/charivari and the state of exception) noting that during the carnival 'criminal behaviour is considered licit or, in any case, not punishable' (2003, 71). The carnival or charivari, then, is a time of legalised anarchy when popular justice is given free reign, potentially including acts of expulsion or eradication of certain sections of the community deemed to have wronged the collective (72).

To continue with the obvious but rarely stated, the carnival is clearly evident in *The Act of Killing* – for instance, in the scenes where the former gangsters prepare for their acting scenes, getting made up and reflecting on their acting styles. The entire documentary may be considered a string of carnivalesque set pieces, including brightly coloured and glitzy costumes, feather-festooned headdresses, drinking and dancing, songs accompanied by dancing girls, TV chat show appearances, and so on: ghoulish as I appreciate this kind of interpretation may sound. The gangsters' way of remembering and memorialising the historical moment of the exceptional 'non-place' is by recreating a time when their movie fantasies could be lived out, and when they became heroes for it. Their world turned upside-down, as per the inversion one expects during the carnival, and low-life ticket tout gangsters were transformed into celebrities credited with saving the nation from communism. Hence, Congo's musical fantasy includes the ghosts of those he murdered, thanking him for sending them to heaven (even handing Congo a medal), precisely echoing colonial modernity's excusing of the genocide and enslavement of indigenous and African Americans via the Christian argument that those who died actually benefitted by having their souls saved. The gangsters' sick movies, then, *The Act of Killing* illuminates, are not necessarily dissimilar to many from Hollywood in this respect.

The gangsters ask us to 'remember' with them how they inhabited a surreal world of legitimised murder, akin, it seems, to living in a film for a period of your youth. By becoming film stars in Oppenheimer's documentary, Congo and his colleagues attempt to relive the moment when they first acted as such, during their murderous spree. Where else, but in the state of exception, can you 'imagine' being given free licence to kill without censure and consequently be considered the hero of a national story, just as a character can be in a gangster film, musical, horror movie, or western? As is evident in the horrifying aesthetic of the film, as death squad members in movie star make-up discuss their murderous deeds, this is precisely as one would expect of the world-inverting carnival.

The past that the film provides us with an encounter with is thus not one of the privatisation of public space, as Žižek argues, but the suspension of the laws that normally govern such a space. This does lead to the becoming-actual of the private dreams of the gangsters in the public sphere, it is true. But this is because of the mechanics of the state of exception as it eradicates the memory of the other pasts that it occludes. Žižek may be right in arguing that the *consequence* of the killings was the space they created for the economic shift which followed – as is evident in the film's repeated shots of Medan's commercial streets and the shops which now exist where murders were previously committed. However, what we see in the film is an older idea of the state of exception, that of the carnival.

Žižek's focus on globalisation actually risks depoliticising what the filmic references indicate in *The Act of Killing*. The projection of the gangsters' (cinematic) fantasies into public space is not a vision of privatisation so much as it is of the licence given to the lords of misrule during the carnival. After all, the black-market ticket tout gangsters acted to boost their business interests by eradicating the threat of communism to the market (communists who had boycotted Hollywood films, harming the gangsters' profits (Brink and Oppenheimer 2012, 2)), during a time which they memorialise through their present-day carnivalesque performances. This is the way in which a particular story of history is maintained as a straight line through time. And it is this maintenance of official history which the film investigates with its crystalline structure.

Crystalline carnival: Encountering the state of exception

The past is forever haunting the present in *The Act of Killing*, as is most obviously apparent when Congo confesses that he struggles to sleep, fifty years on, due to the insistence of memories of this period. By recreating the past in the present, in the form of movie-like re-enactments, *The Act of Killing* foregrounds this crystalline nature of time. What it shows in this way is the perpetual struggle that is required to ensure that only one facet of the crystal is visible, only one story of history is told. Congo's stated desire, to record his role in history for posterity, is assailed by the perpetual threat of the ungrounding of his view of history by the memories of forgotten pasts upon which its contemporary dominance is predicated.

There are numerous moments when this becomes evident. The most apparent is the tipping point in Congo's seeming journey of self-discovery. Earlier in the film, Congo, who boasts about the many murders he committed using a garrotte, falters during the shooting of an execution scene in the style of a gangster movie, when a garrotte is placed around his own neck. He is unable to go on after seemingly realising the fear that his victims felt at the point of death. Towards the end of the film, Congo watches the footage again, at his own request, and professes to know how fearful his victims felt at that moment: to which the off-screen Oppenheimer responds that his victims felt far worse than he did, as he was only acting in a film whereas they faced certain and imminent death. Congo, glancing uneasily at the camera as tears begin to well up in his eyes, says: 'Is it all coming back to me? [...] I don't want it to.' Congo, quite literally, is hesitating with respect to his previous belief as to the veracity of the story of history in which his whole life is embroiled. The following scene is of the violent retching on the rooftop where many murders were committed, in which his sensory-motor continuity is interrupted by his physical spasms, as though the ghosts on the rooftop were attempting to re-emerge in the present.

Both scenes are crystalline, and make evident the coexistence of virtual past with actual present. Firstly, there is the footage – on the television – of the re-enacted killings, the past rendered virtual, which creates an emotion-inducing circuit with the present for Congo. The past rather literally is coming back to haunt Congo in the present. Secondly, in the much-discussed rooftop sequence, the verso is given. This time the virtual past is absent from the screen, but present in Congo's physical actions, due to the haunting nature of this murderous space from his past.

Yet, in spite of these moments, the film is best considered a 'flawed crystal', as per Deleuze's taxonomy. In the flawed crystal, the attempt to replicate the truth of history in the actual present (such that it is perpetually stored and re-stored as affirming of the present when it becomes virtual past, as seen in the cinematic recreations of the carnivalesque state of exception) suddenly reveals a crack. In formulating this very specific crystalline image, Deleuze discusses how, in Jean Renoir's classic French movies, class hierarchies are shown to perpetuate historically until a flaw or crack appears in the societal structure, completely shattering the crystal (1985, 82–85). In *The Act of Killing*, similarly, the gangsters take pains to ensure that the two sides of the crystal should be always truth-affirming and match completely. The past is an epoch during which alternative pathways through time were eradicated, therefore the present needs to be the exact mirror of the truth of history which was established then. Only this exact mirroring can retain the singular, linear truth of this history. Thus by focusing on the perpetrators of the murders, the documentary rarely if ever shows a glimpse of the disappeared pasts which haunt them. Instead, we see the state of exception (the past) relived in the carnivalesque cinematic formats through which it was experienced by the killers (the present matching the past). Even when Congo has his seeming revelation when taking part in one such re-enactment, the crystal does not crack: past and present remain in synch even then. As Congo states, he does not want the past to return, or at least not in any other form than the reincarnation he is comfortable with – the memory which matches that of the official story of history. Thus the film's investigation of the past considers how the state of exception, as carnival, eradicates the virtual past which might have been so as to maintain the veracity of a single pathway through time. A crack does finally appear in the crystal, though, in the much-discussed sequence in which the stepson of one of their victims, Suryono, a neighbour of Congo, is integrated into a torture scene.[12]

Suryono takes the place of one of the gangsters' victims in a torture scene, and as he begs for mercy (for a chance to speak to his family one last time), he breaks down. His grief at what seems an imagined version of what his step-father's last moments alive might have been like seems entirely genuine in a film in which emotions at times seem anything but. Suryono is bound as his step-father seemingly was, and has previously (or at least, we understand from the editing that it took place prior to his acting in the scene) explained his step-father's abduction: how he found his body unceremoniously dumped under half a barrel by the side of the road, how only he and his grandfather were willing to be involved in its unofficial burial, and how his family was forcibly relocated to a shantytown, ensuring that he was excluded from formal education and had to teach himself to read and write. Whether any of this scene is genuine or not, we have literally no way of knowing. Yet as the gangsters discuss the reality of history which their story obscures (that it was they who were cruel and not the communists, as was claimed at the time), Suryono sits dressed as their prisoner in the film-within-a-film, his face contorting as he quietly weeps.

In Suryono's grief we see the crack in the crystal. In this crack we glimpse the co-presence of the eradicated past with the present, as his lost legacy is momentarily evident – as though Suryono's step-father speaks through him in the re-enactment – before this haunting presence is silenced once again by the (fictional) garrotting scene which follows. In this flawed crystalline moment, it becomes evident that the persistence of a dominant story of history is predicated upon the perpetual eradication of the virtual past. The repetition of the same is required to confirm, in the present, the veracity of the past as a series of actual moments. Yet even within this obsessively reiterated historical narrative, just the very glimpse of an eradicated past reveals the flaw in the crystal, and shatters it. Suryono's emotional collapse during the fake garrotting, noticeably, prefigures that of Congo, whose own personal demons from the past will not leave him alone either.

As a flawed crystal of time in which we see the persistence of the re-emergence of the virtual past (such that its suppression needs perpetual repetition in the present), *The Act of Killing* illustrates how the state of exception is, in fact, a constant (and constantly failing) process of eradicating other times. The carnivalesque mise-en-abyme does not just illustrate the constructed nature of history and the fact that the winners always write the record of the past. It also shows the resurgence of lost pasts which undermine this history, most evidently in the harrowing re-enactment by a son of his step-father's torture and death in the past, at the hands of the very killers he faces in the present. The crystal history on display here is one in which attempts to perpetually ensure correct alignment of past with the present create virtual images which, unwittingly, illuminate the impossibility of maintaining history in this way. The crack in the crystal, ultimately, is that of Suryono's personal memories, the unexpected return from the past of something other than the official story of history in which the gangsters were and are national saviours. This underside of Indonesian history is only retained in personal memories (contra the official story of history which dominates public space), but its resurgence is what ensures that we see how, in Indonesia as in many places, the Cold War is not over, but only in a process of decomposition.

The Act of Killing, as noted, is the exception to the rule in this respect. The importance of this personal archiving of the past *as primary focus* is what is investigated in Oppenheimer's accompanying documentary *The Look of Silence*, as it is in the trend for time-image documentaries, globally, of which *At the Foot* is taken as a prime example for analysis here.

At the Foot of the White Tree

The Uruguayan documentary *At the Foot of the White Tree* concerns the recent recovery of photographs, considered lost since the dictatorship, belonging to the communist newspaper *El Popular* (1957–1973). Aurelio González Sacedo, a photographer with the paper during the onset of military rule, hid the paper's archive of negatives (seventy-nine cans covering the period of the paper's existence, including many of González's own shots) in the Palacio Lapido/Lapido Building in Montevideo. The paper occupied several floors of the building before it was closed by the military in 1973. González escaped into exile in the late 1970s, spending time in Mexico, the Netherlands, and Spain before returning to Uruguay in 1985. The recovery of the lost negatives, hidden away for thirty-three years, in 2006 is an 'against-the-odds' recapturing of the past, rendered all the more unlikely by the physical transformation undergone by the Lapido Building in the interim. The negatives were discovered in an underground garage, where they were walled in at some point in the past. This was not their original hiding place. González stashed the negatives in a duct between the interior walls in 1973, and the mystery that the documentary uncovers is the reason for their reappearance in the building's basement. This is not, however, a story of the newspaper's past, or its archive, but of González's extremely personal relationship to the archive – its creation, hiding, and recovery – and how it now informs the official record of Uruguayan Cold War history.

Military rule in Uruguay lasted from 1973 to 1985. This is a country which, for much of the Twentieth Century, saw relative stability under democracy, a welfare state, and economic prosperity which only began to decline from the mid-1950s. The situation in Uruguay in the years prior to the dictatorship was one of increasing guerrilla activities, especially on the part of the Movimiento de Liberación Nacional/Movement for National Liberation, 'The Tupamaros' (from 1967 onwards). The Tupermaros took their popular name from the rebellious indigenous leader of the Eighteenth Century (in what is now Peru), Túpac Amaru. Their activities included assassinations of torturers, bank rob- beries, prison breaks, but most notoriously, the kidnapping and murder of US advisor Dan Mitrione, the subject of the Costa-Gavras film *État de siège/State of Siege* (France/Italy/West Germany, 1972). Mitrione's suspicious presence in Uruguay (it is alleged that he was a CIA operative, teaching torture methods to the national security forces) is likely indicative of the USA's involvement in back- ing totalitarian governments across Latin America during the Cold War, albeit the military intervention in Uruguay – as elsewhere in Latin America – was also due to the desire of established national interests (on the right of the political spectrum) to quash movements for social justice and wealth redistribution.

The intensifying civil unrest in the preceding years, intermittent but ongoing since 1968 – including the closure of leftist newspapers, increasing state spending on the military and use of torture by representatives of the state – culminated in a four-month long coup (the state of siege) in 1973, and the implementation of military rule (Weinstein 1992, 84–89). During its 'dirty war', Uruguay had the largest number of political prisoners of any Latin American country, amongst whom torture was widespread. In addition, over 300,000 people (then 20% of its population) went into exile (Kohut, Vilella and Julian 2003, 1). This small coun- try, then, provides a clear example of the Cold War political situation described by Kwon, after Agamben, as a local-level indicator of more global forces. As Eduardo Galeano summarises, the military government functioned as

> the armed wing of the International Monetary Fund and the system of privileges that agency embodies and sustains. With the guerrilla threat as a pretext, state terrorism set its gears in motion to cut real wages by half, dismantle the trade unions, and eliminate critical awareness. [...] Every home became a prison cell and every factory, office, and institution of higher education a concentration camp.
>
> *(1986, 103–104)*

Most importantly for the analysis which follows: 'A general obliteration of col- lective memory was decreed' (104). Uruguay's post-Cold War history, then, indicates the continued importance of this period for the nation's collective memory of the past. For example, resonating with Kwon's idea of a decomposing Cold War, Uruguayan President José 'Pepe' Mujica (2010–2015) was a former Tupamaro guerrilla who endured over a decade in captivity under the military regime. It is this consequence of the state of exception which *At the Foot* addresses in its crystal images.

At the Foot uses time-images to create a very particular engagement with place, thereby to examine Uruguay's various lost histories of lives influenced by the dictatorship.[13] As in the global trend of documentaries, in *At the Foot* there is a deliberate focus on recreating history from the perspective of those whose past was disappeared. Crystal images purposefully recreate glimpses of another past that might have been, a re-aestheticisation of the past from the archive. This is possible in *At the Foot* due to the recovered archive of photographs at its heart, but even in the films where this is not possible, re-enactment is used in instances where the archive has disappeared (for instance, using surviving prison guards in *S21*, or through toys and models in *The Blonds* and *The Missing Picture*). *At the Foot*, then, is paradigmatic of the global trend for films which create the opposite effect to *The Act of Killing*. In these films we see a conscious attempt to reclaim public space not from privatisation, but with respect to the private memories of events that took place in such spaces, and their capacity to beat back the history constructed during the state of exception: to offer instead a crystal history. In an era in which the establishment of museums of memory has become of increasing importance in reclaiming the forgotten pasts of the Cold War, these films offer virtual museums of memory designed to provide glimpses of memories of an alternative imagining of the public sphere. This must emerge from the private sphere, of necessity, as the potential collectives that might have held public spaces were defeated in the state of exception. Thus *At the Foot*, like the other documentaries from a world of cinemas, memorialises a past which, officially, never happened. Denied official recognition at the time, this is a past that has been disappeared, a glimpse of which requires a hesitation with respect to the veracity of official history.

This interpretation is in line with the existing scholarly view as to the potential that documentary now has, having shifted its emphasis from the objective to the subjective since the Cold War, to 'resonate with wider social change', inviting 'the embodiment through the camera-eye of the personal as political' (Chanan 2007, 243–246). Rather than dissolving its capacity for effecting meaningful political change, this objective to subjective shift fuels different types of engagement emerging from the personal to influence the public sphere. As Michael Renov observes, in relation to gender, sexuality, race and ethnicity, 'a grounding in the personal and the experiential fuelled the engine of political action' (1995, 4), such that contemporary documentary constructs or 'enacts' individual, personal identities 'while remaining fully embroiled with public discourse' (5). Thus joining a longer tradition of documentaries attempting to document a history that was designed to disappear (Rabinowitz 1993, 129), *At the Foot* uses the time-image to illustrate how the intricate linkages between personal and public can provide a glimpse of a lost Cold War past. This is not to privatise the public sphere, as per Žižek on *The Act of Killing*, but to re-engage the public from the private.

Crystalline Montevideo: Encountering a glimpse of a lost political past

The time-images in *At the Foot* are created by shooting in present-day locations associated with the dictatorship in the recent past. Rather than editing in archival footage of these places, the film creates crystal images which reconstruct links between the virtual past and the actual present. In particular, by filming in locations that had an impact on the life of González, it creates a personal, virtual (in the sense of cinematic rather than physical) 'museum of memory'.

There are three such standout moments which establish a direct link between images retrieved from González's recovered archive of negatives and present-day spaces. In each of these mannered moments, González is depicted in a place of great significance in relation to the events surrounding the transition to military rule in the 1970s holding enlarged photographs taken in these spaces at that time. In each we encounter González, regarding us along with his personal/public archive of the past (see Figure 5.2).

In the first, González revisits the ruins of the Nervión metalworks, where he worked as a younger man and which he visited again in 1973 to show his photographs to the assembled workers during the general strike organised by the Convención Nacional de Trabajadores/National Convention of Workers. He recounts his elation at that time as he used his photos of similar seizures of premises elsewhere to inform the workers that they were not alone in their occupation of the factory. The second takes place outside the Trocadero Theater, a former cinema on the corner of Avenida 18 de Julio and Calle Yaguarón in Montevideo, where González witnessed the Republican Guard, on horseback, sabre-charging protesters prior to the coup d'état of 1973. The third is on Avenida 18 de Julio, where on July 9, 1973, there was a demonstration at five in the afternoon (the time influenced by a line from a poem by Federico García Lorca), in which a peaceful crowd supporting the general strike was broken up by the military using horses, water cannons and tear gas.

In each instance, in a location in which his personal history intersected with that of the nation's history, González holds up an enlarged photograph of the

FIGURE 5.2   Personal/public archive of the (eradicated) past, in *Al pie del árbol blanco/At the Foot of the White Tree* (Juan Álvarez Neme, 2007).

same place that he took as a young photographer in the 1970s. These are the only surviving images of these events, now recovered from the lost archive. In this way, virtual past and actual present are seen to coexist in the moment, clearly defined as different by their contrasting existence as stasis (past) and movement (present), and black-and-white (past) and colour (present). Each time, the image created marks the return of a lost moment from the past to the particular place, thereby providing a potentially informative history for the present. The return of the photographs fills in for the absent official history of events, otherwise (until now) erased from the official record and surviving only in witness testimony, of which the recovered photographs now stand as visual proof. These moments, then, provide the singularities, the events, which constitute a crystal history (see Chapter 2), offering an alternative to the teleology of the official story.

This is not the end of the process. In each instance, as González stands still with the enlarged photograph in his hands, for several seconds the image is transformed into black-and-white. This has a curious effect, as though the present day were being shown in the process of being transformed into an image that suggests a new 'photograph', an archival document akin to the one González is holding. Accordingly, the documentary's narrative flow is momentarily stalled, an effect that is compounded when each such instance is followed by a montage of other photos from the event in question, all of them recovered along with the photographic archive in the Lapido Building. In this way, the film foregrounds its strategy of creating a new virtual archive through cinematography, around González's experiences in present-day spaces associated with the turbulent national past. Each moment crystallizes the process of construction of a virtual museum of memory wherein past and present can coexist and through which a personal history opens up a previously lost public past. Thus the crystals in this film indicate that another past subsists along with the present, and that in time's perpetual splitting there lies the potential of its return.

The present-day 'photograph' that the documentary creates in each of these standout moments is part of the new virtual archive of national history, each new black-and-white image containing shots of the same space in both the past and the present. Although these are themselves images that become 'past' in their very emergence as pseudo-'photographs', in each instance the documentary reconnects the present with its previously occluded past.

Moreover, these three standout crystalline moments, in which spaces are virtually archived, are not the documentary's only temporal anomalies. The narrative of the rediscovery of the archive is itself recounted out of chronological sequence. The film opens and closes with a press conference marking the public exhibition of the archive, in 2006, at the Centro Municipal de Fotografía/ Municipal Center of Photography. In between, it includes visits to several of the locations in which González photographed events during the transition to military rule (including public protests and military and police violence), the story of the military raid on the offices of *El Popular*, González's efforts to hide the photos of the general strike during the raid, and his escape. All of this is interspersed with the story of the recovery of the archive, also told out of sequence, beginning with a glimpse of Enrique Lista (the young man who contacted González about the archive's whereabouts), Lista's recounting of the story of his childhood encounter with the photos, and footage of Operation White Hair, a comical raid to recover the negatives, perpetrated by González and his ageing friends from the Communist Party (an account of which is given by González prior to our seeing hidden-camera footage of the event itself). The jumbled chronology that arises from this structure stresses the manner in which personal histories enable a disorienting but revealing virtual archive of the past. González's story and, to a lesser extent, Lista's (which is also a personal story of his relationship with the Lapido Building), are histories reconstructed in the present as, temporally speaking, rambling autobiographies. Thus the intertwining personal stories are experienced by the documentary's viewer as personal, oral documents that segue between past and present (mirroring the digressive nature of human recollection and, indeed, storytelling) and are here recorded in this virtual, documentary, museum of memory.

This is not to say that the national significance of González's story is eradicated because it engages with the transnational history of the Cold War. In fact, the story of the nationally important archive that arises out of González's personal history is the point of the film. The title of the documentary, *At the Foot*, suggests that the white tree in question is the Lapido Building, in front of which González is pictured standing just before the opening titles and prior to the closing credits. To follow the metaphor, then, the archive is recovered from among the subterranean roots of the white tree, the footage of the retrieval of the negatives being telling in this respect, in that the camera angle used (an aerial view from a camera positioned to give a perspective looking down into the wall cavity where the archive is interred) suggests the discovery of a grave containing virtual evidence of a disappeared (perspective on the) past. This image resonates with the ongoing search for the graves of those killed by the military, whilst the film's metaphor of the tree renders the virtual archive that is uncovered from the Lapido Building's basement suggestive of the physical remains of the disappeared that still await excavation. After all, 'Lapido', the surname of one of the founders of the newspaper, is similar to the word *lápida* (gravestone), and when describing the hiding of the archive (which was originally not underground, but within the building proper), González states that the negatives were 'buried', suggesting a direct correlation between the lost bodies and this newly exposed lost history.

The secrecy surrounding the negatives, then, at once resonates with Uruguay's ongoing search for the bodies of the disappeared, and maintains hope that the ordinary people of the nation are complicit in resisting the eradication of evidence of this military violence. Eventually, it is revealed that it was most likely builders who, rather than disposing of the negatives, saved the archive by simply building the basement's new interior walls around it. In this way, the film indicates the existence of a collective will to resist the destruction of the proof of a past that existed prior to the transformation of Uruguayan society and history under military rule.

Hence, the national import of the recovered archive is repeatedly stressed by the film. For instance, when González was initially unable to locate the archive on his return, he adopted the tactic of telling its story whenever he had an opportunity. The oral history of its existence became public property in this way and ultimately led to its recovery when news of the search reached Lista. Moreover, the national significance of the photos is foregrounded in the opening and closing scenes, which depict González addressing an appreciative crowd and the television crews that have gathered for the public exhibition of the photographs. At the start of the film, as he is applauded and cheered, González modestly (but significantly) responds: 'It's yours, it's yours.' In the closing scene, the camera lingers on individual faces in the crowd as González gives an impassioned speech about the heroism of individuals standing up against military repression. In these bookending moments, triumphal in tone, the mood is set for the documentary – which charts the recovery of a virtual archive belonging to a communist newspaper that is of great national relevance *for its placement in the transnational history of the decomposing Cold War.* This is the case even if the archive's re-emergence is rendered through the virtual museum of memory created around one man, González, his photographs, and his relationship with the physical space of the Lapido Building in both the past and the present: past/present, personal/public, national/transnational, are all intertwined.

It is undoubtedly for this reason that the documentary begins with a scene in González's home in which old photographs and newspapers strewn across his bed suggest the correlation of his personal life with public history. As González introduces us to the photos on his wall, we see shots of him as a baby side-by-side with pictures of him as an adult attending a mass rally of the Frente Amplio/ Broad Front (a left-wing political party). González's role as photographer of images intended for the public sphere has become, with history, a personal quest for his lost archive of a paper now closed. What the archive ultimately reveals is as much González's personal political convictions as it is the paper's communist stance. Moving beyond the national, it is not a coincidence that González's own personal story is not that of a native-born Uruguayan, as he arrived as a stowaway on a ship from Morocco at twenty-two in 1952, his life impacting irrevocably on the preservation of the history of Uruguay in the time he lived there prior to his exile. Thus his photographs preserve a national history, yes, but the manner of their recovery equally indicates the importance of transnational flows of people who are personally invested in a political past – which was itself part of a much broader transnational Cold War history. *At the Foot* is thus akin to Annette Kuhn's findings with respect of the use of family photographs in memory work, that the patching together of history as 'reconstructions out of fragments of evidence' can be facilitated by exploring 'connections between "public" historical events, structures of feeling, family dramas, relations of class, national identity and gender, and "personal" memories' (1995, 4). Personal and public histories are shown as interlocked through González's wall's photographs just as they are in *At the Foot*. Personal histories can and do return collective memory, can and do (re)inform public space, due to their function as virtual museums of memory.

The way in which *At the Foot* uses time-images to recover glimpses of the lost past is part of a larger process of memory reconstruction and retrieval in the public sphere taking place across the decomposing Cold War world. Recent historical developments in the public sphere in South America have seen countries with histories of military rule transforming specific places (for example, former detention centres such as the Escuela Superior de Mecánicade la Armada [Army Mechanics School – ESMA] in Buenos Aires) into public museums of memory (Jelin 2003, 39). A particularly pertinent example is the Museo de la Memoria/Museum of Memory, which opened in Montevideo in 2007. Uruguay's national museum of memory recreates and reconstructs the social turmoil of the state of siege by assembling fragments and scraps of the past (banned books and newspapers, photographs, a printing press, banners from protest marches, prison doors, objects made by prisoners, placards of the disappeared) that, whilst unable to generate a totalising image of the period, indicate the existence of a history of organised social activism, protest, and resistance. Noticeably, the museum prominently features González's photographs, as little else of such relevance exists. Together these scattered fragments of the past evoke as much the impossibility of memorialising a lost collective past as they do that past itself. In both the actual and the cinematic (or virtual) instances (museum and virtual museum), a focus on an individual experience of a significant moment in the national past is deployed in order to reclaim the (private) archived past, so as to rejuvenate the public sphere.

Whilst *The Act of Killing* celebrates the licence given to murder during the state of exception, *At the Foot*, by contrast, and like the other films noted at the start, uses the time-image to remember the state of exception as a moment of historical elimination. It was during this state of siege, after all, that the disappearance of sections of the population coincided with the disappearance from the national archive of the public history of which they were a part. Whereas in *The Act of Killing* the crystal illustrates the difficulty of forever recreating the past in the image of the present, in *At the Foot* the search for a glimpse of a lost virtual past (which can oscillate anew with the present to remind us of an alternative history) occupies the time-image. Both enable a historical understanding of how the social contract was suspended during the Cold War. Both create a glimpse of a time of transformation when the collective nature of public space was radically altered by political forces indicative of the broader Cold War. Indeed, in both instances, a state of exception ensured the maintenance of the inequality inherent to the existing social contract (which communism threatened to equalise, thereby offering an alternative form of modernity), and in so doing, the Cold War dictatorships laid the way open for the even more radical dismantling of the social contract by neoliberalism (the subject of the final chapter). Thus both documentaries, in slightly different ways, deploy a crystal image to, as Kuan-Hsing

Chen has it, 'de-Cold War' national histories ('to mark out a space in which unspoken stories and histories may be told' (2010, 120)). In so doing they contribute, by turns, to the way in which a world of cinemas tells the story of this transnational history. This is not a matter of illustrating how the now privatised nature of public space emerged at that time, necessarily, but of the way in which private and public intertwine in the creation of world history.

To recap this chapter: a traumatised man breaks down emotionally whilst re-enacting the murder of his beloved step-father, creating unease amongst the gangsters who typically write national history by eradicating this perspective on the past, just as they did by killing the political opposition during a murderous state of exception in the 1960s. A photographer for a now-abolished communist newspaper stands facing the camera, holding enlargements of the photographs he took in the same locations during a Cold War state of siege, bringing back this forgotten (virtual) past to inform the present. This chapter has explored these crystalline cinematic encounters with the transnational history of the Cold War, as lost political pasts are recreated from personal archives of memory to (re)inform the public sphere. These are key examples from a trend of documentaries about the Cold War's reformulation of the social contract, which laid the ground for our seemingly one-sided contemporary political situation. In the next and final chapter I bring this exploration of the world history of colonial modernity across a world of cinemas up to date by focusing on the transnational history of neoliberalism and its fostering of individual contracts.

Notes

1 The term 'haunting' is not intended in the Derridean sense, although the resonance is not coincidental. Although rarely mentioned, Deleuze's (earlier) *Cinema 2* haunts Jacques Derrida's *Specters of Marx* (1993), and not only in Derrida's same use of Hamlet's line regarding time being 'out of joint'. 1) Derrida's 'past as to come' (1993, xix) and the future as memory (45) echo Deleuze's Nietzschean formulation of cinema's ability to falsify the past and create the memory of the future (1985, 50, 122–150). 2) Derrida's imagined 'New International', a collective able to struggle against the global hegemony of capital (1993, 62) 'without status, without title, and without name ... without contract, "out of joint", without coordination, without party, without country, without national community ...' (106–107) (critiqued by Terry Eagleton for its vagueness (1999, 87), but rather like the Occupy or Anonymous movements) is extremely reminiscent of Deleuze's 'people yet to come' of modern political or minor cinema (1985, 207–15). Moreover, Derrida's ghosts who silently ask for justice ('victims of wars, political or other kinds of violence, nationalist, racist, colonialist, sexist, or other kinds of exterminations, victims of the oppressions of capitalist imperialism or any of the forms of totalitarianism' (1993, xviii)) are but belatedly realised spectres of Enrique Dussel's excluded others of modernity (see Chapter 2).

2 Kwon's position would not be a revelation for decolonial or postcolonial scholars. It evokes Hannah Arendt's prediction that the Twentieth Century would be 'a century of revolutions' (1963, 8), and Noam Chomsky's writings in the wake of the US war in Vietnam (1980). Kwon's position builds upon Katherine Verdery's recommendation that a 'post-Cold War' study of the empire of the former Soviet Union can integrate with existing postcolonial studies of the third world, thereby enhancing the

global picture of both the Cold War and colonialism (2002, 18). Kwon's decentred view of the global Cold War (Kwon 2010, 53–54) thus brings his work in line with Odd Arne Westad's (2007), which Kwon references regarding the importance of revolutionary and decolonial movements in the Cold War order (Kwon 2010, 7, 24). However, Kwon's aim, which sets it apart, is to dissect 'the whole of the global cold war into different constituent parts ... for the purpose of creating a new image of the whole' (2010, 148). Resonances with Kwon's work are increasingly found in works in History and International Relations (e.g. Lawson, Armbruster and Cox 2010; McMahon 2014), whilst previous works in Modern Languages/Film Studies have analysed, for example, the decomposing Cold War in movies from post-reunification Germany (Cooke 2005, 1–26).

3 Following Jason C. Parker (2013, 125), we can view this as the emergence of the post-Columbian era, a time during which the postcolonial independence movements throughout the third world (predominantly national in orientation and support) became embroiled in the Cold War: 'decolonization served as the main conduit by which the Cold War reached – and in a sense created – the "Third World"' (125).

4 Revolution, for Arendt, is historically a product of Europeans witnessing for the first time the 'abundance' of the Americas and realising that scarcity, want, poverty, and inequality are a social not a natural condition (1963, 13). Despite this, there is a seeming invisibility of indigenous and African Americans in Arendt's argument (potentially aligning it with the myth of Manifest Destiny), which illustrates its unawareness of the racial contract undermining the social contract (even if Arendt acknowledges the importance of slavery for the prosperity of the USA (1963, 61)). The idea of indigeneity in the Americas evoking a state of nature, after all, ignores the extensive shaping of the environment by the indigenous (see the Introduction), and is redolent of the myth that the populations of the Americas lived somehow outside of historical progression. Robert Stam and Ella Shohat provide more nuance on the influence of the European colonisation of the Americas on Europe: 'The concept of the free Indian living in a society without coercion helped spark revolutionary ideas in Europe. Jean-Jacques Rousseau deployed the notion of the "natural good-ness of human beings" and "societies without coercion" as a means of undermining European authoritarianism' (2012, 8). Ironically, of course, it may be that the conti-nent whose people prompted such utopian ideas of this supposed state of nature was home to some of the oldest recorded forms of societal government in human history prior to the arrival of Europeans and smallpox (Mann 2005, 185 and 333).

5 Agamben argues that an 'essential practice' of contemporary politics, indeed the 'dominant paradigm of government', is to promote the voluntary acceptance of a state of exception amongst the general populace (2003, 2) (see Chapter 6).

6 Anomie being, for Émile Durkheim in *On Suicide* (1897), an influential text for Agamben, when 'society's influence is lacking in the basically individual passions, thus leaving them without a check-rein' (209).

7 This, in addition to the ethical difficulty created by a film shot from the perspective of the perpetrators of mass murder: whether to be suspicious of a real-life complicity between filmmakers and subjects (Fraser 2013); or to question the manipulation of the subjects by 'treacherous ally' Oppenheimer to convince them to collaborate in making a film exposing their crimes (Nagib 2016b, 227) (Congo is clearly suffering from post-traumatic stress disorder (PTSD)); or to emphasise the risk the filmmak-ers took with their lives over eight years to expose the psychologies of killers (Nagib 2016b).

8 The ideological divide targeted in this state of exception was entangled with a racial one, as the victims of the violence included many ethnic Chinese and the state vio-lence 'often targeted the collective social units where individuals belonged' (Kwon 2010, 39–40).

9 Benedict Anderson explores the film's exposé of how the repetition of the perfor-mance of barbarous acts is instrumental in the perpetuation of impunity amongst

criminal perpetrators (2012); Shohini Chaudhuri critiques the film for taking a moralistic position on the gangsters, which may prevent viewers from realising that they belong to the same global capitalist order, and that there is a corresponding need for 'ethical reflection on how atrocities happen' (2014, 180). Robert Sinnerbrink sees the film as 'a confronting ethical experiment in imaginative "psychotherapy"' (2016, 171), arguing that through its cinematic references the film offers a 'subtle allegorical evocation of the "cultural imperialist" background to the state-sanctioned killings' as it investigates the 'ideological economy of images' that sustained the murders (175, 178). Lúcia Nagib, drawing on Viveiros de Castro (see Chapter 4) discusses the film's political aim, of 'forcing the perpetrators into the skin of their victims so as to give them a physical sense of the plights they have caused' (2016a, 146).

10 A Hegelian view of self-interested modern civil society, a murder in the USA, a Bertolt Brecht play, an item in a Chinese newspaper, hardcore pornography, etc.

11 Žižek's argument regarding *The Act of Killing* replicates his previously stated position on contemporary society and withdrawal into privacy (2003, 38).

12 As the focus of much analysis on this scene suggests, this may be the most important scene in the film (Hearman 2014; McGregor 2014; Sinnerbrink 2016).

13 *At the Foot* is part of an emerging trend in Uruguayan documentary that explores the recent past, focusing on the period under or following the dictatorship. This includes: *Memorias de mujeres* (Virginia Martínez, 2005), *Siete instantes* (Diana Cardozo, 2007), *El círculo* (José Pedro Charlo and Aldo Garay, 2008), *Es esa foto* (Álvaro Peralta, 2008), *Vacuum* (María Teresa Curzio, 2008), and *Decile a Mario que no vuelva* (Mario Handler, 2008) (Ruffinelli 2013; Martin-Jones and Montañez 2013a).

6

45 YEARS

Neoliberal globalisation, the personal contract, encountering bodily pasts

This final chapter explores two contemporary thrillers, *Carancho/Vulture* (Argentina/Chile/France/South Korea, 2010) and *Chinjeolhan geumjassi/Lady Vengeance* (South Korea, 2005). The time-images in these films illustrate how bodies inhabit a temporal undecidability with regard to the future. As stores of personal pasts, interacting with global forces (after the withdrawal of the social contract), they hold out the offer of an alternative to the (Orwellian) perpetually static present of the so-called end of history.

The transnational history which is engaged with through temporal bodies is that of the forty-five years – and counting – of neoliberalism, if we allow the 1973 coup in Chile to mark the start of its rapid global spread. Commencing in many places with authoritarian rule during the Cold War, under neoliberalism the nation-state was superseded by the border-crossing flows of capital which characterise globalisation. As the latest phase of colonial modernity increasingly creates a universal form of economic precarity, these films indicate how neoliberalism reduces all bodies to the status of meat to be exchanged for money. Bodies, disconnected from an informing past, are resituated in terms of individual contracts, requiring personal debts to be paid in flesh. Under neoliberalism, universal precarity means that the border (as per Étienne Balibar, discussed in Chapter 1) now runs throughout society, just as it does under colonial rule (the minority elite atop the majority impoverished and exhausted). Neoliberalism, as a transnational history, then, is one of neo-colonial economic disparity being propagated as global societal design.

The chosen films emerge from nations with recent histories of transitioning from (US-backed) military rule to democracy, only to swiftly realise a disenfranchising of the populace under neoliberalism (a continuation or worsening of the inequality fostered under military rule). They act as a flash-forward with respect to the implementation of the state of exception during the Cold War (see Chapter 5) that enables global capital to cross national borders without impediment. The global trend of films of which they are a part engages with precarious labour under neoliberalism and its impact upon bodies – beaten, broken, drugged, addicted, abandoned, kidnapped, mutilated, battered, incarcerated, enslaved, tortured, abused and exhausted.

Such films emphasise the two poles of the time-image of the body – their everyday postures (seen here in *Carancho*), their theatrical gestures (in *Lady Vengeance*). This is done to demonstrate the impact of this recent period of world history on individuals. The hesitation offered concerns whether world history might take shape in a different way due to different bodily actions in the present. Thus the films offer encounters with global peaks of the present in which recent histories are embodied in the protagonists. In *Carancho* it is the characteristic postures of the principal characters – slumping and stretching – which show their everyday tiredness but also reveal their personal histories of living under neoliberalism (the presence of a before and after to the static present). These time-images show the physical insistence of the past, its potential to inform a present otherwise determined to shut off an individual's access to history (determined, that is, to enclose the destabilising potential of the pause between perception and action wherein the virtual whole of time, of duration, might otherwise (re)emerge) via perpetual physical exhaustion. In *Lady Vengeance*, the theatrical transformation of the protagonist is emphasised, amidst a flashback structure which throws doubt onto her motives in every present moment. Her everyday postures of penitence indicate the latent ability of bodies constrained by neoliberalism's static present to nevertheless influence history (reconsidering the past – via a trance-like pause in sensory-motor continuity – to better influence the future).

In neither instance do we learn about the history of neoliberalism per se. But we do encounter the awareness that it has denied coevalness to the recent history of those whose abused *bodies* (their movements, their positions) *record* colonial modernity's creation of a perpetual present in the service of neoliberal capital. Indeed, both films explore whether bodies, as physical repositories of time, contain the possibility for a more representative, democratic society to emerge from amidst the individual contracts of neoliberalism. To do so, bodies reconnect to lost pasts: in *Carancho*, exploring whether a remembered national past might re-inform the present; in *Lady Vengeance*, a notion of justice obtained via physical equivalence from the Christian past. In both, however, success is limited, as working within the constraints of neoliberalism to foster collective opposition to it is figured as only enabling of temporary change.

Time-images: Bodily pasts

Deleuze understands the body in time-image cinemas to exist in two states, or rather, at two poles: the everyday and the ceremonial (1985, 182–183). These poles exemplify two modes of existence capable of rejuvenating humanity's connection to the world. Thus, the body in time-image cinema is a way of engaging with the unthought in life ('To think is to learn what a non-thinking body is capable of, its capacity, its postures' (182)), but also to understand the temporal nature of the body. As will be seen, its temporal expression is antithetical to the eternally static present for which neoliberalism aims.

The first pole is the everyday body, whose attitudes (including tiredness, 'fatigue, vertigo and depression' (185)), demonstrate the presence of time as series. For Deleuze:

> The body is never in the present, it contains the before and the after, tiredness and waiting. Tiredness and waiting, even despair are the attitudes of the body. [...] This is a time-image, the series of time. The daily attitude is what puts the before and after into the body, time into the body. [...] The attitude of the body relates thought to time as to that outside which is infinitely further than the outside world.
>
> *(182)*

The other pole, the ceremonial, occurs when the everyday body is made to 'pass through a ceremony' (183), everyday postures and attitudes proceeding through an 'everyday theatricalization' (185) in which they become 'gest'. This latter term, from Bertolt Brecht, is adapted by Deleuze to indicate how a body can become a spectacle in its own right, a 'dramatization' composed of the 'link or knot of attitudes between themselves, their coordination with each other' (185). As Ronald Bogue indicates, what is important for Deleuze (and what we find in the films analysed) is the passage from everyday attitudes to gest: 'each series of interconnected attitudes forms a pattern, a continuous flourish or movement that constitutes a kind of "mega-gesture", or gest' (2003, 158). Gest, then, encapsulates a string of everyday postures, giving an overview of the pattern of attitudes or postures through which the body's existence in time is understood to be a connection of 'attitudes in series' (160).

In *Carancho*, from the postures of the two world-weary protagonists' bodies, overburdened by tiredness, beatings and addiction, emerge the respective gests of slumping (perpetually defeated by labour) and stretching (the need to perpetually re-awaken and labour further). These are the gests which encapsulate theatrically the resilience required of bodies under neoliberalism. Beyond this, ultimately, these bodies become car crash victims, the ultimate 'mega-gesture' of a film focusing on devastated bodies inhabiting a world in which the borders of the hospital have expanded to include all of society.

In *Lady Vengeance*, everyday postures of willing servitude (in particular, kneeling) designed to deliberately manipulate others into a sense of indebtedness that can be called upon in the future, find their ultimate 'mega-gestures' in acts of penitence which are – appropriately, due to the manipulation required by a world in which society and prison are one – aborted (a curtailed attempt to cut off fingers) or fake (symbolic tofu consumption re-enacted with cake).

As opposed to the series of time found in the everyday body, the ceremonial body is a different time-image. It demonstrates duration's peaks of present or sheets of time (Deleuze 1985, 188). The gests of the ceremonial body demonstrate that it is a store of the past (its sheets) or indicates the future potential of the present (its peaks). Thus, for Deleuze, time-image films of the body indicate the ungrounding presence of what he considers 'the pure or empty form of time' (1968, 110) (effectively, the Nietzschean eternal return (Bogue 1989, 66; Deamer 2014, 264)). This empty form of time is one in which the future remains open, to be informed by the potential for newness contained within the virtual whole of time, as distinct from the past as linear history. Put succinctly, the empty form of time indicates the virtual possibility of the past that *is*, rather than the actualised version of the past that *was* which constitutes the official story of history (Martin-Jones 2006, 59). This is, then, a cinema of the powers of the false, in which an awareness of other, supposedly lost pasts, can potentially inform a new idea of the future.[1]

Transnational history: Neoliberalism

Neoliberal doctrine extols the benefits of individual entrepreneurialism and the free market as the most effective regulator of societal wealth distribution. The role of the state in this model is one of limited interference with the market. Historically, neoliberalism is synonymous with globalisation, as multinational capital in the form of transnational corporations encourages: the withdrawal of (often democratically elected) national governments from the managing of states; the privatisation and sale (at times, effectively, stripping) of national assets to foreign buyers; the (often aggressive) promotion of free trade across borders in ways which disadvantage nations economically or indirectly reduce their democratic freedoms; the imposition of austerity measures by the International Monetary Fund (IMF) and the World Bank (damaging in various parts of Latin America and Africa since the 1980s (Klein 2007, 161–167)); and the avoidance of tax payments by multinationals within nations where their operations are based.

Whilst the global spread of neoliberalism accelerated after the Cold War ended in Europe and North America, its roots remain in this preceding conflict (Kiely 2005, 88–119; Westad 2010). The most infamous example is the US-backed coup ousting democratically elected President Salvador Allende in Chile, 1973, where the ideas of US economist Milton Friedman and the 'Chicago Boys' were then put into practice under General Augusto Pinochet. As Chapter 5 showed, this was part of a process of eradicating left-wing political thought, globally, underway in the 1960s and 1970s (Klein 2007, 66–71). In this sense, the way was paved for neoliberalism by the Cold War, as: 'The capitalist world stumbled towards neoliberalization [...] through a series of gyrations and chaotic experiments that [...] converged as a new orthodoxy with the articulation of [...] the "Washington Consensus" in the mid 1990s' (Harvey 2005, 13).

Neoliberalism, then, is class war waged by the richest against everyone else, a system designed to foster global structural inequality by redistributing wealth upwards (Harvey 2005, 16). Accordingly, it has been accompanied by increasingly authoritarian government, limiting of expressions of freedom of assembly and protest, and the consolidation of power in a political elite aligned with the corporate business interests of their backers. The creation of economic precarity for all but the rich (Berlant 2011, 7) indicates the neo-colonial dimension of colonial modernity's most historical era, for Walter Mignolo the latest phase of this five-centuries-old 'civilizing design' (2000, 278–280) (see Chapter 1). With neoliberalism, then, emerge 'new forms of nonterritorial colonialism [...] colonialism without a colonising nation, or global coloniality' (280–281), what Michael Hardt and Antonio Negri dub 'Empire' (2000). The former centres and peripheries of the world, previously so geographically distinct under imperialism, now exist side-by-side in the same spaces (Mignolo 2000, ix). The new neo-colonial border runs right through society, dividing Global North and South, often in the same space.

Under neoliberalism the prevailing contract is not a social contract between individuals and the state, but between individuals understood as corporations. Steven Shaviro summarises: 'For neoliberalism, the legitimate role of the State is precisely to destroy civil society, and instead to incite a war of all against all in the form of unfettered economic competition' (2011, 77). Thus the dominant characteristic which neoliberalism seeks to inculcate in citizens is resilience: the acceptance, endurance and adaptability to a seemingly unknowable world which individuals are unable to change (Chandler and Reid 2016, 1–5). For this reason, neoliberalism emphasises living in a present undisturbed by the past.

The neoliberal body is not supposed to be beholden to, or even linked to, the historical past. Or not in any sense that might allow it to offer access to alternative modes of being which might question the legitimacy of neoliberal orthodoxy. Even the potentially unruly nature of the personal past – as noted in Chapter 5, of great importance in unthinking doublethink – is something which neoliberalism looks to control (Väliaho 2014, 61–88).[2] Neoliberalism is inherently undemocratic, then, in that it plays upon the vastness of globalisation to render uncertain a person's place within the world, fostering 'a resilient, humble, and disempowered being that lives a life of permanent ignorance and insecurity' (Chandler and Reid 2016, 3). This increases voter apathy when confronted by candidates who represent a continuation of the same neoliberal system in different guises (Klein 2017, 114), a disempowerment played upon by unscrupulous politicians who seek to spread hesitation over the truth.

Against such pessimism, Mark Purcell indicates the potential for democratic action that neoliberal bodies nonetheless contain. Within a system composed of individual contracts, the potential always exists for it to be appropriated by these individuals, if they all begin to act in accord (2013, 56–57). As Purcell's Hardt and Negri-inspired analysis illustrates, the same ungrounding potential of the past which Deleuze considers evident in bodies in time-image films, also exists for multitude under conditions of Empire. In theory, according to Purcell, it is no longer necessary to take control of the means of production to constitute a revolution, because people are already dispersed (whilst interlocking individually) within this system. Instead, multitude must assert its power through collectives of its own imagining. Yet in practice, these films show, this is not a simple matter. Although such collectives can be constructed, their potential to function effectively under neoliberalism is limited to isolated, and temporary, instances.

Encountering embodied pasts: The individual contract (in the control society)

The films discussed in this chapter offer encounters with bodies which, in a present seemingly disconnected from the past (bodies at the supposed end of history), attempt to act out the resurgence of a new future from lost pasts.[3] They present this encounter with lost pasts via a focus on the individual contracts which are negotiated in a time rendered static by neoliberalism. Thus they explore whether there might be workable alternatives to the post-Cold War situation of a seemingly unalterable, interminable and ubiquitous global capitalism (what Mark Fisher has dubbed 'capitalist realism' (2009)). What the apparently past-less bodies depicted indicate, then, is the difficulties of functioning effectively in control societies via personal contracts.

The place of the individual contract in the control society requires some unpacking. Deleuze's 'Societies of Control' (1992) outlines how contemporary society is shaped by the 'ultrarapid forms of free-floating control' (4), which replace the institutions that organised life and regulated behaviour in disciplinary societies. As outlined by Michel Foucault, these are the family, school, barracks, and factory, and, Deleuze concludes: 'from time to time the hospital; possibly the prison, the preeminent instance of the closed environment' (3–7). In the control society, the corporation replaces factories, prisons (and so on), using competition and perpetual training to modulate behaviour. The 'man enclosed' of the disciplinary society gives way to the 'man in debt' of the control society (5).

The figure of indebted man has taken centre stage in the society of control (Lazzarato 2011; 2013). With the reduction of the state and the promotion of the entrepreneurial self forever in need of improvement, 'Everyone is a "debtor", accountable to and guilty before capital' (Lazzarato 2011, 7). Neoliberalism, for Maurizio Lazzarato, thus gives the lie to the illusion that society is based on a social contract. The creditor-debtor relationship is now the basis on which societal relations are organised (37). Whether individual firms or public institutions, all are enmeshed in 'a set of *individual contracts* linking different actors who, in the pursuit of their own individual interest, are all equal' (2011, 102). Rights to education, health care, and other state welfare has been replaced with solely the right to credit, the right to accrue debt in the interest of self-development (2013, 66).

The indebted individual Deleuze terms the 'dividual' (1992, 5; Shaviro 2011, 74) to express the multiple and ever-modulating nature of identity. The dividual can accommodate to the flexibility required of post-Fordist capital, demonstrating an entrepreneurial bent, self-asserting competitive targets and training needs. For Lazzarato: 'the "dividual" [...] is infinitely divisible, infinitely dividable, that is, infinitely composable and, therefore, infinitely "amenable"' (2013, 194). Noticeably, it is the body which becomes the locus for measuring self-development under neoliberalism. In lifestyle, how many calories, units of alcohol, miles run in the gym? In the workplace, how productive, successful, resilient? And so on.

Importantly for this book, for Lazzarato, neoliberalism aims to create a 'society without time' (2011, 47). This is done to neutralise the market risk involved in the emergence of an unforeseen future. If future replicates present, after all, credit relations entered into now will have the maximum chance of being paid off later (2011, 45). Replacing the time of progress of industrial (disciplinary) society is the stasis of a static or 'frozen' time – the eternal present – under neoliberalism (49).

In contemporary cinema the impact of neoliberalism on bodies is often figured through personal contracts (Berlant 2011, 161–189; Martin-Jones 2013a). This has been amply explored in scholarship on neoliberalism and global cinema (Kapur and Wagner 2011), especially in work on the body in so-called 'extreme' cinemas which render human bodies as meat (Kendall and Horeck 2011; Brown 2012; Scott 2014; Martin 2015; Del Rio 2016; Frey 2016; Kerner and Knapp 2016). Films exploring neoliberalism through bodies express how this temporal stasis might be challenged, establishing scenarios in which new collectives might be shaped by personal contracts, drawing on disparate, seemingly disconnected pasts which bodies may try to reconnect with. Amidst the ubiquitous possible examples, the two analysed films, set in institutions exemplifying the disciplinary society (prison and hospital, respectively), explore how these institutions no longer function for the collective, their walls having become porous to the flows of global capital.

Instead, the films show how these institutions function differently under neoliberalism than they did previously. They 'are no longer the distinct analogical spaces that converge towards an owner – state or private power – but coded figures – deformable and transformable – of a single corporation that now has only stockholders' (Deleuze 1992, 5). After all, such institutions, for Loïc Wacquant (2009) and Michelle Alexander (2010), are integral to neoliberal societies like the USA.[4] In a context of perpetual indebtedness to capital, the two films explore how the institutions of the prison and the hospital are increasingly disembedded across society. They no longer discipline and observe (regulating the individual within the mass), but only modulate the behaviour of the dividual. They are now sites where individual contracts are made by people who criss-cross their spaces, whose physical bodies provide their exchange value within such institutions. In these films, people are no longer 'prisoners' or 'patients' within institutions, being disciplined or healed. They are dividuals pulled in various directions, physically, by the individual contracts they negotiate. The ultimate limit of entrepreneurial human capital is shown to be, precisely, its physicality: the body.

The individual contract is crucial to both films, which respectively expose how its functioning to perpetuate neoliberalism's divisive competitiveness is a failed enterprise. Instead, in both, the individual contract is deployed to create a rhizomatic assemblage of inter-contractually engaged individuals, each acting for individual gain, who find themselves temporarily working together (without longer-term aims) as default collectives. Through this examination of the individual contract, the time-image indicates what limited (democratic) resistance may be possible to the intolerable 'frozen' time of neoliberalism. This is the encounter offered by these films, then, of the revelation of neoliberalism's (lost) bodily pasts and how they may yet indicate the kinds of new collectives which can potentially form under neoliberalism.

Carancho

Carancho is set in the *conurbano*, the urban sprawl of Greater Buenos Aires. It commences with still images of a car crash, prone bodies glimpsed amongst the wreckage. Intertitle statistics inform us that, concerning traffic accidents, there were '22 deaths a day, 683 a month, over 8,000 a year, 100,000 over the last decade. The compensation market is booming.' Immediately the body is linked to its market value.

We are introduced to Héctor Sosa (Ricado Darín), a former lawyer who lost his licence and is now an employee of the 'Foundation'. The Foundation represents people who have been in traffic accidents, but retains the majority of the insurance pay-out. Sosa spends much of his time at crash sites or in hospitals (falsely) advising victims on how to maximise on their insurance. His activities also stretch to more dubious activities, including helping people to fake accidents and cash in on policies, from which the Foundation takes its substantial cut. *Carancho* means, literally translated, 'vulture', the film's title commenting both on Sosa's dubious ethics and foregrounding a spectre overhanging the inhabitants of neoliberal Argentina. Greater Buenos Aires is depicted as a place where bodies are subject to exhaustive work practices (hospital and insurance workers alike), and where the sight of bloodied, prone figures in the road seems commonplace. By evoking this overhanging shadow of carrion, *Carancho* intimates that under neoliberalism the body is commodified meat, as noted by the association made in the intertitles between the number of deaths and the market for compensation claims.

Sosa's desire to leave the Foundation's employ comes to a head when he inadvertently kills a client, a musician called Vega (José María Rivara) for whom he is trying to help obtain an illegal pay-out. Filled with remorse, Sosa hands over all the compensation money to Vega's grieving wife, much to the chagrin of Casal (José Luis Arias) at the Foundation, who sends his henchmen to beat Sosa and threaten further violence if the Foundation is not paid. When another bereaved family looks set to lose out to the Foundation, Sosa and the young doctor he is courting (his counterpart for much of the film), Luján Olivera

(Martina Gusman), attempt to secure them the entire insurance pay-out. Casal beats Luján with a belt as a warning, and Sosa retaliates by beating Casal to death with the metal tray from a filing cabinet. In the finale, the Foundation pay off the police to ensure that Sosa can secure the insurance pay-out due to the family, which they intend to keep for themselves. Backed into a corner, Sosa sets up a crude sting, a traffic 'accident' involving both himself and the head of the Foundation. This results in several fatalities and leaves Sosa injured. As Sosa and Luján attempt to escape, their standby car is also involved in an accident. The final radio communications of the ambulance on the scene suggests that Sosa may be dead and Luján alive. Like a Shakespearean tragedy, with most central and incidental characters dead, *Carancho* demonstrates that there is no escape from neoliberal Buenos Aires.

This kind of critique of neoliberalism's impact upon society has been a consistent feature of Argentine cinema's resurgence over the past two decades (epitomised by touchstone films like *Nueve reinas/Nine Queens* (2000) and *La Ciénaga/The Swamp* (2001)).[5] This is in large part due to the economic crisis of 2001 that followed the Carlos Menem government's turn to this economic doctrine in the 1990s (Falicov 2007, 95–113; Aguilar 2008, 117–182; Page 2009, 180–194; Rocha 2012, 1–18). What the following analysis of *Carancho* adds to existing scholarship on this topic is a greater understanding of how the body as a temporal site is central to the critique of neoliberalism.

The hospital is everywhere/everywhere is the hospital

In *Carancho*, the main location for much of the action is the municipal hospital. This space is shot so as to indicate the decrepitude of such an institution under neoliberalism. When we first encounter it through the eyes of the newly arrived Luján, there are not enough doctors on call to help her patient, who in any case cannot be admitted due to lack of space. Characters enter and leave via an ill-lit entrance in the rear of the building, the corridors are characterised by the ubiquity of patients on trolleys (there is not even space to quarantine a patient who has tuberculosis), and the cinematography repeatedly decentres humans to focus on overflowing bins and medical waste on the floor, dilapidated paint work, and the dirt which has accumulated on the doors.

The hospital does not function in the manner of a disciplinary institution, as described by Foucault. Rather, illustrative of the control society, flowing across this dilapidated space the individual contracts of neoliberalism are seen to form. Three instances of the negotiation of such contracts are revealing of the film's engagement with the impact of the transnational history of neoliberalism via the exhausted bodies of its protagonists.

Firstly, there is Luján pursuing her career. She is gradually moved up from the ambulance night shift to ER. She works Saturdays, and when a more senior doctor encourages her to take on extra hours in order to get appointed, she also sacrifices her day off on Fridays: this, despite noting that she is generally exhausted.

For Luján the hospital has effectively taken over her entire life. Several scenes commence with her being awoken in the building, in her work clothes, where she has fallen asleep. The individual contract that Luján agrees, then, is one which sees her renounce home and social life for conspicuous production.

Secondly, Sosa plies his trade by preying on unsuspecting relatives of the injured. We see him artfully drop the information that he is a lawyer able to represent victims of accidents to a stranger in a waiting room. Various scenes revolve around the importance of people signing to give the Foundation the power of attorney. This is such a prosaic event in everyday reality that the film does well to make it suspenseful.

Thirdly, in a scene which seems intended solely to illustrate the lack of any national cohesion within the space of the hospital, two men who are badly wounded and bleeding attack each other in ER. It is not made explicitly clear, but they may have been admitted as a result of injuries sustained when fighting each other. Their violence spills out of the treatment room, as the friends of one man attempt to join in the fray, before shots are fired and everyone disperses. It is not clear whether this is a skirmish due to football team loyalties or some other feudal issue, but this particular societal system is shown to be clannish or tribal. Its individual scores also criss-cross the boundaries of the hospital, the same as those of the business deals outlined by the behaviour of Luján and Sosa.

In all three instances, individual interests propel people to act, irrespective of the hospital's actual function (which it struggles to maintain) of tending to the sick and injured. Their individual contracts, scores, and debts intersect in the hospital, but do not function as part of an institution integral to a collective-enhancing social contract. Rather it is a porous space across which the 'open, fluid and rhizomatic' (Shaviro 2011, 77) control society flows, enabling momentary intersections of aspects of each dividual – the career in Luján's case (her debt to be paid in working hours), the job in Sosa's case (the debt he must pay to regain his licence) and the feudal in the case of the anonymous men (their debt to their clan or tribal identities). These 'sides' of the dividual intersect in the hospital, rendering it not a 'closed environment' designed to regulate behaviour, as in the disciplinary society, but a node indicative of how business is done, and of how humans interact more generally without the collective sense of belonging offered by a dedicated welfare state.

The Foundation, for its part, has moved into an empty space created by the withdrawal of the state, and taken on the role of offering a (falsely represented) social service to the families of those in hospital. Ambulance driver Pico (Fabio Ronzano), describes the Foundation as the closest thing that many accident victims will get to a social worker. Indeed, Sosa is repeatedly shown, at his desk, consoling distraught relatives in their stress and grief, and offering his services at funerals. Yet the reality is that the Foundation encourages the commodification of the bodies of those without the education to obtain sufficient money to get by. The scam that Sosa sets up, which leads to the death of Vega, is the pivotal case in point.

Vega agrees to be involved in a fake accident, his consent being shown in his signing of a contract. Sosa then injects Vega with painkillers and breaks his leg with a sledgehammer, before helping him out into the road to be run over by an accomplice. Pico, also in on the sting, is waiting nearby in his ambulance. The accidental death of Vega, however, shows the high-risk nature of both individual contracts and neoliberalism's reduction of bodies to the value of meat to be traded on the market. It is after Vega's death, significantly, that Sosa and Luján (after first breaking up) eventually come to explore a (collective) alternative to the individual contract, of which more momentarily.

Exhausted everyday bodies

How are these time-image bodies depicted? Both Sosa and Luján are characterised by recurring gestures: Sosa, a slumped posture, head hanging or head in hands (he massages his head tentatively after numerous beatings (see Figure 6.1)); Luján by exhausted sleeping, close-ups of injections which disembody her legs and feet, and a slow stretching of her neck muscles. These tired postures demonstrate time as series, but they also provide a glimpse of their (lost) personal pasts.

The opening introduces Sosa, who is being beaten by the family of a man whose funeral he has crashed. As he picks himself up he holds his head, the gesture solidifying a posture we will see him repeat: at work (his head in his hands on the desk), at the hospital after Vega's death (leaning forward on a handrail), after being beaten by Casal's men, and when he finds his car has been torched. This opening montage intercuts with Luján, who is introduced as a dissected body. The first image is of her foot filling the frame in close-up as she injects drugs. Later we see her seemingly disembodied hands tapping pills into cups as she self-medicates, and various close-ups dissecting her body follow (see Figure 6.2). Thus both central characters are bodies moving woozily through life due to the exhaustion of their work, their physical tiredness the result of the perpetual drive of the static present.

FIGURE 6.1 Tired all the time, in *Carancho/Vulture* (Pablo Trapero, 2010).

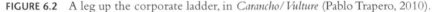

FIGURE 6.2   A leg up the corporate ladder, in *Carancho/Vulture* (Pablo Trapero, 2010).

Both bodies also speak of how their respective pasts are embodied in these everyday postures. It transpires that Sosa's recurring slump is due to regret: at losing his license and having to work for the Foundation, and over the deaths he profits from. Luján, for her part, repeats certain micro gestures (including her neck stretches, along with the pressing together of her lips) after injecting herself with drugs. Luján's movements relate to her arrival in Buenos Aires, when she met an anaesthetist who started her drug habit. Her posture, then, indicates the self-inflicted numbness she requires to cope with the environment, and her gruesome and exhausting career treadmill. These are the glimpses of (lost) pasts found in the encounter with bodies in cinema under neoliberalism.

As both characters are attempting to 'rise' within society (Luján to a more permanent appointment, Sosa to return to his former practice), their respective 'trademark' postures become gests which demonstrate the difficulties they have in the present, due to their respective pasts. Thus the postures these bourgeois professionals repeat in their moments of tiredness are indicative of the series of time which insists along with (but, untapped, is subordinate to) neoliberalism's manufacture of an eternal, static present.

Neither Sosa nor Luján is able to adopt the correct posture to conform to the debt economy, in which, Lazzarato notes, the '"debtor" is not expected to reimburse in actual money but rather in conduct, attitudes, ways of behaving' (2011, 104). Instead, Sosa and Luján are decidedly deficient in their bodily attitudes. As a result, Sosa ultimately descends into murderous rebellion against the Foundation, whilst Luján torpedoes her career by helping the family of the deceased husband against her boss's wishes. Indeed, it is in this failure of physical conformity that an alternative future is explored, in which a collective will might replace individual contracts. Here the crystal of time becomes all-important.

Sosa and Luján, although estranged after the death of Vega, strike up a new individual contract (again, in the hospital). They agree to help the latest family the Foundation is targeting. The change of direction prompting this contract is emphasised when Luján twice insists that Sosa promise to act honourably, which he duly does, to seal the deal. Consequently, they each explore an altruistic side to their respective positions as dividuals. This is a 'side' to Sosa's (previously vulture-like) personality which he develops on meeting Luján, seemingly in the hope of some sort of redemption from the past he regrets. Luján, for her part, goes against her career-oriented aspect, against the warning she receives from her senior colleague (the hospital, it is intimated, works in league with the Foundation). It is as though Luján is finally acknowledging that the numbness she seeks in drugs is an escape from the compromises and sacrifices she makes to pursue her career.

Noticeably, in this process, the two central characters each adopt the other's trademark posture: they become mirror images of each other, creating a crystalline structure through which they together attempt to reconnect to the (national) past. When Luján is warned off her enterprise by her boss, she leans forward on a table, mirroring Sosa's head-down slump. Indeed, shortly afterwards Luján collapses after an injection. The shot of her foot on the dirty toilet floor, surrounded by hospital detritus, directly equates her via a graphic match with the partially out-of-shot corpses seen in the opening shots of the car crash. For his part, in the final crash scene, before he (along with Luján) ultimately becomes a car crash victim, Sosa injects himself just as we have seen Luján do many times previously. The closing scenes are a sting in which Sosa and Luján thus perform the roles that the other would normally adopt, so as to con the Foundation. In this role-reversal process, their respective trademark postures are rendered, theatrically, as gest. Together they pass through the crystal, escaping their static presents to (re)connect to another past from the virtual whole of time.

Yet, in this instance, by not conforming to the postures expected of professionals under neoliberalism, attempting instead to recreate a social justice no longer considered of value by the state, only returns their bodies to its status as meat. Their attempt to escape is a dead end. The disorienting car crash finale emphasises this, in the recreation of the same scam through which Sosa inadvertently caused the death of Vega, with himself in the role of victim. Formerly a shady entrepreneur 'trading' in bodily injuries, the risk to his own body – that he ultimately has to put on the line as his remaining capital – demonstrates its commodity status. Even so, despite this pessimistic ending, although we witness a failed individual contract unable to out-manoeuvre neoliberalism's commodification of the body as asset (or indeed, the exhaustion of its static present), there is a glimmer of hope amidst the carnage. The 'altruistic' side explored by each character is not entirely for naught. To uncover why, we need to explore the rare moments where a collective is depicted that offsets the emphasis on individuality so beloved of neoliberalism.

Carancho's critique of neoliberalism could be interpreted as functioning within a national allegorical reading, much as films like *Nine Queens* (et al.) before it. When Sosa loses control and beats Casal to death, the Argentine flag is central to the shot, in a rather obvious placement. As Sosa pummels Casal's head into a pulp, he punctuates his blows with the words 'nunca más'. This is the slogan associated with the aftermath of the dictatorship, and the return to democracy in the 1980s. A national allegorical reading, then, would see the film as (morally) equating the neoliberal Foundation, and its robbery of the disenfranchised through insurance scams, with the dictatorship – or at any rate, as a continuation of it. Sosa, for his part, is presumably rather like those who suffered under military rule and protested for a return to democracy, or is their present-day representative. However, if we consider the temporal nature of the bodies on display, a more nuanced reading of engagement with transnational history (i.e. that of neoliberalism more broadly) emerges.

In *Carancho*, the characters attempt to reconnect with the potential of the past to offer an alternative future – the virtual potential of past that *is*, as opposed to the actualised, singular past that *was*. Only, in doing so they connect with a decisive moment in the national past ('nunca más'), the return to democracy, which no longer provides the potential it once did. How so?

The undecidability of the body in time retains the possibility of thinking the unthought, of remembering a past which can inform a new future. Hence, although constrained by fatigue, Sosa regains a memory of resistance, from a time when imagining a new future was at the forefront of collective politics ('nunca más'). In this statement he chooses to reconnect with the national past, as opposed to his own personal destiny (of a static present of Sisyphusian deceptions), via the altruistic aspect that has been activated in Sosa (the dividual) by his contract with Luján. Sosa and Luján's contract, after all, is to believe in a form of collective identity other than that of neoliberal individualism.

This becomes clear when Sosa begins to help the family the Foundation is targeting. Sosa is pictured attending a funeral, as an ally of the family. For the first time he is genuinely involved, rather than just using the family's grief to cynically seek a new deal. His alignment with the family at this point is emphasised by the Foundation's torching of Sosa's car to warn him off their case. In this, the undecidability we initially feel seeing Sosa in the crowd of mourners (as we have previously, in his vulture aspect) is created by a suspicion as to his actual motives. Has he really changed, or is he just trying to woo Luján again with whatever lies he can? Yet this tension is usefully deployed to emphasise that Sosa is, precisely, a body in time, whose very existence is one of undecidability. In short, he has within him the potential to change and, we are ultimately reassured, that is what we are seeing.

As a result of this engagement, Sosa and Luján experience a rare moment of happiness, at the 'Sweet Fifteen'/*Felices 15 Años* celebrations of the family's daughter. Sosa and Luján dance together amongst the other guests, smiling, enjoying the company at the festivities before retiring to (finally) have sex. The collective envisioned in this scene, then, is one of a dedicated professional class (lawyer Sosa, doctor Luján), united in their desire to obtain social justice (as much as one can from a financial pay-out) for the working-class family which – as they themselves assert – does not understand the legal situation they are in. This is an attempt to imagine an alternative form of societal collective, one that brings a relaxed happiness (dancing, smiling, laughing, sex) so contrasting to the tiredness (and numbness to the suffering of others) of individualistic neoliberalism.

This is not entirely a return to a former model of Argentine society, of a united middle and working class. Rather, it is an attempt to create a slightly different collective from amidst the enmeshed individual contracts of neoliberalism. Noticeably, when advising the family on how to best obtain their fair due from the insurance company, Sosa advises them of the need to learn a quality that pertains to the constant pressures of this situation: not resilience to over-production and its accompanying exhaustion (as per neoliberal orthodoxy), but patience. Noting indirectly the financial value of time which mitigates against the working-class family, Sosa states of the Foundation that: 'They have a lot of money, a lot of cases like yours, and they have time. They can wait.' Accordingly, his advice to the family is: 'Just don't be in a rush, that's when you lose. The key is knowing how to be patient.' In contrast to the individual contract, then, is an idea of communal solidarity which can counteract the over-demanding treadmill of the present. Patience will provide, literally, the full value of a life, providing there is a community that can support the family through the time needed to win individual cases. Although this may be only positive in so far as it enables the maximising of the market value of the body as commodity (and indeed, it retains the idea of the family and the market as the primary players, as opposed to any more inclusive sense of society), at least it can enable *this* degree of social equality, which is more than is otherwise possible under the carrion shadow of neoliberalism.

Ultimately the 'altruistic' contract of Sosa and Luján fails. The moment from the (virtual) past (that *is*) which they attempt to connect to ('nunca más') does not have sufficient potential to combat the neoliberal present. Or at least, it can only create a bloody stalemate in which both the Foundation and its discontents recreate in miniature the political violence of the former, recent era. However, if Luján has survived, it may well be that the money will be returned to the family, as she vowed. Indeed, amidst the carnage, the Foundation has been effectively destroyed. Whilst neoliberalism is a 'trap', then, and a situation too large for a single individual contract to irrevocably change (the Foundation are in league with the all-pervasive police and the hospital, and no doubt another 'Foundation' will soon arise), a challenge can be mounted. This, however, requires the fatigued bodies of the neoliberal present to remember that insisting along with their com-modification (the physical status of their bodies as meat) is their temporal unde-cidability as bodies, precisely due to their status as multi-faceted dividuals.

Carancho shows that it is possible for these bodies to recover a past otherwise lost in the static present, and reactivate it via unconventional individual contracts not solely oriented towards self-interest. It is this point which is also picked up by *Lady Vengeance*, in South Korea: how to go beyond a critique of neoliberalism, how to imagine – if not its dismantling – then the use of its own structure (the individual contract) to create new collectives that function contrary to its aims?

Lady Vengeance

Lady Vengeance begins in the present, with the release of Geum-ja Lee (Yeong-ae Lee) from prison. She has served thirteen and a half years for murdering a young boy, Won-mo Park, that she helped kidnap. However, although she confessed to the murder, she is in fact innocent. The film then follows her execution of 'the plan' to take revenge upon her former lover, and school teacher, Mr Baek (Min-sik Choi), who murdered Won-mo (and later, it transpires, four other children). Baek blackmailed Geum-ja into confessing in his stead, by kidnapping her baby daughter. The story takes place predominantly in the present, but is interspersed with numerous flashbacks, especially to Geum-ja's time in prison, and one noticeable flash-forward. Geum-ja's story is that she became pregnant as a schoolgirl at eighteen and, unable to turn to either of her separated parents for help, she walked into the arms of her former teacher, Baek, for support. After the kidnapping of Won-mo led to his death, Geum-ja has spent her years in prison wracked with guilt. Her search for atonement has led her to devise a scheme (referred to by her former cellmates as 'the plan') to take revenge upon Baek.

The flashbacks to Geum-ja's time incarcerated are triggered by reunions she has on the outside with people she encountered inside, including: the Christian preacher (Byeong-ok Kim) who was instrumental in her conversion into a saintly figure when in prison (albeit Geum-ja spurns him immediately on her release); the owner of the cake shop that she goes to work for; and, most importantly for 'the plan', her former cellmates. Each of these women owes Geum-ja a debt from their time in jail, due to a good deed that she did for them then. On the outside they pay back these debts in ways which further her vengeful plan. Indeed, Geum-ja proves hard-hearted in what she is willing to ask of those in her debt.

In addition, Geum-ja is reunited with her daughter, Jenny (Yea-young Kwon), who was given up for adoption by Baek. Jenny has grown up in Australia. Jenny travels to Seoul with Geum-ja. Whilst there, awaking from a dream momentarily, she sees the ghost of Won-mo, who is haunting Geum-ja. Jenny's life is briefly put at risk when Baek attempts to have her abducted, only for Geum-ja to kill the would-be captors.

The film's finale sees Geum-ja assemble the families of all the children that Baek has kidnapped and murdered (who learn that their children were dead before the ransoms were paid). She is aided by Detective Choi (Il-woo Nam), due to the guilt he feels over convicting Geum-ja even though he knew she was not guilty. In an abandoned school the families take it in turns to inflict pain on an incapacitated Baek, using a terrifying array of sharp objects. After Baek's death, Geum-ja encounters Won-mo's ghost, but is not forgiven. Instead, Jenny is called by Won-mo to assist her mother in seeking a new life after completion of 'the plan'.

Lady Vengeance is the third part of Park Chan-wook's Vengeance Trilogy, the second part of which, the internationally renowned *Oldboy* (South Korea, 2003), won the Grand Jury Prize at Cannes. Several works have analysed the first two films, focusing on their complex negotiations of neoliberalism in South Korea (Wagner 2011; Herbert 2012; Diffrient 2013).[6] Such national-allegorical assessments of the Vengeance Trilogy are broadly consistent with the founding body of work (in Anglophone academia at least) which explores how contemporary

South Korean cinema engages with the changes wrought on society by, and after, the IMF crisis of the late 1990s (Kim 2004, 233–258; Shin and Stringer 2005; Gateward 2007).

Yet, other scholars have pointed towards the less nationally specific aspects of Park's films, indicating the trilogy's more transnational engagement with neoliberal globalisation. For example: Park as both national celebrity and transnational auteur indelibly associated with the Cannes brand (Lee 2008); Park's films as constituting a hyperviolent cinema of cruelty which deliberately effaces national history to reach international audiences (Choi 2010, 175–177); *Oldboy* as exploration of the ambiguous relationship of people to personal memories in a context where bodies have been reduced to their commodified worth under neoliberal globalisation (McSweeney 2011, 226); the trilogy as postmodern examination of the end of grand ideologies (e.g. humanism) and as exposition of the surface-level interpretation of the image as image with unknowable interpretive depth (K. H. Kim 2011, 178–199); *Oldboy* as a product of 'international exchanges and borrowings' stemming from the original Japanese manga on which it is based to its Bollywood remake (Smith 2013, 189); and *Lady Vengeance* as a meditation on the possibility of forgiving others, in a global context where considerations of ethics and politics may rely on Western definitions of such concepts (Choe 2016, 201–214). But, as was the case with *Carancho*, what the following analysis adds is the role of the body as a temporal entity in this critique of neoliberalism (whether understood as national-allegorical, or more global in intent) and its negotiation of a world of individual contracts.

Everywhere is prison or school/prison and school are everywhere

The key institutions featured in *Lady Vengeance* are, firstly the prison, and secondly the school. Once again, their former disciplinary functions have been replaced in the control society by the criss-crossing of individual contracts amongst people juggling their various facets as dividuals. However, in *Lady Vengeance* these spaces are also shown to be capable of producing new collectives, even if this is only via the shepherding of various individual contracts towards the same, temporary, goal.

The prison is depicted so as to suggest that its walls have stretched beyond their physical boundary, into society itself. The film opens with Geum-ja's release, where she is greeted by the preacher. He offers her tofu, informing her (and, presumably, the international audience anticipated in the wake of *Oldboy*'s global success) of the tradition that eating tofu on your release enables you to: 'live white and never sin again.' In spite of the preacher's flashback showing Geum-ja's conversion into a model Christian when in jail, Geum-ja very dismissively tips the proffered tofu onto the ground and tells him to go and screw himself. Clearly, with 'the plan' to execute, she does not yet feel herself to have left prison. This is reinforced by her new abode (cell-like in proportion, makeshift within a cramped, single-room, illicit hairdressing salon beneath stairs) and her job, a continuation of the cake making she learned inside (employed by the same teacher). Only in the closing scene does Geum-ja eat a snow-white cake (in the falling snow) that she has baked in the shape of, and decorated to look like, tofu. She eats this with Jenny as though repeating the opening scene, only this time after re-establishing the family which should have greeted her on her release. She tells Jenny, in English: 'Be white, and live white, like this' before burying her head in the cake/tofu. Thus, only with 'the plan' complete, does Geum-ja allow that she has actually left the penitentiary.

Beyond this more obvious reading at the diegetic level, however, is the impli-cation that the distinction between inside and outside of this institution has become very blurred in general. This is most clearly shown in Geum-ja's calling in of her debts from other former inmates, once released. As discussed further below, each time Geum-ja reunites with former cellmates, flashbacks create a montage illustrating how the past in the prison is informing of the present on the outside. Thus, for the individual contracts of the control society, the space of the formerly disciplinary institution is not one isolated from the rest of society. Rather, the film suggests that all of the control society is now akin to a prison, or rather, that there is no longer any way to distinguish between the functioning of contracts within and outwith such disciplinary institutions.

The school, for its part, is an abandoned building wherein Geum-ja gath-ers the families of Baek's victims. Its existence as a derelict space emphasises that its disciplinary function is not what it was. In fact, the film shows children to be people let down by both the institution of the family (Geum-ja cannot turn to her parents when pregnant, Jenny is given up for adoption) and the school (Geum-ja becomes pregnant when a schoolchild, schoolteacher Baek kills schoolchildren for ransom money). It is in the school that Baek's motive is revealed to the parents, when Geum-ja drops the bombshell that he was saving up the ransom money to buy a yacht. What shocks the parents about this, aside from the naked greed of neoliberal aspiration, is that the only possible motive they could previously have conceived of as to why anyone would need so much money is that they had children to raise. The bereaved parents' missed guess, of course, indicates the huge cost of bringing up children in a context where the level (and cost) of education provided is increasingly a matter for individual families, not the state.

Thus there is a debt shown needing to be honoured between parents and children. The abandoned school, like the prison, indicates that individual debts (this time, of parents to the memories of their children) also criss-cross the bor-ders of educational institutions in the control society. This is emphasised when the parents are shown videos Baek made of the murders he committed and the past returns to haunt them, bringing back their grief with it. Whilst the point is made by Geum-ja that Baek targeted the children of schools situated in affluent neighbourhoods, and the families' attire mostly indicates bourgeois wealth, one family stands out in its working-class dress. The daughter of this family (whose brother Baek murdered) notes that: 'My mother had to scrub hotel floors to send my brother to that school. We ran around like dogs to come up with the ransom. Now we've lost our house and the relatives won't see us.' This particular murdered child is shown to be curiously out-of-place, then, a victim of their parents' aspiration for them to join the wealthy elite, which leads directly to death. Via this particular contrast, the indebtedness of children to their parents in the attainment of a decent education under neoliberalism is emphasised, but so too the indebtedness of the parents to their children for not providing for their safety. Moreover, as Choi's presence there further shows, the police did not catch the killer, even when they knew him to still be at large: another failing institution. This generational failing is what, at the film's close, the ghost of Won-mo cannot forgive Geum-ja for. Rather, he briefly binds her – exactly as she previously had Baek – to show her that he has the same rights of vengeance over her as she over Baek. Instead of forgiveness, he indicates that she needs to atone by focusing on Jenny, indicating the importance of the generational debt – parents to children – as primary of all individual contracts.

The way in which individual contracts are figured as criss-crossing these two spaces functions, as it did in *Carancho*, to show how neoliberalism commodifies the body, rendering it so much meat to be traded. This is most evident in the motivation of Baek, who kidnaps and murders to buy a yacht. The children he murdered were stolen, their security (erroneously) traded for cash, their bodies expendable meat. However, this time the film contains a much broader examination of how this neoliberal commodification of the body itself opens a door for the particular form of vengeance that is enacted upon the body of Baek. The commodity value of the body is given an additional dimension in *Lady Vengeance*, in that its worth can only be traded for the equivalent, pound for pound.

Each of the families of the deceased children enters the schoolroom where Baek is bound, and exacts a portion of their revenge upon him with something pointed and sharp. However, they agree to leave the killer blow to the grandmother of one of the children, Eun-joo. Thus their revenge is the extraction of the, literal, 'pound of flesh' they are owed by Baek. This seemingly Old Testament idea, reminiscent of the notion that revenge might imply an equivalence ('an eye for an eye, and a tooth for a tooth'), re-appears in other scenes where debts are considered in bodily terms. For example, on release from prison, Geum-ja visits the parents of Won-mo, and cuts off her little finger in dramatic penance. She intends to remove all her fingers, the voiceover informs us, until she obtains their forgiveness. It is not a coincidence that the sum she has to pay to have her finger sewn back on is equal to every penny she has made whilst working in prison. Geum-ja's debt is, precisely, the value of her time inside, but it is also, just as precisely, the value of one finger of her body.

To make this point clear, the film gives a pivotal speech regarding atonement to Geum-ja, as she explains her story to Jenny. She states: 'My sins are too big and deep. I don't deserve to have a sweet daughter like you. You're innocent, but you had to grow up without a mother. But that's also part of the punishment

I must take. [...] Everyone makes mistakes, but if you sin you have to make atonement for it. [...] Big atonement for big sins, small atonement for small sins.' This speech 'makes sense' of Geum-ja's actions in prison, when apparently converted to Christianity, and, again, of her avenging angel femme fatale theatricality when implementing 'the plan' on her release.

However, it would be a mistake to consider this form of atonement (really retribution) to be the film revelling in a 'retro' idea of brutal justice. It would not make much sense of the film's rather mocking tone with regard to Christianity in general, with the preacher rendered a devious if not spiteful character, who (snubbed by Geum-ja in her avenging angel guise) informs Baek of her release, accepting money in return for the tip-off. Tellingly, the welcome assembly the preacher has arranged for Geum-ja at the start all wear Santa Claus outfits, conflating Christianity with capitalism's cashing in on such religious belief systems. Indeed, the first sight of the preacher is shot in such a way as to render ambiguous his very motivation for attempting to help Geum-ja, whom he sees on a news report. It may, in fact, contain an element of desire for the nineteen-year-old whom he believes is the presence of an angel. In which case, how should we consider this discourse on atonement?

It can be more usefully understood as a way of deploying an idea from the past that *is*, but one which stretches back much further than the national past (as was the case in *Carancho*). Instead, Geum-ja, quite literally, *uses* Christianity (as though an idea from world memory established long before nations were), as her callous dismissal of the preacher at the start shows, to destabilise the dominance of the individual contract. In a static present where everyone is a dividual, variously indebted by interconnecting individual contracts, the very old idea of revenge requiring an equivalent pound of flesh is used to inhabit the individual contract in a more personal and bloody manner. If a life can be valued financially, is but meat that can be weighed in this way, then Geum-ja's contracts are designed to return life to its actual equivalent. Only a body can pay the debt owed to another body. This is the literal meaning of a pound of flesh, a much older idea of justice seemingly submerged in an era of deterritorialised capital, which is re-inscribed by Geum-ja into the individual contracts through which neoliberalism functions. In this way, we see, multitude is able to wrestle agency from within the control society, however briefly, by inhabiting the capitalist system of exchange in a very physical way.

Community-oriented ceremonial body

To understand how re-instatement of physical equivalency is used to create two temporary collectives, in two defunct disciplinary institutions, we need to consider how Geum-ja is depicted, temporally, as a ceremonial body. It is this, crucially, which enables her to (re)connect to an older idea of vengeance from the past that *is*. In the preacher's flashback that accompanies Geum-ja's release, her past connection with him in prison is (re)told. On her arrival in prison, the impressionable young Geum-ja is informed by the preacher that: 'Behind that wicked witch face of yours, I saw the presence of an angel.' Geum-ja then apparently transforms herself into a model Christian, believing that she can summon the presence of an angel. When speaking to the assembled inmates in prison she states: 'The angel inside me only reveals itself when I invoke it [...] the act of invoking an angel, this is what we call prayer.' Yet she transforms herself again, on her release, into a black-clad, pink-eyeliner-wearing, designer-pistol-toting, avenging angel. Geum-ja thus explores how her dividual self can be used to a different purpose, by being a different kind of angel. Transforming from light to dark angel, Geum-ja passes through a crystal (as Deleuze describes of the construction of a ceremonial body) and enunciates herself from a different one of its facets. Geum-ja's passage through the crystal enables her life to change, from existence in the (static) present that passes, to (re)connection with another past from the virtual whole of time (the past that is preserved).

When in prison, as a white angel of life, Geum-ja provides, for the cellmate Yang-hee (a prostitute who killed her pimp), faith in the redeeming power of prayer, in return for a place to live on her release. From Sun-sook, the North Korean spy with Alzheimer's whose body she tends, she receives the blueprint for her stylish pistol and the prompt that she must seek vengeance. For So-young, an armed robber with chronic kidney failure, Geum-ja donates her own kidney, in return for the manufacture of her gun on her release. For Soo-hee, the adulterous artist she saved from a sexually predatory cellmate, she receives the silver-embossed handles for her gun. From Yi-jeong, whom she saved from violent bullying, Geum-ja receives access to Baek via Yi-jeong's prostitution of herself (living as Baek's girlfriend). Through these personal contracts the collective is constructed which helps Geum-ja implement 'the plan'.

Alternatively, for Baek, she is the avenging angel, paying him back for his deeds with the collective she creates from the parents of the murdered children. For each of these families, and Detective Choi, she offers a chance at revenge, the justice for their children that will – following the logic of the ancient human notion of retribution, but here used to differently rearticulate a neoliberal structure of control – return them from commodified meat to sons and daughters once more.

It is very deliberately foregrounded, soon after Geum-ja's release, that she passes through a crystal – transforming from everyday to ceremonial body. From angel of life – seen in the prison with light emanating from her face whilst praying – she becomes the all-in-black avenging angel of death. Here we see her, as Deleuze describes it, entering a masquerade. After being shown her new room by former cellmate Yang-hee (the hairdressing salon being a location marked by mirrors, scissors, combs, the construction of the outside face of identity), an extraordinary extra-diegetic moment sees Geum-ja seated in front of a mirror with bare lightbulbs above it, as though backstage at a theatre. She is depicted laughing wildly to herself, at the knowledge that 'the plan' commenced thirteen

FIGURE 6.3 A time to laugh, in *Chinjeolhan geumjassi/Lady Vengeance* (Cahn-wook Park, 2005).

years ago (see Figure 6.3). This is a moment of spectacle which halts the narrative entirely (Yang-hee disappears from the scene) to revel in the theatricality of Geum-ja's identity. It creates the sense that events are occurring in the empty form of time (with the potential it contains for a change to the future), Geum-ja's laughter acting as a reminder of the ability of the powers of the false to unground time.[7]

Shortly after this, the film's most surreal moment occurs. Geum-ja kneels to pray in front of the shrine she has created to Won-mo. This posture is an everyday one, as she is repeatedly seen kneeling, praying, in prison. Geum-ja's body begins to dip and sway, as she experiences a kind of ecstasy, and slips into a smiling trance in which we see – for the first time – her imagined black-clad avenging angel version of herself. Through a bleak, stormy, mountainous and snowy landscape she drags a strange creature, part dog, part sled, which has the head of Baek. This creature she then executes with a spectacular-looking pistol. Later on, when Baek is tied to a chair and dismembered by the parents of his victims, this fantasy has its material realisation. It is 'the plan' as vision, as is demonstrated when the smiling, black-clad avenging angel Geum-ja in the fantasy is match-cut with the same smile appearing on the entranced face of the white-clad saintly Geum-ja.

In this moment we are given insights into the 'everyday theatricalisation' of Geum-ja's postures (in the prison she repeatedly adopts positions of supplication and subservience – praying, cleaning bodies, feeding people) into gest. Passing through these everyday postures of the angel of life, in prison, she reaches the other side of the crystal as avenging dark angel, one connected to an older idea of vengeance from the past that *is*. This standout moment of laughter, accompanied soon afterwards by the surreal vision, is thus used to demonstrate the theatrical nature of this masquerade. As avenging angel, Geum-ja's body becomes a spectacle in its own right (there is more than one humorous incidence of someone questioning her choice of pink eyeliner) that shows through its postures the sheets of the past to which she connects. This is most clearly seen in the crystal image flashbacks that equate past and present as she reunites with her former cellmates. Here Geum-ja's body demonstrates the 'mega-gesture' of her gest, as she transitions from light to dark angel.

For example, when Geum-ja re-unites with Soo-hee, her appearance in the present is matched with the moment in the prison when Geum-ja interceded to save Soo-hee from sexual exploitation. Seen in the past from the perspective of Soo-hee, Geum-ja walking into a room and holding up the bar of soap she has just used – once more on her knees – to make a bathroom floor slippery, intercuts rapidly with Geum-ja and Soo-hee embracing in the present. Geum-ja has come to call in a favour, and Soo-hee willingly agrees due to her debt from the past. Rather than a static present, then, via the personal contract the past remains alive in the present. Geum-ja's is not the series of time seen in everyday postures of tiredness, as in *Carancho*, but the perpetual splitting of time into (virtual) past that is preserved and (actual) present that passes, seen in her crystalline guises. Moreover, the reconstruction of Geum-ja's past in the film is not only non-chronological, but also almost entirely given from the viewpoint of others. Along with the flashbacks to all the personal contracts, the police reconstruction is Choi's, and even the flashback to Geum-ja's desperation over her pregnancy is not her own. Rather, the entire movie has a voiceover, which we finally discover to be Jenny's. She is actually relating a giant memory within which lies even the story of her own conception.

A deliberately *Rashomon*-like uncertainty over Geum-ja's past is thus introduced, which emphasises the undecidability of her temporal existence. On the one occasion when she does speak about the past and how Won-mo came to be killed and she incarcerated, there is no flashback to show events. Rather, the soundtrack replays the sounds of the past she describes with eyes closed, as though to illustrate how closely it haunts her present. These *Rashomon*-like uncertainties also exemplify how, through gest, the existence of the virtual peaks of the present which Geum-ja's attitudes evidence imply the possible presents that exist in the dividual. The flashback perspectives of others again emphasise that this divided self is both temporally undecideable, as well as a product of Geum-ja's various personal contracts. For each different contract, there is a different Geum-ja and a different past. Hence she is at once illustrative of the past as virtual layering and the present as potentially labyrinthine actuality.

The ceremonial nature of Geum-ja's body is most evident in a particular crystal that emerges late on in the film, which explicitly matches her past and present, via her kneeling body. Firstly, a flashback from the perspective of Choi shows Geum-ja re-enacting the murder (she did not commit) of Won-mo, in a police reconstruction. In this doubly staged masquerade (a reconstruction, with an innocent masquerading as the murderer), Geum-ja requires stage directions from Choi. She does not know which pillow was used to suffocate Won-mo, so Choi taps his watch strap to indicate that she choose the brown one. As the frantic clicks and flashes of press cameras re-emphasise the theatricality involved, Geum-ja defiantly reveals her face whilst kneeling. Her posture and facial expression are then pointedly repeated on a second occasion when she finally captures Baek, and likewise kneels beside his prone body. Having at last brought the real perpetrator to justice, she has fulfilled the actual purpose of the initial re-enactment. This mirroring of the past in the present via Geum-ja's face illustrates once more her crystalline nature as a ceremonial body, passing through a masquerade.

Finally, with the death of Baek, an extended close-up on Geum-ja's face shows a remarkable series of micro-transitions, from grief to maniacal happiness to grief to maniacal happiness, and so on (transitions aided by the passing in front of her of the families tramping down the earth on Baek's grave). It is as though Geum-ja's face were working back and forth between the light and dark crystalline facets of her dividual personality. This scene slowly pixelates until Geum-ja's face dissolves into a television screen showing snow, being watched by Jenny. Thus Deleuze's 'disappearance of the visible body' (1985, 183) that occurs in the crystalline masquerade also indicates the overarching existence of Geum-ja as so many memories of others. She is becoming the memory of the film's voiceover narrator, Jenny, her virtual existence as audiovisual image mirroring that of the murdered children, who insist in the past in Baek's videotapes of their murders, always ready to return and haunt the present.

The shrine before which Geum-ja prays at this pivotal point of transition illustrates also the role of the haunting presence of a child in this space, the child being a figure noted by Deleuze to indicate the temporal undecidability of the body, the coexistence of its past with the present (1985, 196). It is the potential of the child as the insisting unthought that can return from the past which ultimately provides a new way for Geum-ja to engage with life. It is for this reason that Won-mo appears to Jenny initially, conflating his ghostly insistence of past with the present (that which drives Geum-ja's quest for atonement) with Geum-ja's parental debt to Jenny. When Won-mo finally appears to Geum-ja at the film's close, she is applying make-up in a well-lit mirror: for the second time, a space evocative of the theatrical nature of her avenging angel guise. Won-mo there transforms from child to adult incarnation, and leaves Geum-ja sitting bound and gagged precisely in the manner of Baek. For Geum-ja there can be no forgiveness from the past by Won-mo. Her atonement only leaves her entrapped in her ceremonial body. Instead, Won-mo leaves Geum-ja to awaken Jenny, so that she can join her mother in the eating of the cake that functions as her long-postponed tofu. It is only now, in her role as a mother to her daughter, that Geum-ja may be able to atone (by repaying the generational debt) and, as such, to regain a direction in life. In this sense, a different future is envisioned to the static present of neoliberalism, one which can be more clearly understood if we explore the collective which forms around 'the plan'.

The two temporary collectives that Geum-ja create rely upon the dividual nature of people living in the control society. The former cellmates are able to help with 'the plan' as dividuals with personal debts contracted to Geum-ja. They temporarily create a rhizomatic assemblage which, whilst contrary to the divisive aims of neoliberalism, is in no way a cohesive singular entity. Rather, Geum-ja constructs this first collective by creating individual debts for which a pound of flesh can be later extracted. As noted, the prostitute Yang-hee receives (at the very least) the physical embrace of Geum-ja; the robber So-young receives one of Geum-ja's kidneys; the adulterous Soo-hee is saved from the disgust of performing oral sex; Yi-jeong from being physically pummelled; etc. Thus, to form a collective, Geum-ja plays upon the corporeal element of the personal contract which insists along with the financial dimension emphasised by neoliberalism. The body as commodity thereby enters into a form of physical barter, an alternative measure to solely its commodity value as meat. Within the body, moreover, the past is preserved to be called upon to honour its debts in the future as present.

But it is the second temporary grouping, coming together to kill Baek, which makes apparent how dividuals can temporarily work as one for a common end if the physical is emphasised over the financial. For this second collective, it is the debt to the memory of the child (once again, the generational debt) which brings them together in the killing of Baek. In this, the choice of the abandoned school adds to the theatricality of the gesture performed when Geum-ja shows the families the videos of their children dying, and the virtual past returns, along with their grief. This is shown in the use of match-cuts between events in the videos and the room. For instance, when the innocent little girl Eun-joo is brutally hanged by Baek in a video, the pulling away of the chair in the past matches – via an abrupt cut – the collapse to the floor of her grandmother in the abandoned school in the present. Once again, bodies are figured as the stores of the past which returns in the present to require repayment of all debts.

Throughout their negotiations as a temporary grouping of dividuals, the different families emphasise the other aspects of their lives which they must negotiate to temporarily join this collective. This includes their health, marital status (whether still a couple or now divorced), financial situations, loss of liberty should their vengeful deed be discovered, and the effect of the weather on the traffic. Indeed, when they decide to kill Baek they also decide to enter the room for their respective pound of flesh as individual families. What is important is that they decide to execute their revenge on Baek themselves because they do not have faith in the police to do this job effectively. If the state's functionaries cannot handle Baek adequately to repay their debts to their children (Choi is there as living proof of this), they decide to do so in a way that honours personal contracts – generational blood debts – rather than as a unified entity with a social contract to honour or fulfil.

With the two collectives thus acting 'together' for exactly the same reasons, the walls of the prison are indeed shown to stretch around all of the neoliberal control society inclusively. However, within its borders so expanded, it is still possible for collectives to form from the dividuals with their personal debts to honour, when the price is recalculated in flesh and blood, rather than solely money.

As with *Carancho*, the model of envisaged collective under neoliberalism does not move much beyond families and the market (as opposed to imagining a form of more cohesive or democratically oriented social collective, say), but it is at least a temporary collective able to obtain justice in the absence of the state. The first, indeed, indicates how the carceral society fosters conditions in which individual contracts between women (most of whom, like Geum-ja, are incarcerated due to the actions of men) can potentially undermine the sexual contract – that which Carole Pateman exposed as presupposing the social contract, the latter being established upon patriarchal right and the subordination of women by the marriage contract (1988, x; Carver and Chambers 2011, xvi). The collective of families, moreover, is able to coalesce around its shared horror in Baek's personal greed (his desire to buy a yacht), rather than the need for money to raise children of his own. The value of a child is, for them, a different kind of worth than the commodity which Baek made of it. It has a physical, flesh-and-blood dimension. For this debt to be honoured, they accordingly require a pound of flesh. Thus, whilst the dark humour with which the conclusion of this business is framed might suggest that a mercenary logic encompasses all of society (each family sheepishly writes down their bank account details for Geum-ja to return them the ransom money), in fact this is entirely at one with the dividual lives of the families in the temporary collective.

Ultimately, the potential this second collective has to break open the static present is illustrated by its ability to tap into a different temporality via the retrieval of its pound of flesh. This is shown in the montage which accompanies the parents' arrival at the abandoned school. The events that are about to unfold are shown rapidly in a series of still images. As each of the five families sitting in the classroom is introduced, a flash-forward shows – for each – a reaction they will later have to either the video of their child dying, or an action they will undertake during the killing of Baek. In contrast to the previous temporal disturbances of the film (flashbacks to the past motivated by the arrival of Geum-ja's ceremonial body in the present), here it is the temporary collective per se which creates the forward-looking temporal disruption, albeit as a montage collecting their individual reactions to the present. Thus the collective of families, however briefly, comes to function as the ceremonial body in the film. The montage collects together their reactions as a series of poses, turning them into a theatrical performance as a collective. They evidence another *Rashomon*-like construction of the past, wherein no one shares quite the same memories, but in communally watching all of Baek's snuff videos they adhere as a group of individuals with a common need to avenge the past. With memory reinscribed into the present via the body, and the debt it carries weighted in pounds of flesh, the dividual is shown not solely to be distributed across a range of lateral connections to different people in a perpetual present, but also temporally in a present informed by pasts (containing generational debts) stored physically in the dividual.

As is pointed out in their discussion, they cannot each individually decide Baek's fate, it can only be decided once and for all – as it is – by a majority show of hands. This vision of temporary democracy under neoliberalism, then, is one which taps into a much older idea of equivalent justice so as to provide community within multitude. In the execution of Baek, the static present is moved forward into the future due to a collective view on how best to avenge the past. This happens because the coming together of the families occurs through the structures that the neoliberal control society uses to keep them apart: the personal contract (now given a different worth, embodied as flesh and blood) and the static present (now imbued with an insisting past, replanted in the very physicality of those involved in the debt repayment by blood-letting).

Lady Vengeance is not solely a critique of neoliberalism, then, but an attempt to think past its static present. The film considers how a person like Geum-ja, who finds themselves required to be, as Lazzarato has it, 'an entrepreneur of the self' (2011, 145) in a carceral society, can still create collectives able to function towards a mutually agreed-upon end. As in *Carancho*, there is no utopian sense of multitude emerging. Rather, there is an exploration of how democratic actions might be possible, even in spite of the eradication of the past enacted on everyday bodies by the transnational history of neoliberalism.

In *Carancho*, the future is ultimately rendered impossible, as the bodies of the couple at the heart of the story (struggling to escape the uncertainty of their context) are destroyed. Thus the film critiques the damage caused by neoliberalism's insistence on a static present, but cannot formalise an alternative, even if a glimpse of another kind of community is offered via a return to an inspirational democratic moment from the national past. Tragically, this is revealed to be a dead end.

In *Lady Vengeance*, by contrast, the theatrical foregrounding of the (virtual) possibility time offers for dividuals suggests a difficult future for the children inheriting the legacy of neoliberalism. The film's sheets of the past (flashback) structure proposes that there is still another possible future accessible via the archived past stored in the body. This process, however, encapsulated in the notion of vengeance (understood in the film as the righting of a wrong from the recent past), requires a refusal of the definition of a static present upon which neoliberalism thrives. Personal contracts are shown to enable the creation of temporary collectives, in particular constituted by women,[8] motivated by the past and able to create a different future. Layers of time are accessed to inform individual contracts, making them worth more than the personal gain they should serve. This is evident in the way in which the film renders bodies ceremonial, in the manner described by Deleuze as evidencing of their temporal complexity.

To summarise: two exhausted, everyday, slumping and stretching bodies, living without access to informing personal pasts, seek to rejuvenate a collective national past, but to no avail. A vengeful woman, transforming from her everyday postures of penitence, laughs theatrically as she temporarily rejoins the present to an ancient idea of equivalence – a process in which neoliberalism's rendering of the body as so much meat to be traded meets the Old Testament notion (literally translated) of an eye for an eye. This chapter has explored these cinematic encounters with the transnational history of neoliberalism, and its exclusion of personal pasts in the pursuit of a static present. These are key examples from an all-pervasive category of films about the prevalence of the individual contract.

With this brief journey through the eradicated pasts of the world history of colonial modernity thus brought up to date, all that remains to be done – in the Conclusion – is to round off this discussion of transnational histories on film with a return to the opening discussion of their contrariness to doublethink.

Notes

1 The body's temporal aspect, as critique of neoliberalism, is an emerging theme in US independent filmmaking (Stone 2013, 96–99; Backman Rogers 2015, 1–5) and China's Sixth Generation films (Holtmeier 2014, 148–150).

2 The paradigmatic case of this temporal dislocation is Leonard Shelby (Guy Pearce), the amnesiac protagonist caught in a perpetual present in *Memento* (USA, 2000), who uses tattoos on his body and photographs to construct a sense of linear history. For Thomas Elsaesser, *Memento* indicates how contemporary cinema acclimatises viewers to life in the control society, providing an affective training for life in a perpetual present (2009, 31).

3 The connection between control society and the time-image has very recently begun to be explored (Roberts 2017).

4 Contemporary US society has been engineered as a racial caste system which manufactures an 'undercaste' by mass incarceration, a situation not dissimilar to that of 'Jim Crow' in the wake of the abolishment of slavery (Wacquant 2009; Alexander 2010, 4). Propelled by the War on Drugs in the 1980s, the US prison population has risen dramatically: 'mass incarceration is designed to warehouse a population deemed disposable – unnecessary to the functioning of the new global economy – while earlier systems of control were designed to exploit and control black labour' (Alexander 2010, 18). Running prisons for profit solves the difficulty of housing the percentage of society no longer needed to produce goods and services (when there is a cheaper global working class to employ), keeping the nation's share of the globally unemployed and homeless out of the elite's gentrified spaces and unable to assemble and resist (Wacquant 2009, 41–75).

5 For example, Jens Andermann (2012), exploring Trapero's earlier films, details how the conflation of a construction site with a penal colony in *Mundo grúa/Crane World* (1999) is 'only the most extreme expression of labour's exploitation in the age of neoliberal crisis' (66).

6 Examinations of 'the apathy, vileness, and corporate dilettantism of an elite that tout neoliberal policies in South Korea in the 1990s and 2000s' and the impact on individual lives of the 'recklessness of neoliberalization' after the IMF crisis (Wagner 2011, 218–219); of the trilogy as a 'historical narration' of the nation, after Homi Bhabha (Herbert 2012, 183–186); and of how facial expression in *Oldboy* might 'convey the existential dilemmas confronting millions of Koreans in the aftermath of the International Monetary Fund (IMF) crisis' (Diffrient 2013, 115).

7 The scene evokes Nietzschean laughter, in a film by former philosophy student, Park, which characterises the realisation that existence is underpinned by the eternal return and, in spite of all the suffering of life, it should be actively willed again (Nietzsche 1891, 180; Lippit 1992, 41).

8 For an in-depth consideration of female intimacy and the Deleuzian time-image of the body, see Pekerman (2011).

CONCLUSION

One or many faces of the (lost) past?

This book argues that a world of cinemas is engaged in telling the stories of the lost pasts of colonial modernity. Across what Deleuze considers the archive of world memory, groups of films engage with transnational histories that have impacted far beyond, and often long before, any one nation. Yet, to realise this, I argue, entails a racking of critical focus so as to better understand the role of the time-image as entranceway to the labyrinth of the past: to not only world memory, but also world history. It requires a recognition that, at the opening to each such portal lies an encounter not with another, but with another past. This renders the realisation of such transnational histories an ethical concern, akin to that of Enrique Dussel's focus on the need to recognise the excluded of colonial modernity (although I add, specifically, to recognise their excluded pasts which subsist within world history) if colonial modernity is to be transcended.

It is in this sense that cinema can be realised to be unthinking doublethink, positioning itself against the obliteration of different perspectives on history to that of the Eurocentric vision of colonial modernity. Of course, there is a long history of decolonial and postcolonial thought which has had a marked influence on filmmaking around the world, and indeed, on how cinema is understood (even if the way of taxonomising a world of cinemas in this book is unique). Indeed, as indicated in the Preface, to reconsider world history in this way may be more of a revelation for those on the 'winning' side of its long historical trajectory – like the characters Evan (Brionne Davis) in *El abrazo de la serpiente/Embrace of the Serpent* (Colombia/Venezuela/Argentina, 2016) (see the Introduction) or Costa (Luis Tosar) in *También la lluvia/Even the Rain* (Spain/Mexico/France, 2010) (see Chapter 4). Perhaps this is also like that of some readers of this book, in the areas of the world where it will most widely circulate, including in well-funded university library collections like those of Europe and North America. One might even go so far as to argue that this is fitting, as the view of world history being *critiqued* in these films is not necessarily that held in some other parts of the world (by many indigenous populations, for example). But even so, as with the experience of Evan and Costa in the Americas, it is debateable how world-changing such a potentially fleeting revelation may be. There is a little more, then, to (a world of) cinema being against doublethink.

The analysis of the films explored in this book has led, repeatedly, to the same conclusion: that the coloniality of power functions by freeing itself of its past so that it can repeat its former abuses with impunity. Global events over the past five hundred years indicate that whilst a shared history can consolidate an identity within (national) borders, even so, depending on how the story of (transnational) history is told it can – by contrast – pose an inconvenient truth about such borders. If the way the story is told indicates something of the guilt which may attach to genocide and theft on a global scale (the eradication of lost pasts), this has the potential to counter the desire to repeatedly recreate the global inequality of domination. For the coloniality of power to be successful, the existence of an archive of world memory capable of repeatedly reminding of the virtual existence of lost pasts (which also unground the legitimacy of the imagined borders and identity promoted by the nation-state form) is something of a fly in the ointment. Even if this archive cannot successfully show us lost pasts, precisely because they are lost, nevertheless, just by reminding us – in the briefest glimpse – that they are lost, it throws doubt on the centrality of all that we believe to be history. This is why so many 'faces' of the (lost) past address us from the times-images of a world of cinemas: of an endangered species of monkey-spirit (Chapter 3), of a murdered indigenous woman and her massacred tribe (Chapter 4), of the archive of a closed communist newspaper (Chapter 5), of the non-profitable idea of community in general (Chapter 6). To recap the point made in Chapter 1, the encounters they offer are less with the unknowable other, the recognition of which has the power to shake our belief in the centrality of our Cartesian self to the world (as per a Levinasian ethics), than with unknowable other *pasts*, the recognition of which has the power to shake our Eurocentric belief in the *centrality of our pasts to world history* (more in line with a Dusselian ethics).

Why is it, then, not necessarily easy to realise the import of the face-to-face encounters with lost pasts on offer in a world of cinemas? Why this book only now? Precisely because this import is denied by doublethink. *The Act of Killing* (Denmark/Norway/UK, 2012) (see Chapter 5) illustrates the ubiquity and the horror of colonial modernity's several centuries of historical eradication of its crimes. In particular, its re-creation of the torture and murder of a beloved step-father (with the original murderers – now national heroes – re-enacting their crimes upon the grieving step-son) indicates the ever-present, but silenced, nature of these lost pasts (often only preserved now in personal memories). It is not coincidental, I think, that it is from *Hamlet* that Deleuze takes inspiration in his discussion of time 'out of joint' – both in terms of Western philosophy's changing perspective on the nature of being in time (1983, vii) and (in the preface to the English edition of *Cinema 2*) as part of his discussion of the emergence of the time-image (1985, xi).[1] Hamlet's revelation as to what his villainous smiling uncle's face may hide – 'one may smile, and smile, and be a villain' (Shakespeare 1980, 93) – arrives with the realisation that the story of the past which he has known, of his father's death, is in fact a fabrication used to obscure his father's murder. This Hamlet is only able to know, however, from the ghost of his father, the virtual memory of his presence, erupting – one might argue quite cinematically – into the present from the past, to throw time out of joint.

History, as Hamlet learns, has a smiling face. For their part, Deleuze and Guattari conceive of the face in its Eurocentric centrality to world history in a manner which illuminates the doublethink underpinning colonial modernity: 'The face is not a universal. It is not even that of the white man; it is White Man himself, with his broad white cheeks and the black holes of his eyes. The face is Christ. The face is the typical European.' (1980, 176) The most recent of US presidential elections of 2016 brings home with full force the alignment of colonial modernity's historical white supremacist underpinnings (see Chapter 4 on the racial contract and 1492) and its latest phase, neoliberalism (see Chapter 6). As Michael Hardt and Antonio Negri remind us (see Chapters 2, 4 and 5), colonial modernity is a several-centuries-long history of the repeated victory of the counterrevolution. Thus neoliberalism in the USA, for thinkers like Loïc Wacquant (2009) and Michelle Alexander (2010), sees the War on Drugs labelled the new Jim Crow due to its fostering of divisiveness along racial lines, the resulting mass incarcerations leading to an apartheid-style carceral society (see Chapter 6). Today's global apartheid, dividing Global North and South (now existing cheek-by-jowl, globally) is but the latest manifestation of colonial modernity.

For colonial modernity's continuation, such rebranding of former divisions to ensure inequality is perpetuated (e.g. the rebranding of Jim Crow as the War on Drugs) must ensure the repeated re-erasure of the past, the submergence of the many-sided struggle over history which it repeatedly 'wins'. This is the process which a world of cinemas resists, attempting to archive and then illuminate in the time-image: the struggle for coevalness that characterises colonial modernity (revealing the lost pasts of exploited nature, oppressed peoples, political oppositions, exhausted bodies disconnected from the past – and so on – which characterise its transnational histories). The archiving of world memory enacted by a world of cinemas is potentially revolutionary in its evocation that such lost pasts (by definition, unknowable), persist in virtual form. This is paradoxical, we might say, as lost pasts are not remembered and are unknowable. Yet, whilst Orwellian doublethink eradicates inconvenient pasts, somehow or other a world of cinemas keeps them alive – revealing their persistent presence (even if only via but the merest glimpse) in the crystalline construction of history.

This struggle over the remembrance of lost pasts is what the smiling face of history ('not … that of the white man … White Man himself') obscures. It legitimises the wilful eradication of the history of violence through which white supremacy maintains its hegemonic position under the thin veneer of the global promotion of democracy as universally beneficial. In the period of the so-called 'end of history' (see Chapter 1), we are now charged with forgetting not only the ideological struggles of the Cold War, but the whole history of popular rebellion against colonial modernity. There is no clearer evidence of this than (as noted in Chapter 4) the continued attempts to ban books like Howard Zinn's *A People's History of the United States* (1980) from schools in the USA. But what will we do with all the redundant copies of this forgotten history once they have been banned? Burn them? Presumably. And if so, what then of the non-fascist life?

It is not the national histories we find onscreen which will enable struggles for equality in the context of the global apartheid of neoliberal globalisation. National borders, by definition, are established to maintain division. This is evident every time national conflict emerges over the proposed removal of statues commemorating figures whose deeds are no longer considered to chime with the warp and weft of mainstream values (Cecil Rhodes in the U.K. in 2016, Robert E. Lee in the USA in 2017). The removal of statues, after all, is so evocative of Cold War societal changes, whether the toppling of a statue of Joseph Stalin during the Hungarian Revolution of 1956, or the destruction of national heritage during the Chinese Cultural Revolution of 1966–1976 (a state-sanctioned murderous state of exception). In terms of national heritage, perhaps most pertinent to this discussion is the persistence of the White Man overlooking indigenous American lands from Mount Rushmore in the USA. Rather than in national histories onscreen, then, it is the remembering of the transnational histories which unite across and beyond nations which may provide a glimpse of this hoped-for equality.

Colonial modernity, it should be remembered, is entirely precarious. This is due to the manner in which this repetition of violent history takes place. Doublethink asks that we return perpetually to the (mythological) origin, create a repetition of the same, forget the very idea that there could be an alternative possibility, another side to the crystalline history of the world. Yet if it is 'remembered' that the past upon which the present rests was a violently exclusive one, people may well try to act differently, to repeat in difference.

The question is, will this be enough?

A non-fascist life? Under democracy? In the Anthropocene?

It is with no small irony that Orwell's anti-authoritarian *1984*, which was so actively promoted throughout the 'third world' by the UK and the USA during the Cold War as anti-communist propaganda, seems so relevant today. This is especially so considering that Orwell, a contradictory character in so many respects, was far from unblemished in his own complicity with Big Brother (Shaw 2004; Lucas 2004, 1–42; Rodden and Rossi 2012, 98–100; Keeble 2012, 158–161). The novel, it transpires, is as, if not more, applicable to certain democracies (amongst other forms of governance) under neoliberalism as it was to Soviet or Chinese communist regimes during the Cold War. In this, the latest phase in the world history of colonial modernity, the question (or even, expectation) asked so often in the 1990s (as to whether or when countries like China might become more democratic) recedes into the background of global geopolitics. In some prominent, often formerly imperial, Western democracies, members of the ruling class may be wondering whether it might be easier to control a capitalist economy by executive (in favour of an elite class, potentially at the expense of the rights and living standards of the domestic population) than it is by the messier, much slower, process of democracy. Neoliberalism is global neocolonisation by the very wealthy minority, a return to pre-Twentieth Century societal divisions. Thus the return of the idea of Orwellian doublethink to the foreground of popular consciousness is not because of a sudden nightmarish turn in contemporary politics, but because the already several-centuries-long history of colonial modernity has entered a phase in which global apartheid is policed worldwide (US presidents scan their own people and fabricate history even as we witness it in the making).

The lessons of the Cold War, when military regimes directly or tacitly supported by Western powers like the USA terrorised national populations, should not be easily forgotten. Whilst nowadays the economic disenfranchisement of youth in parts of the West (and beyond) under neoliberalism (the creation of prohibitively expensive education and housing markets, coupled with insecure labour markets functioning on zero-hour contracts such as those of the UK and USA) is accompanied by a media campaign to discredit 'Millennials' as snowflakes, it should be remembered that it only takes a small change in government to suddenly see a more brutal eradication of entire youthful generations. As authoritarian regimes know only too well, if you disappear the young, you remove the potential for political dissent. Then one only needs to remove from history the fact that it ever happened.

There are parts of the world where this is known only too well, as is clear in Gabriel García Márquez's fictional evocation of the United Fruit Company's massacre of its workers in *One Hundred Years of Solitude* (1967), which I discussed in the Introduction. Nevertheless, the difficulty which even prominent Western scholars have – from Hayden White to Giorgio Agamben (see Chapters 1 and 6) – putting the Twentieth Century's Holocaust into world-historical perspective indicates that many in the West may live in sheltered ignorance of just what is possible under doublethink.

The destruction of political opposition, whether targeting a scapegoated minority, political organisations or simply the young in general, is not new, and we (anyone) would be foolish to believe that it could never happen to us (anywhere). Within living memory there are numerous examples of brutal acts of state terror against civilian populations, which are suggestive of how difficult it is for anyone to see what is coming around the corner. How many people in Germany in the 1930s refused to believe the stories that were slowly filtering back from the concentration camps? How many mothers and fathers of Argentine children born in the 1950s and 1960s could have foreseen, even imagined in their darkest nightmares, that their young adult children might one day be kidnapped, tortured, murdered and their bodies disappeared forever by the nation's rulers, including for crimes as innocuous as demanding reduced bus fares for students? In the not-too-distant future, writing a book like this, even, having written a book like this, might get a person imprisoned, exiled, disappeared or killed. Even owning a copy might be dangerous.

Does this sound far-fetched? Not in many parts of the world, and certainly not historically. There should be no flippancy implied by this discussion of Shakespeare's smiling (white, male) face of history, noted in a book written during changing political times in the UK and the USA. In fact, the times may be more serious than we even realise. The emergence of the English-language adaptation of *Alone in Berlin* (UK/France/Germany, 2016) – from Hans Fallada's eponymous novel set during the Second World War – seems to encapsulate the growing fears of many in countries like the UK and the USA that similarities increasingly resonate between this former era of single-party state control and our own. How are we to resist, it invites us to question, even amidst so much seeming connectivity via social media (the postcards left by the protagonist for his fellow citizens are so evocative of this difference of epoch in their antiquated nature), if our lives are atomised to the point that we are effectively 'alone' (now that the state has aligned with, or is subservient to, capitalist powers formidably larger than we, and our lives are those of dividuals entangled in the control society)? The horrifying question the film raises on our behalf, is, will the current political direction in countries like the UK and the USA ultimately destroy ordinary families, just as it does that in the film? Or rather, if we know that that was what happened in the past, what can we do now to stop this history from repeating?

In my own lifetime, Dussel was expelled from his position at the National University of Cuyo after his house had previously been bombed in 1973, just prior to the Argentine military dictatorship of 1976–1983 which cost the lives of over 30,000 people to state violence (Martín Alcoff and Mendieta 2000, 21; Mendieta 2003a, xi). Whether the state of exception which presages authoritarian rule emerges because this is the political endgame of neoliberalism, as Agamben thinks, or because – as events in Catalonia in 2017 may perhaps indicate at time of writing – it is the last redoubt of the nation-state attempting to save itself from the regionalism (with global/local connection) encouraged by neoliberal globalisation, the question posed of us may well be the same: whether democracy will remain, or whether national borders will be patrolled by a fascist police state.

Even so, a world of cinemas also indicates that those parts of the world that endured military rule during the Cold War, in some of them as part of a much longer exclusionary settler colonist heritage, may consider the future with some optimism. *Otra Historia del Mundo/Another Story of the World* (Uruguay, 2017) uses a self-reflexive play with light and shadows (self-consciously meditating on cinema's ability to investigate the virtual and actual nature of history) to demonstrate an incredible optimism regarding the power, or at least the potential, of film (the medium of shadow-play) to (re)place, or (re)position rather, those excluded by colonial modernity – whose pasts are wilfully disappeared by doublethink – at the centre of world history. A meditation on the Cold War past of Uruguay, standing in for Latin America more broadly, the film's optimism is, admittedly, in hindsight. But it remains a signal that lessons (hard) learned should be remembered. Democracy was ultimately triumphant, the film emphasises as its message of hope.

Despite this optimism, however, climate change raises a further question of whether a non-fascist life can be maintained in the Anthropocene, even under democracy. Vine Deloria Jr., from the perspective of the indigenous North American underside of colonial modernity, questions whether democracy is entirely compatible with the ecological considerations of our age (Deloria 1972, 59). He may have a point. After all, voting in one's own interests, with only the next five years of the future in mind (whilst embedded and indebted within the network of individual contracts which perpetuate the control society (see Chapter 6)), is unlikely to provide the longer-term, community-oriented (or at least, collective-oriented) mindset required to address the future of and for later generations. Certainly it may well not be sustainable to hold our desires, our needs, even what we may believe to be our rights, over the responsibility to live in a more connected manner with the planet – and indeed, for this possibility to be extended to all as opposed to just those who can afford it.

In the Andean cultures which were colonised by the forces of modernity centuries ago, and whose (lost) pasts it perpetually works to eradicate, this is called 'Pachamama, the right to live in harmony (some would say the right to "live well")' (Mignolo in Sanjinés 2013, xix; see also Mignolo 2011, 165–171). Neoliberalism, the present zenith of colonial modernity, stands directly opposed to this responsibility. Not only does it value profit above all else, it also fosters the deterioration of equality under democracy, due in part to neoliberalism's imbrication with oligarchy (it is no coincidence that, historically, this is the preferred social structure of settler colonist cultures) and the return to a class system more reminiscent of that which existed prior to the Twentieth Century. This, the latest phase of colonial modernity – and, as such, exclusionary by design – can only offer, as Dussel summarises 'the collective suicide of humanity' (1998b, 431). If the Twentieth Century is understood, after Dussel, as a struggle over which vision of modernity manages the world system, then even if capitalism 'won' this war, new ideas may well be necessary.

Ultimately, of the most recent political forms that have been attempted as ways of managing colonial modernity (democracy, communism, fascism), it is hard to see which would seem more suited to the coming years, and, more to the point, which the most likely to triumph as things stand. The difficulty would seem to be that it is colonial modernity itself – the structural inequality of the coloniality of power – which creates the difficulties encountered by any such attempt at managing the system. Harder still, then, would be whether we can imagine something better, or whether fascism will become, once again, the only promising opportunity for many who may feel that they have nothing left to lose. How, then, can we transcend colonial modernity, how can we become transmodern?

In such a context, whilst I am not advocating a return to a pre-Columbian ethics of reciprocity, as though with a nostalgic romanticism, even so the link between realising a liveable future and the history of how we got here needs a much more ubiquitous recognition. Certainly there is a greater need to hesitate – to 'stop and think' – about whether there were, or are, lost pasts (amidst world memory) from which a better future might be rejuvenated. It is for this reason that Deleuze works so well with Dussel, enabling a line of flight towards the transmodern through the time-image (in which we first return to the lost past, in order to move forward again differently into the future). Key to realising such a hesitant ethics for the Anthropocene, and something which a world of cinemas has been grappling with for some time (if we know where, and how, to look) is the need to recognise otherness as also a recognition of other pasts. Or rather, the realisation that there can be ways of seeing the past (indeed history itself) other than as a single, linear, teleological progression – as in Hegel's worldview (see the Introduction). What is crucially required now is a realisation of the place within world history of those on the 'winning' side of colonial modernity – that feeling of being uncomfortable in our own skins noted of postcolonial scholars like Paul Gilroy (see the Introduction) and experienced by characters like Evan and Costa, and perhaps even those viewers for whom such stories create a sense of hesitation before (world) history. Such a hesitation translates, politically, into a question over whose interests I am acting in: my own, or those of the collective? Put another way, whose history am I in the process of making, mine, or ours?

To recognise the end of grand narratives is not to be postmodern in what, Dussel indicates, remains a Eurocentric sense (see Chapter 1) – entailing an inevitable 'end of history' discourse within which nonsensical terms like 'post-truth' start to seem to make sense (see the Introduction and Chapter 1). Rather, following more the 'de-' of decolonial (indicating a critical process ongoing over several centuries of colonial modernity, as far back as Bartolomé de Las Casas (see Chapter 4)) as opposed to the 'post-' of 'postmodernity' or 'post-truth' (both in very different ways suggesting that something which some might consider ongoing has ended) is to realise the need to decolonise worldviews such that a hesitant ethics can emerge – one more suited to the Anthropocene. It is in this sense that a world of cinemas is against doublethink.

If Deleuze identified a new political cinema arising with the time-image, it was, I would argue, due to its potential to deterritorialise Eurocentric world history by indicating a multiplicity of views from the Global South on world history. Films are now every bit as important as Orwell's book, just as ubiquitous (as anyone on a long-haul flight can testify) and no less imbricated in complex geopolitics (as the ambiguities surrounding the festival circuit show). Across a world of cinemas, filmmakers provide stories that give access to the vast archive of world memory, the virtual past that *is* (as opposed to the actualised past that *was* of doublethink). Not that this will save us from fascism, economic collapse, or environmental apocalypse, but it can at least help to demonstrate what needs addressing most urgently if these very real possible futures are to be avoided: the encounter with (lost) pasts which can relativise belief in the centrality of our own – the decentring of Eurocentrism.

We might even go further than this. As *Another Story of the World* indicates, the time-image is optimistic. Whilst the analysis of the films explored here has focused on their (impossible) depiction of lost pasts, the potential of the time-image is in its imagination of alternative possible *futures* which such virtual pasts might inspire. It may be that climate change will return unto dust, unto the Earth, what colonial modernity has built upon the bones of former civilisations. It may be that this, in turn, just leads to more of the same – disaster capitalism, as the practice is now known, such as that which took hold in both the USA and UK as the result of their respective votes in 2016 (see the Introduction) (Klein 2007). Or, it may not. In the time-image there is always hope for another future, built anew upon the virtual past uncovered from world memory. What it will take to realise the impetus for such a systemic change, however, is difficult to foresee.

If 1492 shows us anything, it is that any civilisation, no matter how well established or how dominant within its sphere of influence, may only be a few years away from its sudden and dramatic end. The several centuries of privilege conferred by colonial modernity on the wealthiest in the world could easily be reversed in spectacular ways, most obviously by sudden societal, economic or ecological unravelling and collapse. Thus the most important revelation of all that is offered by a world of cinemas may be that another way of understanding history altogether is necessary for the Anthropocene (see the Introduction). But if there is anyone for whom this is to be a revelation, then it is a character like Evan, or like Costa, or perhaps like the viewer of such films, or the readers (and author) of this book. The broader question which this raises, of how to react positively and meaningfully to such a revelation, is beyond the scope of a book like this. However, what can be concluded from this analysis of a world of cinemas is its importance in keeping alive this particular understanding of world history, against doublethink.

Note

1 The initial work, prior to *Cinema 2* (1985) is Deleuze's *Kant's Critical Philosophy* (1984). It is sometimes said that the *Cinema* books divide into a cinematic history of (Western) philosophy up to Kant (movement-image) and after Kant (time-image).

SELECT BIBLIOGRAPHY

Abu-Lughod, J. L. (1989) *Before European Hegemony*. Oxford: Oxford University Press.

Agamben, G. (1995) *Ho Sacer*. Translated by D. Heller-Roazen, 1998. Stanford, CA: Stanford University Press.

Agamben, G. (2003) *State of Exception*. Translated by K. Attell, 2005. Chicago, IL: University of Chicago Press.

Aguilar, G. (2008) *New Argentine Film*. London: Palgrave Macmillan.

Ahmed, S. (2000) *Strange Encounters*. London: Routledge.

Alexander, M. (2010) *The New Jim Crow*. New York: The New Press.

Al-Saji, A. (2012) 'When Thinking Hesitates.' *The Southern Journal of Philosophy*, 50, 2: 351–361.

Al-Saji, A. (2013) 'Too Late.' *Insights*, 6, 5: 2–13.

Al-Saji, A. (2014) 'A Phenomenology of Hesitation.' In E. S. Lee (ed.) *Living Alterities*. Albany, NY: SUNY, pp. 133–172.

Andermann, J. (2012) *New Argentine Cinema*. London: I. B. Tauris.

Anderson, B. (1983) *Imagined Communities*. Revised ed., 2006. London: Verso.

Anderson, B. (2009) 'The Strange Story of a Strange Beast.' In J. Quandt (ed.) (2009) *Apichatpong Weerasethakul*. Vienna: Synema, pp. 158–177.

Anderson, B. (2012) 'Impunity.' In J. T. Brink and J. Oppenheimer (eds.) *Killer Images*. London: Wallflower, pp. 268–286.

Andrade, O. de (1928) 'Cannibalist Manifesto.' Translated by Leslie Bary. *Latin American Literary Review*, 19, 38 (1991): 38–47

Andrew, D. (2006) 'An Atlas of World Cinema.' In S. Dennison and S. H. Lim (eds.) *Remapping World Cinema*. London: Wallflower, pp. 19–29.

Andrew, D. (2010) 'Time Zones and Jetlag.' In N. Ďurovičová and K. Newman (eds.) *World Cinemas, Transnational Perspectives*. London: Routledge, pp. 59–89.

Anonymous (2015) 'Embrace of the Serpent' Peccadillo Pictures. http://press.peccapics. co.uk/Theatrical/Embrace%20Of%20The%20Serpent/Embrace%20of%20the%20 Serpent%20Press%20Notes.pdf

Appadurai, A. (1990) 'Disjuncture and Difference in the Global Cultural Economy.' *Public Culture*, 2, 2: 1–24.

Appadurai, A. (2006) *Fear of Small Numbers*. Durham, NC: Duke University Press.

Arendt, H. (1963) *On Revolution*. London: Penguin.

Armitage, D. and A. Bashford (eds.) (2014) *Pacific Histories*. New York: Palgrave.

Bâ, S. M. and W. Higbee (2012) 'Introduction.' In S. M. Bâ and W. Higbee (eds.) *De-Westernizing Film Studies*. London: Routledge, pp. 1–15.

Backman Rogers, A. (2015) *American Independent Cinema*. Edinburgh: Edinburgh University Press.

Badiou, A. (1993) *Ethics*. Translated by P. Hallward, 2001. London: Verso.

Badley, L., R. B. Palmer and S. J. Schneider (eds.) (2006) *Traditions in World Cinema*. Edinburgh: Edinburgh University Press.

Bakhtin, M. (1965), *Rabelais and His World*. Translated by Hélène Iswolsky, 1968. Bloomington, IN: Indiana University Press.

Bakhtin, M. (1975) *The Dialogic Imagination*. Translated by Caryl Emerson and Michael Holquist, 1981. Austin, TX: University of Texas Press.

Balibar, É. (2003) *We, the People of Europe?* Translated by J. Swenson, 2004. Princeton, NJ: Princeton University Press.

Balibar, É. and I. Wallerstein (1991) *Race, Nation, Class*. London: Verso.

Barclay, B. (2003) 'Celebrating Fourth Cinema.' *Illusions Magazine*, July.

Barker, J. L. (2013) *The Aesthetics of Antifascist Film*. London: Routledge.

Barker, T. S. (2012) 'Information and Atmospheres.' *M/C*, 15, 3. http://journal.media-culture.org.au/index.php/mcjournal/article/viewArticle/482

Barta, T. (1998) 'Screening the Past: History Since the Cinema.' In T. Barta (ed.) *Screening the Past*. Westport, CT: Praeger, pp. 1–17.

Bazzano, M. (2016) '"All the Rest Is Dance": Another Look at Levinas.' *European Journal of Psychotherapy and Counselling*, 18, 1: 19–38.

BBC (2018) 'Sprawling Maya Network Discovered under Guatemala Jungle.' *BBC News*. 2 February. http://www.bbc.co.uk/news/world-latin-america-42916261

Beardsell, P. (2000) *Europe and Latin America*. Manchester, UK: Manchester University Press.

Beller, J. (2006) *The Cinematic Mode of Production*. Hanover, NH: Dartmouth College Press.

Berghahn, D. (2018) 'Encounters with Cultural Difference.' *Alphaville*, 14: 16–40.

Bergson, H. (1896) *Matter and Memory*. Translated by N. M. Paul and W. S. Palmer, 1912. Mineola, NY: Dover.

Bergson, H. (1907) *Creative Evolution*. Translated by Arthur Mitchell and Henry Holt. Mineola, NY: Dover.

Berlant, L. (2011) *Cruel Optimism*. Durham, NC: Duke University Press.

Bermúdez Barrios, N. (ed.) (2011) *Latin American Cinemas*. Calgary, Canada: University of Calgary Press.

Bernstein, J. M. (2012) 'Movement! Action! Belief?' *Angelaki*, 17, 4: 77–93.

Berressem, H. (2011) 'Crystal History.' In B. Herzogenrath (ed.) *Time and History in Deleuze and Serres*. London: Continuum, pp. 203–228.

Berry, C. (2009) 'Jia Zhangke and the Temporalities of Postsocialist Chinese Cinema.' In O. Khoo and S. Metzger (eds.) *Futures of Chinese Cinema*. Bristol, UK: Intellect, pp. 113–128.

Beugnet, M. (2007) *Cinema and Sensation*. Edinburgh: Edinburgh University Press.

Beugnet, M. (ed.) (2017) *Indefinite Visions*. Edinburgh: Edinburgh University Press.

Beverley, J., M. Aronna and J. Oviedo (eds.) (1995) *The Postmodernism Debate in Latin America*. Durham, NC: Duke University Press.

Blaine, P. (2013) 'Representing Absences in the Postdictatorial Documentary Cinema of Patricio Guzmán.' *Latin American Perspectives*, 40, 1: 114–130

Bogue, R. (1989) *Deleuze and Guattari*. New York: Routledge.

Bogue, R. (2003) *Deleuze on Cinema*. London: Routledge.

Bogue, R. (2010) 'To Choose to Choose.' In D. Rodowich (ed.) *Afterimages of Gilles Deleuze's Film Philosophy*. Minneapolis, MN: Minnesota University Press, pp. 115–133.

Boljkovac, N. (2013) *Untimely Affects*. Edinburgh: Edinburgh University Press.

Bonneuil, C. (2015) 'The Geological Turn.' In C. Hamilton, C. Bonneuil and F. Gemenne (eds.) *The Anthropocene and the Global Environmental Crisis*. London: Routledge, pp. 17–31.

Bonneuil, C. and J. B. Fressoz (2016) *The Shock of the Anthropocene*. Translated by D. Fernbach. London: Verso.

Booth, A. (1999) 'Development.' In D. K. Emmerson (ed.) *Indonesia Beyond Suharto*. Armonk, NY: East Gate, pp. 109–135.

Boothroyd, D. (2013) *Ethical Subjects in Contemporary Culture*. Edinburgh: Edinburgh University Press.

Bordwell, D. (1979) 'Art Cinema as Mode of Film Practice.' *Film Criticism*, 4, 1: 56–64.

Boucher, D. and P. Kelly (1994) 'The Social Contract and Its Critics'. In Boucher D. and P. Kelly (eds.) *The Social Contract From Hobbes to Rawls*. London: Routledge, pp. 1–34.

Braidotti, R. (1994) *Nomadic Subjects*. New York: Columbia University Press.

Braudel, F. (1949) *The Mediterranean and the Mediterranean World in the Age of Philip II*. Translated by S. Reynolds, 1972. Reprint 1995. Berkeley, CA: University of California Press.

Braudel, F. (1969) *On History*. Translated by Sarah Matthews, 1980. London: Weidenfeld and Nicolson.

Braudel, F. (1987) *A History of Civilizations*. Translated by R. Mayne, 1993. New York: Penguin.

Braudel, F. (1998) *Memories and the Mediterranean*. Translated by S. Reynolds, 2001. London: Vintage.

Brink, J. and J. Oppenheimer (2012) 'Introduction.' In J. T. Brink and J. Oppenheimer (eds.) *Killer Images*. London: Wallflower, pp. 1–11.

Brown, T. (2012) *Breaking the Fourth Wall*. Edinburgh: Edinburgh University Press.

Brown, W. (2014) 'Minor Cinema.' In W. Buckland (ed.) *Routledge Encyclopedia of Film Theory*. London: Routledge, pp. 290–294.

Brown, W. (2016) 'Non-Cinema.' *Film-Philosophy*, 20, 1: 104–130.

Brown, W. (2018) *Non-Cinema*. London: Bloomsbury.

Burgoyne, R. (1997) *Film Nation*. Revised ed. 2010. Minneapolis, MN: University of Minnesota Press.

Burgoyne, R. (2008) *The Hollywood Historical Film*. Oxford: Blackwell.

Burgoyne, R. (ed.) (2010) *The Epic Film in World Culture*. London: Routledge.

Burt, J. (2002) *Animals on Film*. London: Reaktion.

Butler, A. (2002) *Women's Cinema*. London: Wallflower.

Butler, J. (2004) *Precarious Life*. London: Verso.

Canny, N. and P. Morgan (eds.) (2011) *The Oxford Handbook of the Atlantic World*. Oxford: Oxford University Press.

Carlsten, J. M. and F. McGarry (eds.) (2015) *Film, History and Memory*. London: Palgrave MacMillan.

Carr, E. H. (1961) *What Is History?* Reprint 1990. London: Penguin.

Carrington, D. (2016) 'The Anthropocene Epoch.' *The Guardian*, 29 August. https://www.theguardian.com/environment/2016/aug/29/declare-anthropocene-epoch-experts-urge-geological-congress-human-impact-earth

Carver, T. and S. A. Chambers (2011) *Carole Pateman*. London: Routledge.

Caughie, J. (2018) 'Depicting Scotland.' In J. Caughie, T. Griffiths and M. A. Vélez-Serna (eds.) *Early Cinema in Scotland*. Edinburgh: Edinburgh University Press, pp. 147–165.

Ceballos, G. et al. (2015) 'Accelerated Modern Human-Induced Species Losses.' *Science Advances*, 1, 5: e1400253.

Césaire, A. (1955) *Discourse on Colonialism*. Translated by Joan Pinkham, 1972. Reprint 2000. New York: Monthly Review Press.

Chakrabarty, D. (2000) *Provincializing Europe*. Princeton, NJ: Princeton University Press.

Chakrabarty, D. (2009) 'The Climate of History.' *Critical Inquiry*, 35: 197–221.

Chakrabarty, D. (2015) 'The Anthropocene and the Convergence of Histories.' In C. Hamilton, C. Bonneuil and F. Gemenne (eds.) *The Anthropocene and the Global Environmental Crisis*. London: Routledge, pp. 44–56.

Chanan, M. (2007) *The Politics of Documentary*. London: BFI.

Chandler, D. and J. Reid (2016) *The Neoliberal Subject*. Lanham, MD: Rowan and Littlefield.

Chang, K. (1999) 'Compressed Modernity and Its Discontents.' *Economy and Society*, 28, 1: 30–55.

Chaudhuri, K. N. (1990) *Asia Before Europe*. Cambridge: Cambridge University Press.

Chaudhuri, S. (2005) *Contemporary World Cinema*. Edinburgh: Edinburgh University Press.

Chaudhuri, S. (2014) *Cinema of the Dark Side*. Edinburgh: Edinburgh University Press.

Chen, J. (2014) 'China, the Third World and the Cold War.' In R. J. McMahon (ed.) *The Cold War in the Third World*. Oxford: Oxford University press, pp. 85–100.

Chen, K. H. (2010) *Asia as Method*. Durham, NC: Duke University Press.

Choe, S. (2016) *Sovereign Violence*. Amsterdam: Amsterdam University Press.

Choi, J. (2010) *The South Korean Film Renaissance*. Middletown, CT: Wesleyan University Press.

Choi, J. (2014) 'The Ethics of Contemplation.' In J. Choi and M. Frey (eds.) *Cine-Ethics*. London: Routledge, pp. 79–95.

Choi, J. and M. Frey (2014) 'Introduction.' In J. Choi and M. Frey (eds.) *Cine-Ethics*. London: Routledge, pp. 1–14.

Chomsky, N. (1980) 'The Old and the New Cold War.' In N. Chomsky (ed.) (1987) *The Chomsky Reader*. New York: Pantheon, pp. 207–219.

Chomsky, N. (2016) *Who Rules the World?* London: Hamish Hamilton.

Chow, R. (1998) *Ethics after Idealism*. Bloomington, IN: Indiana University Press.

Christenson, A. J. (2003) 'Translator's Preface.' In A. J. Christenson (trans.) *Popol Vuh*. Norman, OK: University of Oklahoma Press, pp. 14–25.

Christian, D. (2004) *Maps of Time*. Berkeley, CA: University of California Press.

Chung, U. (2012) 'Crossing over Horror', *Women's Studies Quarterly*, 40, 1/2: 211–222.

Cilento, F. (2012) 'Even the Rain.' *Arizona Journal of Hispanic Cultural Studies*, 16: 245–258.

Clavin, P. (2005) 'Defining Transnationalism.' *Contemporary European History*, 14, 4: 421–439.

Colman, F. (2011) *Deleuze and Cinema*. Oxford: Berg.

Columpar, C. (2010) *Unsettling Sights*. Carbondale, IL: Southern Illinois University Press.

Constanzo, W. V. (2014) *World Cinema through Global Genres*. Oxford: Wiley-Blackwell.

Cooke, P. (2005) *Representing East Germany Since Unification*. Oxford: Berg.

Cooper, S. (2006) *Selfless Cinema?* London: Legenda.

Cooper, S. (2007) 'Moral Ethics.' *Film-Philosophy*, 11, 2: 66–87.

Cooper, S. (2007) 'The Occluded Relation: Levinas and Cinema.' *Film-Philosophy*, 11, 2: i–vii.

Copjec, J. (2004) *Imagine There's No Woman*. Cambridge, MA: MIT Press.

Corner, J. (2017) 'Fake News, Post-Truth and Media–Political Change.' *Media, Culture and Society*, 39, 7: 1100–1107.

Coronil, F. (2000) 'Towards a Critique of Globalcentrism.' *Public Culture*, 12, 2: 351–374.

Coronil, F. (2008) 'Elephants in the Americas?' In E. Dussel, M. Moraña and C. A. Jáuregui (eds.) *Coloniality at Large*. Durham, NC: Duke University Press, pp. 396–416.

Cranston, M. (1984) 'Introduction.' In J.-J. Rousseau (1755) *A Discourse on Inequality*. Translated by M. Cranston, 1984. London: Penguin, pp. 9–53.

Crosby, A. W. (1972) *The Columbian Exchange*. Reprint 1994. Westport, CT: Greenwood.

Crosby, A. W. (1986) *Ecological Imperialism*. Cambridge: Cambridge University Press.

Crutzen, P. J. (2002) 'Geology of Mankind.' *Nature*, 415: 23.

Cubitt, S. (2005) *EcoMedia*. Amsterdam: Rodopi.

Dabashi, H. (2015) *Can Non-Europeans Think?* Chicago, IL: University of Chicago Press.

Dangl, B. (2007) *The Price of Fire*. Edinburgh: AK.

Dargis, M. and A. O. Scott (2011) 'In Defence of the Slow and Boring.' *The New York Times*, 3 June.

Daston, L. and G. Mitman (eds.) (2006) *Thinking with Animals*. New York: Columbia University Press.

Davis, A. (2018) 'Laser Scanning Reveals "Lost" Ancient Mexican City "Had as Many Buildings as Manhattan".' *The Guardian*. 15 February. https://www.theguardian.com/science/2018/feb/15/laser-scanning-reveals-lost-ancient-mexican-city-had-as-many-buildings-as-manhattan

Davis, G. (2016) 'Stills and Stillness in Apichatpong Weerasethakul's Cinema.' In T. de Luca and N. B. Jorge (eds.) *Slow Cinema*. Edinburgh: Edinburgh University Press, pp. 99–111.

De Goeje, C. H. (1943) *Philosophy, Initiation and Myths of the Indians of Guiana and Adjacent Countries*. Leiden: E. J. Brill.

De Landa, M. (1997) *A Thousand Years of Nonlinear History*. New York: Swerve.

De Luca, T. and N. Barradas Jorge (2016) 'Introduction.' In T. de Luca and N. B. Jorge (eds.) *Slow Cinema*. Edinburgh: Edinburgh University Press, pp. 1–24.

Deamer, D. (2009) 'Cinema, Chronos/Cronos.' In J. A. Bell and C. Colebrook (eds.) *Deleuze and History*. Edinburgh: Edinburgh University Press, pp. 161–187.

Deamer, D. (2012) 'An Imprint of *Godzilla*.' In D. Martin-Jones and W. Brown (eds.) *Deleuze and Film*. Edinburgh: Edinburgh University Press, pp. 18–36.

Deamer, D. (2014) *Deleuze, Japanese Cinema and the Atomic Bomb*. London: Bloomsbury.

Deamer, D. (2016) *Deleuze's Cinema Books*. Edinburgh: Edinburgh University Press.

Del Rio, E. (2016) *The Grace of Destruction*. London: Bloomsbury.

Deleuze, G. (1968) *Difference and Repetition*. Translated by P. Patton, 1994. New York: Columbia University Press.

Deleuze, G. (1983) *Cinema 1*. Translated by H. Tomlinson and B. Habberjam, 2005. London: Continuum.

Deleuze, G. (1984) *Kant's Critical Philosophy*. Translated by H. Tomlinson and B. Habberjam, 1995. Continuum edition, 2008. London: Continuum.

Deleuze, G. (1985) *Cinema 2*. Translated by H. Tomlinson and R. Galeta, 2005. London: Continuum.

Deleuze, G. (1986) *Foucault*. Translated and edited by S. Hand, 1999. London: Athlone Press.

Deleuze, G. (1990) *Negotiations*. Translated by M. Joughin, 1995. New York: Columbia University Press.

Deleuze, G. (1992) 'Postscript on Societies of Control.' *October*, 59: 3–7.

Deleuze, G. and F. Guattari (1972) *Anti-Oedipus*. Translated by R. Hurley, M. Seem and H. R. Lane, 1977. Minneapolis, MN: University of Minnesota Press.

Deleuze, G. and F. Guattari (1980) *A Thousand Plateaus*. Translated by B. Massumi, 1987. London: Athlone.

Deleuze, G. and F. Guattari (1991) *What Is Philosophy?* Translated by H. Tomlinson and G. Burchill, 1994. London: Verso.

Deloria, V. (1972) *God is Red*. Golden, CO: Fulcrum Publishing.

Dennison, S. (ed.) (2013) *Contemporary Hispanic Cinema*. Woodbridge, UK: Tamesis.

Dennison, S. and S. H. Lim (eds.) (2006) *Remapping World Cinema*. London: Wallflower.

Derrida, J. (1967) *Writing and Difference*. Translated by A. Bass, 1978. London: Routledge.

Derrida, J. (1993) *Specters of Marx*. Translated by P. Kamuf. London: Routledge.

Diffrient, D. S. (2013) 'The Face(s) of Korean Horror Film.' In A. Peirse and D. Martin (eds.) *Korean Horror Cinema*. Edinburgh: Edinburgh University Press, pp. 114–130.

Doane, M. A. (2002) *The Emergence of Cinematic Time*. Cambridge, MA: Harvard University Press.

Downing, L. and L. Saxton. (2010) *Film and Ethics*. London: Routledge.

Drabinski, J. (2011) *Levinas and the Postcolonial*. Edinburgh: Edinburgh University Press.

Durham Peters, J. (2003) 'Space, Time, and Communication Theory.' *Canadian Journal of Communication Studies*, 28: 397–411.

Durie, R. (1999) 'Introduction.' In H. Bergson, *Duration and Simultaneity*. Edited by R. Durie. Manchester, UK: Clinamen.

Durkheim, É. (1897) *On Suicide*. Translated by R. Buss, 2006. London: Penguin.

Ďurovičová, N. and K. Newman (eds.) (2010) *World Cinemas, Transnational Perspectives*. London: Routledge.

Dussel, E. (1971) *Philosophy of Liberation*. Translated by A. Martinez and C. Morkovsky, 1985. Eugene, OR: Wipf and Stock.

Dussel, E. (1974) *Ethics and the Theology of Liberation*. Translated by B. McWilliams, 1978. New York: Orbis.

Dussel, E. (1986) *Ethics and Community*. Translated by R. Barr, 1988. Eugene, OR: Wipf and Stock.

Dussel, E. (1988) *Towards an Unknown Marx*. Translated by Y. Angulo, edited by F. Moseley, 2001. London: Routledge.

Dussel, E. (1992) *The Invention of the Americas*. Translated by M. D. Barber, 1995. New York: Continuum.

Dussel, E. (1995) 'Eurocentrism and Modernity.' In J. Beverley, M. Aronna and J. Oviedo (eds.) *The Postmodernism Debate in Latin America*. Durham, NC: Duke University Press, pp. 65–76.

Dussel, E. (1996) *The Underside of Modernity*. Translated and edited by E. Mendieta. New York: Humanity.

Dussel, E. (1998a) 'Beyond Eurocentrism.' In F. Jameson and M. Miyoshi (eds.) *The Cultures of Globalization*. Durham, NC: Duke University Press, pp. 3–31.

Dussel, E. (1998b) *Ethics of Liberation*. Tranlated by E. Mendieta, N. Maldonado-Torres, Y. Angulo and C. P. Bustillo. Edited by A. A. Vallega, 2013. Durham, NC: Duke University Press.

Dussel, E. (1999) '"Sensibility" and "Otherness" in Emmanuel Levinas.' *Philosophy Today*, 43, 2: 126–134.

Dussel, E. (2000a) 'Epilogue.' In L. M. Alcoff and E. Mendieta (eds.) *Thinking from the Underside of History*. Lanham, MD: Rowman and Littlefield, pp. 269–290.

Dussel, E. (2000b) 'Europe, Modernity and Eurocentrism.' *Neplanta*, 1, 3: 465–478.

Dussel, E. (2002) 'World-system and "Trans-Modernity"'. *Nepantla*, 3, 2: 221–244.

Dussel, E. (2003a) *Beyond Philosophy.* Edited by E. Mendieta. Lanham, MD: Rowman and Littlefield.

Dussel, E. (2003b) 'Philosophy in Latin America in the Twentieth Century.' In E. Mendieta (ed.) *Latin American Philosophy.* Bloomington, IN: Indiana University Press, pp. 11–53.

Dussel, E. (2006) 'Anti-Cartesian Meditations.' Translated by C. Ciccariello-Maher. *Poligrafi*, 41–42: 5–60.

Dussel, E. (2008a) 'Philosophies of Liberation, The Postmodern Debate, and Latin American Studies.' In E. Dussel, M. Moraña, C. A. Jáuregui (eds.) *Coloniality at Large.* Durham, NC: Duke University Press, pp. 335–349.

Dussel, E. (2008b) *Twenty Theses on Politics.* Translated by G. Cicccariello-Maher. Durham, NC: Duke University Press.

Dussel, E. (2011) *Politics of Liberation.* Translated by T. Cooper. London: SCM Press.

Dussel, E. (2013) 'Agenda for a South-South Philosophical Dialogue.' *Human Architecture*, 11, 1: 3–18.

Dussel E., M. Moraña, C. A. Jáuregui (eds.) (2008) *Coloniality at Large.* Durham, NC: Duke University Press.

Eagleton, T. (1999) 'Marxism without Marxism.' In M. Sprinkler (ed.) *Ghostly Demarcations.* London: Verso, pp. 83–87.

Edwards, D. (2013) 'Cinematic Scar Tissue.' *Senses of Cinema*, 67, September. http://sensesofcinema.com/2013/feature-articles/cinematic-scar-tissue-an-interview-with-joshua-oppenheimer-on-the-act-of-killing/

Egerton, D. et al. (2007) *Atlantic World.* Wheeling, IL: Harlan Davidson.

Elden, S. (2009) *Terror and Territory.* Minneapolis, MN: Minnesota University Press.

Eleftheriotis, D. (2001) *Popular Cinemas of Europe,* London: Continuum.

Eleftheriotis, D. (2016) 'Cosmopolitanism, Empathy and the Close-up.' In Y. Tzioumakis and C. Molloy (eds.) *The Routledge Companion to Cinema and Politics.* London: Routledge, pp. 203–217.

Elsaesser, T. (2005) *European Cinema.* Amsterdam: Amsterdam University Press.

Elsaesser, T. (2009) 'The Mind-Game Film.' In W. Buckland (ed.) *Puzzle Films.* Chichester, UK: Wiley-Blackwell, pp. 13–41.

Elsaesser, T. (2011) 'Politics, Multiculturalism, and the Ethical Turn.' In B. Hagin et al. (eds.) *Just Images.* Newcastle upon Tyne, UK: Cambridge Scholars.

Elson, R. E. (2008) *The Idea of Indonesia.* Cambridge: Cambridge University Press.

Escobar, A. (2010) 'Worlds and Knowledges Otherwise.' In W. D. Mignolo and A. Escobar (eds.) *Globalization and the Decolonial Option.* London: Routledge, pp. 33–64.

Espinosa, J. G. (1969) 'For an Imperfect Cinema.' In M. T. Martin (ed.), 1997. *New Latin American Cinema.* Detroit, MI: Wayne State University Press, pp. 71–82.

Fabian, J. (1983) *Time and the Other.* New York: Columbia University Press.

Falicov, T. (2007) *The Cinematic Tango.* London: Wallflower.

Fanon, F. (1952) *Black Skin, White Masks.* Reprint 2008. London: Pluto.

Fanon, F. (1961) *The Wretched of the Earth.* Translated by C. Farrington, 2001. London: Penguin.

Ferrari, M. (2012) 'Primitive Gazing.' In Khatib L. (ed.) *Storytelling in World Cinemas Vol. I.* New York: Wallflower, pp. 165–176.

Ferro, M. (1977) *Cinema and History.* Translated by N. Greene, 1988. Detroit, MI: Wayne State University Press.

Ferro, M. (1981) *The Use and Abuse of History.* Translated by N. Stone and A. Brown, 1984. Revised edition 2003. London: Routledge.

Fisher, M. (2009) *Capitalist Realism.* Ropley, UK: Zero Books.

Fisher, A. and I. R. Smith (2016) 'Transnational Cinemas.' *Frames Cinema Journal.*
http://framescinemajournal.com/article/transnational-cinemas-a-critical-roundtable/
Flaxman, G. and E. Oxman (2008) 'Losing Face.' In I. Buchanan and P. MacCormack
(eds.) *Deleuze and the Schizoanalysis of Cinema.* London: Continuum, pp. 39–51.
Flory, D. (2008) *Philosophy, Black Film, Film Noir.* University Park, PA: Pennsylvania
State University Press.
Flusser, W. (2014) *Gestures.* Minneapolis, MN: University of Minnesota Press.
Foster, J. B., B. Clark and R. York (2010) *The Ecological Rift.* New York: Monthly
Review Press.
Foucault, M. (1977) *Language, Counter-Memory, Practice.* Edited by D. F. Bouchard.
Translated by D. F. Bouchard and S. Simon. Oxford: Basil Blackwell.
Franco, J. (1993) 'High-Tech Primitivism.' In J. King, A. M. Lopez and M. Alvarado
(eds.) *Mediating Two Worlds.* London: BFI, pp. 81–94.
Frank, A. G. (1998) *ReOrient.* Berkeley, CA: University of California Press.
Frank, A. G. and B. K. Gills (1993) *The World System.* London: Routledge.
Frankopan, P. (2015) *The Silk Roads.* London: Bloomsbury.
Fraser, N. (2013) 'We Love Impunity.' *Film Quarterly,* 67, 2: 21–24.
Frey, M. (2016) *Extreme Cinema.* New Brunswick, NJ: Rutgers University Press.
Fukuyama, F. (1989) 'The End of History?' *The National Interest,* Summer: 3–18.
Gabriel, T. H. (1979) *Third Cinema in the Third World.* Reprint 1982. Ann Arbor, MI:
Umi Research Press.
Gaddis, J. L. (1992) 'The Cold War, the Long Peace and the Future.' In M. J. Hogan (ed.)
The End of the Cold War. Cambridge: Cambridge University Press, pp. 21–38.
Galeano, E. (1971) *Open Veins of Latin America.* Translated by C. Belfrage, 1973. Reprint
1997. New York: Monthly Review Press.
Galeano, E. (1986) 'The Dictatorship and its Aftermath.' In S. Sosnowski and L. B.
Popkin (eds.) (1992) *Repression, Exile and Democracy.* Durham, NC: Duke University
Press, pp. 103–107.
Galt, R. (2013) 'Default Cinema.' *Screen,* 51, 1: 62–81.
Gandolfo, D. I. (2013) 'Liberation Philosophy.' In S. Nuccitelli, O. Schutte and O. Bueno
(eds.) *A Companion to Latin American Philosophy.* Chichester, UK: Wiley-Blackwell,
pp. 185–198.
García Márquez, G. (1967) *One Hundred Years of Solitude.* Translated by G. Rabassa.
London: Penguin.
Gates, P. and L. Funnell (eds.) (2012) *Transnational Asian Identities in Pan-Pacific Cinemas.*
London: Routledge.
Gateward, F. (ed.) (2007) *Seoul Searching.* Albany, NY: SUNY.
Geist, K. (1994) 'Playing with Space.' In L. Ehrlich and D. Desser (eds.) *Cinematic
Landscapes.* Austin, TX: University of Texas Press, pp. 283–298.
Gilroy, P. (1993) *The Black Atlantic.* Cambridge, MA: Harvard University Press.
Gilroy, P. (2005) *Postcolonial Melancholia.* New York: Columbia University Press.
Girgus, S. B. (2010) *Levinas and the Cinema of Redemption.* New York: Columbia
University Press.
Glavin, T. (2006) *Waiting for the Macaws.* Toronto: Viking.
Glendinning, S. (2006) *The Idea of Continental Philosophy.* Edinburgh: Edinburgh
University Press.
Glissant, É. (1990) *Poetics of Relation.* Translated by B. Wing, 1997. Ann Arbor, MI:
University of Michigan Press.
Goni, U. and J. Watts (2013) 'Pope Francis.' *The Guardian,* 14 March. https://www.
theguardian.com/world/2013/mar/14/pope-francis-argentina-military-junta

Gordon, L. R. (2013) 'Thoughts on Dussel's "Anti-Cartesian Meditations."' *Human Architecture*, 11, 1: 67–72.

Gordon, R. A. (2009) *Cannibalizing the Colony*. West Lafayette, IN: Purdue University Press.

Graeber, D. (2011) *Debt*. Brooklyn, NY: Melville House.

Grønstad, A. (2016a) 'Slow Cinema and the Ethics of Duration.' In T. de Luca and N. B. Jorge (eds.) *Slow Cinema*. Edinburgh: Edinburgh University Press, pp. 273–285.

Grønstad, A. (2016b) *Film and the Ethical Imagination*. London: Palgrave MacMillan.

Groys, B. (2009) 'Comrades of Time', *e-flux*, 11. http://www.e-flux.com/journal/11/61345/comrades-of-time/

Guattari, F. (1989) *The Three Ecologies*. Translated by I. Pindar and P. Sutton, 2000. London: Bloomsbury.

Guneratne, A. R. and W. Dissanayake (eds.) (2003) *Rethinking Third Cinema*. London: Routledge.

Gunning, T. (1986) 'The Cinema of Attractions.' *Wide Angle*, 8, 3/4.

Gutiérrez, G. (1971) *A Theology of Liberation*. Translated and edited by C. Inda and J. Eagleson, 1988. Maryknoll, NY: Orbis.

Hageman, A. (2013) 'Ecocinema and Ideology.' In S. Rust, S. Monani and S. Cubitt (eds.) *Ecocinema Theory and Practice*. London: Routledge, pp. 63–86.

Hamilton, C., C. Bonneuil and F. Gemenne (2015) 'Thinking the Anthropocene.' In C. Hamilton, C. Bonneuil and F. Gemenne (eds.) *The Anthropocene and the Global Environmental Crisis*. London: Routledge, pp. 1–14.

Hand, S. (2009) *Emmanuel Levinas*. London: Routledge.

Hardt, M. and A. Negri (2000) *Empire*. Cambridge, MA: Harvard University Press.

Hardt, M. and A. Negri (2005) *Multitude*. London: Penguin

Harvey, D. (2005) *A Brief History of Neoliberalism*. Oxford: Oxford University Press.

Hearman, V. (2014) '"Missing Victims" of the 1965–66 Violence in Indonesia.' *Critical Asian Studies* 46, 1: 171–175.

Heckenberger, M. J. (2005) *The Ecology of Power*. Routledge: New York.

Hegel, G. W. F. (1837) *The Philosophy of History*. Translated by J. Sibree, 1900. New York: Willey.

Hendrix, G. (2006) 'Vengeance is Theirs.' *Sight and Sound* 16, 2: 18–21.

Herbert, D. (2012) 'Trilogy as Third Term.' In C. Perkins and C. Verevis (eds.) *Film Trilogies*. London: Palgrave Macmillan, pp. 181–197.

Herzog, A. (2008) 'Suspended Gestures.' In I. Buchanan and P. MacCormack (eds.) *Deleuze and the Schizoanalysis of Cinema*. London: Continuum, pp. 63–74.

Hickel, J. (2016) 'To Deal with Climate Change We Need a New Financial System.' *The Guardian*, 5 November. https://www.theguardian.com/global-development-professionals-network/2016/nov/05/how-a-new-money-system-could-help-stop-climate-change

Higbee W. and S. H Lim (2010) 'Concepts of Transnational Cinema.' *Transnational Cinemas*, 1, 1: 7–21.

Higson, A. (2000) 'The Limiting Imagination of National Cinema.' In M. Hjort and S. Mackenzie (eds.) *Cinema and Nation*. London: Routledge, pp. 63–74.

Hirsch, M. (1997) *Family Frames*. Cambridge, MA: Harvard University Press.

Hjort, M. (2010) 'On the Plurality of Cinematic Transnationalism.' In N. Ďurovičová and K. Newman (eds.) *World Cinemas, Transnational Perspectives*. London: Routledge, pp. 12–33.

Hobsbawm, E. (1962) *The Age of Revolution*. London: Abacus.

Hole, K. L. (2016) *Towards a Feminist Cinematic Ethics*. Edinburgh: Edinburgh University Press.

Holland, E. (2011) 'Non-Linear Historical Materialism.' In B. Herzogenrath (ed.) *Time and History in Deleuze and Serres*. London: Continuum, pp. 17–30.

Holtmeier, M. (2014) 'The Wanderings of Jia Zhangke.' *Journal of Chinese Cinemas*, 8, 2: 148–159.

Holtmeier, M. (2016) 'The Modern Political Cinema.' *Film-Philosophy*, 20: 303–323.

Holtmeier, M. (2018) *Modern Political Cinema*. Edinburgh: Edinburgh University Press.

Hoskins, J. and V. Lasmana (2015) 'The Act of Killing.' *Visual Anthropology*, 28, 3: 262–265.

Hughes-Warrington, M. (2011a) 'Introduction.' In M. Hughes-Warrington (ed.) *The History on Film Reader*. London: Routledge, pp. 1–12

Hughes-Warrington, M. (2011b) 'Shaping historical film'. In M. Hughes-Warrington (ed.) *The History on Film Reader*. London: Routledge, pp. 61–64.

Hulme-Lippert, M. (2015) 'Negotiating Human Rights in Icíar Bollaín's *También la Lluvia*.' *Journal of Latin American Cultural Studies*, 25, 1: 105–140.

Huntington, S. P. (1996) *The Clash of Civilizations and the Remaking of World Order*. New York: Simon and Schuster.

Hutchens, B. C. (2004) *Levinas*. London: Continuum.

Huyssen, A. (1986) *After the Great Divide*. Bloomington, IN: Indiana University Press.

Huyssen, A. (2003) *Present Pasts*. Stanford, CA: Stanford University Press.

Ingawanij, M. and MacDonald R. (2006) 'Blissfully Whose?' *New Cinemas*, 4, 1: 37–54.

Iordanova, D. (2010) 'Migration and Cinematic Process in Post-Cold War Europe.' In D. Berghahn and C. Sternberg (eds.) *European Cinema in Motion*. London: Palgrave, pp. 50–75.

Iordanova, D., D. Martin-Jones and B. Vidal (eds.) (2010) *Cinema at the Periphery*. Detroit, MI: Wayne State University Press.

Iriye, A. (2013) *Global Transnational History*. New York: Palgrave.

Ivakhiv, A. (2013a) *Ecologies of the Moving Image*. Waterloo, ON: Wilfrid Laurier University Press.

Ivakhiv, A. (2013b) 'An Ecophilosophy of the Moving Image.' In S. Rust, S. Monani and S. Cubitt (eds.) *Ecocinema Theory and Practice*. London: Routledge, pp. 87–106.

Iwabuchi, K. (2002) *Recentering Globalization*. Durham, NC: Duke University Press.

Jaffe, I. (2014) *Slow Movies*. London: Wallflower.

Jaising, S. (2015) 'Cinema and Neoliberalism.' *Jump Cut*, 56: 1–6.

Jameson, F. and M. Miyoshi (eds.) (1998) *The Cultures of Globalization*. Durham, NC: Duke University Press.

Jelin, E. (2003) *State Repression and the Struggles for Memory*. Translated by J. Rein and M. Gofoy-Anativia. London: Social Science Research Council.

Jennings, J. (1994) 'Rousseau, Social Contract and the Modern Leviathan.' In D. Boucher and P. Kelly (eds.) *The Social Contract*. London: Routledge, pp. 115–131.

Jeong, J. J. (2011) 'Memories of Memories.' *Cinema Journal*, 51, 1: 75–96.

Jeong, S. H. (2012) 'The Surface of the Object'. In D. Martin-Jones and W. Brown (eds.) *Deleuze and Film*. Edinburgh: Edinburgh University Press, pp. 210–226.

Jeong, S. H. (2013) *Cinematic Interfaces*. London: Routledge.

Jones, E., L. Frost and C. White (1993) *Coming Full Circle*. Boulder, CT: Westview Press.

Kaldor, M. (1990) *The Imaginary War*. Hoboken, NJ: Blackwell.

Kaplan, E. A. (1997) *Looking for the Other*. London: Routledge.

Kapur, J. and K. B. Wagner (2011) 'Introduction.' In J. Kapur and K. B. Wagner (eds.) *Neoliberalism and Global Cinema*. London: Routledge, pp. 1–17.

Kara, S. (2014) 'Beasts of the Digital Wild.' *Sequence*, 1, 4: 1–15. http://reframe.sussex. ac.uk/sequence/files/2012/12/SEQUENCE-1.4-2014-_-SEQUENCE-One.pdf

Kara, S. (2016) 'Anthropocenema.' In S. Denson and J. Leyda (eds.) *Post-Cinema*. Falmer, UK: Reframe.

Keeble, R. L. (2012) 'Orwell, *Nineteen Eighty-Four* and the Spooks.' In R. L. Keeble (ed.) *Orwell Today*. Suffolk, UK: Abramis, pp. 151–161.

Kendall, T. (2016) 'Staying On, or Getting Off (the Bus).' *Cinema Journal*, 55, 2: 112–118.

Kendall, T. and T. Horeck (eds.) (2011) *The New Extremism in Cinema*. Edinburgh: Edinburgh University Press.

Kerner, A. M. and J. L. Knapp (2016) *Extreme Cinema*. Edinburgh: Edinburgh University Press.

Khan, S. (2017) 'Republican Introduces Legislation to Ban Howard Zinn's Books from Publicly Funded Schools.' *Independent*, 4 March. http://www.independent.co.uk/news/world/americas/us-politics/republican-lawmaker-legislation-howard-zinn-kim-hendren-arkansas-a7610986.html

Kiely, R. (2005) *Empire in the Age of Globalisation*. London: Pluto.

Kim, J. (2010) 'Between Auditorium and Gallery' In Galt R.and Schoonover K. (eds.) *Global Art Cinema*. Oxford: Oxford University Press, pp. 125–141

Kim, J. H. (2011) 'Learning about Time.' *Film Quarterly*, 64, 4: 48–52.

Kim, K. H. (2004) *The Remasculinization of Korean Cinema*. Durham, NC: Duke University Press.

Kim, K. H. (2011) *Virtual Hallyu*. Durham, NC: Duke University Press.

King, A. (2014) 'Fault Lines.' In J. Choiand M. Frey (eds.) *Cine-Ethics*. London: Routledge, pp. 57–75.

Kirchgaessner, S. and J. Watts (2015) 'Catholic Church Warms to Liberation Theology as Founder Heads to Rome.' *The Guardian*, 11 May. https://www.theguardian.com/world/2015/may/11/vatican-new-chapter-liberation-theology-founder-gustavo-gutierrez

Klein, N. (2007) *The Shock Doctrine*. London: Penguin.

Klein, N. (2017) *No Is Not Enough*. London: Allen Lane.

Kohut, D., O. Vilella, and B. Julian (2003) *Historical Dictionary of the Dirty Wars*. Oxford: Scarecrow Press.

Kuhn, A. (1995) *Family Secrets*. London: Verso.

Kwon, H. (2010) *The Other Cold War*. New York: Columbia University Press.

Lam, S. (2016) 'It's about Time.' In T. de Luca and N. B. Jorge (eds.) *Slow Cinema*. Edinburgh: Edinburgh University Press, pp. 207–218.

Lampert, J. (2006) *Deleuze and Guattari's Philosophy of History*. London: Continuum.

Landsberg, A. (2004) *Prosthetic Memory*. New York: Columbia University Press.

Landsberg, A. (2009) 'Memory, Empathy, and the Politics of Identification.' *International Journal of Politics, Culture, and Society*, 22: 221–229.

Landy, M. (1996) *Cinematic Uses of the Past*. Minneapolis: University of Minnesota Press.

Landy, M. (ed.) (2001) *The Historical Film*. London: Athlone.

Landy, M. (2009) 'The Historical Film: History and Memory in Media.' In M. Hughes-Warrington (ed.) *The History on Film Reader*. London: Routledge, pp. 42–53.

Landy, M. (2011) 'Comedy and Counter-History.' In H. Salmi (ed.) *Historical Comedy on Screen*. Chicago, IL: University of Chicago Press, pp. 175–198.

Landy, M. (2015) *Cinema and Counter-History*. Bloomington, IN: Indiana University Press.

Las Casas, B. de (1552) *A Short Account of the Destruction of the Indies*. Edited and translated by N. Griffin, 1992. London: Penguin.

Latour, B. (1991) *We Have Never Been Modern*. Translated by C. Porter, 1993. Cambridge, MA: Harvard University Press.

Latour, B. (2004) 'Why Has Critique Run Out of Steam?' *Critical Inquiry*, Winter: 225–248.

Latour, B. (2015) 'Telling Friends from Foes in the Time of the Anthropocene.' In C. Hamilton, C. Bonneuil and F. Gemenne (eds.) *The Anthropocene and the Global Environmental Crisis*. London: Routledge, pp. 145–155.

Lau, J. K. W. (2003) 'Introduction.' In J. K. W. Lau (ed.) *Cinemas and Popular Media in Transcultural East Asia*. Philadelphia, PA: Temple University Press, pp. 1–10.

Laverty, P. (2011) *Even the Rain*. Pontefract: Route.

Laverty, P. (2012) Interview with David Martin-Jones, 6 September. Edinburgh.

Lawson, G, C. Armbruster and M. Cox (eds.) (2010) *The Global 1989*. Cambridge: Cambridge University Press.

Lazzarato, M. (2011) *The Making of the Indebted Man*. Translated by J. D. Jordan, 2012. Pasadena, CA: Semiotext(e).

Lazzarato, M. (2013) *Governing by Debt*. Translated by J. D. Jordan, 2015. Pasadena, CA: Semiotext(e).

Lee, N. J. Y. (2008) 'Salute to Mr. Vengeance!' In L. Hunt and L. Wing-Fai (eds.) *East Asian Cinemas*. London: I. B. Tauris, pp. 203–219.

Lessnoff, M. (ed.) (1990) *Social Contract Theory*. Oxford: Backwell.

Levinas, E. (1947) *Time and the Other*. Translated by R. A. Cohen, 1987. Pittsburgh, PA: Duquesne University Press.

Levinas, E. (1961) *Totality and Infinity*. Translated by A. Lingis, 1969. Pittsburgh, PA: Duquesne University Press.

Levinas, E. (1967) *Difficult Freedom: Essays on Judaism*. Translated by S. Hand, 1990. Baltimore, MD: Johns Hopkins University Press.

Levinas, E. (1971) *Otherwise than Being*. Translated by A. Lingis, 1988. Pittsburgh, PA: Duquesne University Press.

Levinas, E. (1989) 'Ethics and Politics.' In S. Hand (ed.) *The Levinas Reader*. Oxford: Basil Blackwell, pp. 289–297.

Lewis, S. L. and M. A. Maslin. (2015) 'Defining the Anthropocene.' *Nature*, 519: 171–180.

Lim, B. C. (2009) *Translating Time*. Durham, NC: Duke University Press.

Linera, A. G. (2004) 'The Multitude.' In O. Olivera (ed.) *¡Cochabamba!* Cambridge, MA: South End, pp. 65–86.

Ling, A. (2011) *Badiou and Cinema*. Edinburgh: Edinburgh University Press.

Lippit, J. (1992) 'Nietzsche, Zarathrustra, and the Status of Laughter.' *British Journal of Aesthetics*, 32, 1: 39–49.

Lovatt, P. (2013) 'Every Drop of My Blood Sings Our Song.' *The New Soundtrack*, 13, 1: 61–79.

Lovelock, J. (2009) *The Vanishing Face of Gaia*. London: Allen Lane.

Lowenthal, D. (1985) *The Past Is a Foreign Country*. Cambridge: Cambridge University Press.

Lu, S. (ed.) (1997) *Transnational Chinese Cinemas*. Honolulu, HI: University of Hawaii Press.

Lu, S. (2007) *Chinese Modernity and Global Biopolitics*. Honolulu, HI: University of Hawaii Press.

Lu, S. and E. Y. Yeh (eds.) (2005) *Chinese-Language Film*. Honolulu, HI: University of Hawaii Press.

Lucas, S. (2004) *The Betrayal of Dissent*. London: Pluto Press.

Lundy, C. (2011) 'Deleuze and Guattari's Historiophilosophy.' *Critical Horizons*, 12, 2: 115–135.

Lyell, C. (1930–33) *Principles of Geology*. Edited by J. A. Secord, 1997. London: Penguin.

Macfarlane, R. (2016) 'Generation Anthropocene: How Humans Have Altered the Planet Forever.' *The Guardian*, 1 April. https://www.theguardian.com/books/2016/apr/01/generation-anthropocene-altered-planet-for-ever

Maffie, J. (2013) 'Pre-Columbian Philosophies.' In S. Nuccitelli, O. Schutte and O. Bueno (eds.) *A Companion to Latin American Philosophy*. Chichester, UK: Wiley-Blackwell, pp. 9–22.

Mann, C. C. (2005) *1491*. London: Granta.

Mann, C. C. (2011) *1493*. London: Granta.

Marho (1976) *Visions of History*. Edited by H. Abelove, B. Blackmar, P. Dimock, J. Schneer. Manchester, UK: Manchester University Press.

Marks, L. (2000) *The Skin of the Film*. Durham, NC: Duke University Press.

Márquez, I. (2013) 'Liberation in Theology, Philosophy and Pedagogy.' In S. Nuccitelli, O. Schutte and O. Bueno (eds.) *A Companion to Latin American Philosophy*. Chichester, UK: Wiley-Blackwell, pp. 297–311.

Marshak, S. (2015) *Earth*. 5th edition. New York: W.W. Norton.

Martin, D. (2015) *Extreme Asia*. Edinburgh: Edinburgh University Press.

Martin, M. T. (ed.) (1997) *New Latin American Cinema*. Detroit, MI: Wayne State University Press.

Martín Alcoff, L. and E. Mendieta (2000) 'Introduction.' In L. M. Alcoff and E. Mendieta (eds.) *Thinking from the Underside of History*. Lanham, MD: Rowman and Littlefield, pp. 1–26.

Martin-Jones, D. (2006) *Deleuze, Cinema and National Identity*. Edinburgh: Edinburgh University Press.

Martin-Jones, D. (2009) *Scotland*. Edinburgh: Edinburgh University Press.

Martin-Jones, D. (2011) *Deleuze and World Cinemas*. London: Continuum.

Martin-Jones, D. (2013a) 'The Dardennes Brothers Encounter Enrique Dussel.' In M. Conceição Monteiro, G. Giucci and Neil Besner (eds.) *Além dos limites: ensaios para o século XXI/Beyond the Limits: Essays for the XXI Century*. Rio de Janeiro: State University of Rio de Janeiro Press, pp. 71–105.

Martin-Jones, D. (2013b) 'Archival Landscapes and a Non-Anthropocentric "Universe Memory" in *Nostalgia de la Luz/Nostalgia for the Light* (2010).' *Third Text*, 27, 6: 707–722.

Martin-Jones, D. (2014) 'Remembering the Body.' *Journal of Chinese Cinemas*, 8, 2: 111–122.

Martin-Jones, D. (2016) 'Trolls, Tigers and Transmodern Ecological Encounters.' *Film-Philosophy*, 20, 1: 60–103.

Martin-Jones, D. and W. Brown (eds.) (2012) *Deleuze and Film*. Edinburgh: Edinburgh University Press.

Martin-Jones, D. and M. S. Montañez (2013a) 'Uruguay Disappears.' *Cinema Journal*, 53, 1: 25–51.

Martin-Jones, D. and M. S. Montañez (2013b) 'Personal Museums of Memory.' *Latin American Perspectives*, 40, 1: 73–87.

Martin-Jones, D. and D. H. Fleming (2014) 'Deleuze and Chinese Cinemas.' *Journal of Chinese Cinemas* (special issue), 8, 2.

Martin-Márquez, S. (2011) 'Coloniality and the Trappings of Modernity in *Viridiana* and *The Hand in the Trap*.' *Cinema Journal*, 51, 1: 96–114.

Marx, K. and F. Engels (1848) *The Communist Manifesto*. Edited by J. C. Isaac, 2012. London: Yale University Press.

Matsuda, M. K. (2012) *Pacific Worlds*. Cambridge: Cambridge University Press.

Mazrui, A. A. (1997) 'Racial Conflict or Clash of Civilizations?' In S. Rashid (ed.) *The Clash of Civilizations?* Oxford: Oxford University Press, pp. 27–38.

McAuley, L. K. (2013) 'What's Love Got to Do with It?' In R. A. Rosentone and C. Parvulescu (eds.) *A Companion to the Historical Film*. Hoboken, NJ: John Wiley and Sons.

McGregor, K. (2014) 'Inside the Minds of Executioners.' *Critical Asian Studies*, 46, 1: 189–194.

McMahon, L. (2014) 'Beyond the Human Body.' *Alphaville*, 7: 1–18.

McMahon, R. J. (ed.) (2013) *The Cold War in the Third World*. Oxford: Oxford University Press.

McSweeney, T. (2011) 'Memory as Cultural Battleground in Park Chan-Wook's *Oldboy*.' In A. Sinha and T. McSweeney (eds.) *Millennial Cinema*. London: Wallflower, pp. 222–238.

Meillassoux, Q. (2006) *After Finitude*. Translated by R. Brassier, 2008. London: Bloomsbury.

Mendieta, E. (2003a) 'Introduction.' In E. Dussel, *Beyond Philosophy*. Edited by E. Mendieta. Lanham, MD: Rowman and Littlefield, 1–20.

Mendieta, E. (2003b) 'Introduction.' In E. Mendieta (ed.) *Latin American Philosophy*. Bloomington, IN: Indiana University Press, pp. 1–8.

Mendieta, E. (2008) 'Remapping Latin American Studies.' In E. Dussel, M. Moraña and C. A. Jáuregui (eds.) *Coloniality at Large*. Durham, NC: Duke University Press, pp. 286–306.

Menzies, G. (2002) *1421*. London: Bantam.

Mignolo, W. D. (1998) 'Globalization, Civilization Processes, and the Relocation of Languages and Cultures.' In F. Jameson and M. Miyoshi (eds.) *The Cultures of Globalization*. Durham, NC: Duke University Press, pp. 32–53.

Mignolo, W. D. (2000) *Local Histories/Global Designs*. Princeton, NJ: Princeton University Press.

Mignolo, W. D. (2003) *The Darker Side of the Renaissance*. Ann Arbor, MI: University of Michigan Press.

Mignolo, W. D. (2008) 'The Geopolitics of Knowledge and the Colonial Difference.' In E. Dussel, M. Moraña and C. A. Jáuregui (eds.) *Coloniality at Large*. Durham, NC: Duke University Press, pp. 259–285.

Mignolo, W. D. (2010a) 'Delinking.' In W. D. Mignolo and A. Escobar (eds.) *Globalization and the Decolonial Option*. London: Routledge, pp. 303–368.

Mignolo, W. D. (2010b) 'Introduction.' In W. D. Mignolo and A. Escobar (eds.) *Globalization and the Decolonial Option*. London: Routledge, pp. 1–21.

Mignolo, W. D. (2011) *The Darker Side of Western Modernity*. Durham, NC: Duke University Press.

Mignolo, W. D. (2015) 'Foreword.' In H. Dabashi, *Can Non-Europeans Think?* Chicago, IL: University of Chicago Press, pp. viii–xlii.

Mignolo, W. D. and A. Escobar (eds.) (2010) *Globalization and the Decolonial Option*. London: Routledge.

Mills, C. W. (1997) *The Racial Contract*. Ithaca, NY: Cornell University Press.

Minnich, N. H. (2005) ' The Catholic Church and the Pastoral Care of Black Africans in Renaissance Italy.' In T. F. Earle and K. J. P. Lowe (eds) *Black Africans in Renaissance Europe*. Cambridge: Cambridge University Press, pp. 280–302.

Moore, J. W. (2003) '*The Modern World-System* as Environmental History?' *Theory and Society*, 32: 307–377.

Moore, J. W. (2015) *Capitalism in the Web of Life*. London: Verso.

Moretti, F. (2001) 'Planet Hollywood.' *New Left Review*, 9, May–June. https://newleft review.org/II/9/franco-moretti-planet-hollywood

Moretti, F. (2013) *Distant Reading*. London: Verso.

Morton, T. (2013) *Hyperobjects*. Minneapolis, MN: University of Minnesota Press.

Mulhall, S. (2001) *On Film*. London: Routledge.

Mullarkey, J. (2006) *Post-Continental Philosophy*. London: Continuum.

Mullarkey, J. (2013) 'Animal Spirits.' *Angelaki*, 18, 1: 11–29.

Murray, R. L. and J. K. Heumann (2009) *Ecology and Popular Film*. Albany, NY: SUNY.

Mutis, A. M. (2018), '*El abrazo de la serpiente* o la re-escritura del Amazonas dentro de una ética ecológica y poscolonial.' *Hispanic Research Journal*, 19: 1, 29–40.

Naficy, H. (2001) *An Accented Cinema*. Princeton, NJ: Princeton University Press.

Nagib, L. (2006) 'Towards a Positive Definition of World Cinema.' In S. Dennison and S. H. Lim (eds.) *Remapping World Cinema*. London: Wallflower, pp. 30–37.

Nagib, L. (2007) *Brazil On Screen*. London: I. B. Tauris.

Nagib, L. (2011) *World Cinema and the Ethics of Realism*. New York: Continuum.

Nagib, L. (2016a) 'Non-Cinema, or the Location of Politics in Film.' *Film-Philosophy* 20: 131–148.

Nagib, L. (2016b) 'Regurgitated Bodies.' In Y. Tzioumakis and C. Molloy (eds.) *The Routledge Companion to Cinema and Politics*. London: Routledge, pp. 218–230.

Neale, S. (1981) 'Art Cinema as Institution.' *Screen*, 22, 1: 11–39.

Newman, K. (2010) 'Notes on Transnational Film Theory.' In N. Ďurovičová and K. Newman (eds.) *World Cinemas, Transnational Perspectives*. London: Routledge, pp. 3–11.

Nietzsche, F. (1874) 'On the Uses and Disadvantages of History for Life.' In *Untimely Meditations*. Edited by F. Breakeale, translated by R. J. Hollingdale, 1983. Cambridge: Cambridge University Press, pp. 57–124.

Nietzsche, F. (1891) *Thus Spoke Zarathustra*. Translated by R. J. Hollingdale, 1961. London: Penguin.

Noortwijk, A. (2014) 'Heddy Honigmann's Contemplations on *Ars Vitae* and the Metamordern Turn.' In Choi J. and M. Frey (eds.) *Cine-Ethics*. London: Routledge, pp. 111–124.

O'Hara, A. (2012) 'Mysterious Object of Desire.' In P. Gates and L. Funnell (eds.) *Transnational Asian Identities in Pan-Pacific Cinemas*. London: Routledge, pp. 177–190.

Olivera, O. (2004) *¡Cochabamba!* Cambridge, MA: South End Press.

Oppenheimer, J. (2012) 'Perpretrator's Testimony and the Restoration of Humanity.' In J. T. Brink and J. Oppenheimer (eds.) *Killer Images*. London: Wallflower, pp. 243–255.

Oppenheimer, J. and M. Uwemedimo (2012) 'Show of Force.' In J. T. Brink and J. Oppenheimer (eds.) *Killer Images*. London: Wallflower, pp. 287–310.

Ortiz, F. (1940) *Cuban Counterpoint*. Translated by H. de Onis. Reprint 1995. Durham, NC: Duke University Press.

Orwell, G. (1949) *Nineteen Eighty-Four*. Penguin edition 1989. Reprint 2000. London: Penguin Modern Classics.

Pagden, A. (1992) 'Introduction.' In B. de Las Casas (1552) *A Short Account of the Destruction of the Indies*. Edited and translated by N. Griffen, 1992. London: Penguin, pp. xiii–xli.

Page, J. (2009) *Crisis and Capitalism in Contemporary Argentine Cinema*. Durham, NC: Duke University Press.

Pandian, A. (2011) 'Landscapes of Expression.' *Cinema Journal*, 51, 1: 50–74.

Parikka, J. (2014) *The Anthrobscene*. Minneapolis, MN: University of Minnesota Press.

Park, P. K. J. (2013) *Africa, Asia, and the History of Philosophy*. Albany, NY: SUNY.

Parker, J. C. (2013) 'Decolonization, the Cold War, and the Post-Columbian Era,' In R. J. McMahon (ed.) *The Cold War in the Third World*. Oxford: Oxford University Press, pp. 124–138.

Pateman, C. (1988) *The Sexual Contract*. Cambridge: Polity.

Pateman, C. and C. W. Mills (2007) *Contract and Domination*. Cambridge: Polity.

Patton, P. (2009) 'Events, Becoming and History.' In J. Bell and C. Colebrook (eds.) *Deleuze and History*. Edinburgh: Edinburgh University Press, pp. 33–53.

Paul, H. (2011) *Hayden White*. Cambridge: Polity.

Pekerman, S. (2011) 'Framed Intimacy.' PhD Dissertation, University of St Andrews, UK.

Peña, R. (1995) 'How Tasty Was My Little Frenchman.' In R. Johnson and R. Stam (eds.) *Brazilian Cinema*. New York: Columbia University Press, pp. 191–199.

Peranson, M. and K. Rithdee (2010) 'Ghost in the Machine.' *Cinema-Scope*, 43. http://cinema-scope.com/spotlight/spotlight-ghost-in-the-machine-apichatpong-weerasethakuls-letter-to-cinema/

Pérez de Miles, A. (2013) 'An Oppositional Reading of Patriarchy, Love, Neo-Colonialism, and Anthropophagy in Nelson Pereira dos Santos's Film "How Tasty Was My Little Frenchman."' *Visual Culture and Gender*, 8: 104–113.

Pick, A. and G. Narraway (eds.) (2013) *Screening Nature*. Oxford: Berghahn.

Pilkington, E. (2017) 'A Journey through a Land of Extreme Poverty: Welcome to the USA.' *The Guardian*, 15 December. https://www.theguardian.com/society/2017/dec/15/america-extreme-poverty-un-special-rapporteur

Pines, J. and P. Willemen (eds.) (1989) *Questions of Third Cinema*. London: BFI.

Pinker, S. (2012) *The Better Angels of Our Nature*. London: Penguin.

Piotrowska, A. (2014) '*Zero Dark Thirty* – "War Autism" or Lacanian Ethical Act?' *New Review of Film and Television Studies*, 12, 2: 143–155.

Pippin, R. B. (1991) *Modernism as a Philosophical Problem*. 2nd edition, 1999. Oxford: Blackwell.

Pisters, P. (2003) *The Matrix of Visual Culture*. Stanford, CA: Stanford University Press.

Pisters, P. (2012) *The Neuro-Image*. Stanford, CA: Stanford University Press.

Ponzanesi, S. and M. Waller (eds.) (2012) *Postcolonial Cinema Studies*. London: Routledge.

Pope Francis (2013) *Evangelii Gaudium*. Vatican City: Catholic Church.

Pope Francis (2015) *Laudato Si'*. Vatican City: Catholic Church.

Prager, B. (2010) 'Landscape of the Mind.' In Harper G. and J. Rayner, *Cinema and Landscape*. Bristol, UK: Intellect, pp. 91–102.

Purcell, M. (2013) *The Down-Deep Delight of Democracy*. Hoboken, NJ: Wiley.

Pynchon, T. (2003) 'Introduction.' In G. Orwell (1949) *Nineteen Eighty-Four*. Penguin edition 1989. Reprint 2000. London: Penguin Modern Classics, pp. v–xxv.

Quandt, J. (2009) 'Resistant to Bliss.' In J. Quandt (ed.) *Apichatpong Weerasethakul*. Vienna: Synema, pp. 13–103.

Quijano, A. (1995) 'Modernity, Identity, and Utopia in Latin America.' In J. Beverley, M. Aronna and J. Oviedo (eds.) *The Postmodernism Debate in Latin America*. Durham, NC: Duke University Press, pp. 201–216.

Quijano, A. (2000) 'Coloniality of Power, Eurocentrism and Latin America.' *Neplanta*, 1, 3: 533–580.

Quijano, A. (2008) 'Coloniality of Power, Eurocentrism, and Social Classification.' In E. Dussel, M. Moraña, C. A. Jáuregui (eds.) *Coloniality at Large*. Durham, NC: Duke University Press, pp. 181–224.

Quijano, A. (2010) 'Coloniality and Modernity/Rationality.' In W. D. Mignolo and A. Escobar (eds.) *Globalization and the Decolonial Option*. London: Routledge, pp. 22–31.

Rabinowitz, P. (1993) 'Wreckage upon Wreckage.' *History and Theory*, 32: 119–137.

Renov, M. (1995) 'New Subjectivities.' *Yagamata International Film Festival DocBox*, 31 July. http://www.yidff.jp/docbox7/box7-1-e.html

Retamar, R. F. (1971) *Caliban and Other Essays*. Translated by E. Baker, 1989. Minneapolis, MN: University of Minnesota Press.

Richards, K. J. (2011) 'A Shamanic Transmodernity.' In N. Bermúdez Barrios (ed.) *Latin American Cinemas*. Calgary, Canada: University of Calgary Press, pp. 197–222.

Roberts, P. (2017) 'Control and Cinema.' *Deleuze Studies*, 11, 1: 68–94.

Robinson, A. and S. Tormey (2010) 'Living in Smooth Space.' In S. Bignall and P. Patton (eds.) *Deleuze and the Postcolonial*. Edinburgh: Edinburgh University Press, pp. 20–40.

Rocha, C. (2012) *Masculinites in Contemporary Argentine Popular Cinema*. New York: Palgrave Macmillan.

Rocha, G. (1965) 'An Esthetic of Hunger.' In M. T. Martin (ed.) (1997) *New Latin American Cinema*. Detroit, MI: Wayne State University Press, pp. 59–61.

Rockhill, G. (2017) 'The CIA Reads French Theory.' *The Philosophical Salon*, 17 February. http://thephilosophicalsalon.com/the-cia-reads-french-theory-on-the-intellectual-labor-of-dismantling-the-cultural-left/

Rodden, J. and Rossi J. (2012) *The Cambridge Introduction to George Orwell*. Cambridge: Cambridge University Press.

Rodowick, D. N. (1997) *Gilles Deleuze's Time Machine*. Durham, NC: Duke University Press.

Rodowick, D. N. (2007) 'An Elegy for Theory.' *October* 122: 91–109.

Rodowick, D. N. (2010) *Afterimages of Gilles Deleuze's Film Philosophy*. Minneapolis, MN: University of Minnesota Press.

Roosa, J. (2006) *Pretext for Mass Murder*. Madison, WI: University of Wisconsin Press.

Rosenstone, R. A. (1988) 'History in Images/History in Words.' In M. Hughes-Warrington (ed.) (2009) *The History on Film Reader*. London: Routledge, pp. 30–41.

Rosentone, R. A. (1995a) 'Introduction.' In R. A. Rosenstone (ed.) *Revisioning History*. Princeton, NJ: Princeton University Press, pp. 1–14.

Rosenstone, R. A. (1995b) *Visions of the Past*. Cambridge, MA: Harvard University Press.

Rosenstone, R. A. (2006) *History on Film*. Harlow, UK: Pearson Education.

Rosenstone, R. A. and C. Parvulescu (eds.) (2013) *Companion to the Historical Film*. Oxford: Wiley-Blackwell.

Ross, M. (2010) *South American Cinematic Culture*. Newcastle upon Tyne, UK: Cambridge Scholars.

Ross, M. (2011) 'The Film Festival as Producer.' *Screen*, 52, 2: 261–267.

Roth, M. S. (2014) 'Foreword.' In H. White (1973) *Metahistory*. 40th anniversary edition, 2014. Baltimore, MD: Johns Hopkins University Press, pp. ix–xxiii.

Rousseau, J.-J. (1750) *The Social Contract*. Translated by M. Cranston, 1968. London: Penguin.

Rousseau, J.-J. (1755) *A Discourse on Inequality*. Translated by M. Cranston, 1984. London: Penguin.

Ruffinelli, J. (2013) 'Uruguay 2008.' Translated by M. Olivarria. *Latin American Perspectives* 40, 1: 60–72.

Rushton, R. (2013) *The Politics of Hollywood Cinema*. London: Palgrave Macmillan.

Rust, S. and S. Monani (2013) 'Introduction.' In S. Rust, S. Monani and S. Cubitt (eds.) *Ecocinema Theory and Practice*. London: Routledge, pp. 1–14.

Sachsenmaier, D. (2011) *Global Perspectives on Global History*. Cambridge: Cambridge University Press.

Sadlier, D. J. (2003) *Nelson Pereira dos Santos*. Urbana, IL: University of Illinois Press.

Said, E. W. (1978) *Orientalism*. New York: Pantheon Books.

Sanford, J. (2003) 'French Philosopher Calls for New Critical Attitude in Academia.' *Stanford Report*, 16 April. http://web.stanford.edu/dept/news/news/2003/april16/latour talk-416.html

Sanjinés, C. J. (2013) *Embers of the Past*. Translated by D. Frye. Durham, NC: Duke University Press.

Santaolalla, I. (2012) *The Cinema of Icíar Bollaín*. Manchester, UK: Manchester University Press.

Schutte, O. (1993) *Cultural Identity and Social Liberation in Latin American Thought*. Albany, NY: SUNY.

Schutte, O. (2013) 'Philosophy, Postcoloniality, and Postmodernity.' In S. Nuccitelli, O. Schutte and O. Bueno (eds.) *A Companion to Latin American Philosophy*. Chichester, UK: Wiley-Blackwell, pp. 312–326.

Scott, K. (2014) 'Cinema of Exposure.' PhD Dissertation, University of St. Andrews, UK.

Serres, M. (1992) *The Natural Contract*. Translated by E. MacArthur and W. Paulson, 1995. Ann Arbor, MI: University of Michigan Press.

Serres, M. (2008) *Malfeasance*. Translated by A. Feenberg-Dibon. Stanford, CA: Stanford University Press.

Sessions, G. (ed.) (1995) *Deep Ecology for the Twenty-First Century*. Boston, Ma: Shambhala.

Shakespeare, W. (1980) *Hamlet*. London: Penguin.

Shannon, T. J. (2004) *Atlantic Lives*. New York: Pearson.

Shaviro, S. (2009) *Post-Cinematic Affect*. Ropley, UK: Zero Books.

Shaviro, S. (2010) 'Slow Cinema vs Fast Films' (blog post). http://www.shaviro.com/Blog/?p=891

Shaviro, S. (2011) 'The "Bitter" Necessity of Debt.' *Concentric*, 37, 1: 73–82.

Shaviro, S. (2014) *The Universe of Things*. Minneapolis, MN: University of Minnesota Press.

Shaw, D. (2013) 'Deconstructing and Reconstructing "Transnational Cinema."' In S. Dennison (ed.) *Contemporary Hispanic Cinema*. Woodbridge, UK: Tamesis, pp. 47–65.

Shaw, T. (2004) 'Some Writers Are More Equal than Others.' In R. Mitter and P. Major (eds.) *Across the Block*. London: Routledge, pp. 143–170.

Shaw, T. and D. J. Youngblood (2010) *Cinematic Cold War*. Lawrence, KS: University Press of Kansas.

Shih, S. (2005) 'Towards an Ethics of Transnational Encounters.' In F. Lionnet and S. Shih (eds.) *Minor Transnationalism*. Durham, NC: Duke University Press, pp. 73–108.

Shin, C. and J. Stringer (eds.) (2005) *New Korean Cinema*. Edinburgh: Edinburgh University Press.

Shohat, E. (2013) 'The Sephardi-Moorish Atlantic.' In E. Alsultany and E. Shohat (eds.) *Between the Middle East and the Americas*. Ann Arbor, MI: The University of Michigan Press, pp. 42–61.

Shohat, E. and R. Stam (1994) *Unthinking Eurocentrism*. London: Routledge.

Shohat, E. and R. Stam (2003) *Multiculturalism, Postcoloniality, and Transnational Media*. New Brunswick, NJ: Rutgers University Press.

Simpson, B. R. (2014) 'Southeast Asia in the Cold War.' In R. J. McMahon (ed.) *The Cold War in the Third World*. Oxford: Oxford University Press, pp. 48–62.

Sinnerbrink, R. (2008) 'Simon Glendinning, the Idea of Continental Philosophy.' *Australasian Journal of Philosophy*, 86, 4: 696–697.

Sinnerbrink, R. (2011) *New Philosophies of Film*. London: Continuum.

Sinnerbrink, R. (2016) *Cinematic Ethics*. London: Routledge.

Skrbina, D. (2007) *Panpsychism in the West*. Cambridge, MA: MIT Press.

Smith, I. R. (2013) 'Oldboy Goes to Bollywood.' In A. Peirse and D. Martin (eds.) *Korean Horror Cinema*. Edinburgh: Edinburgh University Press, pp. 187–198.

Smith, I. R. (2017) '"For the Dead Travel Fast."' In I. R. Smith and C. Verevis (eds.) *Transnational Film Remakes*. Edinburgh: Edinburgh University Press, pp. 66–84.

Sobchack, V. (1996) *The Persistence of History*. London: Routledge.

Solanas, F. and O. Getino (1969) 'Towards a Third Cinema.' In M. T. Martin (ed.) (1997) *New Latin American Cinema*. Detroit, MI: Wayne State University Press, pp. 33–58.

Sparrow, T. (2013) *Levinas Unhinged*. Alresford, UK: Zero Books.

Spivak, G. C. (1988) 'Can the Subaltern Speak?' In C. Nelson and L. Grossberg (eds.) *Marxism and the Interpretation of Culture*. Champaign, IL: University of Illinois Press, pp. 271–315.

Staden, H. (1557) *Hans Staden's True History*. Edited and translated by N. L. Whitehead and M. Harbsmeier, 2008. Durham, NC: Duke University Press.

Stadler, J. (2008) *Pulling Focus*. London: Continuum.

Stam, R. (1997) *Tropical Multiculturalism*. Durham, NC: Duke University Press.

Stam, R. and E. Shohat (2012) *Race in Translation*. New York: New York University Press.

Steele, S. (2006) *White Guilt*. New York: Harper Collins.

Stelter, B. and F. Pallotta (2017) 'Publisher Printing More Copies of George Orwell's "1984" After Spike in Demand.' *CNN*, 25 January. http://money.cnn.com/2017/01/25/media/george-orwell-1984-best-seller/

Stone, R. (2013) *The Cinema of Richard Linklater*. London: Wallflower.

Stone, R. and P. Cooke (2016) 'Crystallising the Past.' In T. de Luca and N. B. Jorge (eds.) *Slow Cinema*. Edinburgh: Edinburgh University Press, pp. 312–323.

Stone, R., P. Cooke, S. Dennison, and A. Marlow-Mann (2018) 'Introduction.' In R. Stone, P. Cooke, S. Dennison, and A. Marlow-Mann (eds.) *The Routledge Companion to World Cinema*. London: Routledge, pp. 1–20.

Strausz, L. (2017) *Hesitant Histories on the Romanian Screen*. London: Palgrave Macmillan.

Suter, J. (2013) 'Apichatpong: Staging the Photo Session.' *Asian Cinema*, 24, 1: 51–67.

Sutton, D. and D. Martin-Jones (2008) *Deleuze Reframed*. London: I. B. Tauris.

Teh, D. (2011) 'Itinerant Cinema.' *Third Text*, 25, 5: 595–609.

Thomas, R. (1985) 'Indian Cinema.' *Screen*, 26, 3: 116–131.

Thompson, K. and D. Bordwell (1976) 'Space and Narrative in the Films of Ozu.' *Screen* 17, 2: 41–73.

Todorov, T. (1970) *The Fantastic*. Translated by R. Howard, 1975. Ithaca, NY: Cornell University Press.

Torchin, L. (2016) 'What Can the Mass "Check-In" at Standing Rock Tell US about Online Advocacy?' *The Conversation*, 4 November. http://theconversation.com/what-can-the-mass-check-in-at-standing-rock-tell-us-about-online-advocacy-68276

Traverso, A. (2007) 'Migrations of Cinema.' In L. E. Ruberto and K. M. Wilson (eds.) *Italian Neorealism and Global Cinema*. Detroit, MI: Wayne State University Press, pp. 165–186.

Treacey, M. (2016) *Reframing the Past*. London: Routledge.

Ukadike, N. F. (1994) *Black African Cinema*. Berkeley, CA: University of California Press.

Väliaho, P. (2014) *Biopolitical Screens*. Cambridge, MA: MIT Press.

Verdery, K. (2002) 'Whither Postsocialism?' In C. M. Hann (ed.) *Postsocialism*. London: Routledge, pp. 15–21.

Villazana, L. (2008) *Transnational Financial Structures in the Cinema of Latin America*. Saarbrücken: VDM Verlag Dr. Müller.

Viveiros de Castro, E. (1986) *From the Enemy's Point of View*. Translated by C. V. Howard, 1992. Chicago, IL: University of Chicago Press.

Viveiros de Castro, E. (2010) 'Intensive Filiation and Demonic Alliance.' In C. B. Jensen and K. Rödje (eds.) *Deleuzian Intersections*. Oxford: Berghahn, pp. 219–253.

Vuola, E. (2000) 'Thinking Otherwise'. In L. M. Alcoff and E. Mendieta (eds.) *Thinking from the Underside of History*. Lanham, MD: Rowman and Littlefield, pp. 149–180.

Wacquant, L. (2009) *Punishing the Poor*. Durham, NC: Duke University Press.

Wagner, K. B. (2011) 'Fragments of Labor.' In J. Kapur and K. B. Wagner (eds.) *Neoliberalism and Global Cinema*. London: Routledge, pp. 217–238.

Wallerstein, I. (1974) *The Modern World System I*. Reprint 2011. Berkeley, CA: University of California Press.

Wallerstein, I. (2000) *The Essential Wallerstein*. New York: The New Press.

Wallerstein, I. (2004) *World-Systems Analysis: An Introduction*. Durham, NC: Duke University Press.

Wartenberg, T. E. (2007) *Thinking on Screen*. London: Routledge.

Wayne, M. (2001) *Political Film*. London: Pluto.

Wayne, M. (2016) 'The Dialectics of Third Cinema.' In Y. Tzioumakis and C. Molloy (eds.) *The Routledge Companion to Cinema and Politics*. London: Routledge, pp. 17–27.

Weerasethakul, A. (2009) 'The Memory of Nabua.' In Quandt J.(ed.) (2009) *Apichatpong Weerasethakul*. Vienna: Synema, pp. 192–206.

Weinstein, M. (1992) 'The Decline and Fall of Democracy in Uruguay.' In S. Sosnowski and L. B. Popkin (eds.) *Repression, Exile and Democracy*. Durham, NC: Duke University Press, pp. 83–100.

Weiser, F. (2014) 'The Conventions of Unconventionality.' *Rethinking History*, 19, 2: 268–284.

Westad, A. (2010) 'Conclusion.' In G. Lawson, C. Armbruster, and M. Cox (eds.) *The Global 1989*. Cambridge: Cambridge University Press, pp. 271–281.

Westad, O. A. (2007) *The Global Cold War*. Cambridge: Cambridge University Press.

Westwell, G. (2007) 'Critical Approaches to the History Film.' *Rethinking History*, 11, 4: 577–588.

Wheatley, C. (2009) *Michael Haneke's Cinema*. Oxford: Beghahn.

Wheeler, D. (2013) 'También la Illuvia/*Even the Rain* (Icíar Bollaín 2010).' In M. M. Delgado and R. Fiddian (eds.) *Spanish Cinema, 1973–2010*. Manchester, UK: Manchester University Press, pp. 239–255.

White, H. (1973) *Metahistory*. 40th anniversary edition, 2014. Baltimore, MD: Johns Hopkins University Press.

White, H. (1966). 'The Burden of History.' *History and Theory*, 5, 2: 111–134.

White, H. (1987) *The Content of the Form*. Baltimore, MD: Johns Hopkins University Press.

White, H. (1988) 'Historiography and Historiophoty.' In M. Hughes-Warrington (ed.) (2009) *The History on Film Reader*. London: Routledge, pp. 53–60.

White, H. (1996) 'The Modernist Event.' In V. Sobchack (ed.) *The Persistence of History*. London: Routledge, pp. 17–38.

White, H. (2010) *The Fiction of Narrative*. Edited by R. Doran. Baltimore, MD: Johns Hopkins University Press.

White, L. T. (1991) 'The Cultural Revolution as an Unintended Result of Administrative Policies.' In W. A. Joseph, C. P. W. Wong, and D. Zweig (eds.) *New Perspectives on the Cultural Revolution* . Cambridge, MA: Harvard University Press, pp. 83–104.

White, P. (2015) *Women's Cinema, World Cinema*. Durham, NC: Duke University Press.

White, R. (2012) 'After Effects.' *Film Quarterly*, 12 July. https://filmquarterly.org/2012/07/12/after-effects-interview-with-patricio-guzman/

Williams, C. (2017) 'Has Trump Stolen Philosophy's Critical Tools?' *New York Times*, 17 April. https://www.nytimes.com/2017/04/17/opinion/has-trump-stolen-philosophys-critical-tools.html?_r=1

Williams, E. (1944) *Capitalism and Slavery*. Reprint 1994. Chapel Hill, NC: University of North Carolina Press.

Willoquet-Maricondi, P. (ed.) (2010) *Framing the World*. Charlottesville, VA: University of Virginia Press.

Wilson, J. (2017) 'Hiding in Plain Sight.' *The Guardian*, 23 May. https://www.theguardian.com/technology/2017/may/23/alt-right-online-humor-as-a-weapon-facism

Wraight, C. D. (2008) *Rousseau's The Social Contract*. London: Continuum.

Xavier, I. (1993) 'Eldorado as Hell.' In J. King, A. López and M. Alvarado (eds.) *Mediating Two Worlds*. London: BFI.

Young, T. R. (2001) 'You Are What You Eat.' In S. Juan-Navarro and T. R. Young (eds.) *A Twice-Told Tale*. Newark, DE: University of Delaware Press, pp. 80–90.

Zalasiewicz, J. et al. (2015) 'Colonization of the Americas, "Little Ice Age," Climate, and Bomb-Produced Carbon.' *The Anthropocene Review*, 2, 2: 117–127.

Zinn, H. (1980) *A People's History of the United States*. New York: Harper Perennial.

Žižek, S. (2000) *The Fragile Absolute*. London: Verso.

Žižek, S. (2003) *The Puppet and the Dwarf*. Cambridge, MA: MIT Press.

Žižek, S. (2006) 'Neighbours and Other Monsters: A Plea for Ethical Violence.' In S. Žižek, E. L. Santner and K. Reinhard (2006) *The Neighbor*. Chicago, IL: Chicago University Press, pp. 134–190.

Žižek, S. (2008) *Violence*. London: Profile Books.

Žižek, S. (2013) '*The Act of Killing* and the Modern Trend of "Privatising Public Space."' *New Statesman*, 12 July. http://www.newstatesman.com/culture/2013/07/slavoj-zizek-act-killing-and-modern-trend-privatising-public-space

Žižek, S. and J. Milbank (2009) *The Monstrosity of Christ*. Cambridge, MA: MIT Press.

Zylinska, J. (2014) *Minimal Ethics for the Anthropocene*. Ann Arbor, MI: Open Humanities Press.

INDEX